P9-CRD-539

Freedom Days

Other Books by Janus Adams

Glory Days: 365 Inspired Moments in African-American History

Books for Young Readers

Cajun Country. USA
A Journey to the Moon . . . and Beyond
Mark Twain's America
Routes 'n Roots: An Explorer's Guide to America
Trailblazing Yellowstone
Underground Railroad Escape to Freedom

Freedom Days

365 Inspired Moments
in Civil Rights History

Janus Adams

John Wiley & Sons, Inc.
New York • Chichester • Weinheim • Brisbane • Singapore • Toronto

This publication is designed to provide accurate and authoritative information in regard to the subject matter covered. It is sold with the understanding that the publisher is not engaged in rendering professional services. If legal, accounting, medical, psychological, or any other expert assistance is required, the services of a competent professional person should be sought.

Library of Congress Cataloging-in-Publication Data

Adams, Janus
  Freedom days : 365 inspired moments in civil rights history / Janus Adams.
    p.   cm.
  Includes bibliographical references (p.   ) and index.
  ISBN 0-471-19212-0 (cloth : alk. paper)
    1. Afro-Americans—Civil rights—History—20th century—
Miscellanea. 2. Civil rights movements—United States—
History—20th century—Miscellanea. 3. United States—Race relations—Miscellanea.   I. Title.
  E185.61.A232   1997
  323.1'196073—dc21   97-21614

Printed in the United States of America

10 9 8 7 6 5 4 3 2 1

To my family—my mother, Muriel Landsmark Tuitt, and my daughters, Ayo and Dara Roach—my love, admiration, and deepest gratitude for walking this steep and rocky road with me.

To Gail Hamilton with her gentle call, to Betty and Stan Katz, Ben McCrae, R. Steven Norman, Sonia Sanchez, and Hattie Winston, I could not have done it without you.

To a special spirit without whose joy . . . well, why bother? . . . my dear "niece," Samantha Diana, keep writing, precious love.

To a network of librarians and researchers in Wilton, Westport, Stamford, and Greenwich, Connecticut; at the Beinecke Archives at Yale University, and at the Schomburg Collection of the New York Public Library, thank you, thank you all.

To Carole Hall who *made a way* for me at John Wiley, to my editor Hana Lane, to my lawyer Joan G. Zooper, I thank you for your *sister power.* To the entire Wiley team, there is no job called "caring"—thank you for that.

And to those who gave their lives to make the stories I was privileged to retell, I thank you for the strength of your shoulders and the pull of your hand. *How we got ovah.*

INTRODUCTION

"Praise the bridge that carries you over," the old folks say. Go down to the river. Cross over to the other side. Praise the bridge, no matter how rough the ride.

Traveling our own stretch on the freedom road, who among us has not grown weary, at times. *How we got ovah,* the song says. How will we get over? we wonder. The voices of the ancestors echo around us. Go to the bridge. For history is like a traveler's diary, surveying all we have seen and done—where we have been and what has become of us as we press along life's route. Those who have come before us have faced the same crossroads we now face and many of the same treacherous twists in the road. We are proof of their success. We are here today because they never lost hope, never gave up on the journey, never lost sight of the destination, never confused trouble with the gift of a new day. *How can you know how to get where you're going, 'til you know how you got where you've been?* the voices beckon. Travel on, and study the route. At the bend in the river, sound the depth. At the crossroads, look to the signposts staked along the way. Our markers point to your Freedom Days.

Such is the method and message of this book, *Freedom Days: 365 Inspired Moments in Civil Rights History*—365 markers along the road from 1936 to 1976 (plus a leap year's lagniappe for a total of 366); 366 days of challenge and choice, the choice to wind a trail to freedom. And what a journey it has been.

As a fledgling collector of African American documents, I struck out on a quest for what I thought to be the ultimate acquisition—a manumission letter, or *freedom papers,* as these rare morsels of history are called. When, at last, I held one in hand, I recognized it at once for what it was—a piece of paper no different in content, construct, or rag than the bill of sale which could alternatively bind a life enchained. Both documents were leaves from the same book. Both were meant to validate the notion that black life was to be bought, sold, and bartered.

Taken together, these documents—the bills of sale and the freedom papers—offer lasting insight, especially in these tremulous days when the nation stands at a crossroads—the intersection of Integration and Segregation. Again, two leaves of the same book validate the notion that black life belongs to a class apart, black life is not real life. Here, at the bridge, the teeter-totter of American history and race relations can definitely be seen as teetering.

Twice before, America has come upon this moral precipice, and twice before—at this same relative moment two centuries in a row—it has plummeted over the edge.

In 1793, the Fugitive Slave Law and the Constitution's degredation of blacks as "three-fifths a man" belied revolutionary ideals and betrayed black patriots who had cast their lot with colonists, hoping to free their entire families from bondage. This, despite the guarantee of individual liberty had they sided with the British. Not until the 1860s with Emancipation, the Civil War, and Reconstruction did "free-born" African Americans along with those enslaved attain a semblance of human rights. Faced with a majority black electorate in many states (like the "majority-minority state" debates of our day), nineteenth-century legislators and demagogues demonized and dehumanized blacks until every black elected official was expelled from office (as this era's redistricting is designed to do by the dawn of the twenty-first century). Then, the Supreme Court institutionalized the "black codes" and Jim Crow segregation with its *Plessy v. Ferguson* decision of 1896. Not until the Voting Rights Act of 1965 were African American rights of citizenship restored (as you'll read on March 15). Hardly a gain, America had merely stopped subverting the constitutional amendments passed a century before. In 1968 (November 5), with voting rights assured and specially drawn majority black districts, African Americans finally began returning to elected office in significant numbers. Twenty years later, another '90s downturn had begun. What course would the nation choose this time—this third time around?

I am not optimistic about the current trends. But this I know. Even in the worst of times—the slavery years—black minds were *stayed on freedom*. Faced with the depravity of those who opposed human rights in the American Civil Rights era, blacks kept our *eyes on the prize* and held on. In a landscape filled with landmines, African Americans still dare a frustrating maze of history, yet we are here. Standing on the bridge, crossing our *River Jordan*, pushing on to the other side.

In business, in science and technology, in the arts, in education, in every field of our endeavor, there is cause to celebrate—to praise our bridges and *how we got ovah*. It is a triumph over evil that resonates throughout the African Diaspora. The restoration of the continent and its tributary peoples of the Caribbean to independence, those stories, too, are here. On January 28, Jomo Kenyatta's parable "Gentlemen of the Jungle," humorously defines the politics of freedom. On March 5, Ghana is free!

On the lecture trail, asked to speak about history and victory, I invariably end up answering questions of race. The more I travel, the more I witness scenes where students are escorted into the auditoriums of America in clumps either all-black or all-white. I do not want to speak always of race, an artificial construct and waste of spirit, I want to move on. I want to share my love of information and revelation, but the more I see of history-in-the-making, the more I see the inescapable truth that the American saga is a study in race and racism.

In small to mid-sized cities with significant black populations I learn that one or two teachers at best are likely to be black; that adult faces of color represent janitors and security personnel; that white parents threaten flight when black children are not tracked into substandard "at risk" classes. A concerned white administrator confides why there is such resistance to multicultural studies: "Parents and teachers are afraid that if they tell children the truth, the children will think their ancestors were bad." And so all across America, the truth is that millions of children of color are being sacrificed daily—made to feel *their* ancestors were bad—for a *white lie*.

Looking back on the events that forged my generation, few dates meant more than May 17, the day the Supreme Court desegregated public schools with its *Brown v. Board of Education* decision in 1954, drawing the era of Jim Crow to a close. The following year I became one of the four "test" children chosen to break New York City's elementary school color bar as you'll discover on February 26. As such, the faces of today's young caged behind the bars of re-segregation reach me very personally. Blessed with wonderful parents and the love of neighbors and elders, I was promised what all the children in the Civil Rights trenches had been promised: that for our sacrifice, no other child would ever suffer what we had endured. *Brown* was our connection with our courageous ancestors who had brought us this far by faith. *Brown* was our gift to carry our length of the relay race. *Brown*, they hoped, was our chance to do something important. And, in the days when adults north and south raged out of control at the sight of children in school, important was about as good as you could feel. *De facto* or *de jure*, UpSouth or DownNorth, *Brown* created a national platform upon which African Americans claimed our god-given birth rights long overdue. In a time of lynchings— real (August 31) and McCarthy-like (September 4)—*Brown* was a glimmer of conscience. Tragically and tellingly, to speak of the promise of *Brown* forty years after is to know the specter of doubt.

Yet, *Brown* was but one of many junctures. Indeed, Civil Rights history is quite broad, though often seen as framed by the *Brown v. Board of Education* decision on May 17, 1954, on one side and the April 4, 1968, assassination of Dr. Martin Luther King Jr. on the other. Most importantly, it reaches quite beyond the bounds of politics to what makes it all worthwhile—laughter, love, and joy. To crop scenes from its rich canvas sets the movement out of context, denying black people our full humanity and our continuity of experience with the Pan-African world.

For the miracles we have performed did not end with the pyramids of Thebes and the Great Zimbabwe. Mrs. Bethune built a college with "$1.50, six little girls, her faith in God, a recipe for sweet potato pie," and the assets enumerated in her last will and testament (January 3). And, at the depths of oppression, didn't Duke Ellington make folks Jump for Joy (April 29)?

Even in its purest political expression, the Civil Rights movement was one part of a global quest for self-determination by people of African descent, in particular relation to the African American experience, and by peoples of color of every nation as related to the global crusade for human rights and independent rule. It was a goal made tangible and viable when Ethiopia's Emperor Haile Selassie mounted the podium of the League of Nations in 1936 (June 30), when Jesse Owens won four gold medals at the Olympics that same year (September 6), and later, when the world's peoples of color gathered for the great Bandung conference of 1955 (April 20). It is a process of symbiotic healing and resurrection in which the challenges and triumphs of one region inspire and support another. Whether throwing off the yoke of colonization or slavery, apartheid or segregation, the mission is the same: self-empowerment, self-determination. It peaks in 1976, when all eyes and energies focus on the greed and brutality of South African apartheid (December 30). It is a vision in which all things seem possible with the first steps of Nelson Mandela's 1990 walk from twenty-seven years of imprisonment to the presidency of South Africa.

The turning point for the struggle comes in the pivotal years 1936–1976 when the prism of electronic technology—radio, newsreels, television—intensifies the look and sound of freedom (February 7), and the hypocrisy of vision that is freedom denied. *Freedom Days* chronicles this extraordinary forty-year period of passion and promise.

And so it is against this backdrop that I have come to see the faces of young and old, of black and white, of people hungry for answers, craving direction. I wonder where the promise of that era has gone. Where has the hope of the Civil Rights movement taken us and left them? I look at the faces forming forsaken questions and answers and I know *Brown* has died in their eyes. Most do not know that every positive development for blacks has improved the nation as a whole. In this political climate, few are willing to tell them. They do not know that the push for black voting rights ended the poll tax and disfranchisement for poor whites (January 12) or that the Civil Rights and Black Power movements forged "affirmative action" for white women (July 13).

I take their faces home with me to tend—young, old, and in-between. For who among us does not welcome the breath of hope, resuscitation of proud truths, the view these signposts reveal? Long before Einstein's theory of relativity, my grandmother, Myra Carlisle Landsmark, used to say: "All things are one." At the font of her wisdom, this book has been baptized— the oneness of the human experience focused through the lens of the African American sojourn, setting the wisdom of that experience to the task of inspiring us now when we need it so much. *Freedom Days* is a book of love and remembrance—a celebration of life.

To go down to the bridge is to know how our ancestors— and those still with us who walk in that noble tradition—loved life hard enough to make *a way out of no way* for us. No matter the winds and the tides, they knew, as my grandfather would say, to "let no one contaminate your mind." That is the knowledge that is ours to treasure. "Praise the bridge that carries you over," we have been told. Come down to the bridge. Let us celebrate our Freedom Days!

JANUARY

The 1920s . . . The Migrants Arrive and Cast Their Ballots (1974). Courtesy of the artist and the Francine Seders Gallery, Seattle, WA.

For more information about Jacob Lawrence, please see May 29 and October 13.

JANUARY 1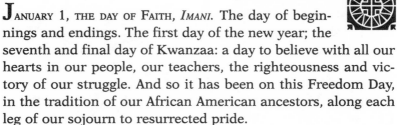

JANUARY 1, THE DAY OF FAITH, *IMANI*. The day of beginnings and endings. The first day of the new year; the seventh and final day of Kwanzaa: a day to believe with all our hearts in our people, our teachers, the righteousness and victory of our struggle. And so it has been on this Freedom Day, in the tradition of our African American ancestors, along each leg of our sojourn to resurrected pride.

In the United States and in international law, January 1, 1808, marked the end of the "legal" slave trade, the first fruits of justice over the most powerful and profitable international cartel of its day. From that tangible victory, the beginnings of a viable African liberation, or emancipation, movement grew. That January 1 became our first Thanksgiving Day, so proclaimed by exslave and cofounder of the African Methodist Episcopal (AME) Church, Absalom Jones. Fifty-five years later, ex-slave, Underground Railroad conductor, and civil war strategist, Frederick Douglass, would achieve confirmation on paper of what was true by nature: the Emancipation Proclamation. January 1, 1863, marked the legal end of slavery, the beginning of making freedom reality. On January 1, 1956, Sudan became the first African nation to retake its independence and it was not naive, as Malcolm X said, to think "the same hand that has been writing on the wall in Africa . . . is also writing on the wall right here in America." Freedom Now! African Americans reasserted on January 1, 1963, as the post-Emancipation century drew to a close at the height of the Civil Rights era. James Baldwin put the period and its objective into perspective: "You know and I know," he wrote to his nephew, "that the country is celebrating one hundred years of freedom one hundred years too soon. . . . [But you come from] men who picked cotton and dammed rivers and built railroads, and in the teeth of the most terrifying odds, achieved an unassailable and monumental dignity. You come from a long line of great poets."

And so we had *come this far by faith*. 1936–1976: the age of Civil Rights, the age of liberation in the African Diaspora. These were our Freedom Days. . . .

JANUARY 2

TIME MAGAZINE had just proclaimed him "Man of the Year!" with a front-cover banner spread. "Nobel Peace Prize laureate!" The international community beamed. As a man, he was on top of the world. As a black man in America, he was at the bottom of the barrel. On January 2, 1965, Dr. Martin Luther King Jr. launched his newest Civil Rights campaign: a voter registration drive.

During the desegregation street wars, the Kennedy administration encouraged the movement to push for voter registration on the theory that elected officials would respond to the issues of a black electorate. Yet, when the Civil Rights Bill of 1964 was passed as a memorial to the assassinated president, voting rights had been negotiated out of the bill in deference to the same segregationists who had caused the violence. Voting rights, therefore, became the next battle. Selma, Alabama, was its first battleground. In Selma, the Dallas County Voters' League (DCVL) had been helping people register by ones and twos since the 1930s. But the harder the DCVL worked to register voters the harder the county, city, and state worked to throw up barriers—tests of literacy and constitutional knowledge, character witness, registrar approval. In 1963, of the fifteen thousand eligible black voters, only 180 blacks were "approved." For help, the DCVL worked with SNCC volunteers, and then with Dr. King's Southern Christian Leadership Conference (SCLC). When King arrived in Selma, it was major news. Speaking at Brown's Chapel African Methodist Church on Saturday, January 2, 1965, he exhorted an overflow crowd:

> When we get the right to vote, we will send to the statehouse not men who will . . . keep Negroes out . . . but men who will uphold the cause of Justice. At the rate they are letting us register now it will take a hundred and three years to register all of the fifteen thousand Negroes in Dallas County who are qualified to vote. . . . But we don't have that long to wait. . . . Our cry to the state of Alabama is a simple one: *Give us the ballot.* . . . We are not on our knees begging for the ballot. *We are demanding the ballot.*

Voting Rights   Expectations

JANUARY 3

As Mary McLeod Bethune would say, "I believe in God, and so I believe in Mary Bethune." Together, God and she had worked miracles, raising her from the cotton fields of South Carolina to found the National Council of Negro Women (NCNW) and to become a member of President Franklin D. Roosevelt's "Kitchen Cabinet" and special adviser to President Harry S. Truman. She had also parlayed $1.50, five girls, the trust of their families, faith, and her recipe for sweet potato pie into Florida's first school to educate blacks beyond the elementary grades—Daytona Educational and Industrial Institute, which she founded in 1904 and developed into Bethune-Cookman College. She was richly rewarded by a life well lived in service to others, though her financial assets were few. But, early in 1955, almost eighty years of age, she felt death nearing and decided to leave her possessions for posterity in a "Last Will and Testament." Excerpted here, it appeared posthumously in *Ebony's* August 1955 issue and was later published in book form:

> Sometimes as I sit communing in my study I feel that death is not far off. I am aware that it will overtake me before the greatest of my dreams—full equality for the Negro in our time—is realized. . . . Already, I have begun working on my autobiography. I have deeded my home to the Bethune Foundation for research, interracial activity and the sponsorship of wider educational opportunities. Sometimes I ask myself if I have any other legacy to leave. . . . My worldly possessions are few. Yet, my experiences have been rich. From them, I have distilled principles and policies in which I believe firmly, for they represent the meaning of my life's work. . . . Here then, is my legacy: I leave you love. I leave you hope . . . , the challenge of developing confidence in one another, a thirst for education, a respect for the uses of power, faith, racial dignity, a desire to live harmoniously with your fellowmen. I leave you finally a responsibility to our young people.

The legacies bequeathed by Mrs. Bethune underlie each of the daily essays in *Freedom Days*. For a full listing, see the Index of Inspirational Themes.

JANUARY 4

On January 4, 1962, the jails of Albany, Georgia, were filled with demonstrators. Imbued with hope and a sense of possibility, many were arrested only to march in protest again and again. As the Civil Rights movement blazed trails across the country, it was the music of the movement, the Freedom Songs, that kept pace with the times. What people could not say, they sang, adapting the Spirituals for current needs. Their powerful voices told the story: "Ain' Gonna Let Nobody Turn Me 'Round"; "I know one thing we did right, was the day we began to fight, keep your eyes on the prize, hold on, hold on." Armed with the gospel of freedom, whole families and former strangers held on to each other and bravely marched off to "battle" in courts, lunch counters, schools, and jails.

> We are soldiers in the army
> We have to fight although we have to die
> We have to hold up the bloodstained banner
> We have to hold it up until we die.
>
> My mother, she was a soldier . . . My father . . . my brother
>
> I am a soldier
> I have my hand on the gospel now
> One day when I'm old, and I can't fight anymore
> I'll say, I'll stand here and fight on, anyhow. . . .

"This little light of mine, I'm gonna let it shine," people sang, preserving a long tradition. It was a favorite of slave leader Harriet Tubman and her modern incarnation, sharecropper leader Fannie Lou Hamer. The African American saga from slavery to freedom was still being written—and rewritten. Bernice Johnson Reagon was a college student when the Albany Movement began (see November 17):

> The voice I have now I got the first time I sang in a movement meeting, after I got out of jail. I did the song "Over My Head I See Freedom in the Air," but I had never been that me before. And once I became that me, I have never let that me go . . . a transformation took place inside of the people. The singing was just the echo of that.

Music   Messages

JANUARY 5

THE IDEA OF BUILDING black theater on adaptations of Euro-American drama always presents a cultural dilemma. By rewriting the insights of other people and other times, there is a hole in the culture where the African American voice should be—a void in the documentation of our unique experiences.

But those who doubt the liberating effects of *The Wonderful Wizard of Oz*, L. Frank Baum's seventy-five-year old story, reincarnated as an African American musical didn't see Geoffrey Holder's costumes and staging, hear Charlie Smalls's score and Harold Wheeler's orchestrations, witness George Faison's choreographic humor, or climb the heights of hope fulfilled with the towering voice of Stephanie Mills when *The Wiz* opened on Broadway on January 5, 1975.

In the metaphor of Dorothy's coming-of-age and search for "home" was a story of our people and time. Her journey was one families could share—inspiring conversations on conquering doubt and fear. Struck down many a time by a torrent of storms, blacks now found themselves in a different place, making their way in a new world. It was a time to "Ease on down the road—'Cause there may be times when you think you've lost your mind—and the steps you're taking, leave you three, four steps behind—just you keep on keepin' on the road that you choose and—don't you give up walking 'cause you gave up shoes . . ." Things that seemed one way were quite another: the "mean ole lion" was outdone when faced with the strength of a teenage girl. How like the school boards, governors, and lunch counter lions who had been faced down by young marchers and sit-ins. "Can't you feel a brand-new day?" A valuable lesson had been learned in Oz: "Believe in yourself, right from the start, believe in the magic that's inside your heart, believe what you see, not what life told you to, believe in yourself." The search for "home" arrived at a comfort zone deep within.

JANUARY 6

On Friday afternoon, January 6, 1961, as Charlayne Hunter returned to her dormitory at Wayne State University, she was called to the phone. "Congratulations," she heard an unfamiliar voice blurt out. It was a New York newspaper reporter with news that, after two years of court challenges, Federal Judge William Bootle had ordered the University of Georgia to admit her. She and Hamilton Holmes would be the first African Americans to attend the school in its 176-year history. Within moments the Wayne State switchboard was jammed; reporters were everywhere. Three days later, on Monday, January 9, Hunter and Holmes registered—and what seemed the end of a long ordeal proved to be only the beginning.

Charlayne and Hamilton expected the first days to be tense. But no one would have dared to predict forty-eight brutal hours of an unchecked campus riot that included cross burnings, burnings in effigy, and a man who came looking for Charlayne with a loaded gun, which led to the suspension of Hunter and Holmes "for their own good." Seated in the back of a Georgia State Patrol car, "a statue of the Madonna provided my only solace," she wrote, "when the unfairness and finality of it all hit me and I burst into angry tears."

How did she rebound from what must have seemed a cruel joke? In her autobiography, *In My Place*, Charlayne Hunter Gault wrote that she and Holmes made their way through the four-year ordeal with the support of their families, friends, and crusading legal team. Even in her childhood, she said, her family had never told her what she could not be, never warned her what she dare not dream. She later wrote about leaving the campus that violent night: "The newfound sense of mission that now motivated [me evolved] out of a natural desire to fulfill a dream I had nurtured from an early age. With a passion bordering on obsession, I wanted to be a journalist. . . . I would not let anything stand in the way." Several rounds later, the two graduated from Georgia in 1963. And Charlayne became the Peabody Award–winning journalist noted for her years with *The NewsHour* on public television.

"TONIGHT WE COME TOGETHER for a very special purpose. This inauguration is . . . the positive reaffirmation that all Atlantans can work together for the good of our City." On January 7, 1974, with this first speech, Maynard Jackson took office as the first African American to be elected mayor of a southern city since Reconstruction. "Tonight we are witnessing a People's Inauguration. Over the next four years we shall work to create a People's administration, one that will afford even the poorest and most destitute person an alternative to agony. No longer will we necessitate Langston Hughes's plaintive cry of the masses, 'I swear to the Lord—I still can't see—Why Democracy means—Everybody but me.'"

Jackson had been well schooled in the art and science of politics with lessons from his grandfather's days with the Atlanta Negro Voters' League. As in other cities where blacks voted, while they could not run candidates of their own, they could help sway the vote on a white slate. So respected was the league that when it issued its "ticket" at 12:01 A.M. on election day, ninety-nine percent of the black vote supported it. Heading the league were Jackson's grandfather, John Wesley Dobbs, a Republican, and Austin T. Walden, a Democrat. How these two men deftly played segregation politics became known as "the Atlanta style." Their legacy evolved into the politics of inclusion, empowered a new generation of African American Atlantans, and paved the way for Jackson's election. As Jackson recalled in an interview for the book, *Voices of Freedom:*

> The white leadership would say, "We have decided to back Joe Blow for mayor; and we want you all to help us out and support our candidate." The black leadership then, with the spokespersons being Dobbs and Walden, would say, "We hear you. And we'll certainly be happy to give them consideration. But first, we need a high school. We need so-and-so streets paved . . . sewers. . . ." They'd have to bargain for the things for which they were already paying taxes. But that's how we got . . . the first black high school in the city of Atlanta, in 1924. That's how we got most of the improvements. . . . It's called the Atlanta style.

JANUARY 8

JAMES HASKINS WROTE, "From my classroom window I have seen fall turn into winter, and winter to spring. Nothing in this block ever changes, except the seasons. The same faces are always here, with their look of despair."

In 1967, Haskins, one of the few African Americans on Wall Street, left his job hoping to teach and to contribute to the "larger human experience." A teacher's strike that year divided faculty along racial lines. One reason for this was the leadership of United Federation of Teachers President Albert Shanker, who rallied his troops with inflammatory anecdotes from his days as a math teacher. In one, the "only way" Shanker could interest students in math was to use an example of "poisoning one's relative." As Haskins noted, "Let's hold no grudges against the UFT president," who was clearly limited as a teacher. . . . "Rather feel pity and disgust for him and for those like him, who believe they must go to extremes to be effective with black children."

Haskins spent that school year teaching at Harlem's P.S. 92 on 134th Street. Like many African American teachers, he crossed the picket line to teach the children. He kept a journal of that year; this excerpt is from his entry for January 8, 1968:

> Jesus' parents keep him out two to three times a week, the excuse usually being that he did not have a clean shirt. Yet he is one of the two children in the class whose families are not on welfare. . . . I know what the problem is. In the winter ghetto children seldom have hot water or heat, so many sleep in their clothes. In the morning the house is so cold that they don't want to undress to put on clean clothes. Like most of the children in my class and in the school in general, Jesus wears dirty underclothing and seldom takes time to wash properly.

As the strike escalated the next year, Haskins, like most of the city's black faculty, kept teaching. His journal was later published as *Diary of a Harlem Schoolteacher.*

JANUARY 9

In January 1938, Lois Mailou Jones was far from the oppressive racial clime of Washington, D.C., living in a light, airy, tri-level penthouse apartment in the Montparnasse section of Paris. Physically, emotionally, intellectually, artistically, she felt, at last, "shackle free." Having sailed to Paris and freedom the previous August, she was that rare African American who had come not as an expatriate but to study for a year, then return to Howard University, where she had been an art professor since 1931. In January 1938, halfway into her sabbatical, she would venture from her adopted haven to take daily forays into the city.

In the great French tradition, she took to painting outdoors. Painting from natural light and natural life, her movable feast of "studios" took her from parks to the banks of the Seine and sundry outdoor vistas. She took classes at Académie Julien, where Henry Ossawa Tanner, the late-nineteenth-century African American painter whose work so inspired her, had found his own painterly voice years before. In class and on the street, her work attracted admirers, some of whom became friends. With their encouragement, she submitted her paintings for an exhibition at the Salon of the Société des Artistes Français and the Société des Artistes Indépendants, where they were accepted. As she wrote, "It was like being free for the first time—my paintings were exhibited . . . purely on merit."

It was a prolific period in which Jones was as free to explore her inner vision as she was to investigate the French scene. "When I took *Les Fétiches* to my professors to see," she said, "it didn't look like a Lois Jones painting. They couldn't understand how I could do such a thing, because it dealt with cubism and the masks. And then I reminded them that Picasso, Matisse, and Modigliani had made great use of African art, and I asked if they didn't think that Lois Jones, whose heritage is Africa, has more right to do so. And they had to smile." In Paris that year, Lois Mailou Jones found freedom to see and to be seen, to be influenced by Africans and by Europeans, to discover the works of others the world over, to be herself.

Art   Empowerment

JANUARY 10

In 1955, when Rosa Parks kept her historic bus seat (see December 5), she phoned her mother from jail and her mother called E. D. Nixon. Nixon called a white attorney and friend, Clifford Durr, and his wife, Virginia, and the three then bailed out Parks. Virginia Durr shared this story with *Eyes on the Prize* researchers:

> [In January 1956] the mayor issued an order that all the black maids had to be dismissed to break the [Montgomery Bus] Boycott. Well, [white women said], "Tell the mayor to come and do my work for me, then." So the white women went and got the black women in the car. They said they did it because the bus had broken down, or any excuse you could possibly think of. And then the black women, if you picked one of them up who was walking, they'll tell you that they were walking because the lady that brought them to work, her child was sick. So here was this absurd sort of dance going on. A woman that worked for my mother-in-law they were asking, "Do any of your family take part in the boycott?" She said, "My brother-in-law, he has a ride every morning and my sister-in-law, she comes home with somebody else, and they just stay off the bus and don't have nothing to do with it." And so I said to Mary, "You know, you had been really the biggest storyteller in the world. You know everybody in your family's involved in the boycott." And she says, "Well, you know, when you have your hand in the lion's mouth, the best thing to do is pat it on the head."
>
> [There's] such a terrible load of shame and guilt that we won't acknowledge. . . .

A footnote: The mayor's order and social disaster of no black maids inspired *Day of Absence*, the play that launched the Negro Ensemble Company (see November 25).

JANUARY 11

FOURTEEN MONTHS into the Albany Movement, Martin Luther King's nonviolent campaign had failed to bring about real change. City officials always seemed to know more than they should. When a report ended up in the hands of the police chief, it prompted SCLC's taskmaster, Rev. Wyatt Tee Walker, to turn a lemon of a situation into lemonade. He bailed Dr. King out of jail and the SCLC out of town for a few days. They returned with renewed vigor, but nagging doubts remained. The campaign had drained more than it had gained (see July 23). Why? Leaving Albany months later, King was visibly depressed. Since his baptism-by-fire with the Montgomery Bus Boycott (see December 5) he had been cleaning up disasters. Assessing his career, he said, "I don't want to be a fireman anymore." What was learned? Succinctly, the four P's—planning prevents poor performance. He immediately dispatched Walker on a secret mission: draft a detailed plan for SCLC's next campaign. Walker called it "Project C"—C for Confrontation.

On January 11, 1963, SCLC leaders—King, Ralph Abernathy, Dorothy Cotton, Wyatt Walker, Andrew Young, and seven others, including Rev. Fred Shuttlesworth—were on a three-day retreat in Dorchester, Georgia. Refining Project C, they drafted a strategy tailored to the next frontier: Birmingham.

In Albany, a major mistake had been "to scatter our efforts too widely." Now they would focus on humiliating segregated lunch counter policies in "the country's chief symbol of racial intolerance." As "Bombingham" went, so went the South. With Easter, the second biggest shopping season of the year, coming up, loss of black spending power would be felt by the downtown business community. When would they start? Immediately after the upcoming special election to avoid its becoming a campaign issue. And unlike in Albany they would research the laws on parade permits and incorporate that into the plan. In the interim, they would raise every possible dollar for bail by the target date: April 3. Onward!

Strategy   Rising from Defeat

JANUARY 12

WHAT IS OFTEN IGNORED by those who fight to uphold a racially unjust society is the cost of racism to whites. In order to circumvent the Constitution, laws have been enacted to mask racism with the appearance of propriety. One such example was the poll tax. Enacted in the 1880s as part of the "Black Codes," which suppressed blacks, the poll tax also excluded poor whites who could also ill afford it.

A six-year attempt at legislative relief finally led, in January 1943, to an anti–poll tax bill in the House of Representatives, H.R. 7, which passed that May. Sent on to the Senate for ratification, it was derailed by a southern filibuster. As the poor of every race were drafted to fight a war that poll tax laws kept them from voting to end, the filibuster dragged on. That was the reality of the situation as senators refused to invoke cloture, limit debate, and take a vote. On January 12, 1944, the NAACP upped the pressure with thousands of flyers circulated north and south:

> **What Is the Poll Tax?** The poll tax is imposed upon citizens of eight southern states to limit the number of persons voting. . . . [During the Depression, poll taxes were one or two dollars when infrequent wages were only cents per hour.]
>
> **Why do Poll Tax Laws Exist?** At one time the united interests of sharecroppers, poor whites, and Negroes threatened to destroy the power of the Democratic Party in the South. Poll tax laws were enacted to prevent this.
>
> **10,000,000 Americans Disfranchised.** Six million white and four million Negro citizens are disfranchised by the poll tax. . . . Negro and white laborers . . . who need legislation to secure better educational, housing, and health facilities have no voice in determining who shall represent their interest. Of 13,600,000 adults in the southern states in 1940, only 3,000,000 or 22% paid the poll tax and voted.

Twenty years later, on January 23, 1964, the twenty-fourth amendment to the Constitution finally struck down the poll tax. It was one more demonstration of the positive effects of the black freedom fight on the nation as a whole.

Voting Rights   Initiative

JANUARY 13

O<small>N</small> J<small>ANUARY</small> 13, 1961, Dick Gregory finally got the break he'd been working for. When another performer was unable to go on, Gregory was ready for his chance at center stage in a major club—Hugh Hefner's Playboy Club.

Arriving at the club, however, he was told by the management that he could not go on after all; a convention of southern whites was in the audience that night. What did Dick Gregory do? He literally broke through the barriers set before him, moving quickly past the manager. "I broke onto stage anyway," he later recalled. "And, after some hectic moments, received a rollicking response." He was a hit, and went on to achieve the success that inspired the next generation of greats, like Richard Pryor, who followed him.

Since his earliest days, something that has kept Dick Gregory so funny is that he is so very serious. In the early 1960s, despite the financial rewards of working the Playboy Club circuit and other major venues, he was nearly broke. He had been arrested in so many Civil Rights demonstrations, paid so much in legal fees, and bailed out so many others, that he was running out of cash. Friends told him he could accomplish more as a comedian than as an activist. His response was typically on target. "They didn't laugh Hitler out of existence, did they?" he said, continuing his freedom fight with every weapon at his command—from humor to hunger strikes to a health food regimen for the clinically obese.

"I went from the depths of poverty to the pinnacle of financial success," said Gregory. "Having experienced both, I had to find what really was the meaning to a man's life. People always ask, 'Have demonstrations hurt your career?' but the only relevant question for me is 'Is my career getting in the way of demonstrations?' Active involvement in the struggle for human dignity is the real value in life. A career is secondary."

JANUARY 14

Even before the official U.S. entrance into the war, blacks could see the same old World War I monster raise its ugly head: the expectation that blacks should sacrifice their lives in a segregated army for freedoms they could not call their own. On January 14, 1941, a federal suit stood poised to force a desegregated military.

In the fall of 1940, as war escalated in Europe, U.S. Secretary of War Henry Lewis Stimson wrote in his diary, "The Negroes are taking advantage of this period just before [the] election to try to get everything they can in the way of recognition from the army." With resentment building on both sides, President Franklin D. Roosevelt directed Stimson to appoint a black civilian adviser to the military. Howard University Law School Dean William H. Hastie was named, and his appointment was well publicized. After the election, as a reward for black votes, the Army Air Corps announced an "experiment": an all-black fighter squadron. To some it was better than nothing. To the *Crisis* it was a "step, [but] by no means the answer to the demand of colored people for full integration into all branches of the armed services." But to Hastie, who blasted it at full throttle, to question the ability of blacks to fly an airplane was an insult. And he didn't stop there. On January 15, 1941, the test case of Howard University student Yancey Williams versus the Army Air Corps went forward. But his move was trumped the very next day when the army announced the opening of the first flying school for blacks at Tuskegee Airfield. The decision proved a mine field. Hateful whites could not tolerate the idea of having, much less training, an elite black flying corps in their midst. Even General George Marshall admitted: "one of the greatest mistakes I made during the war was to insist the colored divisions be trained in the South."

At home, the pilots trained under constant threat of violence. Abroad, the performance of the 99th Fighter Squadron made history for the Tuskegee Airmen. Flying hundreds of missions and never losing a bomber in their escort, they became known as the legendary "Red-Tail Angels."

JANUARY 15

On January 15, 1950, as more than four thousand delegates from one hundred national organizations gathered in Washington, D.C., for the National Emergency Civil Rights Conference, no one could say that progress had not been made on matters of race. But neither could one say that the blockade of white supremacy had been broken in any substantive way. It seemed as impervious as ever. And, no matter how earnest and well intentioned the speakers at such events, the facts of life for most African Americans were often overwhelmed by oratory.

Three years earlier to the day, the official news organ of the Food and Tobacco Workers' Union, the *FTA News*, had published a statement that spoke to issues of everyday life with simple eloquence. On the subject "Why I need a pay raise," Mrs. Estelle Flowers, an hourly worker and sole support of four children, responded directly and with dignity. In 1947, as a Piedmont Leaf Tobacco Company employee in North Carolina, she was paid $21 a week. "Food takes about all of my wages," she said. "What do we eat? Beans, collards, cornbread. I can't afford milk for the children. My six months old baby has to have milk—one can of evaporated milk—15¢ a can a day. It takes $2 a week for coal and that doesn't keep the home warm. What would I do with more wages? Buy the clothes the children need—more food and I could give more to the church."

As solutions to society's ills are proposed, education is always seen as the way out of low-paying jobs. But is that really a solution to the workers' plight? If one is doing a job, it is a job that needs doing by someone. Aren't those who give that job their best entitled to adequate compensation? Getting to the core issue, the solution to the "National Emergency" in Civil Rights seemed simple: do the right thing. For Mrs. Flowers and so many others, it was time for deeds, not words. In straightforward testimony, Mrs. Flowers had long ago outlined the underlying economic factors, stated her rationale, offered a solution, and even provided a spiritual base.

JANUARY 16

IT WAS FITTING that playwright Lorraine Hansberry should have departed this world in a blizzard, for in her brief life she had taken the theater world by storm. Inspired by a Langston Hughes poem—"What happens to a dream deferred? Does it dry up like a raisin in the sun? Maybe it sags like a heavy load. Or does it explode?"—her dream of a play, *A Raisin in the Sun*, exploded on the stage in 1959. For the first time in forty years of Broadway history, the powerful human drama of an African American family, healthy and whole, was up there in lights. With that play—and its later screen adaptation and posthumous staging as a musical—she achieved national acclaim as Broadway's first black woman playwright and the first black dramatist honored with a Drama Critics' Circle Award. With that play, she changed the history of Broadway. No longer could it be said—as it had for years—that an African American play was the "kiss of death" to box office success. For that, the worlds of theater and Civil Rights owed her a debt of gratitude. Tragically, cancer exacted repayment only six years later at age thirty-four. And so it was that six hundred mourners, including the greats of theater and the Civil Rights movement, braved a blizzard to pack the sanctuary of Harlem's Church of the Master on January 16, 1965.

Delivering the eulogy was one of the greats of both worlds, Paul Robeson. Still weak from his own bout with illness, he led the mourners in praise: "Her roots were deep in her people's history. As an artist she reflected the light and struggles of our day." Quoting a spiritual, he concluded, "'Sometimes I feel like an eagle in the air.' As Lorraine says farewell, she bids us keep our heads high and to hold on to our strength and powers, to soar like the eagle."

Among the mourners was Malcolm X. He and Robeson, mutual admirers, had never met. Malcolm hoped to do so at Hansberry's funeral, but word came that the elder preferred to wait for a "less stressful" time. It was not to be. One month later many of the same people would mourn the loss of Malcolm himself (see February 21).

FOR AFRICAN AMERICANS, the official entrance of the United States into World War II tolled bitter echoes of World War I. Again, black men were being called upon to ensure for others the very freedoms they themselves were being denied. On the embattled homefront, African Americans had to wage war for jobs (see June 25) and for respect as soldiers (see July 6). Considering all this, a January 17, 1942, headline in the *New York Age* came as little surprise: "Negroes Not Backing War Effort Fully."

That week, delegates from twenty national organizations had convened at the Harlem YMCA as the National Coordinating Committee. William H. Hastie, the first black federal judge, asked those assembled for their personal views on the war and their sense of opinions in the wider community. As the *Age* reported, "the question produced an embattled controversy among some of the race's most prominent leaders." The outcome of a vote on whether to support the war effort was a resounding nay. Reflecting the mood on the street, this anonymous quote best summed up feelings nationwide: "Just carve on my tombstone, 'Here lies a black man killed fighting a yellow man for the protection of a white man.'"

But many men did go to war, as had every generation of African Americans since the Revolutionary War began in 1776. Fighting two enemies—the declared foe and their racist countrymen—they served honorably. Among them: Dorie Miller, America's first World War II hero, who was awarded the Navy Cross for distinguished service at Pearl Harbor; the Tuskegee airmen who amassed eighty-eight Distinguished Flying Crosses; the 332nd Fighter Group and the 99th Pursuit Squadron, which together earned a presidential citation and eight hundred medals. Equally impressive, the man who gave the greatest peace to the greatest number beyond caste and class was a civilian, Dr. Charles Drew. This African American doctor's pioneering dissertation, "Banked Blood," became the model for World War II's blood banks and still saves countless lives.

JANUARY 18

"**P**LANT A TREE, A SHRUB, OR A BUSH" Lady Bird Johnson urged. As first lady, she had launched a campaign to beautify America. But, thrust against a backdrop of cities enflamed by riot and Vietnamese rice paddies fertilized with napalm, her program had become fodder for bad jokes. In a new initiative, Mrs. Johnson hosted a White House luncheon on January 18, 1968, at which she sought to enlist women in the fight against urban crime. Johnson planted a seed for discussion: "What Citizens Can Do to Insure Safe Streets." But as she spoke, what took root in one of her guests—singer-actress Eartha Kitt—were seeds of rebellion.

War was igniting the streets, charged Kitt. "You send the best of this country off to be shot and maimed. They rebel in the street . . . because they're going to be snatched off from their mothers to be shot in Vietnam." Stunned, the first lady countered, "Because there is a war on . . . that still doesn't give us a free ticket not to try to work for better things such as against crime in the streets, better education and better health for our people." But Kitt was on a different plane. "I have lived in the gutters," said poverty's child and high achiever. "The children of America are not rebelling for no reason."

Kitt's remarks were not received well. A poor player in a high-stakes political drama, she had misjudged her role. Blacklisted in a reputed presidential backlash, she self-exiled in Europe. The White House had squandered another chance to work with its critics. Six weeks later, in a live televised address that surprised even his closest associates, President Lyndon Johnson added his own name to the list of war casualties. "I will not seek and I will not accept . . ." Johnson declared, rejecting nomination to a second term. As the nation warred on at home and abroad, Johnson's retreat marked a turning point in the battle for Civil Rights. Through voting rights, affirmative action, and the "war on poverty," Lyndon Johnson's impact on everyday black life was arguably second only to Abraham Lincoln's. But both had merely acknowledged human rights duly ours.

JANUARY 19

SNCC's DIRECTOR OF COMMUNICATIONS, Julian Bond, once observed that not only was a picture worth a thousand words, it was worth thousands of dollars to the cash-poor freedom movement. On January 19, 1965, one of those pictures captured Alabama Sheriff James Clark's brutal arrest of Amelia Boynton during a peaceful voting rights march. The photo ran in the next day's *Washington Post* and *New York Times*.

In the South, where slavery's legacy was still borne out by its majority-black populace, preserving white supremacy meant keeping blacks away from the polls. In the 1870s, after the Civil War, when the Constitution was amended to guarantee citizenship and voting rights for black men, whites had tasted what the power of a black electorate could do as black governors, senators, congressmen, and local officials took office. When women got the vote in 1920, keeping blacks down became even more of an issue. Any common-interest, common-sense vote by oppressed blacks and women would upset the power structure. Poll taxes, grandfather clauses, and literacy tests were the tactics of choice to impede the black vote. When each was struck down in the courts, blacks were simply refused by registrars. When all else failed, there was intimidation and violence. In Selma, Amelia Boynton was one of the few registered black voters. An activist, she taught others to fill out intricate, prohibitive questionnaires, and escorted aspiring voters to the registrar and personally vouched for their characters: she was pivotal in Selma's voting rights showdown. As a leader of the Dallas County Voters' League, she was Clark's "Public Enemy #1."

She was also the movement's celebrated new poster person. With wry humor, SCLC's Rev. Abernathy nominated Clark for honorary membership in the Dallas County Voters' League for services rendered in publicity and fund-raising above and beyond the call of duty. Clark's brutality was real; so was the need for cash to carry on the freedom fight. Both increased with the spread of the photo.

Photography   Images

JANUARY 20

O<small>N</small> J<small>ANUARY</small> 20, 1970, Dr. Benjamin E. Mays was elected president of the Atlanta Board of Education. As congratulations arrived by the barrel load, one lone rotten apple could not spoil the bunch: "Dear nigger: How does it feel to get elected to a job strictly on your color?" This, to the president emeritus of Morehouse College, an elder statesman of theology and education, an adviser to President John F. Kennedy, a mentor-eulogizer to Dr. King, and the recipient of twenty-eight honorary doctorates.

This occurred sixteen years after *Brown v. Board of Education* legally desegregated schools (see May 17, May 31). Just months after Atlanta elected Maynard Jackson its first black mayor (see October 16). As a soulful lyric of the day promised, "change was gonna come . . ." That change, based on Dr. Mays's philosophy of education, was best stated in his own words as written in his autobiography, *Born to Rebel:*

> If integration means or implies that one must forswear his identity as a Negro, I reject it. . . . The current emphasis on black studies is a tribute to the black heroes of history who died fighting for freedom and equality during slavery and since emancipation, men who were never ashamed of being black. It is a tribute . . . especially to Carter G. Woodson, who spent his life . . . researching the Negro, past and present, and publishing books on the Negro at a time when white historians were degrading the black man and denying him his rightful place in history, and while many Negroes were denying their African heritage. I believe in black studies. American education is incomplete and partially false unless it gives due credit to the contributions that Afro-Americans have made to the development of this great country. . . . Frankly, it doesn't matter to me how this is done— whether there are departments of black studies, majors in black studies, schools of black studies, or an honest-to-goodness integrated curriculum which gives black men their rightful place in the history of this country. This needs to be done not only to give the Negro a sense of worth and well-being, but also to set the historical records straight and to enlighten the mind of white America.

Education   Purpose

WE SPEAK OF crosses burnings, and we envision
southern terrain. We speak of segregation and terror,
and again the South comes to mind. These pictures have been
historically cropped to distort the truth: not one U.S. state is
without a history of institutionalized violence against people
of color by whites who feel entitled and empowered to commit
brutal acts with total impunity. The difference between the
South and the North is actually one of degree and decree.

By degree, the scapegoating of blacks for social ills in the
South was compounded by generations of anger over the loss
of the Civil War. An economy based on exploitation by slavery
was rebuilt into an economy based on exploitation by segregation—an underpaid majority-black labor force was over-
charged for minimal services and terrorized into submission.
The North pitted a minority-black population against newly
arriving low-cost European immigrant labor and extended the
privileges of racism to whites. It was a pattern codified by the
Supreme Court in its Dred Scott ruling of 1857: a black man
had no rights a white was bound to respect. Simply stated: the
South practiced de jure segregation—segregation as a matter
of law.

The North was short on law, long on custom. Its segregation was de facto—a matter of fact. On January 21, 1954, a
New York Times headline read: "Fires Force Negro to Sell Long
Island Home." Amid growing violence, a black family announced that they would not move into their new home in
suburban New York. After the house suffered two arson-
ignited fires in eight days, the bank reneged on an already-
signed mortgage; insurance company retreat was expected to
follow. Fearing for the lives of their young sons, the parents
could no longer continue their "brave stand" on "principle."
With this incident in mind, why would a black family seek its
"better life" in a white neighborhood? Because, as distinct
from the segregated South, there were no suburban black areas in the ghettoized North. That too, a missing part of the picture now restored to truth.

JANUARY 22

In January 1971, a letter received by *Ebony* magazine's associate editor, Peter Bailey, changed his life and gave the gift of a better life to a child.

"In May, Reggie will be five," wrote Sister Rita Conyers, director of public relations at New York Foundling Hospital. "If we do not find adoptive parents for him by that time it will be necessary for us to transfer him to another institution." Little Reggie, whose photo was enclosed in the letter, had become a ward of the hospital just months after his birth. If *Ebony* could do a story on him, the letter implored, perhaps he could be adopted before being condemned to a cycle of endless foster homes and public institutions—a life of guaranteed failure. "He had been there all that time, waiting for someone to like him enough to adopt him as their child," thought Bailey, who had always been aware (in a back-of-the-brain sort of way) that all too many children were in need of loving homes. But something about Reggie—his plight, his picture, his bright smile and bright red suit, his need for love—tugged at Bailey, who knew he would have to help find a home for Reggie. Four months later he found that home—his.

For years, Bailey had been politically active. He'd been there when Malcolm X rallied Harlem. He'd talked the talk of black manhood and pride. He'd been devout about the Black Liberation Movement position that "black people must look out for each other." Now it was time to turn ideology into practice. But Bailey was a bachelor and didn't think he could adopt a child. Yet, the better he got to know Reggie, the more he loved him. When Sister Rita assured Bailey that single people could indeed adopt and that he had already demonstrated the all-important qualities of caring and love, things came together for Peter—not for the sake of a cause but for the love of *his* child. On June 7, 1971, Malcolm Reginald Bailey came home for good. In April 1972, Peter and Reggie Bailey became by law what they had been in spirit for a year—daddy and son.

JANUARY 23

COMMENTING ON JOB OPTIONS for black women, Hattie McDaniel, the first black Oscar-winner, once quipped, "I'd rather play a maid for fifteen hundred dollars a week, than be one for fifteen." It was a sentiment shared by the best-known black stage and screen actors of the day. With their roles restricted to buffoons and butlers, mammies and maids, the only difference was that the theater paid less. Against this backdrop, a *Philadelphia Record* article dated January 23, 1947, was great news. "In theaters the country over—and this includes some cities below the Mason and Dixon Line," it reported, "audiences are accepting Negro actors, not because they are quaint, but because they are actors." Significantly, this meant better jobs for black actors and better images for the black community.

The turning point had come slowly in the mid-1940s with the success of *Anna Lucasta*, an American Negro Theatre (ANT) production originally staged in the basement of Harlem's 135th Street library. The play soon moved to Broadway, where it enjoyed a three-year run. One reason reported for its success was that "the Negro actors play it straight, without appeal to race." A better reason was the quality of the cast, which featured some of the best actors of the day: Hilda Simms (in the role that made her famous), Frederick O'Neal (cofounder of ANT and the first black actor elected president of Actors' Equity, the actor's union), Alice Childress (a noted author), and Earle Hyman (who achieved TV renown on *The Cosby Show* of the 1980s. Later casts and road companies featured Ossie Davis and Ruby Dee (whose fifty-year careers have spanned film, theater, television, and the lecture circuit), and the legendary Canada Lee.

Interestingly, Canada Lee pioneered in the push for non-traditional casting of black actors in roles not specifically written for African Americans. After *Anna Lucasta*, Lee played Caliban in Shakespeare's *A Midsummer Night's Dream* without the audience's knowing that he was African American. A dark-skinned man, Lee wore light makeup for the role.

JANUARY 24

I T HAD BEEN FIVE MONTHS since the lynching of four-teen-year-old Emmett Till (see August 31, September 22). The dust had yet to settle on the story. Who could forget the bashed-in face of the mutilated child? But, as familiar as people thought they were with the story and the awful history of lynching in the United States, most were surprised that no one had ever asked the men acquitted of the crime if they had done it. The community assumed they had, and that it was their job to clear the two. A defense attorney even admitted that because he did not want to lie to his wife and say they were innocent, he never asked. Author William Bradford Huie did. On January 24, 1956, *Look* magazine published his report, "The Shocking Story of Approved Killing in Mississippi."

Huie was doing a book and film about the Emmett Till case, and offered the acquitted men $4,000 for "portrayal rights" to their story. But if he found them to be lying, he wouldn't pay a dime. That was the deal. "Facts which the prosecution had been unable to present at the trial, I found easily; the scene of the slaying . . . the time of the disposal of the body. Moreover— and to some . . . this sounds incredible—[J. W.] Milam and [Roy] Bryant were not reluctant to talk." Yes. They'd killed Emmett Till. The boy had "wolf-whistled" Bryant's wife, and they had done what any "real American" "red-blooded, Anglo-Saxon southern white man" would do. "I didn't intend to kill the nigger when we went and got him—just whip him and chase him back up yonder," said Milam. "But what the hell! I counted pictures o' three white gals in his pocketbook before I burned it. What else could I do? No use lettin' him get no bigger!"

A year later, *Look* published Huie's follow-up, "What Hap-pened to the Emmett Till Killers?" People who had supported and defended Milam and Bryant now shunned them. Said one such citizen, "They're a tough bunch. And you know there's just one thing wrong with encouraging one o' these pecker-woods to kill a nigger. He don't know when to stop—and the rascal may wind up killing you."

JANUARY 25

The exact date is in dispute, but the event itself is secure in Antiguan history and lore. On or about January 25, 1951, on a colonial plantation somewhere near the village of Bethesda, V. C. Bird, a young man who would be transformed from union organizer to national hero, perched beneath a now-legendary tamarind tree and changed the future. There, before him, huddled a mass of overworked and grossly underpaid cane-field workers. There too was the managing director of Antigua Sugar Estates, with all the might of Great Britain on his side. The workers, bent low from inhumane labor conditions and unspent rage, clothed in tattered rags, had reached the end of the line on exploitation. No more.

Staring down his powerful foe and lifting the crowd to action with his words, Bird vowed that his people would no longer work for a shilling a day. They would strike until they were accorded better conditions and better pay. It is said that like an Old Testament prophet, he raised his great arm and thundered, "We will eat cockles and the widdy widdy bush. We will drink pond water." An old man interviewed years later recalled the managing director's response: "I will crush you into subjection. I will beat your head against a wall." To this, V. C. Bird repeated with defiance, "We will eat the widdy widdy bush," again referring to a local plant as prickly and unsatisfying as the predicament in which the workers found themselves. After all, as the strikers saw it, what did they have to lose? One hundred seventeen years after slavery ended in the Caribbean, they were no better off than before.

One year later, despite the predictable hardship of the workers' resistance, they won a 25 percent pay raise. Because wages had been so low to start, the victory amounted to little in actual cash. But it was the beginning of the end for British rule and a defining moment in Antigua's history. Thirty years later, in 1981, three hundred years after Britain seized the island and enslaved their ancestors—with V. C. Bird as prime minister, Antigua gained independence.

Labor

JANUARY 26

ONE EXPECTS TO view abortion as an issue of women's liberation. But, by Friday, January 26, 1973, as people sorted through the implications of the *Roe v. Wade* decision legalizing abortion with which the Supreme Court opened the week, it was apparent that the people most liberated by it would be black men. As those who understand history well know, abortion is one of those issues that takes on a different hue when African American history is excluded from the picture.

Historically, rape has been a difficult crime to prove in all instances but one: when the alleged rapist is black and the alleged victim is white. When abortion was illegal, what should have been a private matter could be sadistically propelled into a sordid, racist, political affair and worse—*a good-ole time for good-ole boys.* Bluntly stated, the all-too-frequent scenario went something like this: a white woman with an unwanted pregnancy alleged rape by a black man. If she did not identify such a man directly, one would be supplied. She got an abortion. He got lynched.

Given the much less fractious episodes excluded from American history, it is no surprise that this rape/abortion scenario has been expunged. But Ida B. Wells-Barnett, the noted writer/lecturer, addressed it in her antilynching campaigns. So did the reparations campaigner Queen Mother Moore. And in 1995, a poignant account came from Jibreel Khazan (formerly Ezell Blair Jr.), one of the original Greensboro student sit-ins (see January 31).

Speaking at the Smithsonian Institution in 1995, Khazan tearfully recounted an experience that had haunted and motivated him for forty years. He was eleven and living in Greensboro when "a poor African American laborer got accused of raping a white woman. He didn't do it. But Mr. Scales died in the gas chamber. Then the white man's wife confessed he did it and put it on this African American man. I remember my two friends crying every night for their father."

JANUARY 27

BRAVO! ON JANUARY 27, 1961, Leontyne Price made her long-awaited debut at the Metropolitan Opera House in New York. With her performance as Leonora in *El Travatore*, she joined a very short list of African Americans who had walked that stage, and became the first black woman to achieve international recognition as "prima donna assoluta."

Now this is what all of this means. That historic night, the curtains were slowly reined down, a woman of extraordinary ability and grace walked center stage to receive her well-deserved adulation, and an audience of thousands of sophisticated opera aficionados applauded and cheered her nonstop for *forty-two minutes!*

As the incomparable diva was quoted in *I Dream a World:*

My proudest moment, operatically speaking, was my debut at the Metropolitan. It was my first real victory, my first unqualified acceptance as an American, as a human being, as a black, as an artist, the whole thing. I was the first black diva that was going to hang on. My being prepared is the reason I didn't go away. That is really the substance of my pioneering. Marion [Anderson] had opened the door. I kept it from closing again. . . .

I don't love anything more than hearing my own voice. It's a personal adoration. Listening to my recordings is like filling your pores with inspiration, and where better to get it from than yourself, because that substance is a combination of everyone who contributed something, your mama, your papa, the community, your teachers, everybody and everything. Applause is the fulfillment. From Mississippi to the Met. That's the pinnacle. That forty-two-minute ovation was like having climbed the mountain. . . .

JANUARY 28

How to tell the history of African colonization in the midst of brutal oppression. That was the challenge Jomo Kenyatta, anthropologist and Kenya's future president, faced as he wrote his 1938 classic, *Facing Mount Kenya*. In the tradition of his Kikuyu ancestors, he related a parable, "The Gentlemen of the Jungle":

> Once upon a time a heavy thunderstorm broke out, elephant went to his friend, a man, and asked to slip just his trunk inside the man's hut to protect it from the rain. The hut was barely big enough for the man, but he considered elephant a friend and said yes. Before long, elephant squeezed in his trunk and everything else belonging to him. As the man grumbled, in shock, jungle creatures came from near and far. He grumbled so loud, he even attracted King Lion. You have done well to make friends in the jungle, lion told the man and commanded his ministers, of whom elephant was one, to appoint a Commission of Enquiry. Relieved, the man awaited his hearing. On the appointed day Mr. Rhinoceros, Mr. Buffalo, Mr. Alligator, Mr. Leopard, and The Rt. Hon. Mr. Fox as chairman heard the case. Speaking animal to animal, elephant said that the man had asked him into the hut to save it from a hurricane. Unoccupied at the time they spoke, his weight could better secure it. How could he, elephant, do any less than help the man? Of course, he had turned it to better use. Shocked, the man wanted to tell the true story. No need, the commission said, elephant had explained the events. The only issue was this: had he or had he not ever exited his hut? After a delicious lunch provided by elephant, the commission rendered its verdict: the man had lost title to the hut, but he could build another elsewhere. Angry, but fearful of the many-clawed animals, the man moved on and built another hut. Soon came rhinoceros, who took it for his snout; then another brought buffalo, and on down the line. "*Ng'enda thi ndagaga motegi*," the man said to himself: "You can't fool a man forever." With that he built the biggest and best hut ever. As the jungle lords battled over it, he set it afire and burnt it to the ground. "Peace is costly, but it's worth the expense," he said, and lived happily ever after.

Historiography   Wisdom

JANUARY 29

WHILE THE GREAT DEPRESSION hit the country in 1929, economic depression had long been a way of life for blacks. Nowhere was that more visible than in housing, where forced poverty, segregated communities, and official contempt locked people into substandard dwellings. Those fleeing the agricultural South in search of better days soon found themselves in the teeming tenements of the industrial North. But in 1936, along with President Franklin D. Roosevelt's "New Deal," came new hope for low-income families. In New York, the former-governor-now-president's home state, federal funds for low-cost housing were earmarked for Harlem—at last! But while the need was estimated at $100 million, only $5 million was allocated. The Harlem River Houses—a network of four- and five-story walk-ups, containing forty-six three- and four-room apartment units for 552 families—was one of the nation's first "projects." How to decide which families to house, that was the question.

On January 29, 1936, a *New York Herald Tribune* article proposed an answer: "Choice of Tenants Urged!" Groundbreaking on the Harlem River Houses had broken new ground on candor as well. A report prepared by New York City's Housing Authority had stated that the project could not "accomplish solution of the Harlem slum situation." The article also confirmed what was usually denied: "discrimination against Negroes in legitimate employment." Then, blaming the victim for the crime, the paper reported that "many Negroes who might apply for apartments were engaged in illegal enterprises, such as bootlegging, the numbers game, [and] drug peddling. . . . These persons were often better able to pay, the report said, than the elevator operator or porter, but they should not be admitted to the development 'because they might exploit the tenants from within.'"

Another thirty-six years would transpire before a presidential order addressed fair housing in 1962 (see November 20). Yet, most projects remain segregated and the historic causal maze linking employment and housing is still overlooked.

JANUARY 30

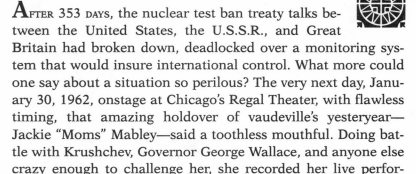

Aᴘᴛᴇʀ 353 ᴅᴀʏꜱ, the nuclear test ban treaty talks between the United States, the U.S.S.R., and Great Britain had broken down, deadlocked over a monitoring system that would insure international control. What more could one say about a situation so perilous? The very next day, January 30, 1962, onstage at Chicago's Regal Theater, with flawless timing, that amazing holdover of vaudeville's yesteryear—Jackie "Moms" Mabley—said a toothless mouthful. Doing battle with Krushchev, Governor George Wallace, and anyone else crazy enough to challenge her, she recorded her live performance, *Moms Mabley at the Geneva Conference:*

> I was fixin' to come here to Chicago sooner, ya know. But one mornin' 'bout two-thirty in the ᴀ.ᴍ., I got a call from John and Jackie at the White House. And to get a call from them at that time in the mornin' like to scare ole Moms to death. I thought it was something about my granddaughter, Caroline. . . .
>
> Well, they want me to see if I could do something to stop those folks from bustin' those bombs. Well, in my travels, in my time, I've met so many foreign people, ya know. I met Georgiaonians, and Alabamians, Mississippians, all them kind a foreign folks, ya know. . . .
>
> Well, then, first I go to Paris. Go to Paris, yeah. Go to Paris. I met so many young men. And every time they'd *parlez-vous* I'd *français.* . . .
>
> Then I grabbed the plane and I went over to meet Krusch. And I said to him, "You wanna fight us? Do you want to fight us?" And he started talkin' 'bout how many men he got up in the stratosphere. How many men he got up there on the moon. And I said, "Damn that, fool. We ain't gon' fight up there, we gonna fight down here. Alabama, Mississippi, or any other foreign country you wanna fight in. I say in my estimation you ain' nothin' but a little short sawed-off FBI (fat, bald, and impossible). . . .

And Moms reigned on. She was taking care of business. . . .

JANUARY 31

ON SUNDAY, JANUARY 31, 1960, four North Carolina A & T College freshmen sat in a Greensboro dormitory stewing over an incident that had happened earlier that day. Returning to campus from a weekend in Wilmington, Joe McNeil couldn't get anything to eat at the segregated bus terminal. Angered by the racism confronting them each day and energized by the courage displayed by so many other Civil Rights demonstrators, the four friends wanted to do something. But what? Together, they cooked up the plan they would act on the very next day.

On Monday, February 1, 1960, Ezell Blair Jr. (see January 26), Franklin McCain, Joseph McNeil, and David Richmond headed downtown. In Woolworth's they purchased school supplies and patiently waited for a receipt. Then, they sat down at the lunch counter and did a perfectly normal thing—they ordered coffee and doughnuts. When they were told to leave, they asked why they could be served at one counter and not another. Their cool logic was too much to handle. Employee confusion turned from hostility to confusion again. There was simply no protocol for the situation. In taking seats at that lunch counter, the four young men made an enduring place for themselves in the history of the human rights struggle worldwide.

In fact, sit-ins did not begin in Greensboro. In 1942, Civil Rights sit-ins had been waged by the Congress of Racial Equality (CORE) at Stoner's Restaurant in Chicago. But what seized the imagination and headlines in Greensboro was the initiative of the four A & T students acting completely on their own. Their action forged a movement that rocked the South to its core. Never before had segregationists been faced with this dilemma—their money or their way of life. If sit-in protesters weren't served, they would block the counter. When they were dragged off and arrested, the commotion deterred other patrons. By mid-February 1960, the sit-in movement had spread to fifteen cities in five states. And by mid-October, things had begun to change for the better (see October 17).

Sit-ins   Initiative

FEBRUARY

Julian Bond. Photographer unknown. Courtesy of the author.

For more information about Julian Bond, please see April 1 and October 16.

FEBRUARY 1

IN SELMA, ALABAMA, each volunteer had a story to tell, like this one about an elderly man:

> We went up to the registrar, and as he began to write in a very unsteady way . . . the registrar said, "Now, you're going across the line, old man. You failed already, you can't register, you can't vote, you just as well get out of line." The old man looked at him and said, "I own a hundred and forty acres of land. I've got ten children who are grown and many of them are in a field where they can help other people. I've got a man who's a preacher and a man who's a teacher . . . and I took these hands that I have and made crops to put them through school. If I am not worthy of being a registered voter, then God have mercy on this city."

That man, like most, was never registered. Added to registrars, another deterrent was Sheriff James Clark. A photo of his arrest of Amelia Boynton (see January 19) was national news. Now Clark was news again. Asked why so few blacks were allowed to register, Clark boasted to the press that it was "largely because of their mental IQ." But when a similar question was posed to the judge who issued an order banning meetings of more than three blacks at a time, it was the judge's intelligence that came into question. Judge James Hare explained that blacks couldn't vote because, "You see, most of your Selma Negroes are descended from the Ebo and Angola tribes of Africa. You could never teach or trust an Ebo back in slave days, and even today I can spot their tribal characteristics. They have protruding heels, for instance.

Knowing the power of nonviolence to bring out a segregationist's true nature, one of King's goals was to expose Clark and company. "In the name of decency," he counted on "Americans of conscience" to call for federal aid. On February 1, 1965, Clark arrested Dr. King as per King's strategy. In 1963, his inspired "Letter from a Birmingham Jail" (see April 16) had proven so effective that he wrote "Letter from a Selma Jail" before his planned arrest. Its publication as a *New York Times* ad on February 5, 1965, coincided with his release from jail.

Voter Registration   Determination

FEBRUARY 2

On February 2, 1970, Maya Angelou burst on the literary scene with the publication of her memoir of childhood, *I Know Why the Caged Bird Sings*. A St. Louis childhood rape had rendered her mute for five years. But she was brought back by the healing love of a grandmother in Stamps, Arkansas, the tough love of a teacher who started her speaking again, and the teenage motherhood that even gave her something to sing about. Said Angelou, "Love affords wonder."

Over the years, she would reclaim her voice and expand the human vistas of her audience with the power of her pen. In her acknowledgments to *Caged Bird*, she wrote, "I thank my mother, Vivian Baxter, and my brother, Bailey Johnson, who encouraged me to remember. Thanks to the Harlem Writers' Guild for concern and to John O. Killens, who told me I could write." Write she could—and there would be so much to write about. For by the time she wrote that first book, Angelou also had been a dancer, a Tony Award–nominated actress, a Civil Rights worker with SCLC at Dr. King's invitation, an expatriate newspaper writer living in Ghana and Egypt, and a repatriated television producer. After the book, she would become a screenwriter, the first black woman to direct a Hollywood-backed feature film (*Georgia Georgia*, 1973), author of a dozen books, playwright, university professor, and Pulitzer Prize nominee. By 1993, she would add to her credits being asked to write the inaugural poem for President William Jefferson Clinton.

Said Angelou:

> One of the unfortunate results of living a legendary life and dying a legendary death is that when the person is written about, more often than not he is made larger than life. The human qualities of humor, being wrong, sometimes gauche, losing, forgetting, these wonderful qualities we all have are never mentioned. Well that's not true. I don't tell everything I know but what I do tell is the truth. . . . I weep a lot. I thank God I laugh a lot, too. The main thing in one's own private world is to try to laugh as much as you cry.

FEBRUARY 3

FOR INTEMPERATE CLIMATE and stifling heat, summer was no match for February in Alabama that year of 1956. Despite a steady diet of violence and intimidation, never before had the brutality of racism been more desperate or taken less effect. In Birmingham, singer Nat King Cole was attacked by thugs who jumped onstage and later seized another man whose genitals they mutilated. In Montgomery, the bus boycott was ten months from victory, but blacks could already claim success for their unity and steely will. When the trial of Rosa Parks, whose arrest had launched the boycott, was kept off the docket to thwart a challenge of segregated buses in the state courts, five women circumvented the ploy by filing a federal suit. At a Montgomery rally, as Mississippi Senator James Eastland railed against the NAACP, his supporters distributed their "declaration of independence":

> When in the course of human events it becomes necessary to abolish the Negro race, proper methods should be used. Among these are guns . . . slingshots and knives. We hold these truths to be self-evident—that all whites are created equal with certain rights, among these are life, liberty and the pursuit of dead niggers. . . . We will soon wake up and find Reverend King in the White House.

It was in this environment that Autherine Lucy desegregated the University of Alabama at Tuscaloosa on February 3, 1956. A graduate of Miles College, she had wanted to attend graduate school. A three-year NAACP Legal Defense Fund fight paved her way to admission. Three days later, students shouting "Let's kill her" erupted in riot. She was sequestered for *their* safety. When she charged the university with conspiring with the mob, she was expelled. That June, the state of Alabama outlawed the NAACP for activities injurious to the peace.

In 1988, the university overturned its expulsion and invited Lucy to re-enroll. A more appropriate effort would have included an honorary doctorate for having risked her life only to be denied a degree and justice. But it's never too late. . . .

FEBRUARY 4

FEBRUARY 4, 1965, found Malcolm X in the Bible Belt South, where his politics and his religion were lightning rods for conflict with two establishments—one white, one black. White response was predictable. As Nation of Islam leader Elijah Muhammad often noted, if 20 million African Americans allied with 500 million Moslems worldwide, the threat would shatter the Christian West. What he hadn't said was that many black Christians were similarly alarmed.

Malcolm had long made the point that when blacks were being segregated and abused no one had stopped to ask our religion: we were enslaved and segregated solely based on color. So was there really cause for alarm on the part of black Christians? As historian John Henrik Clarke said of Muhammad's Nation, "He didn't steal [followers] from the little church, big church, or the lodges, he found a haven for the people who had no haven. He was the king to those who had no kings, and he was the messiah to those who some people thought unworthy of a messiah." From this root, Malcolm X founded mosques and built a following by "fishing," as he called it, for the souls of the lost with a consciousness-raising form of Islam tailored to the needs of the northern black ghettos.

But by 1965 the South's needs were different, and Malcolm had changed, too (see October 18). He hadn't come to Selma on a "fishing" trip. He had come to build alliances with other black leaders. At the invitation of SNCC's Stokely Carmichael, he was in Selma to deliver his first Civil Rights speech. Dr. King was also in Selma that day—jailed for a voting rights demonstration. Addressing an overflow crowd, Malcolm said the right thing at the right time: "White people should thank Dr. King for holding people in check. There are others who do not believe in [nonviolence]. If the white people realize what the alternative is, perhaps they will be more willing to hear Dr. King." Whether by coincidence or providence, that very day a federal judge ordered Selma's registrar to process at least a hundred black applicants daily.

Leadership   Purpose

FEBRUARY 5

F ROM FEBRUARY 3 TO 5, 1961, as SNCC leaders met at Atlanta's Butler Street YMCA to chart the new year, the student movement was at a crossroads. Meeting on the first anniversary of the Greensboro student sit-ins (see January 31) that had inspired the founding of their Student Nonviolent Coordinating Committee, SNCC, they now felt firsthand what their movement elders had experienced the year before: student activism could be followed and aided, but it could not be led by traditional top-down methods. Even as they met, the Rock Hill Jail-In was taking the movement to new heights. A phone call from a jailed warrior served notice and requested backup troops. In a death-defying move—given the brutal treatment of other jailed black dissidents—students arrested for a Rock Hill, South Carolina, lunch counter sit-in rejected the old jail-in-bail-out strategy. They had taken thirty days of hard labor in lieu of paying a $100 fine.

The movement would have to adapt to these needs-based power shifts, counseled Rev. Kelly Miller Smith of Nashville's First Baptist Church, a local movement headquarters. As Christian soldiers themselves, perhaps they could take comfort in knowing that they had taught their children well. (A little too well, thought some.) Assuaging his flock of fearful elders and parents, Smith advised those who could not well suffer the power shift to, at least, appreciate its precedent:

> The students sat at the lunch counters alone to eat and, when refused service, to wait and pray. And as they sat there on that southern Mount of Olives, the Roman soldiers, garbed in the uniforms of Nashville policemen and wielding night sticks, came and led the praying children away. As they walked down the streets, through a red light, and toward Golgotha, the segregationist mob shouted jeers, pushed and shoved them, and spat in their faces, but the suffering students never said a mumbling word. Once the martyr mounts the Cross, wears the crown of thorns, and feels the pierce of the sword in his side there is no turning back. . . . And there is no turning back for those who follow in the martyr's steps.

FEBRUARY 6

"As late as 1945, Portland was known as the 'Worst City in Race Relations North of the Mason Dixon Line,'" wrote Edwin W. Berry, executive secretary of the Urban League of Portland, Oregon. It was "a Northern City with a Southern Exposure." Four years later, the city had a different look and feel. But had it really changed? Hoping for a success story for their February 1949 "Brotherhood Month" issue, editors of the *Christian Register* asked Berry for an update.

Berry could cite a decline in police brutality and gains in jobs, public service, home purchases, public schools, and newspaper coverage of blacks in stories unrelated to crime and sports. Portland had a new appellation, the "Nation's Most Improved City in Race Relations." But being the "most improved" and being the "best" were two different things. In 1945, Berry credited "greed, hate, and vested interests" with keeping segregation alive. In 1949, Jim Crow was down but not out. "He's existing in an oxygen tent," wrote Berry. "Most Americans are a part of the great army of 'bystanders' . . . neither a part of the forward looking citizens, nor of the reactionaries. Overwhelmingly possessed with inertia [they are] governed by tradition rather than by conviction."

So what helped create the new atmosphere in Portland? Nature and time. In 1948, a flood destroyed the nearby city of Vanport. Twenty-two thousand people had had to be relocated within minutes, and there was simply no time for the Red Cross to implement segregation. Emergency interracial contact helped forge change. When CIO labor leaders made desegregated facilities a condition for Portland's becoming their 1948 convention city, restaurants and hotels changed for the good of their businesses. Then there was the issue of vigilance. City policy was regularly decided on the "crude premise that you'll holler when you're hurt." With 300,000 individual pieces of educational material on race relations, a PR campaign to broadcast media, a speakers bureau, and library tables well stocked with handouts, the Urban League had decided to holler—loud and often.

FEBRUARY 7

ON FEBRUARY 7, 1968, in Washington, Dr. King held a press conference to announce the Poor People's Campaign (see June 19). As crews packed their equipment, veteran television reporter Daniel Schorr (see February 11) noticed that King appeared "disconsolate." Asked why, King replied mournfully, "I don't know if you are aware of [what you people in television] are doing, but you keep driving people like me, who are nonviolent, into saying more and more militant things, and if we don't say things militantly enough for you, we don't get on the evening news. . . . And secondly, you're putting a premium on violence."

It was true. The Civil Rights era had come of age in the infancy of television, and the camera's craving for action had been satisfied by increasing levels of violence. The better the picture, the more likely it was for those pictured to make the evening news. Segregationists and desegregationists both depended on the medium to address and elicit support from far-flung constituencies. But whereas the camera afforded a measure of protection for Civil Rights demonstrators, it was often an unwanted method of detection for violent racists.

That very day, February 7, 1968, the guns of war were being aimed toward the next day's "Orangeburg Massacre." Black students from South Carolina State and Claflin College were protesting a segregated bowling alley. The National Guard had been called in to assure national observers of the state of "law and order." But when students continued their protest on February 8, police opened fire, killing three students and injuring twenty-eight. Most had been shot in the back.

There was a lot to be angry about in the killing fields of 1968: the lack of human and civil rights; the escalating war in Vietnam, into which those who benefited least from America's best were the first to be drafted; the assassinations of Dr. King and pro–Civil Rights presidential candidate Robert F. Kennedy; the summer riots by police and people of all races in cities coast-to-coast. Through it all, the camera partnered the scene. And what it said about America was less than kind.

Social History   Collective Responsibility

FEBRUARY 8

Sɪxᴛʏ ʏᴇᴀʀs ᴀɢᴏ, people were as puzzled about the sources of drugs in black communities as they are now. If legal black businesses were impeded by racism, how could a multibillion-dollar black-owned international drug ring flourish with ease? People were stumped until two mysteries were solved by one trunk on February 8, 1945.

Mystery #1: In 1939, a steamer trunk marked "furs" was shipped to Harlem from Cape Girardeau, Missouri, via Railway Express. Unclaimed and unopened for a year, the trunk was auctioned off to the highest bidder. What the buyer found upon receipt of the trunk was a lot more than he had bargained for: two million marijuana cigarettes packed in camphor balls so the odor of the marijuana would be undetectable. His immediate return of the trunk and its contents launched a five-year investigation into Mystery #2: where had the drugs come from and who had shipped them?

Analyzing similar shipments over the years, investigators reported their findings to U.S. Attorney John F. X. McGohey. Five shipments had been sent to Harlem from Missouri. Each of four contained 500 pounds of "mary-jane," as the marijuana was called on the street. One shipment, traced in 1943, contained 120 pounds and was sold to a Harlem distributor for $6.20. Total street value for the 320 pounds: over $2.5 million in uninflated 1945 dollars.

After trailing this high-profit, high-risk business to its source, investigators uncovered not a clandestine foreign operation but a home-grown business straight from the heartland—a farm in Chaffee, Missouri. The distributors were four whites. The two men and two women were indicted in New York on this day in 1945.

FEBRUARY 9

IN ARETHA FRANKLIN'S HOME is a statue of ancient Egypt's
Queen of the Nile, Nefertiti, a woman venerated for
her beauty. In 1967, the Queen of Soul, renowned for the
beauty of her voice, rounded a bend in her own life's stream.

Eleven years into the career that began at age fourteen, she
had achieved little financial success as a recording artist. She
was signed by Columbia's John Hammond, the producer
known for his associations with Bessie Smith and Billie Holiday, but the songs chosen for her cast her as a pretender to the
blues or jazz throne. Although Franklin's voice beheld the history, the passion, and the tradition of African American music
and its queens, her own unique sound was unappreciated. In
1966, the contract lapsed by mutual agreement.

In early 1967, she was brought to Atlantic Records by another major producer, Jerry Wexler. But Franklin disappeared
in the middle of her first session. Side one of the single "I
Never Loved a Man (the Way I Love You)" had been recorded.
It was so good that Wexler later commented, "I had to get used
to that kind of greatness!" But there was no side two and no
Aretha Franklin. Temperament hadn't disrupted her work, observers noted; sadness had. Her marriage was souring; her career was uncertain. Then, as suddenly, she was back. On February 9, 1967, she was in the studio with her sister, Carolyn.
They were experimenting with a sound—an outrageousness of
sorts, a freedom let loose around a phrase they had created:
"sock it to me, sock it to me." They began working the line on
the piano, working it through on an Otis Redding song. Five
days later, on Valentine's Day, what came out was pure gold.
Setting free her own unique style, appreciating the beauty distinctively and instinctively her own, she soared. It was the
take-charge, never-look-back moment in an extraordinary career. Aretha delivered the lines that would become the anthem
of the freedom movements of blacks and women: R-E-S-P-E-C-T.
Just a little *respect*. That's what she deserved. That's what she
wanted. And, with her rallying cry of the decade, that's what
she got.

Music   Respect for One's Power

FEBRUARY 10

R<small>EADERS OF</small> *L<small>IFE</small>* <small>MAGAZINE</small>'s mid-February 1963 issue were in for a treat as pugilist-poet Cassius Clay (Muhammad Ali) modestly declared, "I Am The Greatest":

> This is a story about a man
> With iron fists and a beautiful tan.
> He talks a lot and he boasts indeed
> Of a powerful punch and blinding speed.
> The fight game was dying
> And Promoters were crying
> For someone to come along
> With a new and different song.
> Patterson was dull, quiet and sad,
> And Sonny Liston was just as bad.
> Then along came a kid named Cassius Clay,
> Who said, "Liston, I'll take your title away."
> This colorful fighter is something to see,
> And heavyweight champ he's certain to be.
> You get the impression while watching him fight
> That he plays cat and mouse, then turns out the light.
> What a frustrating feeling I'm sure it must be,
> To be hit by blows you can't even see.
> Where was he first? Where was he last?
> How can you conquer a man so fast?
> I'm sure his opponents have tried their best,
> But one by one on the canvas they rest.
> Everyone knew when Cassius wasn't around,
> For quietness descended on the town.
> If Clay says a mosquito can pull a plow,
> Don't ask him how—Hitch him up!

FEBRUARY 11

THE HISTORY OF THE AFRICAN independence and U.S. Civil Rights movements was full of destabilizing lurches forward and back. Then, on February 11, 1976, the code was cracked on otherwise unfathomable occurrences with the publication of the Pike Papers—named for New York Congressman Otis Pike, chairman of the House Select Committee on Intelligence. Readers of the transcripts in the *Village Voice*'s supplement were shocked by the covert (and ofttimes illegal) CIA and FBI activities that had shaped history. After a major eruption, the source of the leak to the *Village Voice* was found to be CBS television news reporter Daniel Schorr. But the issue was not the source, it was the substance of "The CIA Report the President Doesn't Want You to Read":

On Angola:

> A task force composed of high U.S. experts on Africa strongly opposed military intervention . . . last April they called for diplomatic efforts to encourage a political settlement among three factions to avert bloodshed. Apparently at the direction of National Security Council aides, the task force recommendation was . . . presented to NSC members as merely one policy option. . . . Control of resources may be a factor. Angola has significant oil deposits and two American multinationals, Gulf and Texaco, operate in the offshore area. . . . Pursuant to Section 662 of the Foreign Assistance Act of 1974, the President has found that the Angola action program is "important to the national security."

On surveillance:

> In August 1972, an [FBI] agent collected some [Institute for Policy Studies] garbage. . . . Eight used typewriter ribbons were found. [Al]though there were no signs of crimes, and despite the fact that IPS itself was not suspected of crimes, FBI devoted time and money to the expensive process of reconstructing the documents that had been typed by the ribbon. . . . FBI officials told Committee staff, under oath, that personal information . . . is discarded if it does not bear on a crime. That was not true. Information from the trash retrieval, including the sexual gossip, was incorporated into a number of reports [and] attributed to "a source who has supplied reliable information in the past."

Human Rights   Foundations

FEBRUARY 12

On this day—February 12—in 1926, Dr. Carter G. Woodson launched the first Negro History Week. For the greater part of American history, most blacks had been forbidden to read and write by law. When the laws were changed, we were still unable to read about our historic selves because historians had systematically expunged the black presence from scholarship. Standing in the shade of our own sun, most blacks neither knew the history of our people, nor knew that there was a history to be known. So successful had the "mis-education," as Woodson called it, been that those who condemned blacks as being devoid of a culture and without a past predating slavery were actually believed. Woodson sought to uplift an intellectually devastated people—reinforming the way African Americans saw themselves by filling in the missing pages of history.

In her autobiography written sixty years after that first Negro History Week, South African singer Miriam Makeba reflected upon the death of her mother and its impact on her view of history and self. It is worth noting how different is her sensibility—her sense of the past not as a burden but a balm:

> My mother. She was an extraordinary woman, an *isangoma* [medicine man or woman]. Though she died in 1960, she is still a very real part of my life. What is 1960? A date. A number. It has no meaning in my culture. In the West the past is like a dead animal. It is a carcass picked by the flies that call themselves historians and biographers. But in my culture the past lives. . . . Death does not separate us from our ancestors. . . . We make sacrifices to them and ask for their advice and guidance. They answer us in dreams or through a medium we call *isangoma*. When a Westerner is born, he or she enters a stream of time that is always flowing. When a point in life is passed, it is finished. When a Westerner dies, he leaves the stream, which flows on without him. But for us, birth plunges us into a pool in which the waters of past, present, and future swirl around together. Things happen and are done with, but they are not dead. After we splash about a bit in this life, our mortal beings leave the pool, but our spirits remain. I close my eyes . . . I look at the past and I see myself.

Historiography   **Self-affirmation**

FEBRUARY 13

On Saturday, February 13, 1960, inspired by Greensboro's spontaneous, successful, and fast-spreading sit-in movement (see January 31), Nashville launched its own sit-ins. Just the night before, Rev. James Lawson had convened what became the sit-in movement's first mass meeting. The next morning he activated a plan in which five hundred students participated. From Baptist Seminary, Fisk University, Meharry Medical, and Tennessee State, students descended on Nashville's First Baptist Church. Then neatly dressed rows of students were dispatched to downtown sit-in sites.

Who was this Rev. James Lawson—this spiritual guide to the student sit-ins? Of all the Civil Rights leaders, Lawson was the most devout, thoroughly grounded disciple of nonviolence. In 1951, when he was a Ph.D. candidate at Vanderbilt University's predominantly white divinity school, president of the United Methodist Youth Fellowship, and a conscientious objector, Lawson had refused military induction during the Korean War and gone to prison for his beliefs. Paroled to sponsors in the Methodist ministry, he went to India as a missionary. In India, he studied the philosophy of nonviolence with disciples of Gandhi and first read of Dr. Martin Luther King Jr. in the Nagpur *Times*.

Returning home, Lawson enrolled in Oberlin College's divinity school. In February 1957, King, fresh from his Montgomery Bus Boycott triumph, spoke at a dinner party held in his honor, and Lawson was among the guests. Lawson wanted to start a nonviolent movement in America. King wanted to replicate the success of Montgomery across the South. By evening's end, King had asked Lawson to come south to train others in nonviolent philosophy. Lawson agreed to come after completing school. "But we need you now," urged King. From these roots, Lawson and King would be brothers in the struggle to the end. Years later, as pastor of a Memphis church, Lawson agreed to help organize striking sanitation workers. Ironically, it was Lawson's call for support that brought King to Memphis, where he was tragically assassinated in 1968.

FEBRUARY 14

On this Valentine's Day, what could be more special than the love of a child—or, better still, the love of thousands of children—in other words, the story of the Boys Choir of Harlem and its founder, Dr. Walter Turnbull.

Walter Turnbull knew the transformative power of music. It had taken him from the cotton fields of Mississippi to the concert stages of the world. A graduate of Tougaloo College and Manhattan School of Music, he wanted to share his love of music. "My childhood may have been different from the one children experience nowadays in New York City," he said. "But we share poverty and a sense of hope and a desire for better things to come." In 1967, he began a small boys choir at Harlem's Ephesus Church while teaching in the New York City schools. When a teacher's strike (see September 9) divided loyalties and put children "at risk" in the cynicism of the adult crisis, Turnbull (like most of the black and nonunion teachers) taught throughout the strike. When he found himself faced with a music appreciation class of one hundred students, his choir idea came to the rescue and expanded his pool of students to audition for the church choir. But when fire gutted the church, the boys choir barely lumbered along. Then, in 1974, Turnbull was advised to set up a nonprofit corporation to attract the necessary funds to nurture his idea. For that, however, he needed a strong board of directors. As chairman, he hoped to attract Franklin Williams—a former Civil Rights lawyer and ambassador to Ghana—who was then president of the Phelps Stokes Fund. Williams didn't feel the idea was right for him. But he offered to help attract others.

On February 14, 1975, a seven-year-old Boys Choir of Harlem finally got its "start" with a Williams-hosted reception at the Fund. Attracting board members, fans, and funds, the choir performed its first major concert seven weeks later. Said Turnbull, "Music is very magical, able to transform children with no more than lint in their pockets and honey in their throats into grand performers on the world stage." His love of music had done just that. *Love will find a way. . . .*

Love   Tenacity

FEBRUARY 15

Since the century's rise, Dr. W. E. B. Du Bois had been at the forefront of the freedom fight—giving voice, setting the agenda for black liberation. In 1899, he journeyed to Europe as a graduate student. There, contrary to his experience at Harvard, he "heard Africa mentioned with respect." He heard the term "Pan-Africanism" and gained insight that fueled his lifelong quest to know Africa. As historian; cofounder of the NAACP (the oldest Civil Rights organization); editor of its magazine, *The Crisis;* and author of seminal works of history, sociology, and five autobiographies, he researched and rewrote the story of Africa and her diaspora for sixty years. With unique authority, on February 15, 1960, a ninety-two-year-old Du Bois addressed "The Lie of History as It Is Taught Today."

Born just after the Civil War, Du Bois knew ex-slaves and the ongoing ravages of a postslavery economy and society. A century later, he saw the omission of slavery from history texts as a cover-up that continued to corrupt the American psyche: "With no guidance from the past the nation marched on with officers strutting, bands playing and flags flying to secure colonial empire and new cheap slave labor and land monopoly in Asia [and Africa]." He tolled America's war debt in human resources and dollars: 550,000 dead in two world wars and Korea, more wounded; a $284 billion war debt still due. Yet, said Du Bois, in those same years "we have spent only $14 billion for education," an education that could have prevented such losses.

"Possibly, the main moral of all this is the failure of history as it is taught today even to attempt to tell the exact truth or learn it. Rather, so many historians conceive it their duty to teach as truth what they or those who pay their salaries believe to have been true. Thus we train generations of men who do not know the past, or believe a false picture of the past, to have no trustworthy guide for living and to stumble doggedly on, through mistake and mistake, to fatal ends. Our history becomes 'lies agreed upon' and stark ignorance guides our future."

Historiography   Understanding

FEBRUARY 16

WERE IT NOT FOR the emblem of race, the February 14–16, 1936, gathering of 817 National Negro Congress (NNC) delegates in Chicago would be time-honored history to this day. Never before (and rarely since) has there been such an assemblage representing working- and middle-class Americans. With this historic formative meeting, America's grass roots began sprouting new political maturity. Representing 585 organizations with a total one-person-one-vote membership of 1.2 million, these delegates from 28 of the then-48 states spanned 81 religious congregations, 83 trade unions, 71 fraternities and sororities, and 26 youth, 2 farm, 23 women's, and 14 educational organizations across the political, professional, and business spectrum. Most significantly, the NNC's first president was the labor leader A. Philip Randolph (see March 3, June 25).

From the founding of the historically black colleges right after the Civil War through the launch of the major Civil Rights organizations that began with the Niagara Movement of 1910, the relationship between Civil Rights and labor had been uncomfortable. It was a tension rooted in the unholy alliance of blacks and big business. Whether Booker T. Washington and his so-called wizardry at Tuskegee or his arch-rival Dr. W. E. B. Du Bois and his *Crisis* at the NAACP, the survival of most African American organizations (with the exception of the church), relied on the favor and charity of wealthy whites. As sociologist and one-time Howard University dean Kelly Miller caustically noted, "Logic aligns the Negro with labor, but good sense arrays him with capital."

Among Civil Rights leaders, A. Philip Randolph alone had broken the stranglehold on self-emancipation. The twelve years he had spent organizing the Brotherhood of Sleeping Car Porters often left him threadbare and too poor to make it home. But that first black labor union achieved National Labor Board recognition in October 1937, and its labor contract with the Pullman Company was the first negotiated and signed by and for black men in U.S. history.

Organizing   Building Dreams

FEBRUARY 17

In the winter of 1970, dancer-choreographer Diana Ramos, one of the most unique "voices" of the period, was in metamorphosis. "All through our lives we look for meanings," said Ramos. "What does this mean and how does it fit into our lives?" There were fewer "pretty pictures" in her dances, more contortions. Unknown even to her, what she had begun to dance was the inner life of the Black Power struggle.

On the faculty of Spelman College in the pre–Dr. Johnnetta Cole days as sister-president, she was on shaky ground. People did not understand what she was doing; she didn't understand what she was doing. Campus guards would find her in the studios past midnight—a woman possessed by a mission. To have stopped her, she would later say, would have meant to drag her off in chains, binding her hand and foot—perhaps not even that. For she had already danced those chains in Eleo Pomare's "Hex," broken through ropes in her own choreography to Max Roach's, "Tryptich." Now, here she was, like a sculptor, whittling away all the passions for which there was no longer space in this new world life.

She had already choreographed Coretta King in "Woman in a Window," the inner life of women who watch their beloved partners brutalized and sacrificed. *And Diana danced. . . .* She had done the parting of Winnie and Nelson Mandela, who would never again touch each other, and the extrapolated meaning of their plight and that of others in the long-term struggle for our people. Then, having read an article by Kathleen Cleaver, the Black Panther activist and wife of Eldridge Cleaver, she was seized by the rage of womanhood that so possessed her in the Spelman studios: "Kathleen I" and "Kathleen II." "With the death of Martin, my heart fell to pieces," said Ramos. Now she was putting her heart back together. In "Kathleen I," she is carrying a bench and the weight of the world on her back. In "Kathleen II," she ends her sorrow by flinging a chair, the only prop, to the side and moving on her raw, silent journey. "I was Kathleen, Angela, Coretta, all those women." *And Diana danced . . . and danced . . .*

FEBRUARY 18

PICTURED ON THE COVER of *Time* magazine's February 18, 1957, issue was Dr. Martin Luther King Jr., the Montgomery Bus Boycott's twenty-eight-year-old hero. In its lead, the story touted "the scholarly Negro Baptist minister who in little more than a year has risen from nowhere to become one of the nation's remarkable leaders of men." Not only had King not come from "nowhere," as the son of a prominent Atlanta pastor-father and musician-mother he had come from the pride of a people who, thirteen years later, wondered where all the promises they had suffered so much to exact had gone.

On February 18, 1970, Connecticut Senator Abraham Ribicoff spoke out. "We seem to have lost sight of the fact that the purpose of education is to help the child," he said. With this Senate speech, he attempted to correct the course of northern de facto school desegregation:

> The Senator from Mississippi [John Stennis, Dixiecrat/Democrat, and ardent segregationist] has argued that if segregation is wrong in the public schools of the South, it is wrong in the public schools of all other states. . . . Perhaps we in the North needed the mirror held up to us . . . in order to see the truth. . . . Our problem is not only the dual systems of education which [still] exist . . . it is the dual society that exists in every metropolitan area—the black society of the central city and the white society of the suburb. Massive school segregation does not exist because we have segregated our schools but because we have segregated our society and our neighborhoods. . . .
>
> We can talk all we want about rebuilding the "ghetto," better housing, tax incentives for job development, and massive funds for education. Hopefully, we may even do this. But improving the "ghetto" is not enough. One reason is that it fails to offer to the black man something we have heard much about in this chamber recently: freedom of choice.

That August, as a similar mirror reflected the North's public university system, the City University of New York inaugurated its "open admissions" policy.

O<small>N</small> F<small>EBRUARY</small> 19, 1958, this editorial appeared in the *New York Post:*

> Our Town has long been a haven for refugees from all over the world. Their number will now be increased by one Negro American from Little Rock. Like all the others, Minnijean Brown . . . will be looking for equality of opportunity. She will complete her year's education as a scholarship pupil at the New Lincoln School. . . . When a Negro girl is so drastically penalized for reacting as a human being under fire (and her attacker goes unpenalized), it is no wonder that white youngsters in the school feel safe to resume the business of bullying. The school board, in expelling Minnijean, has put its stamp of approval on the segregationist strategy of terror. . . . But part of the education she gets in Our Town will be the knowledge that we too practice racial discrimination. . . . The difference between New York and Little Rock is not as great as it should be. . . . Little Rock's loss is our proud acquisition.

From the first violent days of the Little Rock school crisis (see September 3), the "Little Rock Nine" had been mobbed, beaten, kicked, knocked down, and offered up to a lynch mob—all this by white students, their parents, and teachers. Counseled against fighting back, Minnijean had taken enough by February. "After provocation of girl student," wrote a school administrator, "she called the girl 'white trash' after which the girl threw her purse at Minnijean." A victory card dispatched among students said it all: "ONE DOWN . . . EIGHT TO GO." Of the Little Rock Nine, there were now eight: Minnijean Brown had been expelled. Saving her required immediate action. Through the NAACP network help came from Drs. Kenneth and Mamie Clark, the team of psychologists whose work had been critical to the Supreme Court desegregation order that had inspired Minnijean's heroism.

And, that same year, Daisy Bates, head of the Arkansas NAACP, and the nine students were awarded African America's highest honor—the NAACP's Spingarn Medal.

How to impart positive, creative images of the African diaspora on the screen, that was the question. In 1958, such black film pioneers as Oscar Micheaux (see September 2) were gone—and with them "race movies" by and for U.S. black audiences; Hollywood's racist stereotypes tainted all too many screens; Africa and Caribbean filmmakers were still combating colonialism. And so, when an impoverished French filmmaker, Marcel Camus, took to the streets of Rio de Janeiro during Carnival—February 18–20, 1958—with his crew to actually celebrate the African-rooted cultural experience, the film he brought to the screen was so fresh, so pure, so needed, and so welcome—it was called *Black Orpheus*.

During the making of the film, Camus—down to his last seventeen dollars—was so broke and so driven that he slept on the beach, unable to afford a hotel. But, as he later said, "The poverty was not such a bad thing in the long run. I spent so much time trailing around on foot, just looking, that in the end I had a deep awareness of Brazil. With money, I would never have made the same film." The benefits of his experiences show in his love for the film's real star—Afro-Brazilian culture.

Based on the legend of Orpheus and Eurydice, *Black Orpheus* was adapted from a play by Brazilian poet and playwright Vinicius de Moraes. In its haunting samba of life, two lovers are chased by death and by the very pulse and rhythm of life, as we hear in the ever-pounding beat of ancestral drums. Without comment, the paradise that is Rio is shown against the ugly poverty perilously hidden above on Morros, the steep mountain bluffs above the city. Out of shacks made from old discarded oil drums tucked together with bits of wood step two beautiful lovers—played by the dancer Marpessa Dawn and by Bruno Mello, a Brazilian soccer player—wedged like the wood between the heaven of their love and a daily hell. Like the costumes of Carnival, *Black Orpheus* is rich in imagination, surely one of the most beautiful films ever made. (In 1959, *Black Orpheus* won the coveted Palm d'Or grand prize at the Cannes Film Festival.

Film   Passion

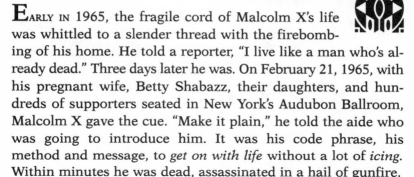
Eₐʀʟʏ ɪɴ 1965, the fragile cord of Malcolm X's life was whittled to a slender thread with the firebombing of his home. He told a reporter, "I live like a man who's already dead." Three days later he was. On February 21, 1965, with his pregnant wife, Betty Shabazz, their daughters, and hundreds of supporters seated in New York's Audubon Ballroom, Malcolm X gave the cue. "Make it plain," he told the aide who was going to introduce him. It was his code phrase, his method and message, to *get on with life* without a lot of *icing.* Within minutes he was dead, assassinated in a hail of gunfire.

In her grief, the poet and educator Sonia Sanchez wrote a tribute, "Malcolm," excerpted here:

> Do not speak to me of martyrdom
> of men who die to be remembered
> on some parish day.
> I don't believe in dying
> though I too shall die
> and violets like castanets
> will echo me. . . .
>
> and in each winter
> when the cold air cracks
> with frost, I'll breathe
> his breath and mourn
> my gun-filled nights. . . .
>
> Do not speak to me of living.
> Life is obscene with crowds
> of white on black.
> Death is my pulse.
> What might have been
> is not for him/or me
> but what could have been
> floods the womb until I drown.

FEBRUARY 22

In 1827, THE BLACK PRESS burst on the American scene with this declaration of independence: "We wish to plead our own cause." A century and a half later, true to tradition, the black press did just that with its support of Paul Robeson's autobiographical testament, *Here I Stand*. Even those newspapers that listed the most obscure books in daily roundups ignored Robeson, who had been figuratively tarred and feathered by the establishment for his politics. So much of a "threat" was he, that his book's publishing history can be documented by FBI files and wiretap transcripts—all authorized by FBI Director J. Edgar Hoover, the same man who branded Dr. King "the most dangerous man in America."

On February 22, 1958, Baltimore's *Afro-American* broke the blockade. "*Here I Stand* is a program of action for colored Americans," wrote Saunders Redding in his review. "But no American of whatever color can really quarrel with Robeson's principles and his program. . . . It is a challenge to fulfill the American dream." The *Afro-American* serialized the book in nine installments. From there, the world press took notice. India's *Blitz* published a four-page insert on the book headlined "Black Voice of God." In its editorial, the paper wrote, "We must take Robeson's slogan, 'The Time is Now,' and arrange mass demonstrations to show that we . . . solidly support the cause of the American Negro."

High-risk publication had turned to triumph for Othello Associates, a small Harlem-based press. Its first printing sold out in six weeks. A year later, 25,000 copies had sold. In a rare show of strength, the book's success was derived from black institutions—the press and the church. As the *Afro-American*'s George Murphy Jr. wrote to Essie Robeson, Paul's wife [see August 3], "With the two biggest Negro papers in the country behind Paul . . . with the Negro church, our most important political institution, increasingly behind him, and with Sister Essie Robeson in there methodically pitching every day . . . how can our Paul fail?" He didn't. With *Here I Stand* Paul Robeson's bold baritone was back.

Publishing   Tenacity

JUMP UP! It's Carnival on the Caribbean isle of Trinidad! An explosion of music and color run riot this Jouvay morn, Tuesday, February 23, 1971.

Every year, just before the Lenten season of austerity, a ritual unfolds. This jewel in nature's paradise—an island nation of one million people with its sister isle, Tobago—"explodes in a kaleidoscope of sound and color," as Caribbean dancer-historian Dr. Percival Borde described it. "The festivities have their own vocabulary. Steel bands—most at least one hundred 'panmen' strong—sweep through the streets of Port-of-Spain in melodious clangor; impromptu dancers 'jump up' in their wake, costumed troupes of revellers 'play mas' [mask], and for the two days prior to Ash Wednesday virtually all Trinidad abandons itself to 'bacchanal.'" And so it was this day in 1971, when the incendiary beat of ancient tamboo-bamboo drums, once outlawed by colonial powers, came alive.

A feast for the soul, there was Calypso by the Mighty Bomber, with his satiric commentary on everyday scenes: the fire engines ablare, the donkeys asnort, and the foxes that are hard enough to catch on four legs, much less when they turn politician and run on two. There was Shango in ritual evoking the ancient West African religion and its Haitian counterpart in voodoo. The song "Rosebud" memorialized a Tobago tragedy—a beauty kidnapped by Spanish sailors and taken out to sea. Then, "like a salvo of sound, the music of massed pans bursts from the stage of Port-of-Spain's Queens Park Savannah during the . . . contest for steel band supremacy. For this yearly moment, the panmen practice for ten months, most memorizing each note. Ten long months wrote one, 'of trying to say with my hands what I have seen with my eyes and felt within my soul.'" And then it was done, packed away until the next year.

FEBRUARY 24

W<small>HAT A MONTH</small> F<small>EBRUARY</small> 1957 was for the twenty-eight-year-old Martin Luther King Jr. In mid-month, he made his first appearance on the cover of *Time* magazine (see February 18). Within days, his wife, Coretta Scott King, surprised him with news that she was pregnant. Days later, the couple received a gift straight from the heart of his pastorate at the Montgomery, Alabama, Dexter Avenue Baptist Church. That Sunday, February 24, 1957, the congregants could hardly contain themselves as they handed their heroic young pastor a purse containing twenty-five hundred dollars so he could take his wife on a vacation to Europe. Days later, he received another thousand-dollar gift from the Montgomery Improvement Association, sponsors of the now-historic bus boycott (see December 20), which he had so nobly led to victory just two months earlier.

Martin and Coretta King had been the newest pastor-and-wife team in town when the decision was made to support Rosa Parks's courageous "seat" for Civil Rights. In fact, their newness was one of the reasons longtime resident and activist E. D. Nixon "volunteered" King to lead the crusade. The Kings took the brunt of an unbelievable ordeal that included the firebombing of their home. In accepting leadership of the struggle, King had even gone against his father for the first time in his life; Atlanta's venerated elder King had correctly feared for his son's life. Now, with these two monetary gifts, the Kings' adopted city was saying a special thank-you. The right thing to do at just the right time, it sent the Kings on a new course.

The independence celebration of the first modern African nation to retake its freedom was scheduled for the very next week (see March 5). The Kings joined a delegation of African Americans accepting the invitation of Ghana's president to attend. Aboard the plane, the captain invited the young pastor into the cockpit. There, at the helm, King saw a vast world stretched in front of him. But unlike the pilot, who had a flight plan and a vast array of controls, King would venture into uncharted ground.

FEBRUARY 25

ON FEBRUARY 25, 1964, the pugilist-poet Cassius Clay made history when he knocked out Sonny Liston to become the World Heavyweight Boxing Champion. "I am the greatest!" Clay declared with customary humor and humility (see February 10). He was right. And it was a good thing he knew who he was, for the next day he would become the lowest of the low.

On February 26, 1964, he issued a statement: "I believe in the religion of Islam. I believe in Allah and peace . . . I'm not a Christian anymore." With that the nation that had canonized "freedom of religion" in its first constitutional amendment two hundred years before turned pathological. From that moment, Clay faced a treacherous route. Said Malcolm X, "Cassius is the black man's hero. Do you know why? . . . The white press wanted him to lose . . . because he is a Muslim. You noticed nobody cares about the religion of other athletes. But their prejudice against Clay blinded them to his ability." For six years, a political and professional lynch mob hounded Clay across the globe. His associates were constantly harassed, his contracts were cancelled, his life was threatened, his phone was tapped by the FBI. In what seemed more than coincidence, just as the Vietnam War escalated, Clay—world champion, top moneymaker for the sports and tourism industries—was reclassified 1-A and was called up for the draft (see April 28). His sincere refusal of induction as a matter of conscience and the legal battle that ensued erupted into such furor that more than a few Civil Rights leaders shunned him, fearing certain reprisal from the same forces plaguing Clay.

Mentored in Islam by Malcolm X, Clay had undertaken a spiritual journey, and the insight gained into his history as an African American man ushered him to a new place of awareness about himself and his world. His name was no longer Cassius Clay, he said. He was now Muhammad Ali. It was the Arabic name given him by his spiritual leader, the Honorable Elijah Muhammad of the Nation of Islam. It meant "worthy of praise." And he was.

FEBRUARY 26

On February 26, 1956, four soldiers in the school desegregation wars were encamped at New York's all-white P.S. 98, having left behind their all-black P.S. 133.

Nearly two years after the Supreme Court desegregated public schools (see May 17), this test broke the city's "neighborhood school plan," which maintained de facto segregation below the high school level. With a family car for their school bus, these eight- and nine-year-olds—Janus Adams, Robert Burns, Theodore Burrell, and Linda Scott—had been selected and counseled by Margaret S. Douglas, principal of P.S. 133 and one of the North's first black administrators. Unlike the South, no loosely harnessed dogs erupted at the children's heels, no troops stood with ready bayonets, no photographers memorialized the scene. And so, as is often the case with such things, it may have seemed that nothing happened. It did. A scan of history texts would lead one to believe that northern schools were never desegregated. They were. Adults spat, screamed, and tore at the clothes of the children. Teachers rearranged their classrooms to keep the blacks "in their place." At P.S. 98, one lone teacher, Rose Zir, put the children first. The strength of the children's families empowered their survival.

The scene harkened back to the dilemma argued by Dr. W. E. B. Du Bois in his 1934 essay, "Separation and Self-respect": "A black man born in Boston has a right to oppose any separation of schools by color, race or class," wrote Du Bois. "But this black man in Boston has no right . . . to send his own helpless immature children into school where white children kick, cuff or abuse him, or where teachers openly and persistently neglect or hurt or dwarf his soul. . . . Let the NAACP and every upstanding Negro pound at the closed gates of opportunity and denounce caste and segregation; but let us not punish our own children under the curious impression that we are punishing our white oppressors. Let us not affront our own self-respect by accepting a proffered equality which is not equality." While the past is prologue and done, the real tragedy is how current our segregated school woes remain today.

FEBRUARY 27

On February 27, 1965, a funeral cortege drove onto the grounds of Ferncliff Cemetery in Hartsdale, New York, bearing the body of the man born Malcolm Little, who had come to be loved, revered, feared, and slain as Malcolm X. On his pilgrimage to Mecca the year before, he had found special peace, and would this day take his eternal rest as El Hajj Malik el Shabazz. As gravediggers stood at the ready to receive him, shovels in hand, the mourners said "no." They would bury Brother Malcolm themselves. They would dig a place of rest for "our prince," as he had been eulogized in poetic elegy just hours earlier by his friend, the noted actor Ossie Davis. "Here at this final hour, in this quiet place—Harlem has come to bid farewell to one of its brightest hopes, extinguished now, and gone from us forever." Davis intoned to the international, interfaith, interracial assemblage of mourners at Faith Temple Church:

> Many will ask what Harlem finds to honor in this stormy, controversial, and bold young captain—and we will smile. Many will say turn away—away from this man, for he is not a man but a demon . . . and an enemy of the black man—and we will smile. . . . They will say that he is of hate. . . . And we will answer and say unto them: Did you ever talk to Brother Malcolm? Did you ever touch him or have him smile at you? Did you ever really listen to him? Did he ever do a mean thing? . . . For if you did you would know him. And if you knew him you would know why we must honor him: Malcolm was our manhood—our living, black manhood! This was his meaning to his people. And in honoring him, we honor the best in ourselves. . . . Consigning these mortal remains to earth, the common mother of all, secure in the knowledge that what we place in the ground is no more now a man, but a seed, which, after the winter of our discontent, will come forth again to meet us. And we will know him then for what he was and is—a prince—our own black shining prince!—who didn't hesitate to die, because he loved us so.

FEBRUARY 28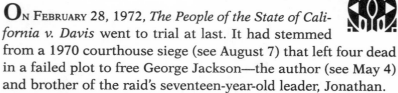

On February 28, 1972, *The People of the State of California v. Davis* went to trial at last. It had stemmed from a 1970 courthouse siege (see August 7) that left four dead in a failed plot to free George Jackson—the author (see May 4) and brother of the raid's seventeen-year-old leader, Jonathan.

In the prisoners' rights movement of the late 1960s, the elder Jackson's plight was championed, and he and his family were befriended, by Angela Davis—a young UCLA professor of philosophy infamous in her own right as a political target of the then-governor of California, Ronald Reagan. Her principled refusal to sign a loyalty oath as a term of her contract made her perfect cannon fodder. When Reagan's attack yielded threats on her life, she purchased and legally registered a gun for her own protection—a gun later used in the courthouse siege. She was charged with murder and kidnapping, and a warrant was issued for her arrest. Knowing the charge to be political, she fled and was posted on the FBI's "Ten Most Wanted" list of felons. In a national dragnet, women with natural Afro hairstyles coast-to-coast were harassed in the name of the law. In October 1970, Davis was captured in New York, extradited, and imprisoned (often in solitary) to await trial and, as detractors hoped, execution for a crime all knew she had not committed. Just five days before her trial, the state supreme court abolished the death penalty—and with it the grounds upon which she had been denied bail. She was released. Two days later, she appeared at the trial of the two surviving Soledad Brothers to lift spirits and thank "all the sisters and brothers who had fought for my freedom."

On June 4, those days of trial were over for her when the jury returned its verdict confirming what was known from the start. She was "not guilty." In her autobiography, the section on her trial is entitled "Bridges," taken from a quote, "Walls turned sideways are bridges." Having scaled the wall to her own freedom, within a week of her vindication she embarked on a speaking tour—her wall had been turned on its side to become a bridge to raise legal defense funds for others.

FEBRUARY 29

FEBRUARY 29, 1952: the deadline black South Africans had set for repeal of the "six unjust laws," the pillars of apartheid; the launch of the modern independence movement when South Africa's empowered white minority refused to budge in terms of its total, oppressive control.

South Africa was at a crossroads in 1952—the intersection where its past and present pointed the way to the future. In the lives of two women—Katie Makanya and singer Miriam Makeba—is the tale in human, rather than political, terms. Like Makeba, Makanya possessed a singing voice that was her ticket to escape South Africa. Like Makanya, Makeba left her family and homeland to travel the world. Makeba was born in the early 1930s and stayed away, riding the wave of a changing world to fight for freedom on the world stage as performer and diplomat, paying the price with twenty years in exile. Makanya, born in 1873, went back to South Africa, knowing her struggle in the heyday of colonialism and segregation was much the same the world over, paying the price with a family life constricted by apartheid and its enforced poverty. In 1952, Makeba's voice was taking her to see the world. In 1952, Makanya was dictating *The Calling of Katie Makanya*, the story of her freedom days as a teenager on tour in London with the African Native Choir.

As the first "kaffir choir," as they were ignorantly called (the word *kaffir* being akin to *nigger*) the "novelty" group gave a Jubilee year command performance for Queen Victoria on July 24, 1891. They visited with Baroness Burdett-Coutts, who insisted on having shoes made for them for fear that by walking barefoot they would catch pneumonia and die. Primped and patronized, they were often the newest exhibits in the zoo. When a kindly older woman, Mrs. Keithley, came to visit one day, she noticed the redness in young Katie's eyes. Realizing the problem, she gave her the gift of her lifetime—glasses. Her headaches gone, her vision clear, Katie Makanya could, at last, truly *see the world* . . . and she chose to return home, where the Katies gave birth to the generation of Makebas.

MARCH

Katie Makanya in London (1898). Courtesy of
Margaret McCord, from *The Calling of Katie
Makanya*, published by John Wiley & Sons, 1997.

For more information about Katie Makanya, please
see February 29.

MARCH 1

I̲ᴛ ꜱᴇᴇᴍᴇᴅ ᴛʜᴇ ᴇɴᴅ of the Civil Rights–era "second Reconstruction" had come even before it had fully begun. On March 1, 1967, by a vote of 307 to 116, the House of Representatives expelled Harlem's Adam Clayton Powell Jr. Charged with high absenteeism and defaming the character of a known "bag woman" (numbers runner), the fiery Powell had long been a thorn in the Establishment's Achilles' heel, and the House seized upon the opportunity afforded by his mishaps.

Powell just wouldn't be "a Negro." Well-educated, he was uppity and unapologetic, handsome and charismatic. He loved the nightlife almost as much as his day job as an activist/reformer. A man of privilege, he led the Depression-era "Buy-Where-You-Can-Work" Boycott on segregated stores in Harlem. His celebrity marriage to jazz singer/pianist Hazel Scott caused a stir, so did his sermons as one of the most riveting Baptist preacher/orators of his day. As the first northern black congressman, he refused to demure in the face of segregation; rejecting racial bans on House facilities, he encouraged his staff to do the same. Best of all, his Committee on Education and Labor passed more major legislation than any other committee in the House. Desegregating the military, ending Jim Crow travel, a new child welfare law, upgrading the minimum wage, Manpower: all these were credited to Powell. Born forty-three years after Emancipation, he was the grandson of a slave. At the age of ten, he saw his grandfather's slave brand. That memory had motivated him for life.

Six weeks after Powell's expulsion, Harlem returned him to Congress. The special election established the right of a district—and of a people, given the fact that there were only five African Americans in this pre–Voting Rights–era Congress—to choose its own leaders. By 1969, the Supreme Court concurred. But the damage had been done. Powell (and a nation of underrepresented blacks) had lost his seniority, his committee chairmanship, and his place in line of succession to the presidency. A twenty-four-year veteran and the ranking majority leader, he had been third in line.

MARCH 2

WITH THE ENTRANCE OF the United States into World War II, racial clashes between white soldiers and civilians and black soldiers plagued the South—especially in those towns with military bases. In Little Rock, Arkansas, area businessmen eager to profit from the spending power of thousands of soldiers had pushed to reopen the long-dormant Camp Robinson. But with the camp and greater prosperity came increased police brutality against blacks. Beating black soldiers off base was the latest sport. And despite protests, nothing changed.

On Sunday, March 2, 1942, at 5:45 P.M., the predictably unthinkable happened: city police killed a soldier in cold blood. Patrolman A. J. Hay did not like hearing a black sergeant question Military Police about a private known to be in custody. Interfering with the MPs and the sergeant, Hay knocked the black man to the ground with his stick, then riddled his body with five shots. As is usual in such situations, nothing is done until *something* happens to "the wrong person." In this case, that person was Sergeant Thomas P. Foster, a respected, well-liked man. As the same police force that murdered him went through the motions of "its investigation," a distraught black soldier wept openly, threw his neatly pressed army cap to the ground, and stomped it to death. "Why should we go over there and fight?" he grieved. "These are the sons of bitches we should be fighting!" As the crowd slowly dispersed, the man stood alone, in so many ways, still stomping his cap, until a fellow soldier gently led him to the bus for Camp Robinson.

Although barely moved by the incident, local businessmen were upset by the coverage the story received from veteran journalist Daisy Bates in the *State Press*—the newspaper she ran with her husband, L. C. Bates. Within five days, every downtown store cancelled its ads. But the community so appreciated the paper's courageous ongoing crusade that circulation doubled within months. After that, the ads returned as well. The buying power of so many black consumers was too good for even white businesses to lose out on.

Journalism   Self-worth

MARCH 3

In 1941, A. Philip Randolph (see February 16, November 10) succeeded in integrating war industry jobs. In 1948, he picked up where he left off before the war. This time, targeting the army itself, he called for civil disobedience against the draft. On March 3, 1948, under threat of being charged with treason, Randolph sat before the Senate Armed Services Committee to account for his transgression. He said, "Our country has come out before the world as the moral leader of democracy. . . . If this country does not develop the democratic process at home and make the democratic process work by [including] the very people whom they propose to draft in the army to fight for their democracy, then that democracy is not the type of democracy that ought to be fought for . . ."

The NAACP's Walter White telegraphed support: "Those who expect [Negroes] to be enthusiastic fighters should remember that their memories of mistreatment in the last war are bitter green. Negro veterans returned home to be terrorized in Tennessee; lynched in Walton County, Georgia; denied the ballot in most southern states; barred from taking GI courses . . . and slandered on the floor of the U. S. Congress. The remedy is not to threaten treason trials but to give these loyal citizens the democracy they are expected and asked to defend."

Also testifying in support was New York Congressman Adam Clayton Powell: "If the finger of treason can be pointed at anyone, it must be pointed at those of you who are traitors to our Constitution. . . . If you threaten our leaders, then the sixty thousand pulpits of the colored church will thunder through their ministers against the immoral hypocrisy of you. I dare you to arrest the sixty thousand ministers of God in order to whitewash your un-Americanism."

In 1948, President Harry Truman signed Executive Order No. 9981, desegregating the military—the first presidential order on race since the Emancipation Proclamation of 1863.

MARCH 4

A MEMO FROM FBI Director J. Edgar Hoover dated March 4, 1968:

> For maximum effectiveness of the Counterintelligence Program, and to prevent wasted effort, long-range goals are being set.
> 1. Prevent the coalition of militant black nationalist groups. . . . An effective coalition of black nationalist groups might be the first step toward . . . the beginning of a true black revolution.
> 2. Prevent the rise of a "messiah" who could unify, and electrify, the militant black nationalist movement. Malcolm X might have been such a "messiah"; he is the martyr of the movement today. Martin Luther King, Stokely Carmichael and Elijah Muhammad all aspire to this position. Elijah Muhammad is less of a threat because of his age. King could be a very real contender for this position should he abandon his supposed "obedience" to "white, liberal doctrines" and embrace black nationalism.

For years the FBI had kept the Civil Rights movement under surveillance—driven by investigations of possible links to communism and Hoover's personal hatred for and obsession with Dr. King. Through the FBI's Counterintelligence Program (COINTELPRO) (see April 6), the Bureau campaign engaged in largely illegal activities to derail the freedom train: spies, wiretaps, room bugs, break-ins, forged signatures, counterfeit documents, and false information to the press. Yet, by its own assessment, the FBI had failed to destroy the movement.

In 1964, desperate FBI agents urged Dr. King toward suicide: "You have just thirty-four days. . . . You are done. . . . There is but one way out. . . . You better take it before your filthy fraudulent self is bared to the nation." Still no "success." But a month to the day after the March memo, Dr. King was assassinated. As revelations poured in, the House Select Committee on Assassinations reported, "the Domestic Intelligence Division's COINTELPRO campaign against Dr. King [the FBI] grossly abused and exceeded its legal authority and failed to consider the possibility that actions threatening bodily harm to Dr. King might be encouraged by the program."

"GHANA IS FREE!" Just before midnight on March 5, 1957, on a path lit by a triumphal arch of colored lights that beamed from endless rows of flowers, the parade of dignitaries began; Ghanaian chiefs from every region looked exquisite in their royal robes as they were joined by representatives from fifty-six countries, including African America's Ralph Bunche (Undersecretary of the United Nations and Nobel Peace Prize laureate), Coretta and Martin Luther King (see February 24), Congressman Adam Clayton Powell, publisher John H. Johnson, and labor leader A. Philip Randolph. At midnight, the Union Jack was lowered on British colonial rule; the red, yellow, and green national flag of a new-day Ghana took its rightful place. The ancestral home of the Ashanti was free. "At long last the battle has ended!" the new nation's liberator and president, Kwame Nkrumah, declared in front of a crowd of one hundred thousand. "Ghana, your beloved country, is free forever," he said to "the chiefs . . . the youth, the farmers, the women, who have so nobly fought and won this battle."

The national anthem was officially heard for the first time, and a roar went up from the crowd, cheering as one: "Ghana is free!" "Once upon a time," Nkrumah said, invoking the spirit of the Pan-Africanist Marcus Garvey (see August 13), "he looked through the whole world to see if he could find a government of a black people. . . . He did not find one, and he said he was going to create one. Marcus Garvey did not succeed. But here today the work of [many] illustrious men who have gone before us has come to reality at this present moment."

That night a lone bugler blew taps, marking nightfall on the colonial Gold Coast and daybreak in Ghana and a new Africa—the start of a long, arduous awakening from five centuries of European invasion and plunder. Ghana was the first of the colonized territories to take back its freedom. For the entire African diaspora, this was the moment for which generations had fought, died, and been sacrificed to slavery. "Ghana is free!" they celebrated into the night. *"Ghana is free!"*

MARCH 6

I**T WAS THE LATE** 1930s, and Richard Wright was making his way in Chicago:

> I received an invitation from a group of white boys I had known in the post office to meet . . . and argue the state of the world. . . . I was amazed to discover that many of them had joined the Communist Party. I was dubious . . . Sol, a Jewish chap . . . had joined a revolutionary artists' organization, the John Reed Club. Sol . . . begged me to attend the meetings of the club, but I always found an easy excuse for refusing. . . . I felt that communists could not possibly have a sincere interest in Negroes. I was cynical and I would rather have heard a white man say that he hated Negroes, which I could have readily believed, than to have heard him say that he respected Negroes, which would have made me doubt him. I did not think that there existed many whites who, through intellectual effort, could lift themselves out of the traditions of their times and see the Negro objectively.
>
> One Saturday night . . . bored with reading, I decided to appear at the John Reed Club in the capacity of an amused spectator. . . . A dark stairway led upwards; it did not look welcoming. . . . I mounted the stairs to a door that was lettered: THE CHICAGO JOHN REED CLUB. I opened it and stepped into the strangest room I had ever seen. Paper and cigarette butts lay on the floor. A few benches ran along the walls, above which were vivid colors depicting colossal figures of workers carrying streaming banners. The mouths of the workers gaped in wild cries; their legs were sprawled over cities. "Hello." I turned and saw a white man smiling at me. . . . "You're welcome here," the white man said. "We're not having an affair tonight. We're holding an editorial meeting. Do you paint?" . . . "No," I said. "I write." "Then sit in on the editorial meeting of our magazine, *Left Front*," he suggested. "I know nothing of editing," I said. "You can learn. . . ." My cynicism—which had been my protection against an America that had cast me out—slid from me and, timidly . . .

So began the literary coming-of-age of one of the twentieth century's finest writers. This account was posthumously published in his book *American Hunger.*

Literature   Opportunity

MARCH 7

THE FIRST WEEKS OF 1965 had mobilized Selma for the voting rights movement. In one demonstration, Reverend C. T. Vivian was blocked at the courthouse by Sheriff Clark. Vivian tried to spark conscience in the deputies: "There are those who followed Hitler like you blindly follow this Sheriff Clark. . . . You're racists in the same way Hitler was a racist. . . ." With that, Clark ordered TV crew lights off. In the darkness, Clark hit Vivian so hard he fractured his own hand. Days later, Vivian preached about the incident, and the night ended in tragedy. As people left the church, the streetlights suddenly went out and the people were rushed and beaten by a mob of police and angry whites as panicked news crews struggled to capture the siege. One demonstrator, Jimmie Lee Jackson, vainly tried to drag his mother and elderly grandfather out of the fray. The family was attacked by troopers and Jackson was shot. He died a week later.

In response, a protest march from Selma to Montgomery was set for March 7, 1965. Beyond the need to publicize the incident, the long march also allowed time for the story to appeal to the national conscience. For SCLC's Rev. James Bevel the march was deeply rooted in Gandhi's teachings: "When you have a great violation of the people and there's a great sense of injury, you have to give people an honorable means and context in which to express and eliminate that grief. . . . Otherwise the movement will break down in chaos."

Dr. King was not expected in Selma that day. A coin toss among SCLC deputies put Hosea Williams in the lead with SNCC's chairman, John Lewis, as his second. After a prayer assembly at Brown's Chapel, marchers walked eerily silent, empty streets and started across the Pettus Bridge. At its crest, two hundred police on horseback rained terror upon the hundreds of defenseless marchers. In the carnage, they were teargassed and trampled; the day would become known in infamy as "Bloody Sunday." As news footage swept the air, thousands of outraged people headed to Selma for the defining march of the era (see March 21, March 25).

Marches   Human Spirit

MARCH 8

IF, AS IT IS SAID in the history of the movement, Rosa Parks was "The Mother of Civil Rights" (see December 5), then the grandmother would surely be "Mother Conscience," Septima Clark. To Clark, literacy held the key to freedom. A gifted teacher and organizer, she honed her skills as a South Carolina public school teacher and empowered generations with her innovative citizenship education workshops for adults at the Highlander Folk School in Tennessee. There, in 1955, she trained NAACP activist Parks the summer before her historic arrest.

When Clark was fired for her Civil Rights work in 1956, Highlander's legendary founder, Myles Horton, recruited her to direct the workshops that became known as the "movement halfway house." Her voting rights literacy project kept her in contact with male leaders. She perceived a weakness in the movement and told them so: They were minimizing the role of women. "The work the women did during the time of civil rights is what really carried the movement along. The women carried forth the ideas. . . . [It] would never have taken off if some women hadn't started to speak up." Women were speaking up in every field.

In 1940, Hattie McDaniel won an Academy Award for her portrayal of "Mammy" in *Gone With the Wind;* she was the first African American so honored. Said McDaniel, "I portray the type of Negro woman who has worked honestly and proudly to give our nation the Marian Andersons, Roland Hayeses, and Ralph Bunches" (referring to two opera virtuosi and a Nobel Peace Prize laureate). In 1956, as the Montgomery Bus Boycott that Mrs. Parks's courage had forged reached its successful end, Dr. King quoted an elderly black woman who, when asked if she was tired, spoke for the group when she said, "My feets is tired, but my soul is at rest."

On this International Women's Day, March 8, we honor Clark's daughters, Parks's sisters, McDaniel's mammies—all the women, unnamed and unsung, who made the Civil Rights movement and whose legacies inspire us today.

MARCH 9

On March 9, 1960, as sit-in demonstrators captured the imaginations of students throughout the South, the Atlanta Committee on Appeal for Human Rights launched its local sit-in movement with a paid ad in the *Atlanta Constitution:*

> We, the students of the six affiliated institutions forming the Atlanta University Center . . . have joined our hearts, minds, and bodies in the cause of gaining those rights which are inherently ours as members of the human race and as citizens of these United States. We . . . cannot tolerate . . . the discriminatory conditions under which the Negro is living today in Atlanta, Georgia—supposedly one of the most progressive cities in the South. Among the . . . injustices . . . against which we protest. . . .
>
> 1. Education: [Public schools] for Negroes and Whites are separate and unequal . . . and many Negro children travel ten miles a day in order to reach a school that will admit them.
> 2. Jobs: Negroes are denied employment in the majority of city, state, and federal government jobs, except in the most menial capacities.
> 3. Housing: While Negroes constitute 32% of the population of Atlanta, they are forced to live within 16% of the area of the city.
> 4. Voting: Contrary to statements made in Congress recently by several Southern Senators . . . Negro college graduates are declared unqualified to vote and are not permitted to register.
> 5. Hospitals: Compared with [other] facilities in Atlanta and Georgia, those for Negroes are unequal and totally inadequate.
> 6. Movies, Concerts, Restaurants: Negroes are barred from most downtown movies and segregated in the rest. . . . Even his thirst must await its quenching at a "colored" water fountain.
> 7. Law Enforcement: Negroes are maltreated. . . . An insufficient number of Negroes is employed in the law enforcing agencies. . . . Of 830 policemen in Atlanta only 35 are Negroes.

What blacks saw as grievances, whites simply accepted as law. The power of the nonviolent sit-ins was their ability to sway those who had never thought much about the connection between violence and "law"—violence as a way of life.

MARCH 10

IN MARCH 1948, *Negro Digest* listed "America's Ten Worst Cities for Negroes." Columbia, South Carolina, topped the list, which put it at the very bottom for blacks. Seventh on the list was Birmingham, Alabama—a place so violent to blacks it was known as "Bombingham." This hostility forced blacks to rely totally on each other for every daily need. This same forcible ejection of blacks from the wider society was the negative catalyst that made a multimillionaire of a man known for his trademark line, "Find a need and fill it"— A. G. Gaston.

After serving in World War I, Gaston was a laborer for 31 cents an hour in Birmingham steel country, where people died often and early from mining accidents and "black lung" disease. Collections would be taken up to bury the dead— a custom that became a racket for the unscrupulous. Gaston came up with a simple, honest solution: a burial society. He collected 25 cents for adults, 15 cents for children, and promised a $75 funeral in return. Ironically (and predictably), his first subscriber died when the society had only 25 cents in assets. Gaston convinced a local undertaker to perform the burial on credit. The minister who conducted the funeral was so impressed that he, in essence, became Gaston's "PR man" when he preached that anyone who wouldn't invest 25 cents in his own family wasn't worth a decent funeral. He appointed two members to help Gaston sign up subscribers after the funeral. In that one day, Gaston collected thirty-five dollars— enough to begin paying back his first "partner," the undertaker, and to launch his Booker T. Washington Burial Society.

That base funded the BTW Insurance Company. When Gaston needed trained clerks, the BTW Business College was founded. Then, a loan company for the growing community to buy homes. Each a need, each a solution. In 1963, when war broke out in Birmingham to end segregation, support was needed for the demonstrators. He solved that too, personally guaranteeing bonds of $160,000 and providing accommodations for Dr. King and the SCLC team at the A. G. Gaston Hotel.

MARCH 11

THERE HAD BEEN A national convention movement by blacks for the furtherance of common political interests since 1830. But on the weekend of March 10–12, 1972, when the National Black Political Convention (NBPC) convened in Gary, Indiana, it was the first such conference ever held during two centuries of history when every black adult had a legal right and practical access to the vote.

Thirty-five hundred delegates from forty-four states, and nearly five thousand observers, converged in Gary. In 1967, that city and Cleveland, Ohio, had become the first since Reconstruction, and the first northern cities ever, to elect African American mayors. "This convention can make history," declared Gary's Mayor Richard Hatcher in his keynote address. "Whether it does will depend on what we do here today." With the theme "Unity Without Uniformity," the convention set about the task of formulating its National Black Political Agenda and creating a mechanism by which to implement it.

"The Gary Declaration: Black Politics at the Crossroads" was released to the public on May 19, Malcolm X's birthday. The fifty-four-page document forged the platform upon which every black candidate would campaign and be judged in the 1970s: congressional redistricting to accommodate black representation, national health insurance, community control of school boards, guaranteed minimum annual income, open housing, a prisoner's bill of rights, and a ban on capital punishment. As promising as it was, NBPC would disintegrate within two years, sapped of its unity and strength by the timeless and useless "integration vs. liberation" argument that has torched every initiative since the Back-to-Africa colonization dispute of the 1820s. Still, NBPC was not without its glory, as when Rev. Jesse Jackson drew the hall to its feet by quoting a poem by playwright, nationalist movement leader, and NBPC co-convenor Amiri Baraka (see July 12). This clarion call would become the mantra, if not the message, of the decade. "What time is it? It's Nation Time! Nationtime," they chanted. "Nationtime!"

MARCH 12

In eulogizing Medgar Evers (see June 15), the NAACP's Roy Wilkins charged that "the southern system has its outposts in the Congress of the United States" and that Evers's assassin "must have felt that he had, if not an immunity, then certainly a protection for whatever he chose to do, no matter how dastardly." If ever there was a document to substantiate Wilkins's charge, it was the "Southern Manifesto," released on March 12, 1956. Signed by nearly every southerner in Congress, the Manifesto denounced the Supreme Court's *Brown v. Board of Education* and *Brown II* decisions ending public school segregation and ordering compliance (see May 17, May 31). While it called for resistance by "any lawful means," this ode to racism became an invitation to uphold segregation *by any means necessary*. Just as *Brown* became the rallying cry of the Civil Rights era, the "Southern Manifesto" became the battle cry of an unreconstructed South:

> The original Constitution does not mention education. Neither does the Fourteenth Amendment [see March 15]. . . . When the amendment was adopted in 1868 . . . the twenty-six states that had any substantial racial differences among its people either approved the operation of segregated schools already in existence or subsequently established such schools. . . . This . . . became a part of the life of the people of many of the states and confirmed their habits, customs, traditions and way of life. It is founded on elemental humanity and common sense, for parents should not be deprived by Government of the right to direct the lives and education of their own children. This . . . exercise of power by the court . . . is destroying the amicable relations between the white and Negro races that have been created through ninety years of patient effort by the good people of both races. It has planted hatred and suspicion where there has been heretofore friendship and understanding.

Not only were the signers a congressional minority, they had been elected by minority rule. Had blacks been able to vote, the signers would have been "amicably" defeated by majority rule. The war for voter registration was just ahead.

School Desegregation   Values

MARCH 13

AFTER 170 YEARS in which black soldiers fought U.S. battles, the military was still segregated. The black rank and file were increasingly on the front lines, and black officers were only inching their way into the front offices. A breakthrough finally came on March 13, 1947, when the air force resurrected Ohio's Lockbourne Field with Col. Benjamin O. Davis in command of the 477th Bombardment Group. It was the first time blacks would administer a base within U.S. borders without immediate white supervisory personnel on site.

The news that black servicemen would be stationed at Lockbourne was not unilaterally well received. The racism that led military brass to admit the error of sending the first black pilots to a base in the segregated South (see January 14) loomed once again, and an editorial in the *Columbus Citizen* charged, "The 477th were a bunch of troublemakers." It was a reference to the unit officers' 1945 peacetime mutiny against segregation while stationed in Indiana. But black Ohio was jubilant, determined to give these heroes the welcome they deserved. As the 477th came to town, a sea of cheering faces lined the streets of Columbus to greet them.

At the helm of the 477th was Col. Davis, who came to the post impeccably credentialed. Not since Col. Charles Young graduated West Point in 1889 had there been a black army cadet. In 1932, young Davis was that man. As the twentieth century's first black cadet, he withstood stinging humiliation and loneliness to graduate in 1936, thirty-fifth in a class of 236. Yet despite his academic achievements, when he applied for the army air corps he was advised to attend law school instead. Still, he persisted in his career choice as a military trailblazer. In this, Davis was following in the historic footsteps of his father, Benjamin O. Davis Sr., who, in 1940, had been appointed a general in the army, the first African American general in U.S. military history. In 1954, Benjamin O. Davis Jr. became the first African American appointed a general in the air force.

Military

Spirit

MARCH 14

For the most depraved acts of terrorism against blacks since the "Red Summer of 1919," the NAACP condemned the U.S. human rights record for 1946 as the very worst. At the NAACP's urging, a presidential committee on Civil Rights was appointed. Its 1947 report, "To Secure These Rights" (see October 28) prioritized the need to guarantee the rights of every person "regardless of who he is, where he lives, or what his racial, religious, or national origins are." But what did all the words mean in terms of everyday African American life?

The March 1948 issue of *Negro Digest* responded with an article by Ollie Stewart, staff reporter for the Baltimore *Afro-American*, that ranked cities according to these criteria: incidences of antiblack violence (lynchings, kidnappings, mob attacks), access to public services (schools, hospitals, libraries, parks), community life (churches and youth centers), job opportunities (police, fire, teaching, civil service careers), and nonsegregated transportation. In an article provocatively titled "America's Ten Worst Cities for Negroes," the cities were:

1. Columbia, South Carolina
2. Greenville, South Carolina
3. Alexandria, Louisiana
4. Atlanta, Georgia
5. Jackson, Mississippi
6. Annapolis, Maryland
7. Birmingham, Alabama
8. Miami, Florida
9. Houston, Texas
10. Washington, D.C.

That Birmingham, a place so mean it was called "Bombingham," placed only seventh tells quite a story. Yet, even as this report was going to press, the invention of the mechanical cotton picker, first demonstrated in October 1944, was reaping revolutionary change in the land of King Cotton. Work that once commanded fifty field hands could now be done by one machine. In the largest migration since the dust bowl days of the Great Depression, Black America was on the move. With little to lose and everything to gain, given the national state of affairs, they dared to dream new lives and powered the Civil Rights crusades.

The real hero of this struggle is the American Negro. He has called upon us to make good the promise of America. And who among us can say that we would have made the same progress were it not for his persistent bravery and his faith in American democracy?—Lyndon B. Johnson

Pushed by the shame of Bloody Sunday in Selma, Alabama, eight days earlier, on March 15, 1965, President Lyndon Johnson went before a joint session of Congress and the nation via television to deliver his "We Shall Overcome" speech:

At times, history and fate meet at a single place to shape a turning point in man's unending search for freedom. So it was last week in Selma. . . . There, long-suffering men and women peacefully protested the denial of their rights as Americans. Many were brutally assaulted. . . . Every device of which human ingenuity is capable has been used to deny this right . . . [but] the fact is that the only way to pass these barriers is to show a white skin. . . . Wednesday I will send to Congress a law designed to eliminate illegal barriers to the right to vote. . . . The command of the Constitution is plain. There is no moral issue. It is wrong—deadly wrong—to deny any of your fellow Americans the right to vote. . . . There is no issue of states' rights. . . . There is only the struggle for human rights. . . .

On August 6, 1965, Johnson signed the Voting Rights Act. But it is an awesome fact that what was suffered and sacrificed for in the 1950s and 1960s had been won by the Civil War and inscribed in the Constitution a century before:

Amendment 13—Ratified December 18, 1865: "Neither slavery nor involuntary servitude" shall exist. . . .
Amendment 14—Ratified July 23, 1868: "All persons born or naturalized in the United States" are citizens; "no state shall make . . . any law which shall abridge the privileges . . . of citizens." Provides for federal intervention; empowers Congress to enforce.
Amendment 15—Ratified March 30, 1870: "The right of citizens to vote shall not be denied" by the United States or by any state on account of "race, color, or previous condition of servitude." Empowers Congress to enforce with legislation.

MARCH 16

ON MARCH 16, 1827, the African American press was born with the first issue of *Freedom's Journal.* "We wish to plead our own cause," the opening editorial declared, clearly stating its goal: "to vindicate our . . . brethren, when oppressed." A century and a half later, Benjamin F. Clark, a Howard University graduate student, reviewed coverage of contemporary twentieth-century oppression. How true was the black press to its founding principles? Clark's 1969 doctoral dissertation, "The Editorial Reaction of Selected Black Newspapers to the Civil Rights Movement," reported both good news and bad.

Analyzing newspaper coverage of the 1960 lunch counter sit-in (see January 31) by four North Carolina A & T students, he found local *Greensboro A & T College Register* articles straightforward journalistic presentations of facts. The first article included a somewhat restrained "transcript" of the dialogue between a student demonstrator and the waitress who had refused to serve him.

When whites rioted against black attempts to desegregate a Biloxi, Mississippi, beach, an *Atlanta Daily World* editorial criticized blacks and urged "more mature" approaches. "There is no need for any group to take matters into their own hands in misguided attempts to gain Civil Rights, when these rights have already been guaranteed by the Constitution of the United States," wrote editors. "Such attempts [create] general ill-will and set up situations that endanger the lives and property of everyone," editors insisted, clearly ignoring the fact that without the attempts of demonstrators, rights were guaranteed but unenforced.

In contrast, *Louisiana Weekly* was devout about its historic mandate. "It appears that [students have] learned something from their African brothers. . . . Going to jail in the fight to uphold [principles] is no disgrace. It is a badge of honor and achievement. . . . The students have stood up like men and were counted. Freedom, dignity, and independence are seldom won without some sacrifice. . . ."

MARCH 17

A BRIEF NOTICE IN THE MARCH 17, 1936, edition of the London *Daily Telegraph* reads: "This stage account of the chief liberator of Haiti is written from the heart. But Mr. James is a journalist (he writes about cricket for a great provincial newspaper) and not a dramatist." To say, in 1936, that the Trinidadian scholar-activist C. L. R. James wrote about cricket was, of course, to say, in 1947, that Jackie Robinson was pigeon-toed. A unique part of his winning charm, this fact was most often raised by those who would detract from the man's far greater significance.

In 1936, Ethiopia had been invaded by Italy. James (like thousands of black men on every continent) was actively engaged in her freedom fight as founder of the International African Friends of Ethiopia—with Jomo Kenyatta, (Kenya's future liberator) and Amy Ashwood Garvey (Marcus Garvey's first wife) among its members. Fascism was overtaking Europe; so, too, was intimidation. For the colonized African diaspora, which had long endured fascism as the price paid for the pursuit of democracy by whites, what could be more analogous than the story of the Haitian revolution? Not only had James written his critically defamed play, *Toussaint L'Ouverture*, he was completing *The Black Jacobins: Toussaint L'Ouverture and the San Domingo Revolution*. This seminal work, and his *History of Negro Revolt*, was published in 1938. In much the same way American dramatist Arthur Miller used the story of the Salem witchcraft trials of the 1690s to illuminate the political witchhunts of the 1950s, James found in the history of Haiti both metaphor and icon for a discourse on Ethiopia.

Eighteenth-century Haiti was the twentieth-century's Ethiopia. As Haiti had served notice to oppressor and oppressed alike that the black masses could and would fight to the death for freedom, Ethiopia also proved a jewel in two crowns. The last frontier for Europe's total seizure of the continent, the Ethiopian campaign was, for blacks, the beginning of the end for colonial rule. James was not an aspiring West Indian playwright, he was an aspiring Pan-African liberationist.

Strategy

Aspirations

MARCH 18

IT IS IMPOSSIBLE TO BELIEVE that segregationists did not know how wrong their acts were—especially in the Bible Belt of the South. As Selma mayor Joseph Smitherman said, "You knew [discrimination] was wrong but you would always rationalize: Why were they pushing this and why were they trying to tear up the society. . . . Of course we knew it was wrong to shoot fire hoses and turn dogs loose. . . ." Not one would have pressed for "separation of the races" were another race to do the separating. Despite the rhetoric, the issue was never separation, it was white supremacy. Motivated by fear of the day when whites would be "done unto" as they had done, racism contaminated those who never saw themselves as "good enough" and settled for a wish to be "better than."

In the changing times and changing roles of the Civil Rights era, to look beyond the black-and-white images photographed, televised, historically memorialized, and emotionalized was to meet people neither bound nor gagged by racism, people who realized that the thing at stake was bigger than "separation," bigger than "states' rights"—at stake were their own lives. Millions committed moral, personal, legal, and financial support to the movement. On March 18, 1965—with a permanent stain of Bloody Sunday (see March 7) on their hearts—scores left the security of family and home to trod dangerous ground: the march from Selma to Montgomery. On March 18, violent segregationists who had reserved special contempt for those who abdicated the "privilege" of being white to join Civil Rights demonstrations, were more determined than ever to stop the march. SNCC had organized a student protest the day after President Johnson's voting rights speech. Before the students could begin their protest, they were attacked by what one writer called a "club-wielding posse on horseback." This was personal, as the students soon discovered. Jailed for helping a fellow student to safety, Pam Clemson of Juniata College had to heal physical and emotional wounds. She said she was "seventeen years old and out to save the world." What she was was a courageous young woman.

MARCH 19

FOR MUCH OF the nation's history, not only had Congress excluded blacks, so had its press gallery. In 1929, Chicago's Oscar DePriest became the first African American congressman since Reconstruction, and the first ever from the North. Yet the press that spoke directly to his constituents—the black press—could not observe him on the House floor. Even after Arthur Mitchell replaced DePriest in Congress, this restriction was enforced. Then, in 1947, Harlem's fiery congressman, Adam Clayton Powell Jr., looked up at the gallery one day and thought, "Where are the reporters of the Negro press—the daily papers from Atlanta, the weeklies from Chicago, the magazines—where are they?" He then set out to change the situation.

For years, the Standing Committee of Newspaper Correspondents had refused to give blacks the credentials necessary to cover Congress on the grounds that this privilege was restricted to reporters from daily newspapers. When this rule inadvertently barred whites who worked for weeklies, it was simply bent to accommodate them. Powell went to the Speaker of the House with a logical argument: he had been elected by the same process that elected every representative; his district had as much right as any to know what Congress and its congressman was doing. He was right. Together, Powell and the Speaker took the issue to the Senate Rules Committee, which overrode the restriction. And, on March 19, 1947, Louis Lautier of the *Afro-American* and Washington bureau chief of the Negro Newspaper Publishers Association became the first black reporter credentialed to cover Congress from within its chamber.

Clearly, the desegregation of the press represents a victory over patterns of bias that have impeded black professionals in every field. It also raises issues about the quality of our news and our histories. If the press was so biased in its gallery, how unbiased was its reportage? If researchers rely on sources so "discolored" by racism, what does this say about our history and our truths?

MARCH 20

A POPULAR ANTIWAR LYRIC went, "Well it's one, two, three, what are we fighting for?" In 1968, disproportionate numbers of blacks were drafted to fight for American interests in Vietnam while their draft-deferred peers fought against what they saw as the same "demons" on campus. The year that began with the Orangeburg massacre (see February 7) of students protesting a segregated bowling alley, would soon erupt in the murder of Dr. King. On campus, the freedom fight found voice in demands for academic reform and courses in black studies.

On March 20, 1968, students of historically black Howard University occupied its administration building and made their case: it was hard to be black at a black university. An open letter to President James Nabrit, written weeks before, argued: "Black youth of today have learned that to be 'just like a white man' is to acquire a synthetic identity and to hate one's true self. . . . The Black leader of today must address himself to a new breed of youth and the black university of today must produce a new breed of leaders—leaders who take pride in their true identity and who will instill similar pride in others. Unfortunately, Howard University has not yet committed itself to producing such leaders."

Among their demands: that Howard be made a center for African American thought; that "economic, government, literature, and social science departments [emphasize] how these disciplines may be used to effect the liberation of black people"; and that links to the neighboring black community be formed. The university had dismissed several faculty members for political activism. Students demanded their reinstatement and the resignations of the administrators responsible for the dismissals. Restructuring academic protocol in step with growing national student activism, Howard's students opted to carry the baton for fallen heroes, their peers, and their most precious demand: the right to a future. Six weeks into Orangeburg and the deepening war, they braced for the worst and hoped for the best.

Education   Respect for Youth

MARCH 21

Mᴀʀᴄʜ 21, 1960, Sharpeville: a day of tragedy. March 21, 1965, Selma: a day of resurrection. Two days, two peoples at a crossroads marked freedom.

March 21, 1960, in South Africa was the day set by the people of Sharpeville to fight the "pass law"—the odious rule that "nonwhites" produce, on demand, an insidious passbook. To be without it was to be subject to fine, imprisonment, banishment, or forced labor. As prearranged with officials, ten thousand peaceful protesters gathered at the police station without passbooks to await a promised change of law. Instead, at 1:40 ᴘ.ᴍ., police raged toward them, firing directly into the crowd of stunned men, women, and children. When the carnage was done, 69 blacks had been killed and 180 had been wounded in the historic Sharpeville massacre.

On March 21, 1965, thousands of people gathered in Selma, Alabama, for the five-day Selma-to-Montgomery march. Three weeks earlier, unarmed protesters had been betrayed and stormed by police on what would be known as Bloody Sunday. Now, determined and defiant, they retraced their route as the world looked on. Singing "Ain' gonna let nobody turn me 'round," they crossed the Pettus Bridge. The movement had come to a crossroads. So gratuitous was the earlier violence that an army of foot soldiers twenty-five thousand strong dropped what they were doing, headed for Selma, and joined the freedom fight.

The symbolism of the Christian season of Lent, sacrifice and the promise of redemption, had been lost on few. Washed in the blood of the slaughtered, organizers chose this date for its symbolic link to Sharpeville, the Pan-African struggle, and the world crusade for human rights. For one marcher, Henry Hampton, it was "a dream I have carried with me since I walked the Pettus Bridge in Selma," fulfilled twenty years later with his television series on those Freedom Days, *Eyes on the Prize.* For posterity, it was the defining march of the era.

MARCH 22

*L*IFE MAGAZINE's eminent photojournalist Gordon Parks was onto a story he had to tell. In Brazil, where ten thousand children had died of dysentery the year before, Parks met Flavio Da Silva. "You're too late," a doctor told Parks. "His heart, lungs, and teeth are all bad—all at the ripe old age of twelve." Speaking out of earshot of Flavio, he added, "The poor lad's finished. He might last another year— maybe not." In the favela of Catacumba were too many Flavios. Walking the child back home up the mountain of Corcovado, Parks told Flavio he would be all right. And so it was left to the boy to comfort the man: "I'm not scared of death. It's my brothers and sisters I worry about. What would they do?" The next morning Parks cabled his editor. Two days later came the reply: FLAVIO SOUNDS TRAGIC BUT HE SOUNDS WONDERFUL—INSPIRING —KEEP A DIARY. On March 22, 1961, Parks began:

> Reached shack at 7:30. Zacarias was crawling around naked in the filth outside. Albia and Isabel were swinging in a greasy hammock hung across the room. Flavio was cooking. I stepped backward to photograph the two in the hammock and upset a pot of beans. Flavio started laughing but it brought on convulsive coughing. He became so weak I had to hold him. Later he scraped up the beans and dumped them back into the pot. I can almost see him dying now. I've started buying food for the family.

Sticking with Flavio, Parks took a two-week walk in the valley of desperate lives. When he returned to New York, he was terrified that the story would not see print—that his editors would think it was too depressing. But Secretary of State Dean Rusk fortuitously called for foreign aid to Latin America's poor to deter the lure of Communism, and the story was locked in for mid-June. With publication came unparalleled offers of help, money from readers, and news of Flavio's turn for the worse. Afraid that Flavio might be too ill to pass through Customs, *Life* asked President Kennedy to help and got the nod: "Bring him on." With the blessing of millions, Parks flew to Rio to save his friend. What a story. What vision. What a *Life*.

Photojournalism   Human Spirit

MARCH 23

A PHOTO OF JULIAN BOND, a cofounder of SNCC, and other member/volunteers taken in Atlanta and dated March 23, 1963, tells a story:

Standing in a triangular cluster, thirteen people face directly forward, staring at the camera, bearing witness, documenting their commitment. Julian Bond is at the apex, a white husband and wife are in the second row, two black men are in the third, and the others are fanned out into the fourth and fifth rows so that all the faces are visible. It is a time when such a photo in the wrong hands could turn a SNCC volunteer into a target. It is a time when every person of conscience is a target and a photo in the right hands is the only way to identify the missing, the mutilated, and the murdered. It is the time of the Civil Rights movement, and the question is this: *Which side are you on, brother?* . . .

On the opposite side of the camera that day was top fashion and celebrity photographer Richard Avedon. Avedon had donated time and equipment from his New York studio to train several photographers for SNCC. He told a friend and owner of a camera shop how badly SNCC needed equipment and supplies. The owner, Marty Forscher, began a campaign among his clients and friends that, in the course of three years, donated seventy-five cameras and a supply of film to the movement. Said Forscher, "It seemed to be a wonderful way to put my money where my mouth was." *Which side are you on, brother?* . . .

With a photo, as with a book, to read between the lines, to look beyond the frame, is to know that there is always more than meets the eye. What made being in the movement so special was that whoever you were, wherever you were, you could stand on the side of doing good.

Photography   Purpose

MARCH 24

So MUCH IS SAID ABOUT what African Americans have not done as a people that it is important to take stock of all that we have done. Invariably, we are pleasantly surprised. Beginning on March 24, 1970, and continuing for eight days spread over eight weeks, that pleasure was shared by filmgoers when the Jewish Museum in New York hosted the nation's first black historical film festival.

As a retrospective, the festival revived the work of film pioneers Oscar Micheaux and Spencer Williams; resurrected the images of actors Clarence Muse, Nina Mae McKinney, and the "Negro Valentino," Lorenzo Tucker; and restored to memory a cultural legacy most filmgoers knew nothing about—the history of African American film. Despite the bars on the gates of Hollywood, blacks had appeared in and made films since the early 1900s. For each film in the festival, a dozen others could have been chosen; that was the good news. And although only a few films could be screened, together they told a collective story of the African American film experience, 1929 to 1969. These were a few of the films in the festival:

A Scar of Shame (1929), produced by the Colored Players Corporation, explored black attitudes on color, caste, and class. Paul Robeson had top billing for the title role in *The Emperor Jones* (1933), playwright Eugene O'Neill's classic, which also featured whites in the cast. *Bronze Buckeroo* (1939) was a western with a dashing singing cowboy, Herb Jeffries. *Broken Strings* (1940) was cowritten by its star—law school graduate and veteran stage actor/director Clarence Muse. *Go Down, Death* (1944), a "story of Jesus and the Devil," starred its writer/ director Spencer Williams. *Cry of Jazz* (1958) was Ed Bland's provocative history of America. The documentary *Ephesus* (1965) captured Sundays in a holiness church. And with *Soul Sounds and Money* (1969) producer/director St. Clair Bourne looked at the economics of the record industry. Comedy, drama, music, and adventure; in narrative and documentary short and feature films, we had done it all.

MARCH 25

IT IS ONE OF THE MOST FAMOUS IMAGES of the Civil Rights movement—a ribbon of demonstrators, stretched as far as the eye can see, marches over the horizon as precipitous storm clouds loom overhead. *"Ain't gonna let nobody turn us 'round,"* people sang. That was the spirit and the legacy of the last great march of the Civil Rights era, twenty-five thousand strong. On Sunday (see March 21) four thousand marchers began the fifty-four-mile trek from Selma to Montgomery. There, in a patrol car at the head, were two men who had vowed this day would never come: Major John Cloud, the state trooper who had launched the attack at the Pettus Bridge that turned back an earlier effort to march (see March 7), and the sadistic Sheriff Jim Clark (see January 19). There, too, were National Guardsmen on the lookout for snipers. There were preachers, nuns, and rabbis; fellow Nobel Prize laureate Ralph Bunche, author James Baldwin, and other Civil Rights leaders. There were local people and thousands who had come from all across the nation. There was an amputee on crutches wearing a cowboy hat, and a teenager who had creamed his forehead white and etched a word onto his dark skin: VOTE.

"Ain't gonna let segregation turn me 'round," they sang. Walking in the rain, sleeping in the mud, they kept going on peanut butter sandwiches and faith as their number swelled to twenty-five thousand. On March 25, 1965, their arrival at the capitol climaxed in a freedom rally. From his office window, Governor George Wallace absorbed the scene, knowing that what Dr. King said that day was true: "Segregation is on its deathbed in Alabama and the only thing uncertain about it is how costly the segregationists and Wallace will make the funeral." That night, Viola Luizzo, a white volunteer from Detroit, was shuttling demonstrators back to Selma. Her out-of-state license plates were the magnet that drew four violent men to her side. Within seconds she was dead. Leroy Moton, the event's fifteen-year-old flag bearer, had been driving with her and survived by pretending to be dead, too. *"Keep on a-walkin', keep on a-talkin', marchin' up the freedom trail. . . ."*

Marches

Empowerment

MARCH 26

IN THE FREEDOM FIGHT OF EVERY PEOPLE comes a moment from which there is no turning back. For South Africa and Africans the world over, the Sharpeville Massacre was such a moment (see March 21). As unarmed demonstrators awaited news on passbook laws, police shot directly into their midst, killing sixty-nine people: fifty-one men, ten children, and eight women. Most had been shot in the back. When news reached already-banned ANC President-General Albert Luthuli, he immediately called for a national day of mourning and prayer—a one-day strike.

Five days later, on March 26, 1960, as the eyes of the world looked on through the lens of the press, in an act punishable by imprisonment, Luthuli burned his passbook and encouraged others to do the same. For, as he would later say, "When the white rulers resort to wholesale indiscriminate violence, as they surely will do, it will be the sign that their end as a master-race is begun." A sign too, that the day of liberation is near.

For his nonviolent leadership in the movement that surged after the Sharpeville Massacre and his response in the "no turning back" passbook-burning incident, when the Nobel Peace Prize committee announced its laureate for 1960 that October, it named Albert Luthuli. In December, an embarrassed South African government lifted its banning order to permit him to travel to Norway and accept his prize "on behalf of all the peoples of Africa."

Tragically, Luthuli did not live to see South Africa's freedom day. In 1967, he was killed at a railroad crossing. With the ANC's old guard leadership dead, imprisoned or exiled, it was the end of an era. But hardly the end of the freedom fight. For if Luthuli, the lion, could be struck down by a passing train, what hope could there possibly be for the weak who so desperately clung to apartheid?

MARCH 27

On March 27, 1948, ten days out of jail on a drug possession charge, Billie Holiday walked onto the stage of Carnegie Hall. She was a sellout. And she sang her heart out—thirty-three songs in all. During intermission, a box of gardenias arrived; someone had remembered her trademark. She went back on stage to triumph. Despite the predictions, it looked like she was going to be able to reclaim her career. She tried coming back to life, looking in on friends, many of whom were fearful for their own reputations and rejected the "jailbird." One, Lena Horne, hearing that word, said, "Don't say that!" Horne welcomed her back into the fold with a gentle line: "You've been sick and away for a little while, that's all." But reality set in. She needed to work, especially in New York, but as an "ex-con" she was prohibited from working where alcohol was served—that included nightclubs, the places where singers made their living. What to do next? Her agents came up with a novel idea. One month later, on April 27, "Holiday on Broadway" opened in the Mansfield Theater—a sellout for three straight weeks. It would be a hard climb, but Billie Holiday was headed back to the top.

Her audiences loved her—forgave her. She had given them years of pleasure and they wanted more. "God bless the child that's got his own," she thought, having learned that lesson a long time before. For weeks she had been stewing over a mother-daughter squabble when her mother wouldn't lend her some money. Then, in one flush moment of inspiration, an entire song fell from her head to the page—it became one of the most enduring lyrics of all time:

"God bless the child that's got his own."

Music   Rising from Defeat

MARCH 28

On March 28, 1968, fifteen thousand people gathered in Memphis to march in support of striking sanitation workers. Placards held aloft read: I AM A MAN! It was an old story: the plight of the common working man and woman, dividing and conquering workers by race. And the decision to unionize was long overdue.

The spark that touched off the sanitation strike had been lit in February, when bad weather prevented workers from completing their rounds. All of the white workers were allowed to remain on the job with pay, but twenty-two blacks were sent home and docked for the day. Not only was this case about discrimination, it was about powerlessness and being poor. As Dr. King prepared for his Poor People's Campaign (see June 19), it was felt that the two campaigns—one of the sanitation workers and the other of the multiracial working poor—were one and the same. And when King's longtime associate James Lawson asked him to participate, he couldn't refuse; he even went against the wishes of his own staff to participate. The staff urged him to focus on the Poor People's Campaign. But he felt bound to return the favor of support Lawson had so often given him. On March 28, 1968, King was back in Memphis, as promised, to lead the solidarity march. Even as the men assembled early that day, an air of foreboding descended. Later that day a riot broke out: hundreds were arrested, sixty were wounded, a black teenager was killed by police. Spirited off to a hotel for his protection, King was so exhausted that night that he didn't even awaken when Dr. Ralph Abernathy covered him with a spread. Said King's assistant, Bernard Lee, he was so terribly upset by the events, so sensitive to being criticized for the violence, that "he just slept. He slept his discontent off." A week later, on April 4, he was assassinated in Memphis as he stood on the balcony of the Lorraine Motel.

Today, the Civil Rights Museum occupies the site of the renovated Lorraine Motel. On permanent display is a heap of symbolic trash and placards—a tribute to the cause of the sanitation workers, King's last campaign.

THE FANGS OF RACISM had done so much to quash his daughter's young spirit. On his deathbed, Daisy Bates's father had told her, "Daisy, you're consumed with hatred for white people. If you're gonna hate, make it count for something. Hate segregation in the South." Years later, the newspaper she co-owned with her husband, L. C. Bates, hated racism and loved the opportunity afforded by their subscribers to serve the people. In the 1940s and 1950s, their *State Press* was the voice of conscience—a difficult but rewarding task for a black paper.

In the war years of the 1940s, the U.S. government censored newspapers by keeping such essentials as newsprint in short supply. But while there was a shortage of paper, there was no lack of criticism for the war effort—especially the poor treatment of blacks in the military and in war industry jobs. The *State Press* kept up its banner critiques. But when the Justice Department threatened twenty black editors with charges of sedition, all were forced to acquiesce—even the editors of the *State Press*. The NAACP negotiated a quid pro quo solution on behalf of black press owners: for toning down their opposition, the government would increase their allotment of paper stock and supplies. In 1946, the war was over, paper was back, and with it a vigilant press.

On March 29, 1946, a *State Press* headline read: FTA STRIKERS SENTENCED TO PEN BY A HAND-PICKED JURY. The war in Europe was over, but the war on unions and the press was on. Police came for the Bateses with warrants. They were arrested, booked, fingerprinted, and photographed. Then they were allowed to post bond, but every lawyer they called was "too busy" to take their case. A CIO union lawyer finally came to their defense in a trial by a judge with no jury. The Bateses were sentenced to ten days, fined, denied the right to an appeal bond, and immediately jailed. Seven hours later, however, their lawyer secured their release by Arkansas Supreme Court Justice Griffin Smith. Eight months later, their sentences were officially vacated.

MARCH 30

AS MARTIN LUTHER KING had written in his "Letter from a Birmingham Jail" (see April 16), "when your first name becomes 'nigger,' your middle name becomes 'boy' . . . and your wife and mother are never given the respected title 'Mrs.' . . . then you will understand why we find it difficult to wait." For all the black men and women who had had to wait, Miss Mary Hamilton demanded the dignity that was her due. Literally making a federal case of it, she fought for that right and won a Supreme Court victory on March 30, 1964.

Significantly, Birmingham inspired both King's letter and Hamilton's triumph. In the spring of 1963, she had helped organize the Freedom March. As she told a Pacifica Radio interviewer, "when [the police] see an organizer around, they, if they can, will arrest you. So I had been ordered by the police to stay off the sidewalk. I had really stepped up on a ledge. . . . It was really this simple. I had lost my balance . . . and the minute I stepped down on the sidewalk I was nabbed—and placed in a police car." She was herded into solitary confinement bins along with eighty other young women. As things escalated and they screamed for release, she protested as policemen crowded in again. "I told them, 'The girls have been in here for five hours without bathroom facilities and without water—and you can't treat people this way.'" With that, she was left alone in solitary. When her case came to trial, the prosecutor addressed her on the witness stand as "Mary." She asked to be properly addressed, as "Miss Hamilton." Seeing a wedge to find her guilty of something—anything—the prosecutor pushed the first name issue until the judge sentenced "Mary" to five days and a $50 fine for contempt.

"Mary" appealed her conviction from the state appeals court, to the state supreme court, up to the United States Supreme Court, where a twelve-word decision was handed down on March 30, 1964: "The petition for writ of certiorari is granted. The judgment is reversed." The eyes of the law finally reflected what she had seen in herself all along: "Mary" was "Miss Hamilton" at last.

Believing that "the good lord helps those who help themselves," M. Moran Weston pursued a multifaceted career: state university professor; activist/advocate for moderate- and low-income housing; founder and chairman of the board of Carver Federal Savings and Loan, a black-owned and -operated bank. A respected leader in the National Council of the Protestant Episcopal Church, he was also rector of St. Phillips, New York City's oldest black Episcopal church.

On the most sacred of days in Christian history, it is said that Jesus looked down from the cross and said, "Forgive them, Lord, for they know not what they do." On Good Friday, March 31, 1972, Reverend M. Moran Weston gave his assembled flock his "Declarations of Awareness," which were as earthbound in inspiration as they were heaven-sent:

O God, we acknowledge we do not see clearly, nor fully understand: open our eyes and our perception. O God, we acknowledge we have too often been unwilling to march on the seat of power to cleanse church, government, and the marketplace from corruption which defiles man and defies God. . . . O God, we acknowledge we have too often retreated and given ground under the backlash of the establishment. . . . O God, we acknowledge that too often we have failed under cross-examination on the witness stand; too often we have lost our nerve when prosecutor, witnesses, jury, and judge have conspired with a bloodthirsty mob to render a verdict of "guilty" and a sentence of "death" . . .

O God, we acknowledge that too often we have refused to become involved, we have sought refuge from the battle by being a sightseer or spectator: may we be inspired to follow the example of Thy chosen ones who have been involved until the bitter end, even at the cost of their life. O God, we believe through Thy chosen one Jesus the Carpenter, People's Leader, Chosen One, Prisoner, Defendant, Condemned Man and Confident Man, that good will indeed overcome evil. . . . [May we] go forth into the world with courage and confidence, [and] be ready to confront evil without retreating, knowing that men and women, young and old, chosen and called by God will receive power to stand fast against evil and to triumph day by day.

Prayer   Responsibility

APRIL

Virginia Durr and Ella Baker in Wetumpka, Alabama (1979). Courtesy of Joanne Grant, from *Ella Baker: Freedom Bound,* published by John Wiley & Sons, 1998.

APRIL 1

In April 1959, SCLC needed a new executive director. Only reluctantly, and on an interim basis, was the job given to the best candidate, a woman—Ella Baker (see April 17). Raising the money through SCLC that would launch SNCC, for her guidance and inspiration, Baker would become better known as the "Godmother of SNCC." Always motivating her God's children with questions, training them as organizers with questions, she helped them understand the repercussions of their energetic acts. You can structure a voter registration campaign, she would say, but is the community strong enough to handle it? What support must you put in place? Are there enough available volunteers to tell your adversary that if one is killed, ten more will replace him or her?

Such was her strength as a mentor that SNCC's members, Ella Baker's "godchildren," now continue the work they were trained to do in every endeavor as the ongoing struggle now demands. Among them: Marion Barry has served several terms as the mayor of Washington, D.C.; Julian Bond made history with his election to the Georgia state legislature (and the Supreme Court case that finally allowed him to take his seat) and as a broadcaster; Stokely Carmichael (Kwame Ture) is an author, lecturer, and organizer on the international scene building alliances with African nations; Kathleen Cleaver achieved notoriety for her work with the Black Panther Party and her marriage to Eldridge Cleaver, later graduated Yale Law School, and was part of the legal team that kept up a twenty-seven-year vigil until falsely imprisoned ex-Panther Geronimo Pratt was finally freed in 1997; Jennifer Lawson became director of programming for the nation's public television consortium, PBS; John Lewis is a member of the House of Representatives from Georgia; Dr. Bernice Johnson Reagon is a McArthur "genius award" Fellow on staff at the Smithsonian Institution, and founder of Sweet Honey in the Rock; and Judith Richardson became a producer for Blackside, Inc., the production company that gave us the fourteen-hour documentary series on the Civil Rights movement (including SNCC), *Eyes on the Prize*.

APRIL 2

W ITH THE WORLD embroiled in the madness of World War II, Willard Motley's life was filled with grueling irony. By day, he was a lab technician performing shock experiments on animals. In the failed human experiment called peace, he was awaiting draft reclassification—conscientious objector status as a pacifist. And at night, in his private life, as he confided to his diary on April 2, 1943, he had come to a critical juncture. "This week or next I have to kill Nick," he wrote. "It is not a pleasant thing to look forward to after three years of living with him, knowing him better than I've ever known anyone and—liking him."

As a teenager adamant about becoming a novelist, Motley began his diaries in 1926 at the age of sixteen. "Awful lonesome; need a chum," he wrote on day one. Transposing daily life to the diary and its pages into art, he recorded encounters with chums and invented characters for the next seventeen years. Now, the life of his old chum, Nick, was in danger. "Have pages of notes for these last two chapters," he wrote. "They must be good. They must be powerful. They must have punch—deep impact. In them I have to synchronize everything I've said in the book." And he did. That first book would become the 300,000 copy bestseller *Knock on Any Door*. But first he had to close the book on old friends, and it would be two more months before he was up to the task.

> Nick died at 8 o'clock tonight. So the book is finished now. . . .
> I'm not as happy about ending as I felt I would be. I hadn't realized how long three and a half years are nor how dear Nick had grown to me. I feel as if one of my arms had been cut off. Three and a half years of my life—ten years of Nick's life. Killing him hurt a lot—I ended with tears in my eyes. Started tonight on the next book. . . . Then, thinking about Nick, went out for a few beers. Met Morry. Had a few more—and a couple shots of whiskey. Got drunk.

Whether art had mirrored life or life had mirrored art, the taking of a life—even a fictional one—had taken its toll on him for good, for bad, for sure.

APRIL 3

In what had become a nightly ritual, Joan Frances Bennett chronicled her day—her walk to the Hudson River, stretching out on the lawn to watch the cars go by. The youngest of eleven children, she was eighteen, a Barnard College student from Taylors, South Carolina, on her own in New York. In days, history would drastically alter her life with such events as the seizure of the Columbia University administration building by students protesting racial injustice and the Vietnam War. But this night, April 3, 1968, she completed her Freshman English assignment and unwittingly recorded her last carefree day of youthful wanderings and wonderings.

> I wonder what changes these experiences will make in me. I wonder if I'm being broadened, because I need to be broadened. I probably won't notice any differences in myself. I'll have to be told. I can hear them saying, "Joan! You've changed!" and I'll say, "Naw, it's just me. I'm coming out at last. I was always like this underneath." Perhaps people don't grow up or change, just shed skins like snakes do. Or think of a human being as a clothes dummy, and the different ages as layers of clothing. Youth being the underwear, young adulthood the dress or shirt and pants, and old age the coat. Death being total undress—revelation.

This was her last reflection of herself before she and her world would change with the currents. She would shed the protective skin of her youth the very next day, April 4, 1968.

> Martin Luther King, the "King," was killed tonight. After the shock, what did I think? Well done, Martin Luther, well done. Let the people say *Amen*. Some say his philosophy died with him. I would say that the kind of man who could implement that philosophy died with him. Under him the Civil Rights movement came of age, and the growth cycle doesn't reverse itself. We have passed that point. There won't be a chance for another little black boy in Atlanta, Georgia, to grow up believing in the innate goodness of man. . . . What damn good does it do anybody—man, God, or beast—to be born with an innate capacity for goodness if in his flight through this way the conditions aren't conducive to its development?

APRIL 4

In 1967, as the United States escalated the Vietnam War, Martin Luther King could not stand as one apart, silent. Never one to limit his vision, he refused to constrict his voice: the African American condition was inextricably linked to the human condition of all the world's peoples. Amidst criticism and threats, on April 4, 1967, he gave his courageous, personally dangerous antiwar speech at New York City's Riverside Church. A statement issued by his hosts, Clergy and Laymen Concerned about Vietnam, began, "A time comes when silence is betrayal." King agreed:

> Over the past two years, as I have moved to break the betrayal of my own silences . . . many persons have questioned me about the wisdom of my path. . . . Why are you speaking about war, Dr. King? Peace and Civil Rights don't mix, they say. . . .
>
> . . . A few years ago there was a shining moment in the struggle. It seemed as if there was a real promise of hope for the poor . . . through the Poverty Program. . . . Then came the buildup in Vietnam, and I watched the program broken and eviscerated as if it were some idle political plaything of a society gone mad on war, and I knew that America would never invest the necessary funds or energies in . . . its poor so long as adventures like Vietnam continued to draw men and skills and money like some demoniacal destructive suction tube.
>
> Perhaps the more tragic recognition [was] . . . the cruel irony of watching Negro and white boys on TV screens as they kill and die together for a nation that has been unable to seat them together in the same schools. . . .

He felt the dilemma of dissuading from violence angry, hopeless, young men who saw that they would soon face the violence of war. He ached for the Vietnamese, to whom he felt the United States should "atone" and "make reparations." For many, this speech was the beginning of the end for King—but not for the war, which raged on another eight years. One year to the date from this speech, April 4, 1968, Martin Luther King was assassinated in Memphis, Tennessee.

APRIL 5

O<small>N</small> A<small>PRIL</small> 5, 1941, in its lacrosse match at Annapolis with the U.S. Naval Academy, Harvard University agreed to bench a black lacrosse player, Lucien Alexis Jr. By doing so, the university acceded to the academy's segregation policy, which forbade black players on its publicly funded grounds.

It was a sad replay of the racist games played by whites unwilling to win or lose a fair sportsman's test. In 1917, a seventeen-year-old star athlete at Rutgers University, who had been proclaimed a "football genius" by no less than the *New York Herald*, was similarly benched for the benefit of his racist football opponents—his name was Paul Robeson. Years later, black athletes turned the tables on their adversaries by benching themselves, refusing to play teams that upheld racist practices (see October 7). Together with performing artists, athletes would boycott South Africa's white teams in the fight to end apartheid.

With help from protesters lashing out among the ranks of its faculty, students, alumni, and the wider community, Harvard reconsidered. It had a tradition to uphold as one of the world's leading institutions for the education of world-class leaders—and that included African American leaders. In the mid-1800s, the legendary Underground Railroad conductor Dr. Martin Delany became Harvard's first African American medical school graduate. He was credited with ending the cholera epidemic in Ontario, Canada, in 1856. In 1884, the school graduated ex-slave Robert Terrell. In 1910, he became the nation's first black federal court judge. In 1893, Harvard graduated Clement G. Morgan, the first African American to earn two Harvard degrees—a bachelor's and a master's in law. And in 1895, W. E. B. Du Bois graduated as the university's first black Ph.D.

In its own best interests, and that of its students, on April 21, 1941, Harvard University announced that it would no longer bench its lacrosse players for reasons of race.

APRIL 6

F**OR YEARS**, the Civil Rights movement had experienced uncanny events: misinformation was often fabricated and released to the press, forged letters were mailed between allies, and an anti-Semitic comic book was sent to Jewish leaders under a Black Panther Party imprint. On April 6, 1976, suspicion was borne out in fact: those responsible were FBI Counterintelligence Program (COINTELPRO) agents. As described and authorized by FBI Director J. Edgar Hoover in a secret 1967 memo, their mission was to "expose, disrupt, misdirect, discredit or otherwise neutralize the activities of black nationalists . . . and supporters."

Since the 1920s and Marcus Garvey, the FBI had been obsessed with the freedom movement. But what had begun as an investigation became a systematic pattern of intimidation. As FBI director from 1924 until just before his death in 1972, Hoover had been given unusual latitude during the witch-hunts of the "Red Scare" years. When COINTELPRO came to light at last, no one should have been surprised:

March 8, 1971: Documents stolen from the FBI's Media, Pennsylvania, office on its efforts to thwart black activism are mailed to newspapers, which break the story nationwide.

November 18, 1974: FBI counterintelligence operations against black activists are uncovered.

November 21, 1974: Congress passes Freedom of Information Act, guaranteeing public access to government files. News organizations begin petitioning for release of FBI files.

December 21, 1974: *New York Times* reports Bureau surveillance of ten thousand American Civil Rights and antiwar activists and illegal CIA activity.

December 26, 1974: CIA Director William Colby admits truth of December 21 report.

July 14, 1975: FBI Director Clarence B. Kelley defends illegal FBI burglaries and break-ins as national security—a claim the *Washington Post* quickly disputes with documentation.

And this was only the start (see December 4).

Government   Demons

Hɪꜱ ꜰʀɪᴇɴᴅ ᴀɴᴅ ɢᴇɴᴇʀᴀʟ had been slain at his side. Distraught but not destroyed, Ralph David Abernathy wrote "My Last Letter to Martin."

> In Heaven I know you have so much to do, so many people to see. . . . But look up these black friends and talk to the ones you and I have talked about. Say thanks to those prophets we quoted. Find Mahatma K. Gandhi, the one who inspired us so much in our struggle to free black people. But above all, I want you to see Jesus.

Then Abernathy called the roll of souls to thank: Nat Turner, Frederick Douglass, Marcus Garvey. Find George Lee (see August 2) in heaven, Abernathy reminded his friend. Reverend Lee could hardly read or write, but he died vowing to vote. There was Mrs. Viola Luizzo (see March 25) to see in heaven, the white Detroit homemaker who was killed for her civil rights work. And don't forget Malcom X, he said.

> [Malcolm] may not have believed what we believe but he was a child of God and he was concerned about the welfare of his people.
>
> My dear friend, Martin, I want you to know that black people loved you. It may seem that they are denying our nonviolence for they are acting out their frustration [that] even a man of good, as you were, was killed in such an evil world. They do not see a way out. But I want you to know, Martin, that we're going to point to them a way. That was the frustration of Jerusalem during this same [lenten] season nearly two thousand years ago. But we know, Martin, that, after the venting of frustration, there will be the need for reconciliation. There you will be invisible but real. There has been a crucifixion in our nation, but here in this spring season as we see the blossoms and smell the fresh air we know that the Resurrection will shortly appear. Sincerely, Ralph.

On Sunday, April 7, 1968, this tribute to Martin Luther King Jr. became Dr. Abernathy's Easter sermon at West Hunter Street Baptist Church in Atlanta.

APRIL 8

Just seven years after independence, Nigeria was tragically wracked by civil war. During the war, which lasted from 1967 to 1970, the Nigerian author/dramatist who would become a Nobel Laureate for Literature, Wole Soyinke, was held as a political prisoner for his objection to the self-destructive violence of the war. One year after the war's end, free, visible, and vocal, Soyinke adapted his satirical farce for a film directed by Ossie Davis, the African American actor/ playwright. The film, *Kongi's Harvest*, premiered in Lagos, Nigeria, on April 8, 1971.

In the mythical nation of Isma (so named as a warning against "isms"), President Kongi (played by Soyinke) wields absolute power. Having placed all traditional and spiritual leaders in detention, Kongi puts himself in a bind. Exposed is his own impotence when met with the indomitability of the people themselves, their traditional African values, and their heritage.

"The time has come for Africa to speak for itself," wrote Davis. "*Kongi's Harvest* is a film that does just that, and that is why I made it." Indeed, the determination to "speak for itself" had reached into every phase of the film's production. While editing the film, a very "colonial" moment took place when a suggestion was made that whites might not know what the people were saying or talking about. To that, Davis answered that for years we have had to learn to understand them; now they will learn to understand us. The deference given white viewers over black harkened back to a time when, as Davis said, "those who spoke for Africa were not Africans—anything but that—until at last it was assumed that Africans themselves had nothing to say really worth listening to." With *Kongi's Harvest*, Africans (and African Americans) were speaking for themselves, speaking to each other, and underwriting the process. The film was produced by Calpenny-Nigeria Films of Lagos, Nigeria, and Herald Productions of New York (producers of the African American satire *Putney Swope*), with the sisters of Delta Sigma Theta among its backers.

Film   Cooperative Economics

APRIL 9

WHAT A BEAUTIFUL DAY IT WAS that Easter Sunday, April 9, 1939. Photo pioneers Morgan and Marvin Smith captured the scene. Women in fur jackets and fine hats; men formally attired in morning coats, striped trousers, cravats, gray suede gloves, walking sticks, and spats. This was a Harlem rarely seen. "He is risen!" women said, nodding with a smile and a wave of a white-gloved hand. "He is risen!" gentlemen answered with a tip of a top hat. Arm in arm they strolled, black folks stylin' and steppin', tippin' up Seventh Avenue in the Easter parade—the annual resurrection of hope and tribute to a brighter day.

Things couldn't have looked much brighter in Washington, D.C., that Easter Day. With a break in humiliating clouds of injustice, Marian Anderson, the noted contralto, rimmed by an honor guard of members of the president's cabinet, took a historic step up to the microphone at the Lincoln Memorial and sang to an audience of the faithful, 75,000 strong.

For years, Anderson had been performing concerts at Howard University and Washington's area churches. But when the NAACP named her the Spingarn Medalist for 1939, demand to hear her increased dramatically. Constitution Hall, a venue owned by the Daughters of the American Revolution (DAR), was chosen for its size. But upon word that the hall would be used for an Anderson concert, the DAR refused to lease the space, invoking its segregation policy. Outraged, Howard University and concert impresario Sol Hurok launched a storm of publicity. Only mildly chastened, the DAR offered the hall with the proviso that Anderson not be allowed to set a precedent. Howard and Hurok refused, and under mounting pressure, First Lady Eleanor Roosevelt used her newspaper column to resign her DAR membership as a matter of conscience. But Hurok announced that Anderson would rather perform in the open air than bow to segregation, the secretary of the interior offered the Lincoln Memorial, a projected audience of 7,500 swelled tenfold, and Marian Anderson became an international legend.

APRIL 10

THIS WAS NEWS. Jackie Robinson—the first African American to break the color barrier in modern baseball history—was joining the Brooklyn Dodgers. What was the pivotal moment for Robinson en route from the Negro Leagues (see July 9, August 27) to desegregating the majors? It began when he distinguished himself with the Negro Leagues' Kansas City Monarchs and caught the eye of the *Pittsburgh Courier* sportswriter Wendell Smith.

April 16, 1945: Smith arranged a Boston Red Sox tryout for Robinson and two others, but the Sox management wasn't interested in making history.

August 29, 1945: Robinson and Dodgers owner Branch Rickey had their first historic meeting. "They'll taunt you and goad you," warned Rickey. "They'll do anything to make you react. They'll try to provoke a race riot in the ballpark. This is the way to prove to the public that a Negro should not be allowed in the major leagues." Could Robinson take the abuse and not react openly for one year? Robinson said he could. Two months later Rickey signed Robinson to desegregate his all-white farm team, the Montreal Royals.

April 18, 1946: Robinson plays his first game with the Royals in Jersey City. Despite the pressure, he gets four hits, a three-run homer, and steals two bases. He was so strong that season that adoring Montreal fans chased him three blocks after the season closer.

April 9, 1947: Rickey makes headline news: Robinson is a Brooklyn Dodger! Six days later, April 15, Robinson joins the opening lineup, desegregating major league baseball—a victory for the sport, a coup for the National League.

But perhaps the most inspired day of all was April 10, 1947—the first day of the rest of Jackie Robinson's life. His next weeks would be spent riding a roller coaster from terror to triumph. But on April 10 he awakened in the arms of history and courageously rose to meet his destiny. (Weeks later, on July 5, 1947, history would name Larry Doby the first black player in the American League.)

Sports   Confidence

WHEN CORE LAUNCHED the Freedom Rides in the 1960s, many thought it a new idea. It wasn't. The first Ride, called "The Journey of Reconciliation," took place in 1947, lasted two weeks, and traveled to fifteen cities in Virginia, North Carolina, Tennessee, and Kentucky. Amazingly enough, as the group wound its way through Durham, North Carolina, on a Greyhound bus on April 11, 1947, while they were threatened with arrest, none was actually made. It was a first.

The Journey was inspired by an October 1944 case that began when Irene Morgan was traveling from Virginia to Maryland by Greyhound bus. When asked to move to the back, she refused, was arrested, charged with disorderly conduct in the circuit court of Middlesex County, Virginia, found guilty, and fined $10. With legal aid from the NAACP, she appealed the decision up to the Supreme Court, which found in her favor. Segregated facilities, the Court said, placed an "undue burden" on commerce by forcing both black and white passengers to reshuffle seating between states and bus drivers to act as enforcement agents. With this decision, the Court struck down segregated interstate bus travel on June 3, 1946.

After the Court upheld its decision through several legal tests, CORE and the Racial Industrial Committee of the Fellowship of Reconciliation sponsored the biracial Journey of Reconciliation. Sixteen men—eight black and eight white—left from Washington, D.C., and made twenty-six assaults on what was no longer law but still very much custom. Several arrests occurred, but only in Chapel Hill, North Carolina, did they meet with violence. A group of whites who watched one arrest followed them to the home of a local minister and threatened to stone the house, but they were persuaded not to. Other than that incident, the pattern was the same with each "infraction": the demonstrator was arrested, charged, and fined a nominal sum. How did local judges subvert the Court's order? They declared that although the Journeymen held interstate tickets, they made local stopovers. In those jurisdictions, the local judge declared, state law prevailed.

APRIL 12

W<small>HAT</small> <small>BETTER</small> <small>ENDING</small> could there be for a life so dramatically lived? On April 12, 1975, the final curtain came down on the life of legendary performer Josephine Baker as she lay in a bed strewn with newspapers, bolstered by pillows and reviews for her latest "comeback." Just shy of her sixty-ninth birthday, a hit Paris revue celebrating her fifty years in show business had made of her closing act an endless whirl of celebrity. Resting before a scheduled 5:00 P.M. interview and that evening's performance, she had a good death, if ever there was one. She did not suffer, but fell asleep under a pile of praise and died of a cerebral hemorrhage.

Four days earlier, on April 8, *Joséphine*, her return extravaganza, had opened at the Bobino Theater on rue de la Gaieté in Montparnasse. As her master of ceremonies read opening night congratulatory telegrams from French President Giscard d'Estaing, in the audience were other heads of the realm from the worlds of fashion, politics, and entertainment—her dear friend Princess Grace of Monaco, Pierre Balmain, Alain Delon, Mick Jagger, Sophia Loren, Jeanne Moreau, Madame Sukarno, and General de Boissieu (son-in-law of former president and war hero Charles de Gaulle, who had awarded Baker the Croix de Lorraine and later the nation's highest honor, the Medal of the Resistance, for her wartime service in the French underground). Twelve costume changes later, she relinquished the stage to deafening applause.

All but one of the reviews sang her praise. The exception, published in *Libération*, marked a high of irreverent put-down. Baker, a "vestige of the past and notorious Gaullist," was greeted onstage with "delirium." "The fossils congratulate each other. 'She' is still there, as in 1925 at the Casino de Paris. She is ecstatically emotional about a past of importance only to privileged nostalgics for whom between the wars was that charming period when such a good time was to be had in Monte Carlo." That said, Baker was a hit. With her show sold out for weeks in advance, she died upholding the show business creed: Always leave them wanting more.

APRIL 13

THE ACADEMY AWARDS CEREMONY is a ritual with which almost everyone is familiar—the glamour, the tension, the career-making voice that says "And the Oscar goes to . . ." On April 13, 1964, Sidney Poitier was on the hot seat with a Best Actor nomination for his performance as a handyman upholding a reluctant vow to needy nuns in *Lilies of the Field*. He won—the first African American male actor in the forty-five-year history of the Oscars. What is it like to be there and to win? He answered eloquently in his autobiography, *This Life*.

Seated in the Santa Monica Auditorium: "I thought: Oh, my God, here I am a bundle of nerves—I've got to collect myself and be in control when Albert Finney's name is called." *Waiting:* "I begin making promises to myself in my mind. I say: I can understand that this is an important moment and I have to be here and in fact I want to be here for what it means to us as a people, but I'm never going to put myself through this sh— no more." *Practicing, just in case:* "Think, Sidney, think. . . . After building and discarding a series of opening sentences, I happened upon the phrase 'It has been a long journey to this moment. . . .' A really super, neat phrase, I thought, in a moment of self-congratulation. *When Anne Bancroft said "The winner is Sidney Poitier":* "I ran up on the stage and looked out at those thousands of faces and suddenly forgot my speech."

While celebrating that evening, I paused somewhere in my merrymaking to count my blessings. . . . But a private sadness haunted the celebration and left a place unfilled inside me because I was unable to share it all with the one person most responsible for my being there. Evelyn Poitier's life had come to an end some weeks short of that April evening. She died January 18, 1964, at the age of sixty-eight, after confiding to my sister that she wasn't feeling too well and [saying] "I'm going to lie down for a while." In the few minutes it took my sister to brew a cup of tea and take it into the bedroom, our mother had slipped quietly away to join her Reggie (my father).

APRIL 14

IN THE ANNALS of Civil Rights history, one incident stands out as the moment when a dissident head of a Harlem cult became a religious leader of national renown. That turning point in the story of Malcolm X came on April 14, 1957.

The incident began with a man and a woman arguing on a Harlem street corner. Police arrived and, in front of onlookers, began beating the man. When a witness, Johnson Hinton of Temple #7, attempted to stop the beating, police beat and arrested him as well. In the crowd was another Black Muslim. He quickly notified Malcolm X, who in turn alerted the temple's Fruit of Islam. When Malcolm arrived at the 28th Precinct, he was met by over a hundred Muslim men and women "standing in rank formation," as he recounted in his autobiography. Entering the station, he asked to see Hinton. At first, the police lied, saying he wasn't there. Then, when the group remained unmoved, the officer reconsidered: Hinton was there but Malcolm would not be permitted to see him. Still the Muslims remained. Eventually, the police produced a battered, semiconscious, blood-soaked Hinton. Quietly but firmly, Malcolm demanded that Hinton be taken to a hospital. When the ambulance arrived, the Fruit of Islam walked with it fifteen blocks to the hospital. Once there, they resumed their perfect formation until Malcolm was satisfied that Hinton would receive medical care. At one motion of his hand, members of Temple #7 "slipped away" as a stunned crowd of citizens and police looked on in awe. In that crowd, at Malcolm's request, was James Hicks of the *Amsterdam News*. He reported overhearing a white police captain say of Malcolm X, "No man should have that much power."

Having suffered severe brain injury, Hinton sued the city of New York and won, with help from a Nation of Islam legal team. Malcolm was asked to write a newspaper column that ran in the black press coast-to-coast. And the police and FBI, reasoning that anyone who could stop a riot could also start one, put Malcolm under intense surveillance for the rest of his life.

Strategy   Racial Dignity

TWO HERO-HUSBANDS, two warrior-wives, two nations, one struggle. On April 15, 1963, Coretta and Martin King share a phone call while he is jailed in Birmingham for protesting segregation. On April 15, 1976, Winnie and Nelson Mandela share a letter while he is imprisoned at Robben Island for protesting apartheid.

In 1963, King's jailers had told the FBI that King would be allowed to phone home. When he did, he was wiretapped:

> Martin Luther King: I just read your lovely letter.
> Coretta Scott King: You just got it? . . . I just got a call from the president and he told me you were going to call me in a few minutes. . . . Is your spirit all right?
> MLK: Yes, I've been alone, you know.
> CSK: The [Atlanta Daily] *World* has had front page about every day recently, but it was not accurate. They said the boycott was not effective. . . .

By 1976, Mandela had spent fourteen years in prison for anti-apartheid activities. His letters home were censored and restricted to family matters. He wrote:

> . . . As I woke up . . . I was missing you and the children a great deal as always. . . . Good girl! At last you're back at [school]. But it really shook me to learn that in the evenings you drive to the public library. For the last decade you've been the object of cowardly night attempts on your life. . . . How can you now give them such an ideal opportunity? . . . I almost forgot to say that there're victories whose glory lies in the fact they're known only to those who win them, but there are wounds which leave deep scars when they heal. . . . I dust [your beautiful photo] carefully every morning, for to do so gives me the pleasant feeling that I'm caressing you as in the old days. . . .

Through it all, thousands of miles and years apart, our heroes and sheroes are men and women struggling to live their lives in the tangled web of history.

APRIL 16

Cᴏɴꜰɪɴᴇᴅ ɪɴ ᴀ ɴᴀʀʀᴏᴡ ᴊᴀɪʟ ᴄᴇʟʟ for leading a Good Friday march, on April 16, 1963, Dr. King read a letter from eight clergymen in the *Birmingham News*. Attacking the protest as "untimely and unwise," they urged blacks to wait. Any who've never felt "stinging darts of segregation" might find it easy to wait, wrote King in the margins of the *News* and on scraps of paper he smuggled out. Languishing for weeks, though destined to become a classic of world protest literature, his impassioned 6,500-word "Letter from a Birmingham Jail," was published in the Quaker journal, *Friends*.

> But when you have seen vicious mobs lynch your mothers and fathers at will and drown your sisters and brothers at whim; when you have seen hate-filled policemen curse, kick, and even kill your black brothers and sisters; when you see the vast majority of your twenty million Negro brothers smothering in an airtight cage of poverty in the midst of an affluent society; when you suddenly find your tongue twisted and your speech stammering as you seek to explain to your six-year-old daughter why she can't go to the public amusement park that has just been advertised on television, and see tears welling up in her eyes when she is told that Funtown is closed to colored children, and see ominous clouds of inferiority beginning to form in her little mental sky, and see her beginning to distort her personality by developing an unconscious bitterness toward white people . . . when you . . . find it necessary to sleep night after night in the uncomfortable corners of your automobile because no motel will accept you; when you are humiliated day in and day out by nagging signs reading "white" and "colored"; when your first name becomes "nigger," your middle name becomes "boy" (however old you are) and your last name becomes "John," and your wife and mother are never given the respected title "Mrs."; when you are harried by day and haunted by night by the fact that you are a Negro, living constantly at tiptoe stance, never quite knowing what to expect next, and are plagued with inner fears and outer resentments; when you are forever fighting a degenerating sense of "nobodiness"—then you will understand why we find it difficult to wait.

APRIL 17

ARRIVING IN HIGH POINT, North Carolina, in early February as rows of students began a slow, resolute walk downtown to desegregate lunch counters, Reverend Fred Shuttlesworth saw the future. He phoned Ella Baker, SCLC's executive director, in Atlanta. "You must tell Martin that we must get with this," he told her excitedly. As founder of the Alabama Christian Movement for Human Rights and an SCLC organizer, Shuttlesworth had a well-trained eye. He recognized the potential of the sit-ins to "shake up the world." A new opportunity (and responsibility) presented itself—organizing and training protesters for the escalating violence that would surely come. With an eight-hundred-dollar grant from SCLC, Ella Baker invited student leaders to meet at Shaw University in Raleigh. On April 17, 1960, that conference gave birth to the Student Nonviolent Coordinating Committee (SNCC).

"Just as the sit-ins had skyrocketed or escalated without rhyme or reason," said Baker, "so too the response to the concept of a conference escalated beyond our expectations." One hundred students were expected to attend the conference, "Sacrifice for Dignity." Nearly three hundred came. And although SCLC had underwritten the meeting, it soon became clear that these students who had so passionately and spontaneously forged a new movement would not be bound to an older hierarchy. They did not wish to be a youth division of SCLC or the NAACP. And such was the genius of Ella Baker's leadership that even though she had convened them, she advised and nurtured them into expressing their own identity. For that, she received the enduring respect of the SNCC's young leaders, who soon assumed center stage on a national platform all their own.

From SNCC would emerge such powerful voices as Julian Bond, Stokely Carmichael, John Lewis, and Diane Nash, who praised Baker for "giving direction" to the movement and for "seeing how important it was that the students should set the goals and directions and maintain control of the student movement."

Organizing   Understanding

APRIL 18

FIVE YEARS AFTER the Supreme Court found segregated public schools unconstitutional and thus illegal, little had been done to desegregate schools. Labor leader and Civil Rights activist A. Philip Randolph issued a call to protest. It was billed as the "Youth March for Integrated Schools." On April 18, 1959, 26,000 students of all races answered the call at the Lincoln Memorial. With them came a nationally circulated petition bearing the signatures of 250,000 fellow voices of protest. Among the day's high points were a youth delegation to the White House and speeches by Roy Wilkins of the NAACP and Dr. Martin Luther King:

> ROY WILKINS: The day is long past when what you don't know won't hurt you. . . . The world's [technological] progress has made more necessary than ever before an adequate education in human relations. This resistance [to desegregation] is the plan of adults. . . . Their [old] world is behind them. They don't know and don't care about the difference between . . . Ecuador and Ethiopia. Our segregationists cry, Who cares? So, living in their world of yesterday, they fight the uprooting of segregation and inequality which they nurtured in the land of the free. Yesterday it did not matter much to the rest of the world what the governor of Arkansas did to nine Negro children [see September 3]. Today it matters a great deal. It is your concern because this is the world in which you will have to grow up and serve. . . .

> MARTIN LUTHER KING: As I stand here and look out upon the thousands of Negro faces and the thousands of white faces, intermingled like the waters of a river, I see only one face—the face of the future. . . . As June approaches, with its graduation ceremonies, a thought suggests itself. Whatever career you may choose for yourself—doctor, lawyer, teacher— let me propose an avocation to be pursued along with it. Become a dedicated fighter for Civil Rights. It will make you a better doctor, a better lawyer, a better teacher. It will give you that rare sense of nobility that can only spring from love and selflessly helping your fellow man. Make a career of humanity. Commit yourself to the noble struggle for equal rights. You will make a greater person of yourself, a greater nation of your country, and a finer world to live in.

APRIL 19

From the earliest Nashville sit-ins in February 1960, Z. Alexander Looby, a highly respected African American attorney, had defended demonstrators in court. When white teens assaulted black student protesters, putting out cigarette butts on their backs and pulling them off the lunch counter seats, police arrested the blacks for "disorderly conduct" while their white attackers went free. At trial, the judge was so contemptuous that he actually turned his back on Looby. But just as protesters kept up their sit-ins, Looby kept up his defense of them. Then, at 5:30 A.M. on April 19, 1960, a bomb thrown from a passing car destroyed Looby's home. So severe was the blast that 147 windows were blown out of a nearby building. Amazingly, Looby and his family escaped with minor injuries.

News of the bombing swept the Civil Rights community and the South. When interviewed years later for the book and television series *Eyes on the Prize*, a white Nashville minister recalled, "Mr. Z. Alexander Looby was . . . conservative politically, a Lincoln Republican of many years—no one could accuse him of being a wild-eyed radical politically . . . and when his house was dynamited, I think it solidified the black community and it enraged a segment of the white community in a fashion that nothing else had." Even Nashville's mayor, Ben West, a vocal opponent of the sit-ins, condemned the violence. "You all have the power to destroy this city," he warned, "so let's not have any mobs."

At noon that day, April 19, 1960, twenty-five hundred people marched silently on city hall to protest the Looby bombing. Standing face-to-face with the mayor, sit-in activist Diane Nash asked Mayor West if he felt it was right for blacks to be sold school supplies and makeup at one counter and refused service at the lunch counter. "Mayor West, do you feel it is wrong to discriminate against a person solely on the basis of their race or color?" she asked. Nodding, he admitted it was wrong. The next morning, *Nashville Tennessean* headlines blared the breakthrough, "Mayor Says Integrate Counters."

APRIL 20

From April 18 to 27, 1955, Indonesia hosted the Bandung Conference. This unparalleled event so un-nerved Europe and the United States that it was briskly condemned as "communist"—the code word for self-assertion by peoples of color—and was denounced as "self-segregation" by the U. S. Secretary of State. In his keynote address to Fisk University's Twelfth Annual Institute of Race Relations, Fisk's president, Dr. Charles S. Johnson, put the event into context:

> A conference of twenty-nine recently independent colored nations of Asia and Africa, representing over a billion people, more than half of the population of the world. It was . . . a formal announcement . . . of the determination of the peoples of Asia and Africa . . . to determine their own destinies. They hoped by their stand to preserve the peace of the world against the West.

It was a mission perhaps best stated at Bandung by Chinese premier Chou En-lai:

> The course which we peoples of the Asian and African countries have taken in striving for freedom and independence may vary, but our will to win and to preserve our freedom and independence is the same. However different the specific conditions in each of our countries may be, it is equally necessary for most of us to eliminate the state of backwardness caused by the rule of colonialism. We need to develop our countries independently with no outside interference and in accordance with the will of the people. The people of Asia and Africa . . . know that new threats of war will not only endanger the independent development of their countries, but also intensify their enslavement by colonialism. That is why the Asian and African peoples all the more hold dear world peace and national independence.

During the era of slavery, successful free blacks were regularly threatened with enslavement by angry whites. The charge: "setting a bad example for slaves." A century later, much the same charge was hurled at Bandung conferees. In their successful overthrow of Western domination, they were setting a bad example for those still colonized and segregated—a dangerous thing indeed.

APRIL 21

IF AN AFRICAN AMERICAN congressman faces humiliation on the railroad, what must the average citizen endure? The son of ex-slaves, Chicago's Congressman Arthur W. Mitchell was unrelenting in his fight against injustice. He told his story on the floor of Congress in 1941:

> On the morning of April 21, 1937 . . . while traveling between Memphis and Little Rock . . . I was ejected from the first-class car by the conductor of the Rock Island passenger train on which I was then traveling. The reason for ejecting me was that I was riding in the body of a Pullman car in which there were riding several white passengers. . . .
>
> This fight for the rights of the Negro has been a hard and expensive one, covering a period of more than four years. All expenses incurred in this suit have been borne by me. I think it is well to note that I, with a Negro lawyer, Richard E. Westbrooks, of Chicago, Illinois, have fought the case through all of the courts. We conducted the hearing in Chicago, argued the case before the Interstate Commerce Commission and before the United States District Court in Chicago. We also argued the case before the Supreme Court of the United States, this being the first and only instance where a member of our race has [so] argued his own case. . . . The case before the Supreme Court was heard by the full court, and their decision was unanimous for me, setting aside in strong language the findings of the Interstate Commerce Commission and the decision of the United States District Court of the Northern District of Illinois. I think I should also call attention to the fact that the Attorney General's Office, whose duty it was to appear . . . in behalf of the Interstate Commerce Commission, not only refused to appear and argue in favor of the [commission's findings], but . . . filed with the Supreme Court a very strong memorandum [in favor of my complaint].

The Supreme Court found in favor of Mitchell—separate facilities must indeed be substantially equal. With no black first-class car, Pullman had violated Jim Crow law. Gradually, enforcement of the added burden of separate but equal facilities helped to desegregate interstate travel. But not until the Civil Rights Act of 1964 were all facilities fully desegregated.

APRIL 22

THREE MONTHS AFTER the North Carolina A & T sit-in had ignited young activists, a rapid-fire movement had spread to campuses throughout the South. Five days after the Shaw University conference that led to the founding of SNCC (see April 17), the National Student Conference on the Sit-in Movement was held in Washington, D.C., on April 22 and 23, 1960.

The sit-ins had erupted from the outrage of African American students on historically black southern campuses. The purpose of the Washington meeting—organized in large part by Allard Lowenstein, president of the U.S. National Student Association and a future New York City congressman—was to recruit student volunteers of all races on campuses nationwide. To this end, black student leaders who had already seen action in the trenches of the sit-in wars came to Washington. Enflamed by passion and possibility, they told their stories.

Among them was Bernard Lee, president of the Student Movement at Alabama State College in Montgomery. To Lee, the sit-ins were inheritors of a torch passed from the Montgomery Bus Boycott of 1955–56. Appropriately enough, his local movement had begun with a meeting at the home of one of the boycott's leaders—SCLC's Dr. Ralph Abernathy. The first Montgomery sit-in took place in the belly of the beast—the Montgomery County Courthouse snack bar—and involved thirty-five young men. Furious, the governor vowed to "investigate" the demonstrators, which he did by having nine students expelled from the state-run black campus. Still the movement went on. Leaving the Montgomery battlefield to rally Washington-based troops, this twentieth-century General Lee brought with him a message from his fellow students. Said Lee, "We have taken up the struggle for freedom without counting the costs . . . we are wrestling with a spirit of wickedness in high places. . . . We expect to be thrown in jail on trumped-up charges, but we shall continue to protest and fight for our rights in the court. . . . We have the moral force of the universe on our side and we shall not fail."

IT IS SAID AND—in her life's work as anthropologist, author, and a bit of a conjure woman herself—Zora Neale Hurston found it to be true:

> The Conjure doctor's job is this: Conjure doctors have to diagnose the case, tell the person whether he is conjured or not (he usually is if some of the less ethical members of the profession get hold of him) and to find out who "layed de trick." The "trick" (charm) must be found and destroyed and the patient cured. If the patient wishes we must also be able to turn the trick back upon the one who set it. Besides this, a conjurer truly up in his profession must be able to lay haunts, and to locate buried treasure or a vein of water. The treasure trove may be found by taking a divining rod (a small branch with two side limbs running off in the shape of a V, driving a nail in the end of each branching twig and in the spot where they converge, holding these twig ends in the hands, and marching boldly over the suspected landscape. When you pass over the buried treasure the free end will be pulled suddenly toward the ground. You may put three pieces of brass in your right hand, keeping them well separated. Sniff occasionally and when you pass over the buried treasure you will find that the brass will automatically begin to smell. Water may be located by a similar rod without the nails; or if you observe a tree in the locality with the limbs longer on one side than on the other, the tree bending somewhat in that direction, you may be reasonably sure that a vein of water is located beneath the surface of the earth on that side.
>
> To make the evil move: Take the hair off a dead black cat, fill its mouth with lemons that have been painted with melted red wax crayon. Wrap animal in silver paper, repeat your desire over it, and place it under the house of the person.
>
> If you really want to drive a person crazy, do this: Sprinkle nutmeg in his or her left shoe every night at midnight.

That'll do it . . .

"**N**EVER BEFORE have Negroes been so outspokenly bitter about America's refusal to give them equal status . . . and never before have Negro leaders been so active on behalf of Negro rights," an editorial in the April 24, 1944, issue of *Life* magazine observed. The nation's "great uncured, self-inflicted wound" had become the subject of *The American Dilemma*, a landmark Carnegie Corporation study sponsored by the Swedish sociologist, Dr. Gunnar Myrdal.

The *Life* editorial went on:

> The American creed make[s] all men free and equal in rights. Yet in fact we deny equal rights to our largest minority, and observe a caste system which we not only criticize in other nations but refuse to defend in ourselves. This makes us living liars—a psychotic case among the nations. . . .
>
> Myrdal finds that the chief white fear is the fear of intermarriage . . . fear of personal and social equality, of joint use of schools and other public places, of equal voting, of equality in law courts, and of equal economic opportunity. [The South is] least unwilling to give the Negro an equal right to work; next, to give him legal justice; next, the vote, etc.; but it treasures the Jim Crow laws and it will never, never permit intermarriage. However . . . the Negro ranks his grievances in exactly the reverse order. He wants fair breadwinning opportunities most of all, legal justice and the vote next; but he does not make a major point of segregation, and his ambition to marry whites exists only in the whites' minds. There would, therefore, seem to be basis for progress. But not when all phases of the problem are woven together into a single flag emblazoned white supremacy. The North asks the South: Why won't you let the Negro vote? The South replies, How would you like your daughter to marry a Negro?

In 1944, anyone believing that the main goals of the oppressed were "marrying white" and voting for the "evil of two lessers" was certainly not among society's forsaken. The freedom fight would march forth to its own drum, Civil Rights.

APRIL 25

W̲HY WAS DENZIL DOWELL KILLED? the handwritten headline demanded. It was just one of the ongoing inquiries promised as volume one, number one, of the *Black Panther* newspaper went on sale on April 25, 1967.

Six months after founding the party, the Black Panthers launched their first cooperative business—the publication and distribution of the newspaper. Two legal-size sheets of paper, typed and printed on both sides, the *Black Panther* began with a first printing of ten thousand copies and grew to a circulation of fifty thousand copies within weeks. But the look of the newspaper only added to its credibility—here was a voice of, by, and for the people. That was its mission—as was made clear in a later, more sophisticated, tabloid-size edition of the paper with a masthead proclaiming "Power to the people." A major success, the *Black Panther* became increasingly important to the organization and the community as its profile heightened around the innovative night patrols that tailed police as witness and deterrent to the brutality that killed Denzil Dowell and inspired the first of many high-risk headlines and inquiries. "Denzil Dowell was unarmed" when shot by a Contra Costa County sheriff's officer, and the angle of the bullets suggests that his hands were raised, the paper reported. "So how can six bullet holes and shotgun blasts be considered justifiable homicide?" Justifiable homicide had been the frequent and official response that licensed police to kill blacks with impunity. That was the travesty the Panthers sought to rout.

Who was getting the news and editing the paper? The Black Panther Party's "Minister of Information underground"—a provocative allusion to the parole status of Eldridge Cleaver. Writing for the established *Ramparts* magazine was one thing; editing the *Black Panther* was another. Cleaver knew that his work would target him for retaliation. His fear was later borne out in the parole revocations of several ex-offenders who had become the paper's street vendors. The violation: "failure to maintain gainful employment." It was a sign of the times.

Journalism   Assets

APRIL 26

In POLITICS, there is nothing more rare than straight talk. Rarer still in the red-baiting 1950s, was straight talk on race from an African American point of view. Yet, when the Republican Women's Convention met in Washington, D.C., on the anniversary of the assassination of Abraham Lincoln, straight talk is exactly what E. Frederic Morrow delivered. And while some feathers remained ruffled by his candor two weeks later, on April 26, 1959, the first black presidential aide in U.S. history felt good. As he'd written in his diary, "It is a tremendous relief."

It was an era when being tight-lipped was often the better part of valor, when the "disloyal" were subjected to passport revocation, job loss, and even prison. But, five years after the historic *Brown v. Board of Education* decision outlawing segregation, and a year into the terror inflicted on the Little Rock Nine (see February 19), little had changed. Polite political circles eager to placate southern segregationists now proposed "gradualism" as though 350 years of delay on the civil and human rights of blacks had not been gradual enough. En route to a Detroit speech just two weeks before his Washington appearance, Morrow was asked, "What do we have to do to make friends with the Negro and get his vote?" Angered but restrained, the ex-CBS public affairs staffer answered that until blacks were "permitted to have a voice in party councils and aspire to office, it will be a long time before the party can count on [black] allegiance." For those who evoked the "party of Lincoln" expecting gratitude, Morrow further clarified his feelings with his Washington speech: "Republicans [cannot] expect Negroes to be extremely grateful for what Lincoln did, since in effect he . . . merely returned to them their God-given rights of freedom and personal dignity."

That did it! As Morrow wrote in his diary, "I had hardly finished my speech before hell broke loose. The audience had given me a standing ovation, but . . . the leadership on the platform was pretty sore." He was unapologetic, and it proved a liberating experience for him—about time, and right on time.

Speeches   Opportunity

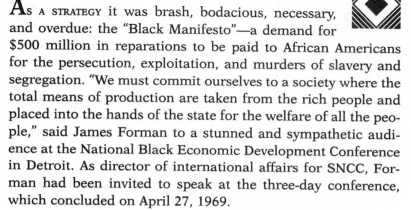

As a strategy it was brash, bodacious, necessary, and overdue: the "Black Manifesto"—a demand for $500 million in reparations to be paid to African Americans for the persecution, exploitation, and murders of slavery and segregation. "We must commit ourselves to a society where the total means of production are taken from the rich people and placed into the hands of the state for the welfare of all the people," said James Forman to a stunned and sympathetic audience at the National Black Economic Development Conference in Detroit. As director of international affairs for SNCC, Forman had been invited to speak at the three-day conference, which concluded on April 27, 1969.

The concept of reparations had precedent in the 1947 Marshall Plan, which rebuilt Europe after World War II, and legal basis in Field Order No. 15, the Civil War–era document issued by Union General William Tecumseh Sherman on January 16, 1865, that set aside "forty acres of tillable land" for each family formerly enslaved. And so, while Forman's call was not new, its resurrection was nevertheless full of surprises. The first surprise was the target of the campaign: America's white churches and synagogues. The second was the active support the campaign received from the National Conference of Black Churchmen, an otherwise conservative group of black clergy in majority-white denominations. Third was the serious attention it received in press and pulpits nationwide.

It was the late 1960s, a time for calling the rolls of the victims and perpetrators of the African American holocaust. That roll call was a first step in healing, which, if it is to happen, must begin with facing truths. The next step was planning for a better future. To that end, the Black Manifesto proposed a nine-point program with budgeted line items for: a southern land bank, communications media interest in publishing and television, educational outreach in a black university, training centers and a research skills center, a labor strike fund and welfare rights, and support for the International Black Appeal, the proposal's fund-raising arm.

APRIL 28

ASKED TO COMMENT in the press on his 1-A draft status, World Heavyweight Boxing Champion Muhammad Ali tossed off the rhyme that would turn his fame into infamy: "Keep asking me, no matter how long—On the war in Vietnam, I sing this song—I ain't got no quarrel with the Viet Cong." A year later, having lost his bout for conscientious objector status on religious grounds, at 8:30 A.M. on Friday, April 28, 1967, he stood before Houston's Local Draft Board No. 61 for induction into the army. Refusing induction could mean five years in prison.

As his attorney, Hayden Covington, commented, Ali's case wasn't like any other. "Joe Namath can get off to play football and [actor] George Hamilton gets out because he's going with the president's daughter, but you're different. They want to make an example out of you." But Ali, it could be argued, was not being made an example, he had set one. Just eight days before induction, he unleashed a political storm even more virulent than the one that had raged when he converted to Islam (see February 25). "No," said Ali, "I am not going . . . to kill and burn other people simply to help continue the domination of white slavemasters over the dark people the world over. This is the day and age when such evil injustice must come to an end." Despite the decision to strip him of his title, the seizure of his passport, and the loss of his source of income, when his name was called in Houston, Ali refused induction. An international symbol of courage, he had chosen to act in service to his country and the world.

Ali was not alone in breaking rank with the status quo that day. In Mississippi, segregationists preaching to the choir of their own racist convictions were still insisting that blacks did not want to vote when the Mississippi Freedom Democratic Party sponsored a practice election on April 28, 1967. Despite the intimidation waged against them, despite losing their jobs and their land, the African American citizens of Sunflower County voted in numbers that foretold the triumph of voter registration on Election Day 1968 (see November 5).

Eᴅᴡᴀʀᴅ Kᴇɴɴᴇᴅʏ Eʟʟɪɴɢᴛᴏɴ was the "Duke," a man without peer, and one of the world's finest composer-musicians. In 1959, African America had awarded him its highest honor, the Spingarn Medal. He had earned world acclaim and fifteen honorary doctorates. Then, on April 29, 1969, came a seventieth birthday party hosted by President and Mrs. Richard Nixon at the White House, the Presidential Medal of Freedom, and an all-Ellington concert performed in tribute. For the admirers of Duke Ellington, the award was poetically just and sweet. Four years before that month, in a cultural and racial affront, he had been denied the Pulitzer Prize over objections from the music committee that had nominated him. Angry resignations by two committee members would prompt a sixty-six-year-old Ellington to write:

> Since I am not too chronically masochistic, I found no pleasure in all the suffering that was being endured. I realized that it could have been most distressing and distracting as I tried to qualify my first reaction: "Fate is being very kind to me; Fate doesn't want me to be too famous too young." Let's say it had happened. I would have been famous, then rich, then fat and stagnant. And then? What do you do with your beautiful, young, freckled mind? How, when, and where do you get your music supplement, the deadline that drives you to complete that composition, the necessity to hear the music instead of sitting around polishing your laurels, counting your money, and waiting for the brainwashers to decide what rinse or tint is the thing this season in your tonal climate?

Ever the connoisseur of a good harmonic line, that word, *masochistic*, harkened back to a story he so loved to tell, "The Tale of the Sadist and the Masochist." "Now, this particular evening, you see, the sadist and the masochist were savoring each other's charms," he'd croon in an elegant baritone. "And the sadist cozied up to the masochist, 'My dear, beat me . . . beat me . . . beat me . . .'" Ellington would relate, snapping his fingers off the beat. "To which the masochist responded, 'My darling, suffer . . . [snap] . . . suffer . . . [snap] . . . suffer . . . [snap].'"

APRIL 30

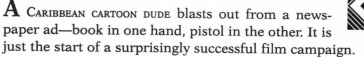

A CARIBBEAN CARTOON DUDE blasts out from a newspaper ad—book in one hand, pistol in the other. It is just the start of a surprisingly successful film campaign.

In February 1973, the opening day ad for *The Harder They Come* blared a cartoonlike melange of action and speed—fast cars, faster motorcyles, a calypsonian, a palm tree, and a double-barreled gangster posed to take on all comers. "Top of the hit parade and number one on the most wanted list!" read the advertising copy. That same day another opening ad ran in up-scale newspapers with a more subtle and suggestive graphic approach: a "palm tree" with switchblade knives for branches in the foreground emulates the more traditional background depiction of a palm tree swept by tropical breezes. "Advance critical acclaim" is offered in such capitalized words as "BEAUTIFUL" and "EXOTIC," with mention of the film's "quiet craftmanship" and "rhythmic validity" in sedate, smaller type.

By October 1973, the two ads had changed, but they were just as determined to draw two decidedly different audiences. This time, the gun-toting figure in the brash ad took on a human persona. "With a piece in his hand. He takes on the man! . . . He makes women and the charts and is on top with both," the copy read against pictures of a singer, a motor-cyclist, a man, and a swooning woman. The second ad was again more conservative and arts-oriented. "DAZZLES YOU— BEAUTIFULLY DONE!" was in bold type. The two palm trees were still there, but the one with the switchblades now looked like a windmill. And these campaigns had indeed spun the wind of cultural change to generate high-energy profits.

So powerful was the added demand for showings of this film that by April 30, 1976, the *New York Times* reported "80TH STRAIGHT WEEKEND FOR REGGAE FILM!" *The Harder They Come* was a breakthrough hit. With two parallel campaigns targeting two audiences, black and white, the first Jamaican feature film ex-ported reggae music to the world and launched a craze that endures.

Business   **Pragmatism**

MAY

The Mother of the Civil Rights Movement,
Rosa Parks at the Poor People's Solidarity March
(June 19, 1968). Photographer unknown.
Courtesy of the author.

For more information about Rosa Parks, please
see June 19 and December 5.

MAY 1

O_N May 1, 1950, Gwendolyn Brooks was awarded the Pulitzer Prize for Poetry. She was the first African American writer so honored. The book that so distinguished her was *Annie Allen*, the story of a young black woman coming of age. The story of the book is also the literary coming-of-age of a poet and her work.

Brooks's first book, *A Street in Bronzeville*, had been published to high acclaim in 1945. But her second proposal was rejected, and two years later she had yet to produce a follow-up. Then, on March 24, 1948, she sent Elizabeth Lawrence, her editor at Harper and Row, poems titled "Hester Allen." The reaction was so mixed among fellow editors that Lawrence sent the poems to another poet for comment on June 8. The painfully adroit verdict: "nothing develops" . . . "lacking a real human story" . . . "no gift for the reader." On July 14, Lawrence sent the full critique to Brooks with a note: "You are too good a poet to have to resort to trick and shock devices." Brooks was confused at the directive but not at the intent. On August 11, she received a contract with an advance of $100. It was only half of what had been offered for her first book, but tangible promise of the journey of author and editor ahead.

On January 14 the next year, Brooks finished her manuscript, now retitled *Annie Allen*, and sent it to Lawrence with a note: "Our funny and sad heroine speaks always in her mature voice (or thought). . . . Here is as much maturity, in attitude and conviction, as we can plausibly expect her range to allow. . . . Undertones of comedy and tragedy but never either to the extravagant degree of more youthful times." What was true of a heroine was true of her poet. That August, *Annie Allen* was published basked in kudos from Langston Hughes, *Poetry* magazine's Stanley Kunitz, Richard Wright in Paris, and other literary lights. And so came these first lines gilded in bronze:

> The birth in a narrow room . . .
> Weeps out of Western country something new.
> Blurred and stupendous. Wanted and unplanned.

MAY 2

THE FRONT PAGE of the *New York Times* for May 2, 1969, reflects a world in chaos:

COLUMBIA REBELS LEAVE; VANDALS ROAM AT QUEENS!—SDS FLEES SHERIFF: About 100 radical Columbia University students fled yesterday from the two buildings they had occupied overnight within minutes after warrants for their arrest had been signed in State Supreme Court. FURNITURE IS SMASHED: Bands of student vandals roamed through the Queens College campus yesterday afternoon, overturning bookcases . . . in the main library. . . .

CORNELL OUTLAWS 'TERROR' TACTICS! Cornell University President James A. Perkins was directed yesterday by the university board of trustees to implement a 10-point declaration affirming that disruption and "tactics of terror" on the campus would be met by "firm and appropriate response." Trustees said, "The university is not a sanctuary from the law. . . ."

169 FINED IN HARVARD SIT-IN; YALE BACKS ROTC CONTRACT—TWO CLEARED AT CAMBRIDGE: In tense proceedings, Judge M. Edward Viola found guilty today all but four of 173 persons charged with criminal trespass in the occupation of a Harvard University building April 9. BREWSTER UPHOLDS PLEDGE: Kingman Brewster Jr., president of Yale . . . told a mass meeting of 4,000 students, faculty members and trustees tonight that the university will not break its legally enforceable promises to the Reserve Officers Training Corps. "We have one year that we must honor, if we have any self-respect as an institution at all. . . ."

One year earlier (see January 18), singer Eartha Kitt had made the infamous White House luncheon remark that forced her untimely exile to Europe. The topic planned was "What citizens can do to insure safe streets." But Kitt cut to a deeper wound than provided for in the script. "[Youths] are angry . . . because there is a war going on that they don't understand, that they don't know why," she said. "They can't get to . . . the president, and so they rebel in the streets." As students, black and white, resorted to increasingly desperate acts, as if to reinforce Kitt's point, there was no stopping the chickens en route home to roost. . . .

MAY 3

T HIRTY DAYS INTO PROJECT C, (see January 11) and two
weeks after Dr. King's imprisonment on Good Friday
(see April 16), Birmingham's black citizens weren't happy
about the "trouble" the freedom movement was "causing." And
that was exactly the way some voiced the situation—as though
the movement had ruined a perfectly good thing. They argued
that the newly elected mayor should first be given a chance to
negotiate. Not so, said Reverend Fred Shuttlesworth, pastor of
Bethel Baptist Church, spiritual leader of the movement, and
victim of a 1956 bombing. To him, the new mayor, Albert
Boutwell, was "just a dignified Bull Connor"—(a reference to
the commissioner of public safety who had refused to inter-
vene in the notorious Mother's Day mob attack on Freedom
Riders two years earlier).

Then, on May 3, 1963, Bull Connor turned a volley of
hundred-pounds-per-square-inch water pressure on a children's
march, slamming them into cars and hosing them down like
just so much trash on a sidewalk. And as if that wasn't enough,
Connor set a team of raging K-9 dogs on the children aged six
to eighteen. At the time, African American millionaire hotel
owner A. G. Gaston was on the phone with a white attorney.
He opposed demonstrations, but he had nevertheless donated
hotel rooms and money to SCLC. Gaston had just finished de-
crying King for "messing up things" when he looked out the
window and stopped in mid-sentence. "But Lawyer Vann," he
said, "they've turned the fire hoses on a black girl. They're
rolling that little girl right down the middle of the street. I can't
talk to you no more." Ambivalent no longer, Gaston and the
naysayers now stood convinced.

Dr. King often spoke of the four basic steps of nonviolent
warfare: fact-finding, negotiation, self-purification (demonstrator survival training), and direct action (marches, demonstrations, civil disobedience). Many who passionately joined the
movement the next day found in the freedom fight keys to a
whole new way in every phase of life—unlocking fears and options sacrificed deep within.

MAY 4

In 1959, at the age of eighteen, George Jackson was a passenger in a car when its owner disappeared into a gas station and robbed it of $70. Although there was no proof of Jackson's participation, he was nevertheless sentenced one year to life. Of his first eleven years in prison, eight and a half years were spent in solitary confinement. While incarcerated, he wrote and read. His collected letters are a diary of his journey from boy to sensitive, angry man—a revolutionary with power in his pen. In 1970, when a guard was thrown to his death in Soledad Prison, Jackson and two others were charged with the murder—a charge they denied and for which there was neither a witness nor evidence to incriminate them. The case of these men, soon known as the "Soledad Brothers," drew national attention and inspired a then-unknown California professor, Angela Y. Davis, to join the prisoners' rights movement. Two days before his trial, Jackson was killed by a guard in an alleged escape attempt from San Quentin's yard.

A prolific, thoughtful writer, his book, *Soledad Brother: The Prison Letters of George Jackson*, was published in 1970. This letter to Jackson's mother is dated May 4, 1968:

> Dear Mother,
> You are correct in all that you say about the problems of men and responsibility, and about the hangers-on, and the foot draggers, the failures . . . the myopic tendencies to squander time and energy in counterproductive efforts. At times I become so depressed seeing it that I feel justified in [wanting to] just take off with you people in tow to some other part of the world where blacks have already come into their own, with an ocean or two between us and this place. . . . I see that the black family unit is in ruins. It is our first and basic weakness. This fact may contribute much to our difficulty in uniting as a people. . . . If we are to understand and heal these effects we must understand the cause. To say that the black family unit is slowly eroding because of pressures from without (poverty and social injustice) and from within (negative response to crisis situations) is to . . . mistake the depth of the issue [and to devalue the] historical factors [which] have produced the present state of chaos. . . . Take care of yourself.—George.

MAY 5

On May 5, 1941, Ethiopia's Emperor Haile Selassie triumphantly reentered the capital city of Addis Ababa, liberating his ancient land, reassuming his throne, and fully overthrowing his Italian invaders.

In 1884, four hundred years after the papal encyclical that granted Europe's kings and queens "title" to lands that were not theirs, the descendants of those same marauders held the Berlin Conference to partition Africa. Their reign of terror had crested in the rape of every part of the continent but one— Abyssinia, later renamed Ethiopia. In 1896, by winning the Battle of Adua, Ethiopia forced the retreat of Italian troops, retaining its sovereignty. In 1935, Italy was back, this time victorious. Selassie had fled to London with his family, and for seven years Ethiopia was under foreign rule, the papal mission fulfilled at last.

When sons of Africa on every continent volunteered support, Selassie rejected help in the hope of assuaging the very European powers that were supporting aggression into his nation—the same powers that were collectively holding the entire continent hostage. In 1936, Selassie royally ascended the League of Nations platform, only to discover what centuries of Africans, Asians, Australians, and indigenous Americans before him had already discovered: Ethiopia's sovereignty as a member state was secondary to that of any European nation. The name of the game was still colors. As individuals of color found themselves second-class citizens in the lands of their birth, countries of color were second-class member states in world affairs. Wizened, as heir and scion to a family whose known history could be traced two thousand years, Selassie liquidated his royal assets—gold, silver, jewels—to alleviate the suffering of his countrymen. In 1940, he met with Ethiopia's chiefs to strategize the victory over Italy. Together on May 5, 1941, they made a triumphant return—returning Ethiopia to freedom and striking the first crack in the armor of Europe that would lead to the resurrection and independence of nation after nation across the continent.

FROM: Bishop Desmond Tutu, Dean of St. Mary's
Cathedral in Johannesburg

To: Prime Minister John Vorster in Cape Town, South Africa

May 6, 1976

I am writing to you, Sir . . . as leader of several thousand Christians of all races in the Diocese of Johannesburg. I am writing to you as one who had come to be accepted by some [Africans, Indians, and Coloreds] as one of their spokesmen articulating their deepest aspirations. . . . I am writing to you . . . because I know you to be a loving and caring father and husband, a doting grandfather who has experienced the joys and anguish of family life. . . . In short, I am writing to you as one human person to another human person, gloriously created in the image of the selfsame God.

I write to you, Sir, because our Ambassador to the United Nations . . . declared that South Africa was moving away from discrimination based on race. . . . I am afraid that very little of this movement has been in evidence so far. I write to you, Sir, to say with all the eloquence I can command that the security of our country ultimately depends not on military strength and a Security Police being given more and more draconian power to do virtually as they please. . . . How long can a people, do you think, bear such blatant injustice and suffering. . . . I am writing to you, Sir, because I have a growing nightmarish fear that unless something drastic is done very soon then bloodshed and violence are going to happen. . . . A people can take only so much and no more. . . . But we blacks . . . are aware that politics is the art of the possible. . . .

Six weeks later came the Soweto Massacre (see June 16).

For his leadership at an excruciating time when most South African leaders were martyred or imprisoned, Tutu was awarded the Nobel Peace Prize in 1984.

As the Authors League of America convened on May 7, 1957, for the first national assembly in its forty-five-year history, onstage at New York's Alvin Theater was Langston Hughes, the only African American panelist. The witch-hunts of the McCarthy era had ensnared more than their share of writers, and the subject was censorship. "Negro writers, just by being black, have been on the blacklist all our lives," said Hughes. Not only had bias constricted opportunities, but many libraries refused to stock books by best-selling black writers— "even as a gift."

"Do you not think it strange that of [a dozen top] writers, at least half of them live abroad, far away from their people, their problems, and the sources of their material?" And he named them and their expatriate locales: James Baldwin, Chester Himes, and Richard Wright in Paris; Frank Yerby in southern France; and Willard Motley in Mexico. "Why? Because the stones thrown at Autherine Lucy at the University of Alabama are thrown at them, too. . . . Because the body of little Emmett Till drowned in a Mississippi river and no one brought to justice haunts them too. One of the writers when I last saw him before he went abroad, said to me, 'I don't want my children to grow up in the shadow of Jim Crow.'"

For that writer's children and all black children, he ended with his 1940s poem "Merry-Go-Round," about a child trying to find a place for herself in the North.

Where is the Jim Crow section
On this merry-go-round,
Mister, 'cause I want to ride?
Down South where I come from
White and colored
Can't sit side by side.
Down South on the train
There's a Jim Crow car
On the bus we're put in the back—
But there ain't no back
To a merry-go-round:
Where's the horse
For a kid that's black?

MAY 8

ON MAY 8, 1970, antiwar demonstrators held a peace rally on Wall Street in New York's financial district. Although the police department (NYPD) had been warned of possible violence, it had failed to take proactive measures. As the rally disbanded, a group of construction workers rampaged, and unprotected demonstrators were badly beaten in the fray. In a written statement, New York City Mayor John Lindsay criticized the NYPD for its mishandling of the incident: It was "most appalling," he said, that "the people of this city witnessed a breakdown of the police as the barrier between them and wanton violence."

With another demonstration planned for the Memorial Day weekend, Wall Street attorney Michael Belknap demanded protection in a suit filed in federal district court. The case was heard by Justice Constance Baker Motley, who ordered the NYPD to inform every officer of his obligation to protect antiwar demonstrators from physical assaults and threats prior to the weekend's events.

This daring and controversial decision made the front pages and was overturned on appeal. But the judgment's sensitivity to the rights of people with minority views was characteristic of Justice Motley. A pioneer in her rulings and in her career, she was the first African American woman named to the federal bench. As she has said, "You can't invent events. They just happen. But you have to be prepared to deal with them when they happen." In 1946, as a Columbia University Law School student, that attitude made her a leading candidate to clerk for Thurgood Marshall, then head of the NAACP Legal Defense Fund team. She was there when he took the *Brown v. Board of Education* school desegregation case to victory. She was also there as a city councilwoman and state senator.

In the coven of politics and debate that whirled about her ruling, the *New York Times* wrote, "Constance Baker Motley's mild manner, soft voice and amiability come as a shock to those who know her only by her formidable reputation."

Asked what he admired most about Paul Robeson, *Ebony* publisher John H. Johnson once commented that Robeson refused to go anywhere or do anything as a celebrity that he could not go to or do as a black man. Determined to hush his crusade for the rights of black men (and women), McCarthyites of the 1950s made sure that Paul Robeson—celebrity and black man—could go nowhere.

In his forty years as an athlete, lawyer, singer, and actor, Robeson's extraordinary talents and achievements had brought him world acclaim. Then the spotlight faded to a blackout as the curtain rose on the McCarthy era in the United States. Lloyd Brown wrote in his preface to Robeson's *Here I Stand* (see February 22), "The blackout was the result of a boycott of Robeson by the Establishment that was meant both to silence him and to deny him any opportunity of making a living. All doors to stage, screen, concert hall, radio, TV, and recording studio were locked against him." Just as the Fugitive Slave Law of 1850 had put the entire nation in service to block the escape of slaves from slaveowners, the McCarthy era passport revocations of the 1950s were meant to prevent escape from the twentieth-century powers-that-be. A century apart, neither effort worked. While definitely crippled, Robeson was still kicking. Among his legendary efforts were the foreign concerts at which he "appeared" by phone. The London *Times* noted, "Robeson is a single-minded crusader for the American Negro . . . and by refusing him a passport for many years, the American government promoted him to the status of a political martyr."

And so May 9, 1958, when Paul Robeson stepped onstage at Carnegie Hall for his first concert in the decade since the blackout began, marked a true Freedom Day for people the world over. He performed to a sold-out house. In triumph, he sang the spiritual *"Didn't My Lord Deliver Daniel."* True to his history, with *the whole world in his hands*, as the internationally renowned Robeson reentered the celebrity spotlight unbowed, with him came Everyman.

MAY 10

BIRMINGHAM WAS IN TURMOIL. After four weeks of protests and one week of negotiations, a "Birmingham Truce" between protest leaders (the SCLC and its Birmingham affiliate, the Alabama Christian Movement for Human Rights) and the business community was signed on May 10, 1963. Within three days after close of demonstrations, fitting rooms would be desegregated. And, once the city government was established by court order, within 30 days signs on wash rooms and drinking fountains would be removed; within 60 days a program of lunchroom counter desegregation would begin; and Negro employment would be upgraded and further steps considered.

It seemed so little progress for so much sacrifice by demonstrators who had each pledged to uphold the Ten Commandments on their signed Commitment Cards:

1. MEDITATE daily on the teachings and life of Jesus.
2. REMEMBER always that the nonviolent movement in Birmingham seeks justice and reconciliation—not victory.
3. WALK and TALK in the manner of love, for God is love.
4. PRAY daily to be used by God in order that all men might be free.
5. SACRIFICE personal wishes in order that all men might be free.
6. OBSERVE with both friend and foe the ordinary rules of courtesy.
7. SEEK to perform regular service for others and for the world.
8. REFRAIN from violence of fist, tongue, or heart.
9. STRIVE to be in good spiritual and bodily health.
10. FOLLOW the directions of the movement and of the captain on a demonstration.

With word of the truce, violence broke out. Bombs struck at Dr. King and his brother, Reverend A. D. King. They had forced a dialogue *and* forced a president and a governor into the showdown that desegregated the University of Alabama and brought scores to the March on Washington.

MAY 11

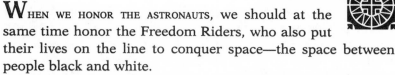

WHEN WE HONOR THE ASTRONAUTS, we should at the same time honor the Freedom Riders, who also put their lives on the line to conquer space—the space between people black and white.

In 1946, the Supreme Court ordered interstate bus travel desegregated. Within months, CORE tested the law with its Journey of Reconciliation (see April 11). In 1955, the Interstate Commerce Commission (ICC) desegregated waiting rooms. By 1961, gone were the signs in depots demarcating spaces "colored" and "white," but firmly fixed were the duplicated facilities, the glaring eyes, and the refusals of service. CORE's new executive director, James Farmer, resurrected the Journey as the Freedom Rides.

On May 11, 1961, the first Freedom Riders were a week into their trip through Virginia, the Carolinas, and Georgia. Nothing had happened—yet. But there were rumors. In the Gandhian tradition, Farmer believed in letting your adversaries or those in power know what you were going to do. He sent letters to all concerned. The Klan also served notice: attack! An informant warned the FBI numerous times. But with Klansmen among the police and FBI, a pact had already been made giving the Klan *15 minutes to kill,* in the word's most violent sense, before police intervened.

On May 14, 1961, Mother's Day, the Riders' bus was mobbed in Anniston and its tires slashed before it could speed on with fifty Klan cars storming behind. When the tires gave out, the mob knocked in windows, blocked exits, and firebombed the bus. Only when a state investigator on board fired warning shots did the mob retreat and the Riders escape the burning bus. Strategically late troopers took the Riders to Anniston Hospital, where they were again attacked and evicted by a hospital staff afraid for its own safety. With all this advance notice, blacks had also prepared. To the rescue came armed black churchmen.

MAY 12

Detention means that midnight knock when all about you is quiet. It means those blinding torches shone simultaneously through every window of your house before the door is kicked open. It means the exclusive right the Security Branch have to read each and every letter in the house. It means paging through each and every book on your shelves, lifting carpets, looking under beds, lifting sleeping children from mattresses and looking under the sheets. It means tasting your sugar, your mealie-meal and every spice on your kitchen shelf. Unpacking all your clothing and going through each pocket. Ultimately it means your seizure at dawn, dragged away from little children screaming and clinging to your skirt, imploring the white man dragging Mummy away to leave her alone.—Winnie Mandela

On May 12, 1969, Winnie Mandela was detained in a raid on black South African townships. She would spend 491 days in detention—many wedged between solitary confinement and a revolving door. In February 1970, the state withdrew all charges against her. But as she turned to leave the courtroom, she was redetained. Finally the following June, with world opinion mounting, charges were brought against her. In September, she was again acquitted. Two weeks later, as she left home to visit with the husband she had not seen in two years, a new banning order restricted her travel and placed her under house arrest each night after work. As she became a cause célèbre in her own right, her days were studded by death threats. For years, while her husband remained locked at Robben Island for life, this was how she lived.

A happier May 12 finally came in 1984, when she, her daughter Zeni, and her youngest grandchild were escorted into the office of the prison warder, Sergeant Gregory, for their first "contact visit" in twenty-two years. "Can you imagine! We last touched his hand in 1962," said Mrs. Mandela. "We kissed Nelson and held him a long time. It is an experience one just can't put into words. It was fantastic and hurting at the same time. He clung to the child right through the visit. Gregory, his warder, was so moved, he looked the other way."

Family   Human Spirit

On May 13, 1961, the Freedom Riders were nine days into their treacherous trip. It is said that a local preacher, afraid for their safety, warned against it. "Go to South Africa, where they've only got apartheid," he advised. "But whatever you do, don't go to Mississippi." Realizing that the Riders were answering a higher call, the preacher delivered this epistle, "God, Man, and Mississippi":

As it is told, there was a black man who lived in Mississippi. Things being what they were, he lived mostly on the run—running from county to county. And when the time came for him to run out of state, he left pretty fast—not by Greyhound, but, as Dick Gregory would say, by bloodhound. Settling up in Chicago, he was happy for a time. Then he got to thinking about his mother and the smooth southern soil under his bare flat feet. As it turned out, he lost his job. For weeks he looked for another with no luck. "Lord," he said, "what do I do now?" And the good Lord said, "Go back to Mississippi." He said, "Lord, you can't mean it. You know what it's like there. There's segregation down there. White folks kill us just for thinking down there. The dogs are mean; the police are worse. Lord, I know what I said about missing my mama, but I'm begging you. Don't send me to Mississippi." And God said, "Go to Mississippi." "Now, Lord," the man bartered, "I know I've got to go if you insist. But will you go with me? Will you be by my side?" And the Lord said, "As far as Cincinnati."

When the Riders arrived in Montgomery on the first lap of the Ride, Attorney General Robert Kennedy asked for a cooling-off period before they continued. Said James Farmer, the guiding force behind the Freedom Rides, "I asked Dr. King to tell Bobby Kennedy that we'd been cooling off for 350 years, and that if we cooled off any more, we'd be in a deep freeze." Heeding the call to go to Mississippi, the Freedom Riders first passed through Alabama. What greeted them was a godless place indeed. But in His place God sent Reverend Fred Shuttlesworth and a convoy of armed black churchmen to rescue the Freedom Riders (see May 10).

MAY 14

"**F**OR ANY OF YOU WHO WOULD LINGER in the cemetery and tarry around the grave, I have news for you," said Dr. Ralph David Abernathy just days after the murder of his fallen leader and best friend, Dr. King. "We have business on the road to freedom. . . . We must prove to white America that you can kill the leader but you cannot kill the dream." With those words, the new leader of SCLC reconnoitered his troops in Memphis and set out for Washington on the Poor People's Campaign. By May 14, 1968, nine convoys of the poor of every race had arrived and erected their Resurrection City of tents and shanties on the Capitol Mall, where a camp planned for one thousand people soon housed twenty-five hundred.

In 1964, President Johnson had waged his War on Poverty and engineered congressional passage of the $1 billion Economic Development Act, which launched Head Start, Upward Bound, and college work-study programs. In 1967, as the Vietnam War overpowered the domestic front, the president and the nation retreated from the needs of the poor. That summer, attorney Marian Wright was headed from Washington back to her NAACP Legal Defense Fund post in Mississippi (see June 10). Two visits she made en route inspired the Poor People's Campaign (see June 19). On a visit with Senator Robert Kennedy at his Virginia home, the two shared frustration over the summer's riots and the president's lack of domestic focus. In parting, she mentioned that she would be seeing Dr. King. Seeking to dramatize the crisis, Kennedy said, "Tell him to bring the poor people to Washington." When she saw King in Atlanta, Wright did just that. "As simply as Bobby Kennedy had said it," she recalled, "King instinctively felt that that was right and treated me as if I was an emissary of grace here, or something that brought him some light."

By late June, when Kennedy, too, was assassinated, the campaign that was to have been led by King became a memorial to both men. It was the end of one era, the beginning of a new one. And the cry of the poor would tear at Marian Wright (Edelman), who founded the Children's Defense Fund in 1973.

"Too OFTEN THE STORY of the southern Negro deals exclusively with those who are timid," wrote Roy Wilkins in *Crisis* magazine. "But [there are some] . . . who dare to speak out and, if necessary, to act. . . . Southern white people, almost unanimously, characterize such Negroes as 'crazy.'"

Such was the case on May 15, 1936, in Gordonsville, Virginia. William Wales and his sister Cora, both in their sixties, held off a lynch mob of five thousand for six hours until a gasoline-soaked torch tossed into the house killed them and burned their home to the ground. Gory details of the siege and subsequent killing of two "crazy" blacks filled local newspapers. Wilkins patched together a truer picture from Associated Press wires and the accounts of area residents. But, what really transcends the brutality in Gordonsville is the courage under fire that the Wales and so many other African Americans have displayed at such terrible times. From Wilkins's editorial:

> Impatiently the mob waited for hours for the embers of the house to cool. Then, the killers rushed in and chopped up the two bodies for souvenirs to carry home. The story behind the slaughter is that . . . efforts had been made over a period of thirteen years to oust [the Wales] from their property. They refused to sell. The city condemned a part of their land to expand the cemetery. [After] their final refusal to vacate their home . . . local whites were forced to fall back upon the time-worn device of dragging some white woman into the quarrel and charging Wales with threatening her, [a charge] she vigorously denied—after Wales was dead. Anyway, the sheriff swore out a warrant charging Wales with lunacy. When the sheriff appeared to serve the warrant he was shot and killed.
>
> Some white people . . . are shamed by Gordonsville. They know there is more to the story than the killing of a sheriff and the destruction of a "crazy Negro." Yes, the *Crisis* defends William and Cora Wales. We think we understand them. . . . We think we know the real criminals in these situations everywhere. Crazy? Wales was not crazy. The two sane people in all that array were in the house. It was five thousand outside who were mad.

Revolt!   Self-defense

MAY 16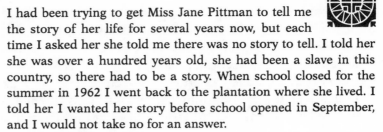

I had been trying to get Miss Jane Pittman to tell me the story of her life for several years now, but each time I asked her she told me there was no story to tell. I told her she was over a hundred years old, she had been a slave in this country, so there had to be a story. When school closed for the summer in 1962 I went back to the plantation where she lived. I told her I wanted her story before school opened in September, and I would not take no for an answer.

"You won't?" she said.

"No, Ma'am."

"Then I reckon I better say something," she said.

"You don't have to say a thing," Mary said.

Mary Hodges was a big brown-skin woman in her early sixties who lived in the same house that Miss Jane did and looked after Miss Jane.

"If I don't he go'n just worry me to death," Miss Jane said.

"What you want know about Miss Jane for?" Mary said.

"I teach history," I said. "I'm sure her life story can help me explain things to my students."

"What's wrong with them books you already got?" Mary said.

"Miss Jane is not in them," I said.

Not only was Miss Jane not in the history books, any other woman vaguely reminiscent of her was missing, too. And even if this Miss Jane Pittman hadn't lived—which she hadn't—that did not mean she was not real. As Reverend Jesse Jackson has said, "My grandmother, who was a slave in Kentucky, told me of things that happened to her as they happened to Miss Pittman. The truth rings truly throughout this book." Miss Jane was the creation of Louisiana-born novelist Ernest J. Gaines. Raised on a Delta plantation, as a child he had worked the fields for fifty cents a day. That's how he knew Miss Jane and had become one of her "children." He recorded her story in his 1971 novel, The Autobiography of Miss Jane Pittman. In 1974, Miss Jane was endeared to millions when Cicely Tyson relived her story for television audiences. For her portrayal of the formidable Miss Jane from a teen to her 110th year, Tyson won two Emmy Awards.

Pᴇᴏᴘʟᴇ ꜱᴀʏ ʏᴏᴜ ᴄᴀɴ'ᴛ ᴄʜᴀɴɢᴇ ᴛʜᴇ ᴡᴏʀʟᴅ, but on May 17, 1954, the NAACP strategy to end segregation did change our world with the *Brown v. Board of Education of Topeka* Supreme Court victory. The court's unanimous decision desegregated schools, officially ushered in the Civil Rights era, and brought to global prominence the NAACP Legal Defense Fund's (LDF) lead attorney and future first African American Justice of the U. S. Supreme Court, Thurgood Marshall.

In a strategic assault on the 1896 *Plessy v. Ferguson* ruling that legalized Jim Crow (see December 11), LDF worked within the law in order to overturn it. Under "separate but equal" law, racially separate schools had to be equal; unequal schools violated the law. That point was tested by four cases that led up to the decision collectively known as *Brown*. In *Briggs v. Clarendon County, South Carolina*, a suit by twenty African American parents, 75 percent of Clarendon's students were black but 60 percent of the budget was spent on whites. By definition the school was unequal. To bolster its case, LDF applied Dr. Kenneth Clark's "doll's study," which established a causal link between segregation and a negative self-concept in black children. Predictably, racists countered with a double-barreled offensive: intimidation and defense of the status quo. With *Briggs* on appeal, LDF headed to Kansas and the actual *Brown* case. Barred from the nearby school, seven-year-old Linda Brown crossed busy railroad tracks and a switching yard to await a bus to an all-black school. Clearly, Linda was unequally imperiled. In Virginia's *Davis v. County School Board*, the state court agreed that there were inequities to be remedied in physical damage to the black school, but let stand the emotional damage to black children. And in Delaware's *Gebhart v. Belton*, a state court ordered blacks admitted to white schools while black schools were upgraded. Deciding the four cases as one, the Court strategically consolidated them under the Middle American *Brown* to make a point: at issue was not North versus South but the Fourteenth Amendment to the Constitution, guaranteeing "equal protection under the law."

MAY 18

In 1962, as the United States assessed its racial views, to many the concern was are you with whites or against us? *Dialogue* magazine challenged the Nation of Islam's Malcolm X and SNCC's James Farmer to a debate. "Separation vs. Integration" was published in the May 1962 issue.

Farmer personalized the theme. Having upheld segregation before joining the struggle against it, he saw himself as complicit in it. But, like him, "the masses of Negroes are through putting up with segregation. They are tired of being pushed around in a democracy that fails to practice what it preaches. . . . The Supreme Court decision in 1954 banning segregated schools has had almost eight years of existence, yet less than eight percent of the Negro kids are in integrated schools." Now, he said, people were determined to make change happen. As a young man had told him, "I myself desegregated a lunch counter, not somebody else, not some big man, some powerful man, but me, little me. I walked the picket line and I sat in, and the walls of segregation toppled."

Malcolm was philosophical. A *New York Times* column by James Reston called for Europe, Russia, and America to unite to ward off the alleged threat of China and the nonwhite world. Still digesting the bitter aftertaste of that propaganda, Malcolm viewed the matter in line with developments at the UN, once dominated by Europe and the United States. Newly independent UN member nations of color could now outvote the white world, said Malcolm. "The same hand that has been writing on the wall in Africa and Asia is also writing on the wall right here in America." He went on: "It is not a case of wanting integration or separation, it is a case of wanting freedom, justice, and equality. Now if certain groups think that through integration they are going to get . . . human dignity . . . [we] go along with the integrationists. But if integration is not going to return human dignity to dark mankind then integration is not the solution. . . . Ofttimes we make the mistake of confusing the objective with the means by which [it] is obtained."

TWO HISTORIC DAYS had passed since the Supreme Court delivered its landmark *Brown v. Board of Education* school desegregation decision. Now, on May 19, 1954, Representative John Bell Williams of Mississippi took to the floor of the House of Representatives to rail against "Black Monday." Expounding upon this, Judge Tom P. Brady, the so-called intellectual leader of segregationists, wrote of the glorious slaveholding South and vowed that "socialism and communism are lethal messes of porridge for which our sacred birthright shall not be sold." At one dollar per copy, his booklet was widely distributed throughout the South:

> "Black Monday" is the date upon which the Supreme Court of the United States handed down its socialistic decision in the segregation cases on appeal from the states of Kansas, South Carolina, Virginia, and Delaware. "Black Monday" is indeed symbolic of the date. Black denoting darkness and terror. Black signifying the absence of light and wisdom. Black embodying grief, destruction, and death. Should Representative Williams accomplish nothing more during his membership in Congress he has more than justified his years in office by the creating of this epithet, the originating of this watchword, the shouting of this battle cry. "Black Monday" ranks in importance with July 4, 1776, the date upon which our Declaration of Independence was signed. It was on "Black Monday" that the judicial branch of our government usurped the sacred privilege and right of the respective states of this union to educate their youth.

So what makes such venom the stuff of an African American Freedom Day? It is this: Brady was right. May 17 did rank in importance with July 4. If Brady and Williams were by-products of American education prior to *Brown*, there was little need for debate on the subject of change. Reeducating America was a must. Our court battles from *Gaines* (see December 11) to *Brown* were steps in staking out our independence. In response—with violence and vitriolic words—America's kings had behaved no differently than England's George III two centuries before. Our revolutionary war was begun.

MAY 20

By 1959, the McCarthy era had ended but Mc-
Carthyism had not. Every effort to end human rights
abuses was met with the same old "red scare" tactic. Worse,
the "communist" epithet was taken seriously, time was lost on
a distraction, and the real issues—segregation and intimidation—were predictably forestalled. When the Youth March (see
April 18) was similarly attacked, Michigan's Congressman
Charles C. Diggs took to the floor of the House of Representatives. From the Congressional Record of May 20, 1959:

> Mr. Speaker, in the RECORD of April 20, 1959 . . . there appear
> comments and several newspaper articles referring to the . . .
> youth march on Washington. Inserted in the RECORD by the
> gentleman from Georgia, these materials are used in an attempt
> . . . to link the youth march with the Communist Party . . . I should
> like to set the RECORD straight on this piece of slander.
>
> The 1959 youth march was fully and objectively covered by
> Washington and other daily newspapers around the country. By
> including among the newspaper clippings an article published in
> the Communist Party's *Sunday Worker* on the subject of the march,
> an attempt is made to infer a connection between the two. Of
> course, the communist press would comment upon this march.
> It, too, is the press and reports on events of national interest. . . .
>
> It is ironic that with those who have some vested interest in
> segregation and oppression of the rights of Negro citizens, any-
> thing having to do with the democratic ideals of justice, equality,
> liberty, and opportunity between and for all men must somehow
> be linked up with communism. It is more ironic that this infer-
> ence and charge should come from such groups when the truth is
> that it is the group's very position on race relations and civil
> rights which is the boon to communism. During my five years in
> Congress, I have observed that small band of vitriolic and dema-
> gogic diehards whose approach to these issues is so completely
> divorced of reason and at such an animalistic level that while
> they defeat their own efforts to sell their blind hatred and bigotry
> to thinking people, they nevertheless make fodder for the com-
> munist cause. The use of inference as a tactic for hurling vitriolic
> unreasoned charges is not subtle and does not escape attention
> and the evaluation it deserves.

MAY 21

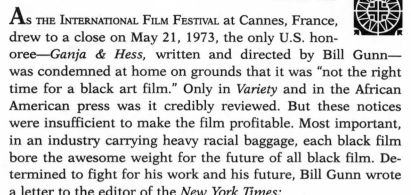

As the International Film Festival at Cannes, France, drew to a close on May 21, 1973, the only U.S. honoree—*Ganja & Hess*, written and directed by Bill Gunn—was condemned at home on grounds that it was "not the right time for a black art film." Only in *Variety* and in the African American press was it credibly reviewed. But these notices were insufficient to make the film profitable. Most important, in an industry carrying heavy racial baggage, each black film bore the awesome weight for the future of all black film. Determined to fight for his work and his future, Bill Gunn wrote a letter to the editor of the *New York Times:*

> There are times when the white [American] critic must sit down and listen. . . . [otherwise] he must not concern himself with black creativity. A children's story I wrote speaks of a black male child that dreamed of a strong white golden-haired prince who would come and save him from being black. He came, and as time passed and the relationship moved forward, it was discovered that indeed the black child was the prince and he had saved his friend from being white. That, too, is possible.
>
> . . . it is a terrible thing to be a black artist in this country. . . . One white critic left my film . . . after twenty minutes and reviewed the entire film. . . . Another wondered where was the race problem. If he looks closely, he will find it in his own review. If I were white, I would probably have been called "fresh and different." If I were European, *Ganja & Hess* might be "that little film you must see." Because I am black, I do not even deserve the pride that one American feels for another when he discovers that a fellow countryman's film has been selected as the only American film to be shown during "Critic's Week" at the Cannes Film Festival. Not one white [American] critic from any of the major newspapers even mentioned it.

But the audience did. In December 1973, the Museum of Modern Art honored the film with two special screenings. Since then, with word-of-mouth praise, the film has become an underground classic and a total sellout at screen revivals.

MAY 22

In 1965, as the Selma march moved toward Montgomery, marchers entered a time warp called Lowndes County, Alabama. As they paraded along Highway 80, the workers in the fields went on hoeing and tilling as though they didn't know the war was over and the Yanks had won. Little had changed in Lowndes over the years. At a time when the national minimum wage was just under $2, and northern families earning $6,000 a year were considered poor, the average black family in Lowndes earned only $985 a year. Of fifteen thousand people, twelve thousand were black, and not one was registered to vote. As Stokely Carmichael and Charles Hamilton wrote in the book *Black Power*, "In the heart of the 'black belt,' that range of Southern areas characterized by the predominance of black people and rich black soil," as in slavery, "black people could come together to do only three things: sing, pray, dance. Any time they came together to do anything else, they were threatened or intimidated."

On the march, Stokely Carmichael vowed he'd come back to Lowndes County. He did. And he brought SNCC's resources and his skills as an organizer. Surveying existing strengths, he found the seeds of a vibrant voter registration drive. Despite the look of things, slavery was over. Of the blacks in Lowndes County, 17 percent worked in nearby Montgomery. There was strong church-based leadership. The few black teachers and two high school principals were respected by blacks and whites. Add a history of resistance. The Selma march had stirred up old powder. Emory Ross's freedom fighter father had been shot and had his house fired on and burned down all in one lesson—a lesson that inspired his son to carry on. John Hulett and seventeen brave others joined with SNCC to register 3,900 people within twenty months. These new voters formed the Lowndes County Freedom Organization (LCFO).

On May 22, 1966, John Hulett spoke at a Los Angeles rally. Sharing the Lowndes story, he inspired daring new dreams with LCFO's symbol—the black panther.

MAY 23

AFRICA WAS BEING REBORN. In 1941, Ethiopia had triumphantly repelled its Italian invaders (see June 30). In 1956, Sudan had become the first modern African nation to regain independence after colonial rule. And by 1963, a majority of the continent was free and indigenous Africans were restored to their rightful positions of leadership. Ethiopian Emperor Haile Selassie invited his fellow Africans to meet at the newly completed Africa Hall in Addis Ababa from May 22 to 25, 1963. In all, thirty-one sovereign nations answered his call, sending delegations led by twenty-nine heads of state. Together they formed the Organization of African Unity, OAU, a loose confederation of nations allied for their political, economic and military interests. For his vision, Selassie was elected honorary president and adopted the role of lead peacemaker for international African affairs.

Thirteen years later, an OAU anniversary celebration hosted by Ambassador Messanvi Kokou Kekeh and his wife, Latre, of Togo hosted five hundred guests from forty-one countries, including twenty-six ambassadors and their wives. With dishes from each of the member nations, the menu was a diplomatic feat and feast. To such traditional treats as goat soup, yam salad, and chicken peanut stew were added these national highlights:

Cameroon: Cassava root foofoo with vegetable soup
Ethiopia: Doro Wot—a stew of chicken, onions, red pepper, and hard-boiled eggs
Ghana: Ginger-flavored fried fish—rock fish
Liberia: Fried plantains in palm butter sauce
Tanzania: Stewed beef with curried green bananas
Togo: Tchatchanga—skewered lamb shank sautéed in ginger and green pepper
Tunisia: Tajines—boneless chicken baked in bread crumbs and grated cheese

A feast of riches.

MAY 24

On May 24, 1960, a reporter for the *Amsterdam News* interviewed Malcolm X on plans for his mass outdoor Freedom Rally later that week. "If the Negro leaders fear they will alienate themselves from the favor and support of their liberal-minded so-called white friends by attending [the rally] simply because it is sponsored one hundred percent by black people in Harlem, how can they continue to expect to be accepted as spokesmen by the fast-awakening black masses?" asked Malcolm rhetorically. His Freedom Rally had fast become the litmus test by which black loyalties were being decided—and divided.

It was 1960, and change was in New York's air. Ghana's President Kwame Nkrumah had visited Harlem. So had Sékou Touré of the newly independent Republic of Guinea. The African diplomatic corps, in its magnificent array of native dress, was everywhere. In this presidential election year, blacks too had presidents, had actually seen them in the flesh, and it was having an effect—some said "too positive" an effect—on the black psyche and sense of possibility. The *New York Times* reported "concern" by unnamed "moderate Negro leaders" on the growing "extremism" of blacks. Harlem itself questioned long-standing white leadership of such Civil Rights institutions as the NAACP. People began looking to black leadership of black organizations. And no one was more vocal about that than Harlem's own Malcolm X.

Malcolm was relentless in his challenge to other black leaders—and to Harlem itself—to take a stand. "Let the people of Harlem hear you voice your personal opinion on the problems that confront them, and to know that you understand their plight and identify yourself personally with their struggle. . . . [Participation] does not mean your endorsement of any other person or groups. It means only that you are . . . taking this opportunity to let the people of Harlem know they are not without true leaders and fearless spokesmen." Significantly enough, Harlem was out in force for the rally that Saturday, but most of its leaders were not.

MAY 25

As DELEGATES THE WORLD OVER convened in San Francisco to draft the United Nations charter, the West Indies National Council (WINC) presented its "Appeal to the UN Conference on Behalf of the Caribbean Peoples" on May 25, 1945. Were these not colonized peoples of color, they might have been more accurately portrayed by historians and political scientists as exiles—involuntary and voluntary. Called "Harlem-based Caribbean immigrants," they set out to craft a politico-cultural identity before the world and free their native island lands.

In 1940, the "Declaration of Rights of the Caribbean Peoples to Self-Determination and Self-Government" was presented to the Pan-American Foreign Ministers' Conference. The resulting Act of Havana endorsed limited democratic rights for Caribbean peoples, but it was never invoked. And, by 1945, as WINC organizer Richard B. Moore wrote in the appeal, although West Indians had "unstintingly" demonstrated support for the UN "in proportion to their size and numbers and the meager actual resources left to them after centuries of colonial retardation and impoverishment," the UN was not similarly inclined to support them. No matter the UN troops, financial support, and essential materials provided, the UN stand remained on the side of the colonial powers over the colonized. Now, with the appeal, WINC proposed a plan that honored the right of Caribbean peoples to self-government and self-determination, the "age-long objective of the West Indian peoples for voluntary federation," a right to participate in regional decision-making, postwar rehabilitation, UN seats for their own delegates, and a guaranteed end to racism.

Dismissing the appeal as an "internal" colonial matter (see December 17), the UN Conference Secretary General protected the imperialistic West and refused to consider the West Indian plea. Nevertheless, the years of organizing and alliances made around the appeal were not for naught. That effort bore first fruits in the independence of Jamaica and Trinidad/Tobago in August 1962.

As Freedom Riders wound deeper south and federal marshals kept watch along the length of the route, a hysterical calm fell on riders and ruffians alike. The Mother's Day attack (see May 11) when mobs firebombed the buses and nearly beat the Riders to death, had politicized and helped recruit new volunteers. One was William Mahoney. A Howard University student embroiled in the semester's end and final exams, Mahoney had dismissed advance news of the Rides until he saw a picture of a fellow student being beaten. Outraged and inspired, Mahoney signed on. His account was published in *Liberation* magazine:

> Friday, May 26, 1961, 11 P.M. I boarded a Greyhound bus in Washington with tickets for Montgomery. . . . At our first stop in Virginia . . . I was confronted with what the Southern White has called "separate but equal." A modern rest station with gleaming counters and picture windows was labelled "White," and a small wooden shack beside it was tagged "Colored." When we entered the White waiting room Frank [Hunt] was promptly . . . asked to leave. Because I am a fair-skinned Negro I was waited upon. I walked back to the bus through the cool night trembling and perspiring. . . . Once across the [Mississippi] state line we passed a couple of police cars, which began to follow us. . . . As we rolled toward Jackson, every blocked-off street, every back road taken, every change in speed caused our hearts to leap. Our arrival and speedy arrest in the White bus station in Jackson, when we refused to obey a policeman's order to move on, was a relief.

Who were these Riders and why did they risk their lives? Significantly, one was John Peck, an original member of the Journey of Reconciliation and heir to the Peck & Peck clothier fortune. With privilege and conscience, he felt it a moral obligation. A black worker's friend had been nearly killed on the first Ride. He joined because he had been chased home "by white toughs once too often." A middle-aged Minneapolis art dealer with "three dollars to his name" joined "because it is one way of fighting a system which not only hurts the Negro but is a threat to world peace and prosperity." Heroes all.

For YEARS, psychiatrist Frantz Fanon had quietly published his observations of oppressed Africans in French-ruled Algeria. By May 27, 1965, his first English-language edition was sweeping the United States. The Martinican doctor had become the philosopher-hero of black liberationists, and his work, *Wretched of the Earth*, had become an instant classic. The African American struggle for Civil Rights could be seen as one with a global Pan-African freedom fight. Fanon's analysis of human responses to mistreatment went beyond validation; it was vindication. Not only had he understood the rage, he had viewed retaliation as a "logical" and "inevitable" process of social revolution. Arriving on the scene two months after the assassination of Malcolm X and one month after Bloody Sunday (see March 7), Fanon was literally and figuratively *all the rage.*

Fanon's prescriptive message was controversial. Those whose ancestors' cries of "Tyranny!" had erupted in the eighteenth-century revolutions in America and France could not relate to the legions they now oppressed worldwide via segregation, apartheid, imperialism, and colonization. Even some of the "wretched" themselves feared Fanon's treatise. But the cost of remaining oppressed and of fighting for one's rights were about the same. The threat of white terrorism was nothing new. Treatment of their ills demanded action—or confrontation, as Fanon called it. And confrontation was in the air.

Confronting history, the oppressed now championed self-empowerment and self-determination. The tree of Fanon's "inevitable" social revolution began sprouting new shoots in the Black Power, black studies, AIM (American Indian Movement), women's liberation, antiwar, Young Lords, Gray Panther, and Appalachian Young Patriots movements. For the "wretched" of the isms of race, gender, and class, the dam had burst on centuries of frustration. A century after the first Civil War, the 1960s saw a second. But would a lasting Reconstruction result in equity for all this second time around? That answer is still under debate.

Psychology   **Empowerment**

St. Augustine, Florida, the nation's oldest city, was, in 1606, the site of the first recorded birth of an African child in the Americas. Under Seminole protection and the Spanish flag, it was a refuge for escaping slaves well into the 1800s. In 1866, a year after the Civil War, it spawned the all-black town of Little Africa, later renamed Lincolnville. For years it prospered, but by 1963, when the Klan nearly burned Dr. R. N. Hayling and three other NAACP members to death, black St. Augustinians had had their fill of segregation. A year later, a determined Dr. Hayling, Reverend C. T. Vivian, and the SCLC developed a plan. Among those arrested attempting to integrate a church and a motel were the mother of the governor of Massachusetts and the wife of a black Episcopal Church bishop. When two black homeowning families tried to enroll their children in white schools, their houses were burned down. Then, on May 28, 1964, at the invitation of black St. Augustinians, Dr. King and the Movement came to town.

In "My Last Letter to Martin" (see April 7) Dr. Ralph Abernathy—Dr. King's first lieutenant and successor—had written: "You remember St. Augustine, Florida, and Hoss Manuei [Holsted Manucy] when he said that he did not have any evil vices whatever? He did not drink liquor, he did not chase after women, he did not smoke. His only hobby was beating and killing niggers."

St. Augustine was so bad that when Dr. King requested federalization of troops, an uncharacteristically demure President Lyndon Johnson said it was "impossible." When blacks saw terrorist segregationists parading in the streets guarded by the troops Dr. King had requested for *their* protection, they knew why even Johnson was stumped: St. Augustine was rough. So entrenched was the racism, the hatred, the police corruption, and the violence that St. Augustine's tower of segregation did not begin to crumble until the Civil Rights Bill was enacted in 1964. When President Johnson signed it into law on July 2, 1964, Dr. Hayling went to court, sued the city for refusing blacks their Civil Rights, and won.

MAY 29

IN MAY 1974, visitors to the Whitney Museum of American Art in New York were invited on a pilgrimage to history via the paintings of Jacob Lawrence.

"Only an artist for whom history is a living issue—a matter of personal fate rather than intellectual choice—could have sustained so protracted a commitment to a vision that contradicts so many [of modern art's] established pieties," wrote *New York Times* art critic Hilton Kramer in his review of this retrospective. Here were Lawrence's famed "series paintings," which had elevated narrative art: *Toussaint L'Ouverture* (1938), forty-one panels on the Haitian Revolution; *This Is Harlem* (1942–43), thirty scenes of his hometown; *Harriet Tubman* (see October 13); *War;* and more—all from the man about whom art historian Dr. David Driskell has written, "Lawrence [looks] at history with the discerning eye of a sensitive critic."

Lawrence's *The 1920's . . . The Migrants Arrive and Cast Their Ballots* (1974) appears on the cover of *Freedom Days;* it is one of several "civil rights" works painted while his retrospective was on tour. Painted thirty-three years after his best-known series, *. . . And the Migrants Kept Coming* (1941), this 1974 painting extends his exploration of black migrants and their impact on history. Of this work Lawrence has written:

> During the post–World War I period, millions of black people left the southern communities of the United States and migrated to settle in the northern cities of the United States. This migration reached its peak during the 1920s just before the Great Depression of the 1930s. Among the many advantages that the migrants found in the northern communities was the freedom to vote. This particular work represents some migrants taking advantage of that opportunity.

Lawrence dropped out of high school during the Great Depression, but he completed his education at Harlem's 135th Street Library, home of the Schomburg Collection—making Lawrence a protégé of the impassioned black bibliophile Arturo A. Schomburg.

MAY 30

BLACK METROPOLIS was a bustling, thriving Chicago community rooted in its own institutions. There, people raised families, built a vibrant economy, and, in the 1930s, returned the first African American to Congress since the expulsion of blacks after Reconstruction. Quinn Chapel of the AME Church, the oldest black congregation in the city, was founded there in 1844. From that strength came Dr. Daniel Hale Williams' Provident Hospital, where he successfully pioneered the world's first open-heart surgery. The black-run Wabash Avenue YMCA served as the social and educational center for the thousands who fled north in the Great Migration of the 1920s. The Overton Hygienic Building, named for a former slave and businessman who erected it in 1923, remains a testament to black entrepreneurism. Headquartered there were Victory Life Insurance, two black periodicals—the *Chicago Bee* and *Half Century Magazine*—and Douglass National Bank, the first black-owned bank to receive a national charter. All of that was there in 1926 when the community mobilized to erect a statue to its heroes of World War I, the "Fightin' Eighth," whose armory was right there, too.

At first the city's South Park Commission rejected the idea, insisting there was no room. But when the *Chicago Defender* launched an editorial campaign urging blacks to "vote no" on every other commission-backed project, the commission recanted. The monument is a gray granite stand with three bronze facings; one depicts a soldier, another womanhood and motherhood, and the third the figure of Columbia (the feminine personification of the United States) holding a tablet and keeping count of the Eighth Regiment's major battles. Symbolically, in its rim of figures facing out, the statue (both battle and victory in itself) paid tribute to the need for blacks to fight on all fronts. "Stay on top of everything," it cried out. And it did that, too. Like that final cherry on the cake, the last figure of the Victory Sculpture—a uniformed African American World War I doughboy—took his place of honor atop the statue at last for the Memorial Day celebration of May 30, 1936.

MAY 31

In the landmark *Brown v. Board of Education* Supreme Court decision of 1954 desegregating public schools (see May 17), Chief Justice Earl Warren wrote:

> It is doubtful that any child may reasonably be expected to succeed in life if he is denied the opportunity of an education. Such an opportunity, where the state has undertaken to provide it, is a right which must be made available to all on equal terms. . . . Does segregation of children in public schools solely on the basis of race . . . deprive the children of the minority group of equal educational opportunities? We believe that it does. . . . To separate them from others of similar age and qualifications solely because of their race generates a feeling of inferiority as to their status in the community that may affect their hearts and minds in a way unlikely ever to be undone. . . . We conclude that in the field of public education the doctrine of "separate but equal" has no place. Separate educational facilities are inherently unequal. Therefore, we hold that the plaintiffs and others similarly situated for whom the actions have been brought are, by reason of the segregation complained of, deprived of the equal protection of the laws guaranteed by the Fourteenth Amendment.

One year later, having reviewed the desegregation plans of the four states named in *Brown*, on May 31, 1955, the Supreme Court issued a supplementary ruling that would become known as *Brown II*. But while *Brown* was known and prized for its simple humanity and clarity of language, *Brown II* was a bit more circumspect in tone and intent. The Court reaffirmed its decision and required implementation of school desegregation plans "with all deliberate speed" to satisfy blacks who had won the case, but also signaled retreat to satisfy whites. The Court gave states time to craft ways to circumvent the decision: "The courts may consider problems related to administration . . . the physical condition of the school plant, the transportation system, personnel, revision of school districts. . . ." *Brown* wedged open the door to Civil Rights, but *Brown II* required blacks to force their way through.

JUNE

JUNE 1

NINE YEARS AFTER the color bar set by the Daughters of the American Revolution (DAR) had prevented the noted contralto Marian Anderson from performing in Washington's Constitution Hall, concert halls and theaters in the nation's capitol were as segregated as ever. Actors' Equity Association, the stage actors' union, came up with a solution. June 1, 1948, was day one of its new policy: Actors' Equity members were forbidden to participate in shows in Washington theaters that barred African Americans.

The precipitating incident had occurred in 1946 when an interracial group of World War II veterans and their guests were refused admission to George Washington University's Lisner Auditorium. In response, the Committee for Racial Democracy enlisted aid from an upcoming benefit production for the American Veterans Committee. The company vowed to help end discrimination in the city's unionized theaters. The all-white company, including the playwright Maxwell Anderson and the actress Ingrid Bergman, originated a resolution requesting Actors' Equity to refuse to perform before segregated audiences. That November, thirty-three member playwrights and producers of the Dramatists' Guild added their voices to the boycott. Because of the actions taken by these unions, within months the university ended segregation in public performances—but it reserved the right to rent the theaters for segregated private events.

At the National, the struggle took a different approach. There, blacks could be onstage but not in the house. Once again the committee took the lead. Buying blocks of seats for whites, they then sent interracial groups to the theater. When blacks were refused, they demanded refunds for the entire group, wreaking havoc on box office receipts. When the management refused all refunds, the committee sued and the theater remained segregated, but returned to its refund policy. The Actors' Equity ban went into effect on June 1 and remained in partial effect until Washington, D.C., fully desegregated public places in the 1960s.

Social History   Respect for Use of Power

JUNE 2

AFTER THE PASSION, PAIN, and prophetic truths witnessed the night before, it seemed a sacrilege to review *for colored girls who have considered suicide/when the rainbow is enuf!* as a play. Review it they did, on June 2, 1976. Ntozake Shange's dramatic evening of poetry, coproduced by Woodie King and Joseph Papp, had opened at the Public Theater in New York, and it was a smash!

Seven ladies walk a dark, bare stage—Lady in Rose, Lady in Yellow, in Red, in Green, in Purple, in Blue. And the Lady in Orange, herself, Shange. From *"dark phrases of womanhood of never havin' been a girl half-notes scattered without rhythm/ no tune . . ."* they wind their way past solitude to *"i found god in myself and i loved her/ i loved her fiercely"* and emerge at *"and this is for colored girls who have considered suicide/ but are movin' to the ends of their own rainbows."* At stops along the way, a Lady finds *"I survive on intimacy and tomorrow."* Another grows in her wisdom of the world: *"I will tell all of your secrets into your face."* In this age of the "black is beautiful" 1970s, these women know what it means to be black and not feel beautiful. They also know that it is time to move on to being black with new feelings: *"I couldn't stand being colored and sorry at the same time—it seems redundant in the modern world."* There was so much more to life:

> at 4:30 AM/ she rose/ movin the arms & legs that trapped her/ she sighed affirmin the sculptured man/ & made herself a bath/ of dark musk oil egyptian crystals/ & florida water to remove his smell/ to wash away the glitter/ to watch the butterflies melt into/ suds & rhinestones fall beneath/ her buttocks like smooth pebbles/ in a missouri creek . . .

With success at the Public, it was on to Broadway with bright mural-size posters of Shange's colorful colored women in the subways. Bequeathing her Lady to another actress, Shange left to pursue new voices and bring us more than *enuf.* . . .

For years, an historic battleground in the fight for labor rights was the R. J. Reynolds Tobacco Company in Winston-Salem, North Carolina. There, in 1943, a black worker complaining of illness was refused relief and dropped dead on the plant floor. In sympathy and solidarity, black women workers staged an immediate sit-down strike affecting ten thousand employees and shutting down the plant. With the founding of Local 22 of the FTA (Food, Tobacco, Agricultural & Allied Workers of America), a CIO-affiliated union, that action led to better working conditions. But four years later, with the contract up for renewal, Reynolds sought and received relief from the government via the actions of a young California congressman eager to make a name for himself, Richard Nixon.

Through his seat on the House Un-American Activities Committee (HUAC), Nixon invoked the Taft-Hartley Act, requiring union officials to sign an anti-Communist loyalty oath. Then he ordered the union to be investigated as an alleged "communist-dominated union" to prove or disprove the validity of their oath. No consideration was given to their demands. But the fact that the union won a twelve-cents-per-hour wage increase, maternity leave, and wage and job classifications gives an inkling of the desperate conditions they had faced before the final settlement.

Making an example of the union by intimidating workers was the order of the day. Enter Moranda Smith. In 1949, this champion of labor reform became the first woman organizer to head the notoriously dangerous southern region for any union. A booming presence, tall, and full-voiced in spirit and determination, she was more than up to the task. Her health wasn't. In 1950, her body gave out at age thirty-four; she had literally worked herself to death for the cause.

On June 3, 1951, Smith's posthumous thirty-sixth birthday, thousands of workers stopped to honor the woman who had given her life in defense of theirs.

JUNE 4

TWENTY YEARS HAD PASSED since A. Philip Randolph successfully moved President Franklin D. Roosevelt to issue Executive Order No. 8802 prohibiting job discrimination in the war industries (see June 25). Blue-ribbon presidential panels had issued several reports and recommendations. Then, in 1963, President Kennedy put forth Civil Rights legislation. But only after his death, and a record eighty-two-day filibuster by southern senators, was a watered-down version of the bill passed in 1964. Yet there were still no concrete goals and standards of accountability for those empowered and entrusted to implement the bill. In 1965, President Lyndon Johnson did just that. With a bow to a 1947 presidential commission report, "To Secure These Rights" (see October 28), he delivered his landmark speech, "To Fulfill These Rights," at Howard University on June 4, 1965.

With that speech, the era of "affirmative action" began. Actually, the term was first used by John F. Kennedy in his Executive Order No. 10925 of March 6, 1961, which established the President's Commission on Equal Employment Opportunity: "The contractor will take affirmative action to ensure that applicants are employed, and employees are treated during their employment, without regard to their race, creed, color, or national origin. . . ." But, said Johnson, "Freedom is not enough. You do not take a person who, for years, has been hobbled by chains and liberate him, bring him to the starting line of a race and then say, 'You are free to compete with all others,' and still justly believe you have been completely fair."

And what did he propose? "We seek not just freedom but opportunity," said Johnson. "We seek not just legal equity but human ability, not just equality as a right and a theory but equality as a fact and equality as a result." That summer Johnson's Executive Order No. 11246 would spell out the terms of affirmative action. Passage of the Voting Rights Act of 1965 would assure blacks the right to run for office and would help enforce affirmative action under the law.

Affirmative Action   Foundations

JUNE 5

In the parade of Supreme Court decisions that steadily chipped away at the legal foundation of segregation, three cases form a collective milestone: *Henderson v. United States*, *Sweatt v. Painter*, and *McLaurin v. Oklahoma State Regents*. Adding to their impact, the unanimous decisions reached in each of the three cases were all handed down on the same day—June 5, 1950.

Henderson v. United States: This transportation case was brought by Alpha Phi Alpha fraternity against Southern Railway Company, which, in its dining car, assigned one table to blacks and reserved the other tables for whites only. Under the Interstate Commerce Act, passengers are equally entitled to facilities appropriate to the class of service for which they have paid. Because "the curtains, partitions, and signs" all called attention to differences in treatment by race, the Court banned dining car segregation.

Sweatt v. Painter: Brought by the NAACP Legal Defense Fund, this case attacked segregated graduate schools. Faced with a legal challenge, the Texas legislature had hastily funded a black law school. But as the decision stated "The University of Texas Law School possesses to a far greater degree those qualities . . . which make for greatness in a law school. . . . It is difficult to believe that one who had a free choice between these schools would consider the question close." The Court was not ready to strike down the doctrine of "separate but equal" segregation, but it ordered Herman Sweatt admitted to the law school under the "equal protection" clause of the Fourteenth Amendment, granting rights of citizenship to blacks.

McLaurin v. Oklahoma State Board of Regents: Further undergirding *Sweatt*, the Court held that once admitted, students could not be segregated within the school. Recognizing such segregation as a handicap to the African American student, the Court finally declared all graduate school racial segregation invalid.

JUNE 6

Newsweek HAD CALLED James Meredith "a black Don Quixote." As he left Memphis for his solo 220-mile march to Jackson, he wore a bush helmet and held a carved ivory-head African walking stick. He tilted at the windmills of segregation and charged on to his "impossible dream": that a black man could walk free in Mississippi. In 1962, he had paved the way in education as the first African American admitted to the University of Mississippi (see September 13). Now, this lone crusader would lead the way to the voting booths with his "March Against Fear."

On June 6, 1966, as Meredith crossed from Tennessee into Mississippi, snaking his way along a parallel route was Aubrey James Norvell, a white unemployed Memphis hardware clerk. Lying in wait just outside Hernando, Norvell slithered from his hole in a thicket of green. Lurching forward and shooting, he was heard to say, "I just want James Meredith." With two blasts to the chest, he got him. First reported dead, Meredith was in satisfactory condition after surgery.

To his side flew SCLC's Martin Luther King, SNCC's Stokely Carmichael and Cleveland Sellers, and CORE's Floyd McKissick. The next day, they continued Meredith's march, determined that its campaign against fear and for voting go on: it was time to deal with the issue of blacks controlling their own destinies. Returning to the hotel that night, they were joined by Roy Wilkins (NAACP) and Whitney Young (National Urban League). The issues: local (vs. national) identity, engaging all-black groups (vs. excluding the Louisiana-based Deacons of Self-Defense), Civil Rights and antiwar (vs. solely Civil Rights), white participation (vs. leadership). As "vs." on each point, the establishment-oriented Wilkins and Young angrily left as quickly as they had come. In their place came activist-comedian Dick Gregory and thirty thousand others nationwide. This was one impossible dream even Meredith never had as he joined his "followers" for the climax of the march in Jackson on June 26.

JUNE 7

Aᶠʳⁱᶜᵃⁿ Aᴍᴇʀɪᴄᴀɴ ᴡʀɪᴛᴇʀs had long nurtured a literary tradition featuring white characters and situations. Among these works were Zora Neale Hurston's *Seraph on the Suwanee*, Charles Perry's *Portrait of a Young Man Drowning*, Ann Petry's *Country Place*, Richard Wright's *Savage Holiday*, and Frank Yerby's *Foxes of Harrow*. Yet, even in these circles, Willard Motley's work (see April 2) stood out for its predominant whites. While race, as an issue, was usually absent from his work, it all but dominated his later life. When his letter to the editor critiquing James Baldwin was published by *Time* magazine on June 7, 1963, it provided rare insight into Motley's own youth.

> Sirs,
>
> We were the only Negro family in the neighborhood. During Chicago's race riot [of 1919] I was a boy and didn't understand why my father had me piling rocks up in the hall by the front door. The curtain was down and he stood behind the door with a rifle. If memory serves correctly, next to him, also with a rifle, stood his white neighbor and friend. The mob came. Perhaps fifty or more. A woman neighbor a block and a half down the street from our house stopped it and wagged her finger under the leader's nose and said, "Don't you dare bother that colored family down the street or you are going to have trouble with all of us." The answer: "No, we're going to the West Side to get some niggers." As they approached our house the woman across the street ran out and stopped them, telling them the same thing. They walked past our house without looking at it.
>
> My experiences are a little different from those of most Negroes in that I have never lived in a Negro neighborhood, instead: Near Maxwell and Halsted, that wonderful place where all nationalities live within a couple blocks of each other. . . . Not bad for Chicago, eh?

Significantly, while this letter provides an unusual portrait of the infamous Red Summer of 1919, it offers rare insight on Chicago and captures the family life of two famed Motleys—Willard and his brother, the Harlem Renaissance painter Archibald Motley.

JUNE 8

DECIDING THE CASE *District of Columbia v. John R. Thompson Company* on June 8, 1953, the Supreme Court upheld earlier bans on segregated public accommodations and found discrimination by restaurants to be illegal. It was an important step en route to desegregation, but the case was most memorable for how it came to be: Mary Church Terrell, the venerated eighty-seven-year-old black activist and feminist, had taken to the picket line in pursuit of justice. She led a group into a Washington, D.C., restaurant, and refused to leave when they were denied service. The group was arrested, providing a test case. On May 24, 1951, the Municipal Appeals Court found in favor of the Terrell group, outlawing segregation in D.C. restaurants. The plaintiffs appealed, and the Supreme Court upheld the decision two years later.

Freeborn to a wealthy ex-slave in 1863, Mary Church graduated from Oberlin College in 1884, studied abroad in Europe, and married Robert Terrell—an ex-slave who had graduated from Harvard, studied law at Howard, and became the first black federal judge. Church was groomed for the life of a "lady," but the 1892 lynching of her friend, Thomas Moss, recast her life. Guilty only of success, Moss was lynched by a mob angered at the loss of black trade to his People's Grocery Store. Moss's lynching sent Mary Church Terrell and Frederick Douglass (the abolitionist, ambassador to Haiti, and family friend) to the White House to lobby President Benjamin Harrison to publicly condemn lynching. Harrison's nay was Terrell's call to activism.

Attacked as a "meddler," in the put-down of the day, Terrell was undaunted. Her article "The Mission of the Meddler" was published in the August 1905 issue of *The Voice of the Negro.* "Everybody who has tried to advance the interests of the human race by redressing wrongs," she wrote, "has first been called a meddler. . . . There is an imperative need of a host of meddlers who will . . . go so far as to interfere officiously . . . where corruption of any kind is apparent and the transgression of the law is clear." Meddling would be her life's work.

JUNE 9

In 1947, Joe Louis was on top, World Heavyweight Boxing Champion of the World, one of the greatest fighters of all time, a gentleman, and a true hero in the African American community. A film starring the champ himself had to deliver box office punch. Veteran film producer William Alexander was so sure of that fact that he invested a healthy wad of his own money to make the film, starring Joe Louis and Ruby Dee. In 1948, he released *The Fight Never Ends*. The film was such a colossal financial flop that Alexander would later say, "Man, we lost our shirts, our underwear, and our shoestrings."

This defeat was a major blow to Alexander, pioneer of wartime newsreels, founder of the Associated Producers of Negro Motion Pictures, and owner of his own company, Alexander Productions. This film—his first full-length feature—should have marked a career milestone. In 1946 alone he had produced four hit shorts. In this post–World War II era, two of those films—*The Highest Tradition* and *The Call of Duty*—were stories about black soldiers. Then, with Hollywood musicals still popular, he made two musical shorts, *Vanities* and *Rhythm in a Riff*. He thought he understood something about selecting the right project for the right time, yet . . .

The skill that ultimately helped Alexander rebound was the one that had been his strongest suit from the start. As his production manager, Harryette Miller, would recall, what stood out about him was "his business awareness, his ability to raise money and to fund these productions—the feature films and shorts. . . . This inside knowledge, knowing the inner workings of the financial side and how to sell his product and ideas . . . gave him an edge." Reflecting on his success years later, he advised others to stress professionalism above all in every area of the business, "not only in front of the camera, but way back at the check-signing stage, gathering of financing and ownership of movies."

JUNE 10

O<small>N</small> J<small>UNE</small> 10, 1963, Marian Wright would soon become Marian Wright-Edelman—all the promising signs were there that day as Yale University awarded her a LL.B. (Bachelor of Law) degree. It could not have come at a more prescient time. For at that very moment, thousands of miles away from the pomp of New Haven, a circumstance was taking place in Mississippi that would bring the first African American woman admitted to the Mississippi bar and future founder of the Children's Defense Fund reams of respect for her lawyering with the Jackson, Mississippi, branch of the NAACP Legal Defense Fund.

On June 10, 1963, Fannie Lou Hamer lay near death in a Mississippi jail, the victim of a sadistic police beating and conspiracy. That day, she was supposed to have begun a week-long workshop in the Highlander Folk School, the school known for empowering the working class with its founding philosophy: "people are not powerless." She never made it. Traveling by bus with Annell Ponder of SCLC and four brand-new teacher-trainers like herself, Hamer got off at the Trailways depot in Winona. Still buoyant from their past week of sessions and such delights as "Freedom Fighting Hot Rolls" and "Brotherhood Punch," the group entered the whites-only waiting room. A waitress called for the police, crying out, "I can't take no more." Two years had passed since the ICC desegregated terminals (see November 14). But that meant nothing in Winona. The freedom group was thrown out. Ponder wrote down police license plate numbers with the intention of filing a complaint. Seeing that, the police dragged them off to the station. Each one was badly beaten. Ponder was repeatedly thrown to the floor and picked up for more blows until her head was swollen. Hamer was thrown face down on a cot and police forced two black prisoners to torture her—one to beat her with a blackjack while the other sat on her legs; then switch places.

This was the type of case that required Wright-Edelman's skill and compassion—and got the best of both when she arrived in Mississippi later that year.

JUNE 11

JﾠUNE 11, 1963: what a day. Alabama Governor George Wallace announced plans to personally block admittance to the University of Alabama of two black students—James Hood and Vivian Malone. Prompted by Wallace's bravado, Dr. King initiated a challenge: "If the governor of Alabama will present his body by standing in the door to preserve an evil system, then President Kennedy ought to go to Tuscaloosa and personally escort the student into the university with his body!" As Wallace appeared, the president did not, but a deputy attorney general and federal troops did.

As this drama climaxed in Tuscaloosa, another unfolded in Boston: parents, the Boston NAACP, and the Massachusetts Commission Against Discrimination versus the Boston School Committee. The charge: a "lack of educational opportunity" for black children. The fast-escalating crisis yielded a one-day school boycott and a bitter northern school desegregation battle that consumed Boston into the 1970s.

Back in Alabama, the two students were admitted and the university was officially desegregated under federal guard. That night, JFK took to the air. Segregation, he told the nation, was morally wrong, and he outlined his proposed Civil Rights Act:

> We preach freedom around the world and we mean it. And we cherish our freedom here at home. But are we to say to the world—and, much more importantly, to each other—that this is the land of the free except for Negroes; that we have no class or caste system, no ghettos, no master race, except with respect to Negroes. Now the time has come for this nation to fulfill its promise.

Civil Rights leaders were ecstatic: the movement had the support for which it had so long sacrificed so much. The victory was short-lived (see June 15). Byron de la Beckwith stalked the night in wait for NAACP field secretary Medgar Evers. Just after midnight, as Evers pulled into his driveway, Beckwith killed him with a shotgun blast to the back. Evers was the first in a tragically long line of martyred Civil Rights leaders.

Desegregation

Demons

JUNE 12

O~N~ J~UNE~ 12, 1970, Max Roach and Janus Adams headed *home*. Reversing the Middle Passage, with its triangular route, they left the Americas for his European concert tour, then journeyed to Africa—the first members of each of their families to touch its soil in more than two hundred years. It was an occasion made ripe for providential awe by two facts: she was pregnant with their twins; and the couple bore with them, in a suitcase, the ashes of her recently departed grandfather.

A Caribbean immigrant from St. Eustatius, her grandfather raised his family to appreciate the opportunity for education in America, but he had never been happy there. Thus, when he died in 1969, it was decided that he should be cremated and returned to his birthplace. Even in death this Grandpa was a motivator and advocate for the impossible dream. A devout follower of Marcus Garvey (see August 13), he was one of Harlem's soapbox philosophers of Mt. Morris Park fame. Left to babysitting chores, the lullaby he sang was the Garvey hymn "Ethiopia, the Land of the Fathers." And so once the impending African odyssey became a reality, the family knew there could be no better resting place for Willie Landsmark than somewhere—anywhere—on the African continent.

Roach and Adams landed in Tangiers for the homecoming as guests of the pianist Randy Weston, and events unfolded like an ancient ritual. Late Saturday night at the water's edge stood a Moroccan emissary, the host, the husband, and the wife bearing the ashes of the grandfather. At midnight, with her long robes whisked to the wind, heavy with the weight of her future and her past, Adams waded toward that bend on the horizon where the waters turn to enfold Africa and delivered Grandpa to the sea. Home, recounting the scene on demand, news reached one of her grandfather's friends. "Willie always said it," he intoned, shaking his head as if seized by a miracle. "'Africa!' Willie always said, 'If my eyes don't see it, my dead ashes will.'" It was the first Max and Janus knew of the prophesy they had just fulfilled.

Family   Ancestors

JUNE 13

I<small>T WAS</small> J<small>UNE</small> 1956, and the Civil Rights movement was just starting to stir things up. Montgomery Bus Boycotters had been walking for six months. Rosa Parks and Martin Luther King were not yet household names. Job opportunities were drowned in the crocodile tears of weeping employers "unable to find qualified Negroes." Trade schools refused black applicants (see September 16). Unions barred black members (see November 10). The average annual income for black men was $2,342—59 percent of that for white males. The average income for black women was lower still. And the Fuller Products Company employed five thousand well-paid predominantly black profit-sharing sales agents.

A doorbell rings, a smart-looking salesperson introduces himself. He's the Fuller Brush Man (or Woman)—just one of a proud network of people in the growing door-to-door direct sales industry. Each "Fullerite," as they call each other, is proof positive of the power of an ultimate "buy-where-you-can-work" campaign. The predominantly black sales force sells the products of a black-owned manufacturer to a predominantly black customer base. At the top of the list of guarantees are these: the highest quality toiletries, cosmetics, and housewares; top-notch customer service; well-treated and well-compensated employees. Top sellers who once barely earned $8 per day now earn $8 per hour. Job security is assured by Fuller's "to brag about" quality and one's own initiative. Avoiding the indignities of segregated travel, Fullerites drive their own cars—the newest and shiniest of which are merit awards to the highest-achieving high-volume salespeople.

With corporate earnings of $90 million, not since the early 1900s—when Mme. C. J. Walker's cosmetics empire empowered a profit-sharing workforce of three thousand—had one person generated so much independence and pride for so many blacks. In the late 1920s, S. B. Fuller had hitchhiked from Memphis to Chicago, found work as a coal hiker, quit when his boss laughed at him for reading about salesmanship, bought $25 worth of soap, started selling, and never let up.

Business   **Cooperative Economics**

JUNE 14

THEIR COURTING DAYS were spent in an endless round of politics, law, school, and survival. But despite one of apartheid's infamous banning orders, Nelson Rolihlahla Mandela, cofounder of South Africa's first black law firm, and Nomzamo Winifred Madikizela, South Africa's first black social worker, were married on June 14, 1958.

They each remembered seeing the other for the first time when the other was unaware. He passed a bus stop, saw her waiting, and tucked her face away as a pleasant memory. She first saw the "imposing" barrister in court when a friend of hers was assaulted by police. They met in his office when she consulted his lifelong partner, Oliver Tambo. Phoning the next day, he asked her to help raise money for the Treason Trial Defense Fund: "It was merely a pretext to invite her to lunch." Nervously, she "took out every schoolgirl's dress" and ultimately wore a friend's dress. From then on they were together—even when they couldn't spend much time. "I was both courting her and politicizing her," said he. "Life with him was always a life without him," said she. At that first lunch, he said, "I knew right there I wanted to marry her—and told her so." Winnie added, "One day, Nelson just pulled up on the side of the road and said, 'You know, there is a woman, a dressmaker, you must go and see her, she is going to make your wedding gown.'" He was given six days' leave of his banning order and paid the traditional bride price (*lobola*) to her father. After the ceremony, a piece of the wedding cake was wrapped up for the bride to bring to the groom's ancestral home for the second part of the wedding. But that was not meant to be. Indicted for treason, he returned to Johannesburg for trial. Six years later, he was sentenced to life.

True to her name—Nomzamo means "one who strives" and "one who undergoes trials"—she, too, endured banishment, prison, and constant upheaval. For twenty-seven years, she was all the world knew of him. Still, she kept the cake—though it "crumbled a bit." It was there when he returned from prison, a hero, in 1990.

Family   Love

JUNE 15

"**I**F I DIE, IT WILL BE IN A GOOD CAUSE," Medgar Evers told a reporter just days before his assassination. "I've been fighting for America just as much as soldiers in Vietnam," said the World War II–vet–turned–NAACP-general in the trench war called Mississippi. On June 15, 1963, thousands gathered to mourn the war hero.

Overflowing the huge Negro Masonic Temple in Jackson that day were others from the front: Daisy Bates from the "Battle of Little Rock," U.N. Nobel Laureate Dr. Ralph Bunche, Rep. Charles Diggs, CORE's James Farmer, activist-comic Dick Gregory, the United Automobile Workers' Walter Reuther, and an SCLC delegation of Dr. Martin Luther King, Rev. Ralph Abernathy, and Rev. Wyatt Tee Walker. Said Dr. T. R. M. Howard, an early ally, "For over a hundred years now, we have been turning first one and then the other cheek. Our neck has gotten tired of turning!" Roy Wilkins, the NAACP executive secretary and delegation leader, gave the charge:

> The lurking assassin pulled the trigger, but in all wars the men who do the shooting are trained and indoctrinated and keyed to action. The southern political system put him behind that rifle. . . . The southern system has its outposts in the Congress. . . . The killer must have felt that he had, if not immunity, then certainly a protection for whatever he chose to do, no matter how dastardly. But nothing can stop the drive for freedom. It will not cease here or elsewhere. [Indeed, three trials and thirty years would go by before Evers's murderer was finally convicted.]

Silently, the mourners walked to the funeral home from which the body would be flown to Arlington Cemetery. From somewhere deep, a voice welled up. "Oh, Freedom," she sang, and was quickly joined for "And before I'll be a slave." Then "This little light of mine." They could not give up Medgar and be silent. With that, a police riot broke out: hundreds of jackbooted, club-swinging police lunged into the crowd, heaving their victims into garbage trucks and hauling them off to jail. As blood flowed in the war-torn streets of Jackson, Medgar Evers did not go down without a fight. The battle of Jackson was on.

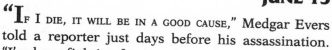

JUNE 16

In the spring of 1976, the South African government declared Afrikaans the official language in the Soweto schools. Now, twenty years after the Sudan had achieved freedom as the first modern African nation, black South Africa was determined to follow the trail to freedom blazed by other African nations. With Steven Biko, a Bantu medical student, as one of its vocal young leaders, the Black Consciousness movement recognized this imposition of language as just one more move to suppress indigenous African languages, a means of intra-African communication, and to destroy indigenous African heritage and cultural integrity.

"The basic tenet of Black Consciousness," said Biko, "is that the black man must reject all value systems that seek to make him a foreigner in the country of his birth and reduce his basic human dignity." On June 16, 1976, twenty thousand schoolchildren empowered by that awareness protested the government decree. "Down with Afrikaans!" their placards read. "If We Must Do Afrikaans, Vorster Must Do Zulu!" they proclaimed, referring to the prime minister. Accounts of who struck the first blow differ, usually by race. But, whether schoolchildren threw a first stone, or machine gun–toting police first taunted them, a thirteen-year-old boy, Hector Petersen, was shot in the back and police fired into a mass of fleeing children. Riots broke out countrywide, and by the end of the uprising 618 were known to be dead (estimates range higher) and 1,500 others were known wounded (most in the back). Said Winnie Mandela, "The thirst for freedom in little children's hearts was such that they were prepared to face machine guns with stones. That is what happens when you want to break those chains of oppression. Nothing else seems to matter." *Amandla!* they had vowed. *Power!*

A second massacre had happened. Never again, people cried. After Sharpeville (see March 21), the ANC's Oliver Tambo (Nelson Mandela's law partner) had fled to train military cadres who now retaliated with raids on police installations.

Wɪᴛʜ ᴛʜᴇ ꜰʀᴇᴇᴅᴏᴍ ꜰɪɢʜᴛ moving forward throughout the Pan-African world, African Americans sought other freedoms: the freedom deep within oneself to be oneself; the freedom to recover for oneself and one's people what was lost, stolen, or denied—but is yet retained in the marrow. Each piece (peace) restored became a precious swatch of rebirth. It forged the spiritual and intellectual cloth of a people's resurgence rooted in their own recovered truths. One of the writers who helped restore that memory patchwork was Julius Lester. His 1968 book, *To Be a Slave*, revived slave narratives. From their words, an intimate view of the "enslaved" emerged—the human being behind the label. His next book, *Black Folktales*, resurrected the literature of the enslaved as preserved in and sustained by the oral tradition. Speaking of his own journey to a special place and time, his involvement with SNCC in the 1960s, the dedication reads: "In memory of Zora Neale Hurston (see June 23), who made me glad I am me, and to H. Rap Brown." In June 1969, he wrote this introduction:

> Folktales are stories that give people a way of communicating with each other about each other—their fears, their hopes, their dreams, their fantasies, giving their explanations of why the world is the way it is. It is in stories like these that a child learns who his parents are and who he will become. . . .
>
> There are many kinds of stories. Stories that partly happened and are partly imagined (but what you imagine can be as real and true as what happens in front of your eyes). . . . Each person who tells a story molds the story to his tongue and to his mouth, and each listener molds the story to his ear. Thus, the same story, told over and over, is never quite the same. But when stories are written in books, people think that this is the only way the story should be and that it cannot be changed. And that is the way a story as a living, growing, changing thing dies. Stories can be changed and should be, as the storyteller feels. The stories don't live otherwise. These stories are told here not as they were told a hundred years ago, but as I tell them now. And I tell them now only because they have meaning now.

Literature

JUNE 18

In 1948, Rev. Gardner C. Taylor was named pastor of Concord Baptist Church, one of New York's largest and oldest congregations. From his earliest days there, he had made a name for himself as an activist and doer. In 1949, he was named to a school board committee. Six years later, his close ties with New York's mayor yielded a seat on an advisory board charged with improving city services. In 1958, four years after the Supreme Court desegregated public schools, he was named to a seat on the Board of Education of the City of New York, the nation's largest school district. In his drive to improve city schools for black children, and because of his frustration with what had come to be called the "all deliberate lethargy" approach to school desegregation, the ever-forthright Mr. Taylor told the board: "The only way to integrate is to integrate."

In 1958, school desegregation crises throughout the South made national headlines. One of the most infamous cities was Little Rock, Arkansas, where the physical and emotional violence inflicted upon nine black children brought international notoriety to the case of the Little Rock Nine. When a newspaper compared New York City to Little Rock (see February 19, February 26, August 29), Taylor was appalled and in total agreement. Born and raised in Louisiana, he found the implications of the story "frightening."

On June 18, 1958, while others declined to be too vocal for fear of offending the powers that be, Reverend Taylor sent the provocative clipping to the New York City Board of Education with a cover letter stating, in part: "I am confident that you will see this as one more instance of the forthrightness with which we must move, in the matter of full and complete integration of New York schools. We condemn the assault on our democracy which came in the infamous attacks on nine little Negro children, and rightly—but Little Rock will never be right until New York is right; and New York will never be right until Little Rock is right."

JUNE 19

JUNETEENTH! On this date in 1865, a Union soldier rode into Galveston, Texas, and announced that slaves were henceforth free. In 1968, June 19, fifty thousand people came to Washington, D.C. for the Solidarity Day March of the Poor People's Campaign (see May 14) and announced that millions were slaves to poverty. In 1865 and since, this was the day of Jubilee. In 1968, there seemed little joy as marchers beheld the shantytown of tents and plywood shacks named Resurrection City. Martin Luther King had been killed a month before. Organizer Bayard Rustin had just resigned. And in a disaster of biblical metaphor, it had rained almost every day during the forty days since the first symbolic poor arrived. Was this what the Civil Rights era had come to: tents flogged by rain, the stench of fertilized fields of green turned to mud, petty violence and despair, a world in tatters and tears?

The march had been planned to affix real faces to the problem of poverty. SCLC would lead a caravan of one thousand people of every hue to the capital, house them on public land, hold empowerment workshops, and lead their troops on daily forays to such enemy camps as the Departments of Agriculture, Justice, and Interior. But it was the wrong effort at the wrong time. As Rev. Andrew Young noted, "If you talked too much economics in the fifties and sixties, you were called a communist. So we clearly avoided the economic issues. . . . When we got around to taking them up in the Poor People's Campaign, that was the time that the war in Vietnam had hit." Rosa Parks, a grieving Coretta King, and other heroes were there. This could not be what King envisioned, people said. Maybe it was. For King said he had seen the antipoverty agenda "broken" like "some idle plaything of a society gone mad on war." Whether it was 1865 or 1968, massa was in the big house refusing to do right by the people. And so they walked off the plantation and set out for a new life. Tents were folded, a mule train bound for the Democratic National Convention headed west, and movement leaders reset the compass for a new course: electing blacks to public office.

JUNE 20

"For months I've drilled myself for this moment," said the man who was about to refuse induction into the army as a conscientious objector. "But I still feel nervous. I hope no one notices my shoulders tremble." That was in April 1967. Now, two painful months later, there was little doubt that the change in the man's draft status had been propelled by his change of religion (from Christianity to Islam), change of name (from Cassius Clay to Muhammad Ali), and newly won title, World Heavyweight Boxing Champion (see February 25).

The Ali issue was about neither the war nor the draft, it was about America—its history, its agenda, its future, and saving face. It was about power. To the powerful, no man—and no black man—was going to have the power to articulate or escalate grassroots hostility to a war for which Dr. King had called upon America to "atone." Risking his life and stature (see April 4), King said the war added "cynicism" to the deaths of its victims on all sides: "Before long [our own troops] must know that . . . none of the things we claim to be fighting for are really involved. . . . The more sophisticated surely realize that we are on the side of the wealthy and the secure while we create a hell for the poor." This was the climate Ali weathered to arrive at his day in court on June 20, 1967. Found guilty of violating the Selective Service Act, he was sentenced to five years in jail and a $10,000 fine. Ali posted bond and descended into a three-year nightmare. Exiled from boxing, time ticked away on his biological athletic clock. For financial and moral support, he took to the college lecture circuit, where the war was extremely personal to his draft-age audiences.

By 1970, the Supreme Court had already rejected hearing his case when two key factors changed his fate: The Court learned that the FBI had illegally wiretapped Ali's phone; and a law clerk convinced one of the justices that Ali's objection to war itself was sincere. The case was heard on a technicality. On June 28, 1970, in the matter of *Clay v. United States*, the Court rendered an 8–0 decision in Ali's favor.

JUNE 21

JUNE 21, 1964. It was the first day of Freedom Summer, Father's Day, and Civil Rights workers from across the country were converging in Meridian, Mississippi, to join local volunteers in a massive voter education and registration project. That day, three workers—James Chaney (a black native Mississippian and CORE volunteer), Andrew Goodman (a white Jewish summer volunteer from New York), and Michael Schwerner (a white CORE field trainer and Jewish New Yorker)—headed toward Neshoba County to investigate the bombing of Mount Zion Methodist Church, where the congregation had volunteered to host a Freedom School. Looking into a terrorist attack was a dangerous assignment. If they did not return by 4:00 P.M., they said, fellow workers should start a search. That search would go on until August 4, when an FBI reward of $30,000 yielded a tip. The three bodies were found in a shallow grave near Philadelphia, Mississippi. The two whites had been shot; Chaney had a fractured skull.

The facts of the murders are sketchy. What is known is that on the evening of June 21, police stopped a car of "mixed-race" occupants and jailed the men for "speeding." They were released that night—most likely into KKK hands.

If any good possibly came from this horror, perhaps it was the courage exhibited by those who were once too fearful to vote, yet who attended a memorial for the three Civil Rights workers at Mount Zion. On August 16, a service honoring the three was held in the burned-out rubble of the church. Standing on a mound of charred brick and wood turned to charcoal, SNCC's Robert Moses spoke about the tragedy of "people who believed in an idea enough to kill for it." "The problem of Mississippi is the problem of the nation and the world," said Moses. "A way has to be found to change this desire to kill." Six days later, Fannie Lou Hamer and Robert Moses would take their historic Mississippi Freedom Democratic Party challenge to the 1964 Democratic National Convention (see August 24). Along with the delegation went photos of the three young martyrs. *Lest we forget . . .*

JUNE 22

In late June 1966, the crusade of those who had picked up the banner for a fallen James Meredith's aborted March Against Fear (see June 6) wound its way toward Jackson, Mississippi, and a triumphant rally there on the capitol steps. On June 22, the second anniversary of the disappearance and murder of three martyred Civil Rights workers—Chaney, Goodman, and Schwerner—Dr. King detoured marchers to Philadelphia, Mississippi, for a prayer memorial.

Arriving in Philadelphia, they were met by Chief Deputy Sheriff Cecil Price. "Are you the fellow that had Schwerner and those fellows in jail?" asked King. "Yes, sir," answered Price, ornery and unrepentant. With that, King knelt down on one knee and led a spontaneous open-air memorial service. As the crowd of hecklers around the marchers grew into a mob, there was reason for fear. King continued, "I believe in my heart that the murderers are somewhere around me at this moment." "You're damn right," Price drawled, nestled in the mob. "They're behind you right now."

King completed the service as camera crews documented the scene. Then, as the marchers attempted to move on, they and the crews were attacked by the mob. With the sheriff and his men at one with the mob, there was no relief to be had that night from the brutal clubbing. Still the marchers carried on— wounded, weary, and determined. They were on a mission, bound for the capitol. It was this kind of horror, repeated again and again, that inspired singer/pianist Nina Simone to write and sing, "Mississippi, God Damn!"

Indeed, an all-new body of activist music would begin to document the struggle.

JUNE 23

IN HAITI IN 1937, healing from a soured love affair, Zora Neale Hurston wrote her masterpiece, *Their Eyes Were Watching God*, in seven breathless weeks. She reflected on that book in her autobiography, *Dust Tracks on the Road:*

> It was dammed up in me, and I wrote it under internal pressure. . . . I wish that I could write it again. In fact, I regret all of my books. It is one of the tragedies of life that one cannot have all the wisdom one is ever to possess in the beginning. Perhaps, it is just as well to be rash and foolish for a while. If writers were too wise, perhaps no books would be written at all. It might be better to ask yourself "Why?" afterwards than before. Anyway, the force from somewhere in Space which commands you to write in the first place, gives you no choice. You take up the pen when you are told, and write what is commanded. There is no agony like bearing an untold story inside you.

When the dam burst on her story of Janie, agony produced three bouts with love that climax in self-love:

> Oh to be a pear tree—*any* tree in bloom! With kissing bees singing of the beginning of the world! She was sixteen. She had glossy leaves and bursting buds and she wanted to struggle with life but it seemed to elude her. Where were the singing bees for her? Nothing on the place nor in her grandma's house answered her.

When Janie comes to understand something about herself:

> So Janie waited a bloom time, and a green time and an orange time. But when the pollen again gilded the sun and sifted down on the world she began to stand around the gate and expect things. What things? She didn't know exactly. Her breath was gutsy and short. She knew things that nobody had ever told her. For instance, the words of the trees and the wind.

And when Janie speaks to us directly with her own full voice:

> Love is lak de sea. It's uh movin' thing, but still and all, it takes its shape from de shore it meets, and it's different with every shore.

Small wonder that thirty years after releasing Janie, when merging tides of the African American and women's literary movements brushed Hurston's shores, the author who died penniless and alone in 1960 was alive with love once more.

Literature   Love

JUNE 24

IT WAS THE END OF AN ERA: June 24, 1968, the last day of the tents and shanties of Resurrection City during the Poor People's Campaign of 1968. As Dr. King had said when he announced the campaign, "The only real revolution, people say, is a man who has nothing to lose." Now King was dead and people with nothing to lose found themselves with nowhere to go. With a crack and a sputter, tear gas canisters erupted, smoking out the last vestiges of the dream as helmeted capital police marched into the crowd in a long blue line. As Rev. Jesse Jackson, SCLC staffer and "mayor" of Resurrection City, recalled, "There was an attempt now to kill the dream itself. . . . Rather than come forth with a plan to wipe out malnutrition, they were wiping out the malnourished."

With the park emptied so traumatically, a crowd of young people gathered just beyond the Washington Mall at the corner of Fourteenth and U Streets with desperation and riot in mind. In an interview with the *Eyes on the Prize* research team, Roger Wilkins—director of the Justice Department's Community Relations Service and nephew of the NAACP's executive director, Roy Wilkins—related the dramatic, fiery baptism of a young leader and watching him soar:

> Up on the back of a flatbed truck there was young Jesse Jackson, who was about twenty-six years old at the time. And he was preaching. And he was saying, "I am somebody. If you're somebody, you don't riot. Say after me, 'I am somebody.' If you are somebody, you go out and you build strong black people. . . ." What Jesse was doing was preaching the riot out of those people. He's preaching, really, pride. "If you are somebody, you build up, you don't tear down." . . . He kept on preaching, he kept on preaching. He was taking quite a risk. 'Cause to preach nonviolence and to preach no rioting to a group of kids who wanted to tear the place down was taking a risk. . . . Jackson took the risk, he preached the people down. They became calm, they went home, there was no riot. It was quite a remarkable performance for a twenty-six-year-old kid.

In 1940, as the United States geared up for war, the nation was counting on the sacrifices of the 1,154,720 African Americans who would eventually volunteer or be drafted into the armed forces. But five million black workers were being shut out of civilian war industry jobs without a thought. Black leaders called upon President Franklin D. Roosevelt to issue an executive order banning discrimination in war-related jobs, and vowed to lead a march on Washington of 100,000 blacks if the ban was not issued. First Lady Eleanor Roosevelt met with the group on her husband's behalf and warned that such a march would breed violence in the streets. To this, A. Philip Randolph, as the group's leader, responded that violence would only occur at the order of the president to the police; the issue was an executive order barring bias. In October 1940, FDR personally met with the group, uttering job promises but no guarantees. On May 1, 1940, with no progress, Randolph called the march and announced a date. On June 18, FDR and Randolph's group met again. The president said he resented the pressure, he wanted the march called off; Randolph refused. One week later, on June 25, Roosevelt issued Executive Order No. 8802, banning job discrimination by federally contracted war-related businesses.

Clearly, Randolph's strategy exacted a coup. Just as clearly, the victory was a cumulative one, strategically built over several years. In telling the story of freedom, pointing up a particular win has its pitfalls. Had the strategy been used earlier, would similar gains have accrued earlier? Was not using the strategy earlier the cause of added years of inequity? Randolph himself would have adamantly answered no to both. Indeed, the greatest of our everyday victories seem more the embodiment of this African proverb: "Mighty rivers are filled one drop at a time." How we generate those drops was perhaps best stated by Frederick Douglass: "Those who profess to favor freedom, and yet deprecate agitation, are men who want crops without plowing up the ground. . . . Power concedes nothing without a demand. It never did and never will."

Strategy   **Respect for Use of Power**

JUNE 26

O~N JUNE~ 26, 1955, three thousand people gathered in an open-air space near the colored township of Kliptown, South Africa, for the Congress of the People. The congress (called by Professor Zachariah K. Matthews, a leading scholar) was as notable for those who came (a full multiracial compliment of organizations) as it was for those who could not come. Those absent included ANC leaders Albert Luthuli and Walter Sisulu, officially banned persons under the laws of apartheid. Significantly, Nelson Mandela, also banned, secretly watched the proceedings from a nearby house as the landmark Freedom Charter was ratified. This document was the working constitution of a government that would achieve dramatic presence and power as Nelson Mandela walked from prison to freedom in 1990. On that prophetic day in Kliptown, with a vote taken by a show of hands, each clause declared aloud was adopted with a cry of acclamation: "Afrika!"

> We, the people of South Africa, declare for all our country and the world to know: That South Africa belongs to all who live in it, black and white, and that no government can justly claim authority unless it is based on the will of the people; That our people have been robbed of their birthright to land, liberty and peace by a form of government founded on injustice and inequality; [Afrika!] . . . We the people of South Africa . . . equals, countrymen and brothers—adopt this Freedom Charter . . . [Afrika! Afrika!] The People shall govern! All national groups shall have equal rights! The people shall share in the country's wealth! [Afrika!] The land shall be shared among those who work it! All shall enjoy equal human rights! The doors of learning and of culture shall be opened! [Afrika!] There shall be peace and friendship! These freedoms we will fight for side by side, throughout our lives until we have won our liberty! [Afrika! Afrika! Afrika!]

Twenty years later, June 26, 1975, marked Mozambique's first full day of freedom after 470 years of Portuguese subjugation. United under the banner of FRELIMO, the people's liberation army was unique for its women soldiers.

JUNE 27

IN THE CIVIL RIGHTS MOVEMENT WARS, pictures were both tools and weapons. For reporters and photographers, injuries could be as inevitable as in any other conflict. But fewer incidents were accidents. Damning some press members as "nigger lovers" for covering a story, police might threaten or beat those who reported their illegal acts in the media. In the twisted scenario of segregation, some police seized photos identifying potential black targets for intimidation and worse. There were also photographers who gave their photos to police, knowing such acts were tantamount to a death warrant for activists. Then there were those who acted as double agents—like Danny Lyon, a white photographer working for SNCC. He palled around with police to better document the story. He recorded an encounter with state troopers in Gadsden, Alabama, in his journal on June 27, 1963:

> I introduced myself as a photographer working for a quasi-fascist news agency in Chicago, and spent the next few hours in quasi-fascist conversation with the police. . . . (We spoke of mutual friends) You know Forman [SNCC executive secretary James Forman]? Is he up in Danville [Virginia]? . . . (I noticed an officer sitting behind the wheel of his car was going through a pile of 8 × 10 photos. . . . He said a *Birmingham News* man was sending him shots. Maybe I could send shots of Danville leaders to check against those in Gadsden?)

Selma's notorious Sheriff James Clark regularly walked lines of demonstrators, taking pictures of his own and asking blacks if their employers knew what they were doing. As Steven A. Kasher noted in his book, *The Civil Rights Movement: A Photographic History 1954–68:*

> Both Mississippi and Alabama set up "Sovereignty Commissions"—These photographers set out to get "dirt" on the movement and often they did that in the most literal way: pictures of dirty feet and overflowing trash receptacles. They also focused on what they considered another kind of "dirt"—physical contact between whites and blacks.

These archives bring a unique perspective to the movement.

Photography   Perspective

JUNE 28

RICHARD WRIGHT had had it with America—especially because his antiracist agitation and biracial
marriage had him wading increasingly troubled waters.

In 1947, as racism worsened after World War II, Wright
and his family sailed for Paris and the expatriate life. There, in
the intellectual capital of the postwar world, he cosponsored
the cutting-edge journal *Présence Africaine*. Paris in the 1940s
was a haven to Africans and Afri-Caribbeans from the French
colonies, and among Wright's friends were the writers of the
Négritude (see August 20) movement: Aimé Césaire of Mar-
tinique, Léon Damas of French Guiana, and Léopold Senghor
of Senegal—each of whom was an elected representative to the
French National Assembly, each of whom would help lead his
colonized nation to freedom. On a trip to London in 1946, a
year before he settled in Paris, Jamaican activist/scholar and
fellow ex-Communist George Padmore had welcomed Wright
to the English-speaking African and Afri-Caribbean community that had birthed Pan-Africanism in 1899 (see December
6). Embraced by this embarrassment of cultural riches, Wright
knew peace and alienation. And both were soon heightened by
his first trip to Africa. "I'm of African descent and I'm in the
midst of Africans, yet I cannot tell what they are thinking and
feeling," he wrote of his visit to Sierra Leone and the Gold
Coast in June 1953. Then, in Accra, he saw Africans dance:

> I'd seen these same snakelike, veering dances before. . . . Where?
> Oh, God, yes; in America, in storefront churches, in Holy Roller
> Tabernacles . . . in unpainted wooden prayer-meetinghouses on
> the plantations of the Deep South. . . . And here I was seeing it all
> again against a background of a surging nationalistic political
> movement! How could that be? . . . I'd long contended that the
> American Negro . . . had been basically altered [by slavery], that
> his consciousness had been filled with a new content, that
> "racial" qualities were but myths of prejudiced minds. Then, if
> that were true, how could I account for what I now saw? And
> what I now saw was an exact duplicate of what I'd seen for so
> many long years in the United States.

"It isn't much, but it's all we've got." For many, this sentiment best expressed the feeling of resignation that came with passage of the Civil Rights Act in the House by a vote of 289 to 126 on June 29, 1964.

Eight days earlier, the Mississippi Freedom Summer campaign to register black voters was rocked by the now-historic murders of three volunteers (see June 21). Despite this tragedy and a Kennedy administration push to sway the movement away from mass civil disobedience in favor of voter registrations, when the Congress passed the Civil Rights Act in memorium of the recently assassinated President Kennedy, it once again sacrificed the justice due people of color for accommodation to a guilty South. Congress "negotiated" voting rights out of the Civil Rights Act of 1964. In summary, the eleven-title bill:

- barred discrimination in public accommodations and publicly owned facilities
- authorized the federal government to positively reinforce school desegregation to those districts engaged in compliance
- barred discrimination in any federally funded program
- prohibited discrimination by employers or unions with more than one hundred employees; in four years, extended coverage to workplaces with as few as twenty-five employees
- directed the Census Bureau to compile voting statistics by race
- extended the term of the Civil Rights Commission

And while the bill barred registrars from applying different voter registration standards by race, it also allowed states the use of traditionally discriminatory literacy tests. In cases where the law was violated, parties could bring suit. In short, the act preserved the status quo by tying up enforcement of already mandated rights in the courts.

On July 2, 1964, President Lyndon B. Johnson signed the beleaguered, hard-won, albeit watered-down, bill into law. Buried in the bill was its greatest legacy—Title VII: Employment, which opened the door to legislation on "affirmative action."

Law   Pragmatism

JUNE 30

O<small>N</small> J<small>UNE</small> 30, 1936, Emperor Haile Selassie of Ethiopia, direct descendant of the Queen of Sheba, appeared before the League of Nations to request that sanctions be imposed against Italy for its 1935 invasion of Ethiopia.

For the diaspora, Italy's trespass was the desecration of sacred land. As the mid-century neared, time ebbed on the mission foreseen in Dr. W. E. B. Du Bois's prophesy, which had bought the first Pan-African Congress to a close in 1900: "The problem of the twentieth century is the problem of the color line." From the earliest years of Marcus Garvey's movement for a liberated Africa (see August 13), *Ethiopia, Thou Land of Our Fathers* had been its anthem and Garvey's charge its battle cry: "Up you mighty race, you may do what you will!" Italy's violation was the diaspora's wake-up call. As the eminent Kenyan scholar Ali Mazrui noted in his television series and companion book, *The Africans:*

> Were the African spirits especially aroused by the Italian invasion of Ethiopia—the remaining proud symbol of Africa's independence—acquiesced to even by those European nations . . . which halfheartedly applied the League of Nations economic sanctions against the aggressor? Indeed, I and other African political scientists and African historians believe that the Second World War did not begin in 1939 following the violation of the territory of Czechoslovakia and Poland. It began in 1935 following the violation of Ethiopia's sovereignty by Mussolini's Italy. The fact that Mussolini succeeded with his own aggression in Africa whetted the appetites of the Nazi and Fascist dictators nearer home. Once again Africa's Curse of Nemesis might have been at work as Europe's external territorial appetites abroad were mercilessly internalised, turning European against European.

This World War II genesis would also initiate the fight for total African independence and manifest itself in the United States as the Civil Rights movement.

Martin Luther King and his Legions March on Chicago (1967). Courtesy of the photographer.
© Roy Lewis, 1967.

JULY 1

A CHANGE WAS GONNA COME. On July 1, 1964, the long-awaited Civil Rights Act, the first national Civil Rights legislation since 1875, was one day from passage. Rev. George Lee had died for it; so had Medgar Evers, John F. Kennedy, and four girls in Birmingham; and so would many more. Atlanta Congressman Charles Longstreet Weltner took to the floor of the House, stunning his colleagues:

> Mr. Speaker, over four months ago, the Civil Rights bill came to this floor. Its stated purpose, equality of opportunity for all Americans, is a proper goal. But I questioned the means, and voted against passage. Now, after the most thorough and sifting examination in legislative history this measure returns for final consideration . . . with the overwhelming approval of both Houses of Congress. Manifestly, the issue is already decided, and approval is assured. By the time my name is called, votes sufficient for passage will have been recorded. What, then, is the proper course? Is it to vote no, with tradition, safety—and futility? I believe a greater cause can be served. Change, swift and certain, is upon us, and we in the South face some difficult decisions. We can offer resistance and defiance, with their harvest of strife and tumult. We can suffer continued demonstrations, with their wake of violence and disorder. Or, we can acknowledge this measure as . . . the verdict of the Nation. Already, the responsible elements of my community are counseling this latter course. And, most assuredly, moderation, tranquility, and orderly processes combine as a cause greater than conformity.
>
> Mr. Speaker, I shall cast my lot with the leadership of my community. I shall cast my vote with that greater cause they serve. I will add my voice to those who seek reasoned and conciliatory adjustment to a new reality. And finally, I would urge that we at home now move on to the unfinished task of building a new South. We must not remain forever bound to another lost cause.

The act passed in the House the next day by a vote of 289 to 126.

JULY 2

O N JULY 2, 1963, six Civil Rights leaders met at New York's Roosevelt Hotel to plan the March on Washington for Jobs and Freedom (see August 28): A. Philip Randolph, whose call to march in 1941 had desegregated war industries (see June 25); James Farmer of CORE; Martin Luther King of SCLC; John Lewis of SNCC; Roy Wilkins of the NAACP; and Whitney Young of the National Urban League.

With only seven weeks left before the march, a goal of one hundred thousand demonstrators, and a budget of $120,000 to raise, they tapped the best organizer around: Bayard Rustin, who immediately set to work in a small Harlem office. Two weeks later, his *Organizing Manual No. One* was ready, and two thousand copies were distributed to local leaders nationwide. Donations began to come in, and Plan B—"official" buttons— yielded results within three weeks: 175,000 buttons had sold at twenty-five cents each. It was the first indication of how successful the march could become. Another 150,000 buttons were ordered and as quickly sold. Forty thousand "official" march programs, to be sold at one dollar each, were published by the Urban League—the programs contained a portfolio of five photo collages with such images as the Birmingham marchers beset by dogs and fire hoses. All across the country, fish fries and car washes raised money for busloads of people to head to Washington. On August 23, the Friday before the march, the biggest event of all—a celebrity benefit to generate funds and major media publicity—was held in the heart of Harlem at the Apollo. Among its headliners were Tony Bennett, Billy Eckstine, Quincy Jones, Carmen McRae, and Thelonius Monk. And in Paris, a solidarity march was hosted by Josephine Baker, James Baldwin, and Burt Lancaster, who would also lead a delegation to Washington for the march.

This groundswell was not lost on President Kennedy, who argued to put off the march to avoid "offending" the very congressmen whose inaction had provoked the march in the first place. *Pass the Civil Rights Bill!* was the demand. Brooklyn CORE began its 230-mile trek on foot. The march was on.

Organizing   Empowerment

Duke Ellington said it best: "I loved and respected Louis Armstrong. He was born poor, died rich, and never hurt anyone on the way." It took a Duke to define the King of Jazz. And, on July 3, 1970, sixty-seven hundred fans nodded their heads, tapped their feet, and clapped their hands in agreement at a tribute to Louis Armstrong at Hollywood's Shrine Auditorium on the eve of his seventieth birthday.

To those who had come of age in the movement years of the early 1960s, haunted and conflicted by the dapper elder grinning at the *Ed Sullivan Show* camera, handkerchief in hand, Armstrong was strutting off the beat of that revolutionary time. He seemed a minstrel, prancing to his gravel-voiced hit "Hello Dolly," sentimental in his ode to martyrs "Abraham, Martin, and John." What this generation didn't know was the man every knowledgeable black musician called "Pops" in deference not to his age but to his extraordinary abilities with a cornet. Lost was Armstrong's similar prowess as a prolific writer and diarist. As the sound of his incredible "Hot Five" horn and the volumes he had written would attest, Pops had reason to smile. Born into desperate poverty, he'd grown up on the streets of New Orleans scrounging for food. Being sent to the Colored Waifs' Home at thirteen was a step up in his life. There, he began to play the cornet in the orphanage's brass band. With immense talent and little training, he honed an inadvertently innovative style. Released at age sixteen, he hung around the legendary Storyville, and was taken in and groomed by such legendary musical elders as Joe "King" Oliver. And from there his star began its ascent.

As he walked on the covered stage of his birthday tribute, his fans were drenched by rain, and yet they refused to leave the amphitheater. Pops hurried through a medley to spare his guests undue exposure. It put the grin in context. Here was a man who had found his way in out of the rain and knew there were others still on the outside looking to him for joy and relief. Obliging them with everything he had to give, he made things better for a time, and somehow lessened the chill.

JULY 4

JUST TWO DAYS EARLIER, a riot by three thousand mostly white upper middle-class young men had brought the 1960 Newport Jazz Festival to a premature close. Outraged at being left outside a sold-out concert, emboldened by drink and daring, they had rushed the gates of Freebody Park. The National Guard was called up, ferries were turned, the town's main bridge was closed off. The elegant seaside town of Newport was occupied territory.

On July 4, 1960, the riot was over, the music silenced, the musicians gone. Only festival founder George Wein and his fellow organizers remained for the post mortem, among them Langston Hughes. But while his allegiance was with the festival, he was seized by the rebelliousness of the young middle-class rioters. His biographer, Arnold Rampersad, wrote:

> In the vented rage of these young whites he saw what a later leader, Malcolm X, would describe as chickens coming home to roost, the whirligig of American history bringing, at long last, a token of its nearing final revenge. The rioters had been like dry tinder, to which black jazz had been a lighted match. In a city of wealth and elegance built on the stinking cargoes of slave ships, and where Langston in the early days of the festival had more than once endured racist snubs, Africa had returned to haunt Europe. The descendants of masters now danced to the music of the descendants of slaves; American "civilization" had begun, in however modest a degree, a fateful slide toward revolution.

Per Rampersad, Hughes began "the most ambitious single poem of his life, "Ask Your Mama: Twelve Moods for Jazz," on that Independence Day 1960 in Newport's Hotel Viking.

IN THE
IN THE QUARTER
IN THE QUARTER OF THE NEGROES
WHERE THE DOORS ARE DOORS OF PAPER
BLOWS A SCRATCHY SOUND.
AMORPHOUS JACK-O-LANTERNS CAPER
AND THE WIND WON'T WAIT FOR MIDNIGHT
FOR FUN TO BLOW DOORS DOWN

JULY 5

In the 1950s, when a "communist threat" allegedly endangered national security, Congress sustained a political witch-hunt that quashed dissent by abrogating constitutionally guaranteed freedoms of speech and assembly. No matter how just the cause—Civil Rights, labor reform, women in the workplace—dissent was deemed subversive. Powerful voices in government and the private sector discredited advocates of change with rumors of "communist ties" (see June 3). Using fear, deliberate misinformation, and the failure of the press to invoke journalistic codes limiting single-source (unsubstantiated) reportage in favor of the sensational, political terrorism swept the nation. This ever-widening net of intimidation destroyed the lives of thousands of people on the political left. This was the McCarthy Era, named for its leading light, Senator Joseph A. McCarthy. When it finally climaxed in his disgrace, some of its scapegoats still languished in jail as political prisoners. Among them was the activist Henry Winston.

In late June 1961, with mounting international pressure to address rightable wrongs, a newly elected John F. Kennedy expended his presidential powers to free Winston. On July 5, 1961, five days after his release, Henry Winston held a press conference to thank his supporters worldwide.

Poor medical care over nearly five years in prison had left him weakened, totally blind, and absolutely committed to the cause for which he had suffered so long and lost so much. Said Winston, "In prison, I followed with special pride the accounts of the magnificent struggle of my people. I regard the Freedom Riders as heroes of our time who are making a contribution not only to the cause of Negro freedom but of democratic rights for all Americans. I return from prison with the unshaken conviction that the people of our great land, Negro and white, need a Communist Party fighting for the unity of the people for peace, democracy, security, and socialism. I take my place in it again with deep pride. My sight is gone but my vision remains."

JULY 6

It was July 6, 1944, wartime on the homefront, and Jackie Robinson was up at bat. In three years he would make a pact with the devil of racism; he would resist striking back at his tormenters as a strategy in desegregating the Brooklyn Dodgers and major league baseball. But on this day in 1944, as he would for the rest of his life, Jack Roosevelt Robinson made history as a freedom fighter.

A second lieutenant in the army, Robinson boarded a military bus near Fort Hood, Texas, where he was stationed. By military law, army base buses had been desegregated. Yet, as Robinson got on with a light-skinned African American woman friend, the bus driver yelled at him to "get to the back of the bus where the colored people belong." Robinson refused. But knowing his rights and protecting them were two different things. MPs marched him off to the guardhouse. Once there, he protested having a civilian stenographer take down the statement of an officer. When a white private couldn't resist taunting "a nigger," Robinson offered to "break him in two." All agreed, the black college boy was "uppity"—the wrong Negro to mess with. And for that, a fellow officer had him transferred to a unit where no one would object to embroiling Robinson in a retaliative court-martial. Because there was no real wrongdoing on his part, a barrage of charges were trumped up: insubordination, conduct unbecoming an officer, disturbing the peace, being drunk, insulting a civilian, and refusing to obey the lawful orders of a superior—a superior officer, that is.

In court, Robinson was given the highest praise a former commanding officer could give—he said Robinson was a soldier he would want with him in combat. Nine judges concurred and found him not guilty in twenty minutes. But "it was a small victory," said Robinson. "I had learned that I was in two wars, one against a foreign enemy, the other against prejudice at home." To look back on the career of Jackie Robinson is to realize that the baseball diamond was but one of the fields on which he played to win for himself and for the good of others.

Military   Self-respect

GROWING UP IN DECATUR, MISSISSIPPI, Charles Evers and his brother, Medgar, had made a pact: "Whatever happened to one of us, the other would carry on." On June 12, 1963, Medgar Evers, then field secretary of the NAACP, was assassinated, becoming the first martyred leader of the Civil Rights era. Six years later, on July 7, 1969, Charles Evers took an oath in both their names to became mayor of Fayette, Mississippi, the first black mayor in Mississippi since Reconstruction.

With their eyes on the same prize, Medgar was the nonviolent one, not Charles. "I'm no Democrat. I'm no Republican. I'm an Independent and a sonofabitch," Mayor Evers would later admit. "I don't care what [people] say. Most of them don't understand a man willing to die for what he believes in." And what he was willing to die for was family and justice. Having encouraged his brother to take the NAACP job, he too was active and endangered. When a woman with the White Citizens Council roared from a parking lot and deliberately rammed his car, police ticketed *him*. The same woman sued for damages, which a judge assessed at five thousand dollars—and he ordered everything Evers owned seized to satisfy the claim. There was no appeal. No lawyer would take the case; this was Mississippi. Moving his family north, Evers ran out of money in Chicago and that's where he planted. As he began to earn money, some of what he earned went to fund Medgar's NAACP work. After Medgar's murder, he even returned to Mississippi from Chicago and took over the job of NAACP field secretary.

On June 3, 1969, election day, as votes were counted—264 for Turnip Green Allen, the white candidate, and 433 for Evers—the new mayor knew he was a symbol for something much bigger than Fayette. "I knew this day in Mississippi would touch folk all over the nation," he said. "I kept thinking of those who'd died for Civil Rights." On Monday, July 7, 1969, "a scorching hot Mississippi day," his inaugural program featured a black hand and a white hand shaking hands with a message: "Let us go forward together." The time had come.

JULY 8

Just as the paranoia of whites who feared repayment for the sins of slavery was responsible for forcing duly elected blacks from legislatures, ending Reconstruction in the mid-1870s, eighty years later it remained the motivating factor preventing a second Reconstruction from ending segregation. In LeFlore County, Mississippi, blacks outnumbered whites three to two, and the level of threat felt by whites was high. As one white voter told a reporter, "We killed two-month-old Indian babies to take this country, and now they want us to give it away to the niggers." One could almost hear the words of SNCC's Robert Moses reverberate across two stagnant years: "I thought to myself that Southerners are most exposed when they boast." When three white men tailed and shot SNCC volunteer Jimmy Travis in the neck, LeFlore County was exposed big time. In the car with Travis was Moses himself and a white Voter Education Project lawyer, Randolph Blackwell. The press was alerted; Blackwell fired off a telegram to President Kennedy, a campaign to register every qualified Negro in the county was announced, and LeFlore County became the destination of choice for a massive influx of demonstrators. The eyes of the world were cast upon Mississippi.

Among those who came to bolster spirits on July 8, 1963, were folk singers Theodore Bikel and Pete Seeger, who invited a newcomer, Bob Dylan, to perform a song he'd written inspired by the movement, "Blowin' in the Wind."

As the song climbed to the top of the pop charts, the ears of the world were tuned to Mississippi, too.

JULY 9

I<small>T WAS OFFICIAL</small>. After twenty-two years in the Negro Leagues, Satchel Paige was a rookie—with the major league Cleveland Indians, that is. On July 9, 1948, at age forty-two, the most famous Negro Leaguer played his first major league game. He was the world's oldest rookie. And with age comes experience. Paige knew how to make an entrance, and he did. It was his moment. Bringing the crowd at Cleveland's Municipal Stadium to a rousing roar, the lanky 6'4" Satchel Paige slowly strode to the mound. "I didn't go fast," he said. "No reason wearing myself out just walking." And another chapter was added to the legend.

Baseball had taken its time, too. "To sign a hurler at Paige's age is to demean the standards of baseball," fumed *Sporting News*. "Were Satchel white, he would not have drawn a second thought from [Indians owner] Veeck." Veeck's retort: "If Satch were white, he would have been in the majors twenty-five years earlier, and the question would not have been before the house." Jackie Robinson broke the color bar in 1947, but many had expected the legendary Paige to be the first. As he had said, "That was my right. I should have been there. I got those [white] boys thinking about having Negroes in the majors." But that kind of backward glance was uncharacteristic of him. He'd always been a forward-thinker. He'd promote exhibition games by boasting that he'd strike out the first nine batters— and he would. He'd have the outfielders sit behind the mound with the bases loaded because he was about to strike out the next batter. He would. He even walked two of the Negro Leagues' best hitters, planning to strike out one of baseball's greatest ever, regardless of race—Josh Gibson. Paige did that, too. Legends about him were legion; the facts even better. So was his philosophy of life: "Don't look back, something might be gaining on you."

In 1971, when baseball looked back on Paige's career, it was a proud day. He was the first player inducted into the Hall of Fame as a Negro Leaguer. His record in an unprecedented forty-year career: 2,600 games, 300 shutouts, and 55 no-hitters.

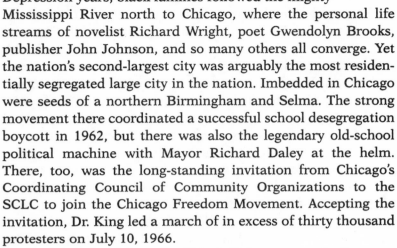
Fleeing the segregated South and the dust bowl Depression years, black families followed the mighty Mississippi River north to Chicago, where the personal life streams of novelist Richard Wright, poet Gwendolyn Brooks, publisher John Johnson, and so many others all converge. Yet the nation's second-largest city was arguably the most residentially segregated large city in the nation. Imbedded in Chicago were seeds of a northern Birmingham and Selma. The strong movement there coordinated a successful school desegregation boycott in 1962, but there was also the legendary old-school political machine with Mayor Richard Daley at the helm. There, too, was the long-standing invitation from Chicago's Coordinating Council of Community Organizations to the SCLC to join the Chicago Freedom Movement. Accepting the invitation, Dr. King led a march of in excess of thirty thousand protesters on July 10, 1966.

To dramatize the needs of black Chicagoans and other people of color, King took inspiration from his medieval namesake, Martin Luther. Just as Luther had posted his "95 Theses" on a church door, this modern-day reformer led his followers to the mayor's office, where they posted "24 Demands" on the door of City Hall.

In *banking*, they demanded that loans be made available to qualified borrowers regardless of race. In *employment*, that unions compile and publish membership and employment statistics by race, job, and salary levels; that there be desegregated job listings; and recruitment of four hundred black and Latino apprentices into the craft unions. Desegregated *housing* and increased unrestricted availability of low-cost units for low- and middle-income families. An end to *police brutality* by creation of a citizens' review board. Finally, just as Martin Luther had criticized the Catholic church for selling its "indulgences," Martin Luther King criticized the city for its system of favoritism and patronage that disfranchised those beyond its scope of indulgence. Finally, they demanded *enforcement of the 1964 Civil Rights Act.*

JULY 11

As THE NAACP CONVENED for its 58th annual meeting on July 11, 1967, it should have been celebrating. NASA had just named Major Robert H. Lawrence Jr. its first black astronaut. Thurgood Marshall, who had led the NAACP Legal Defense Fund to victory in *Brown v. Board of Education* (see May 17), had just been nominated to the Supreme Court—another first. What greater tribute could there be for the nation's oldest Civil Rights organization? But the joy that should have been in the forefront became a mere footnote to the "long hot summer" of 1967 as riots swept the nation: Louisville in April; Jackson in May; Boston, Tampa, Cincinnati, and Buffalo in June; then Atlanta, Baltimore, Cairo, Chicago, Durham, Memphis, Milwaukee, New York, and Washington, D.C.

Why? the nation asked through crocodile tears. In Cambridge, Maryland, SNCC leader H. Rap Brown had allegedly fumed, "The only thing honkies respect is guns." Those words were given more credit for causing a riot than the inhuman living conditions Maryland's own governor blasted as "sick." As city after city erupted with pent-up passion, the same House of Representatives that had been unable to pass a Civil Rights bill in six months within days passed a bill making it a federal crime to cross state lines for the purpose of inciting a riot. Clearly aimed at movement activists, as one white congressman commented, the bill was "neither preventive nor curative"; it was guaranteed to provoke further ire.

In this atmosphere, allies who had so successfully led the March on Washington fell prey to public squabbling. When Dr. King cited cities likely to riot, Roy Wilkins blamed him for trying to "stir up trouble." It was that open door that FBI Director J. Edgar Hoover (see April 6) charged through to condemn King for issuing an "open invitation" to riot. Hoover had cleverly ignored King's true intent—targeting cities in need of remedy, not riot. Racism was equally sacred to the North and the South. The climate would get worse before getting better, as the very next day would prove. Newark, New Jersey, was next. . . .

JULY 12

IT WAS THE SEASON OF OUR DISCONTENT. The nation was aflame with rage. More than a decade of sacrifice had borne legal and political fruit but little change in everyday life—better jobs, income, housing, and schools. In the aftershock of the assassination of Malcolm X, in the quake of Vietnam, people were tired of stacking up empty promises into a great big hill of "not yet." War permeated every facet of life; activists for a new day vowed to "take no prisoners."

There is an old saying, "a thing doesn't necessarily have to happen to be true," and as lives rotted hopelessly in Newark, New Jersey, the thing that didn't happen in fact began with this bit of truth: At 9:45 P.M. on Wednesday, July 12, 1967, police arrested a black cabdriver. The news, inflated by rumor, quickly spread that the driver had been beaten to death in police custody. It was not the first time such things had actually happened. But by the time the driver was found to be alive, the black community had erupted at one last straw on the dung heap of hardship. It was the first major riot since the Watts rebellion of 1965 in Los Angeles. Five days later, when the rage was spent and the area had been secured by the National Guard, twenty-six people were dead, fifteen hundred were wounded, one thousand had been arrested, and property damage totalled in the millions.

Among those arrested was Newark's Amiri Baraka, the poet-playwright. Beaten and held in solitary confinement, Baraka said he knew his fate when Judge Leon W. Kapp told the all-white jury that "the 'boys in blue' (the police, who were the state's principal witnesses against us) 'would never lie.'" The verdict: guilty. Citing Baraka's poem "you can't steal nothin' from a white man, he's already stole it he owes" as "a diabolical prescription to commit murder and to steal and plunder," Kapp sentenced him to three years in prison while others were sentenced to one year. Baraka's real sin: visibility—he was co-convenor of the first Black Power Conference, which had brought a thousand people to Newark one week after the riot. Baraka's conviction and sentence were later overturned.

Revolt!   Truth

O<small>F THE</small> 435 <small>MEMBERS</small> of the House of Representatives in 1971, only twelve were women, one of whom was black—New York's Shirley Chisholm. In the Senate, there was only one white woman. With women a population majority, something had to change. On July 13, 1971, three hundred women gathered in Washington, D.C., to found the National Women's Political Caucus (NWPC). Among those representing African American women were Congresswoman Chisholm, activist (and widow of Medgar Evers) Myrlie Evers, Mississippi crusader Fannie Lou Hamer, National Council of Negro Women president Dorothy Height, and National Welfare Rights Organization vice president Beulah Sanders.

In feminist gatherings as early as the mid-nineteenth century, black and white women had long been divided on the issue of race as most white women opted to hold on to the privileges of "whiteness." Throughout African American history, black men and women were divided on issues related to gender as most black men opted to hold on to the privileges of "maleness." Would anything in this event change these precedents? Boston school board politician Louise Day Hicks had, for years, hostaged that city with her racist opposition to school desegregation. Would the NWPC back her, a woman? A moment of progressive solidarity came when the NWPC told Hicks no, hinging its agenda to human rights.

Taking the conference at its word on women candidates, Congresswoman Shirley Chisholm announced her candidacy for president the following January. The first black woman elected to Congress, now she was the first black woman to run for president. Campaigning on a foreign policy platform that demanded an end to the Vietnam War and an end to the European-American pact thwarting the liberation of peoples of color, she earned surprising grassroots support. Significantly, on July 13, 1972—one year to the date from the founding of the NWPC—when the roll of delegates was called at the Democratic National Convention in Miami Beach, Florida, Chisholm actually won 151 delegate votes!

JULY 14

SOMEWHERE IN THE BADLANDS and bad times of Texas, George McJunkin was born. Papers he later signed when buying a homestead cite 1851 as his birth year, but little more is known. Some say he was slaveborn, others say not. Some say he was from Midland, others say Midway. Some say he lived with blacks, others contradict that. Terrorized by marauding whites too long ago to remember and in a manner still too painful to forget to this very day, few blacks live in the territory where he was thought to have grown up. The world as it was back then did not see the life of a young black man like George worthy of note.

Yet, those who knew him and passed on the details of his later years agree that George McJunkin was a man who could get people talking and sharing. And on July 14, 1971, over a century after his birth, eleven of his admirers did just that. Gathering in Folsom, New Mexico, they shared their latest rediscoveries about the life and lore of an extraordinary man. Then, making a pilgrimage to Wild Horse Arroyo, they visited the ancient site where George McJunkin, an unassuming cowboy, once wandered after a great flood. It was there, in a moment of biblical proportion, that he discovered the bison bones that changed our understanding of the history of the world.

Wandering the arroyo in the late 1890s, McJunkin noticed a crest of thick bones. He was convinced that there was something unusual about his find. He then noticed adjacent spear points that also seemed to be relics. He shared the story of his discovery, and word spread to local archaeologists, who confirmed McJunkin's suspicions. In fact, they exceeded them. Scientifically dating the finds, the archaeologists decoded a story never before told. Earlier archaeological digs had dated the human history of the Americas at four thousand years. But McJunkin's finds proved it extended back at least ten thousand years.

McJunkin, a child the world did not see fit to notice, had become a man who changed the way the world saw itself.

Adventure   Human Spirit

JULY 15, 1963. On this day, as historian Clarence Taylor has noted, fourteen conservative members of New York's black clergy "became revolutionaries." Joining forces with Oliver Leeds, chairman of Brooklyn CORE—at a time when his Congress of Racial Equality chapter was in its heyday as a radical group—the Ministers' Committee for Job Opportunities for Brooklyn took to the streets.

Just blocks from the predominantly black Bedford-Stuyvesant neighborhood, the $25 million Downstate Medical Center construction site had closed out African American and Latino workers. Demanding 25 percent of the jobs, the CORE-led protest turned the site into a battleground over which the issue of fair employment was fought. With congregations to-talling a hundred thousand registered voters, the Ministers' Committee had come armed with the power of numbers.

On Monday, July 15, the fourteen ministers joined other protesters (some of whom were members of their congrega-tions), in picketing the site and agreed to return in two days. As they were about to leave that Monday, a truck approached the gate. Said Leeds in a flash of inspiration, "We can come back Wednesday, but I'm taking this truck today." He sat down, halting the moving truck, and was quickly joined by the minis-ters in singing freedom songs until they were arrested by po-lice. That night, two thousand supporters rallied at Corner-stone Baptist Church, and the Ministers' Committee was formed. For the next twenty-two days civil disobedience dis-rupted the site. On July 23, women with signs reading END WHITE SUPREMACY! JOIN CORE! FREEDOM NOW! sat in, falling limp as policewomen struggled to carry them off to jail. On July 25, demonstrators chained themselves together, forcing police to cut them apart with wire clippers. Each day brought a new tactic. It also brought an increase in violence by people insufficiently committed to nonviolence. In the end, the fight for jobs was not successful, but it was a beginning. Lessons learned strengthened future campaigns.

JULY 16

ON JULY 16, 1970, the Folklore Institute of Indiana University hosted the Conference on African Folklore. It was an important sign of the times. Beyond "relating" to Africa, people now wanted to "know" Africa.

With knowledge of historical African folklore would come revelations from African American culture. To people who had been indoctrinated to believe that they (alone among all the people of the world) "had no culture"; to people who had not only lost touch with home but lost sight of it as well; to people who no longer even knew where home was—East Africa or West, mid-northern Igbo or southern Zulu—what a transformation this discovery was about to unleash. In *nommo*, the word, was proof of vast cultural retentions traceable in the imprint of the distinctively African (and African diasporan) talking animal tales. Decoding the connective tissue of content and metaphor, Brer Rabbit and Ananci traced their roots of ancestry to the moralistic animal fables of Aesop, one of the world's greatest and most enduring philosopher/teachers. The knowledge became ours that *Aesop*—alternately spelled *Esop, Ethiop* (as in *Ethiopia*), and *Aethiop*—means "African." And there was more. Black South Carolinian rice baskets were found in West Africa. Shotgun house architecture had a new pedigree.

"Your mother won't know you, child, if I change your name . . ." African Americans had mourned in the Spirituals. *Nobody Knows My Name*, James Baldwin had written, entitling a book of essays and empowering a quest. And those who had so long sung "Let the circle be unbroken" as more dirge than revelry now got their wish. In an ever-expanding circle of knowledge, African Americans reunited with loved ones much alive on that other shore. And the truths regained in folklore would be amplified by such contemporary voices as Nigerian novelist Chinua Achebe. As a faculty member at the University of Massachusetts in Amherst, he would soon launch *OKIKE: The African Journal of New Writing*.

To HEAR GULLAH SPOKEN is to retrace the odyssey of Africans bound for slavery across linguistic streams. To hear its retained blend of ancient African languages and West Indian patois, along with English words known to have become extinct at least two hundred years ago, is to witness the "ties that bind." In the 1930s and 1940s, the noted linguist Lorenzo Dow Turner, a faculty member of Fisk University, traveled the southern states and Africa, sifting African American dialects for their ancient African essences. His work—and that of the Avery Research Center for African-American History and Culture in Charleston, South Carolina—is considered most responsible for Gullah scholarship and documentation.

In July 1949, Turner met Diana Brown, a black woman born and raised on Edisto Island in South Carolina. In her use of language was the voice of her ancestors preserved. Turner transcribed the prayer she raised, "I Ask You, Jesus, to Take Care of Me."

> Oh, God, I have a chance for another July meet me here. I stagger up and down hills and mountains; but I ask you, Jesus, to take care of me and want you, Master, to be to the head and one be to the foot for the last morning. Oh! stand to the bedside, oh, God! this morning. And Lord, when you see Diana done knock from side to side on Edisto—no mother, no father, no brother, no sister—I ask you, Jesus, to be me mother and be me father for the last morning. Oh, God! stand to me as my hair to my head, because you is the only one I can look upon if I call you. And you is me mother; you is me father; you is all and all I got to depend upon. Oh, God! and take charge of me once more time—on the road, out in the field, up to the fireside; Oh, God! to the well. And I ask you, Jesus, oh, God! be with me once more time; so when I come down to Jordan, oh, Lord, I want to cross over Jordan for meself and not for another.

> Oh, God! this evening, Lord, I didn't expect to be on this side till now; but you is—you is a good captain. You hold to the helm. Oh! I ask you, Lord, when you see me done knock about on Edisto from church to church, from class to class, oh, God! let me die with me right mind, for meself and not for another.

Prayer   Authenticity

JULY 18

I<small>T WAS THE SUMMER OF</small> 1956, and actor-author Julian Mayfield was writing his book, *The Hit*, and capturing cherished street scenes of a vanishing New York:

Noon eased itself into the Manhattan streets. The sun hung high over Harlem, and its heat was heavy as a white cloak over the flat roofs and the gray streets. Children sought the coolness of dark basements and dark hallways. The old people sat near their windows and looked with indifference out onto the shimmering streets. Behind the lunch counters brown girls and yellow girls, irritated by the heat and their own perspiration, grouchily served up frankfurters with sauerkraut, hot sausages with mustard and relish and onion, milk shakes, malteds, coffee, and orange juice; served these to impatient clerks and laborers and helpers' helpers, to shoppers, policemen, and hack drivers. Preachers napped and dreamed of churches larger than the Abyssinian. Lawyers and petty real-estate brokers planned and schemed and gamblers figured. A con man dropped a wallet with a hundred-dollar bill in it to the sidewalk in front of the Corn Exchange Bank and waited for a sucker to fall for the age-old game. A hustler sat in her apartment on Sugar Hill sipping cocktails with a white merchant from downtown who was taking a long weekend, sized him up, estimated his worth. Madam Lawson shuffled her cards, Madam Fatima stared into her silver crystal ball, and turbaned Abdul Ben Said of the ebony skin mumbled an incantation to the black gods of old, and lo! all of them saw glory in the morning if not sooner. There, near the top of Manhattan Island, Harlem sizzled and baked and groaned and rekindled its dream under the midday sun.

In 1962, the "New Frontier" was more than a Kennedy era slogan, it was a common ground yet to be reached by African Americans and the white press. In its then-fifty-four-year history, the National Press Club had prided itself on bringing together newsmakers and the press away from the pressure of breaking news. Yet, the first black reporter was not admitted until 1955. And no African American had ever been invited to speak. That changed on July 19, 1962, with the appearance of Dr. Martin Luther King Jr. as the National Press Club's first African American speaker. So momentous an occasion was it for the club that the exact time of his arrival into the hall was recorded for posterity: 12:35 P.M.

It is logical that an American institution would be infused with the same racism that permeates the rest of society, but it is odd that the press was not more enlightened. This was 1962—the heyday of the Civil Rights era. This was the same press that fed daily coverage on movement progress—or did it? Even in the independent northern press, racism seemed responsible for coverage that jumped from crisis to crisis without context or a sinew of understanding. In his 1997 documentary, *Walter Cronkite Remembers*, the veteran journalist recalled how a local sheriff would pick up some poor black man, beat a "confession" out of him, and call the crime solved. Reporters knew better but looked the other way in their own best interests. Well into the movement, the press still went along with local officials. Only when the blood flowed in front of their eyes did many begin to appreciate the black point of view.

At the press club, Dr. King was greeted with endless ovations. Breaking the color bar was news and history. As Taylor Branch wrote in *Parting the Waters*, "They were proud, too, to sponsor such lofty oratory. This was King's ironic trap up close: he could bring inspiration even to the National Press Club, but he could force his movement into the news columns only by bloodshed or political miracle."

JULY 20

WITH THE ADVENT of World War II, critical battles in the war on racial injustice had been delayed. In 1949, still denied the rights they had helped secure for others, African Americans renewed the crusade just as an amorphous "communist threat" erupted into the Cold War. Once again thwarted, black people whose ancestors had begun the movement 250 years before communism was even imagined, now faced the historically impossible charge that their 350-year-old movement had been "communist-inspired."

For his outspoken views on world peace and freedom, Paul Robeson, son of an ex-slave, had been charged with disloyalty to the United States, had had his passport revoked (see May 9), and had been nearly lynched at Peekskill (see September 4). For the noted actor and Columbia University Law School graduate, the time had come to accuse the accusers. On July 20, 1949, he issued a press release:

> Quite clearly America faces a crisis in race relations. The Un-American Activities Committee moves now to transform the government's Cold War policy against the Negro people into a hot war. Its action incites the Ku Klux Klan, that . . . terrorist organization, to a reign of mob violence against my people. . . . This committee attempts to divide the Negro people one from another in order to prevent us from winning jobs, security, and justice. . . .
>
> The loyalty of the Negro people is not a subject for debate. I challenge the loyalty of the [committee]. Every prowar fascist-minded group in the country regards the committee's silence [on the lynchings of Maceo Snipes and others] as license to proceed against my people, unchecked by government authorities and unchallenged by the courts. Our fight [is] for human dignity . . . for constitutional liberties, the civil and human rights of every American. No country in the world today threatens the peace and safety of our great land. It is not the Soviet Union that threatens the life, liberty, and the property and citizenship rights of Negro Americans. The threat comes from within. I shall not be drawn into any conflict dividing me from my brother victims of this terror. I am wholly committed to the struggle for peace and democratic rights of free Americans.

Politics   Principles

JULY 21

O N July 21, 1965—and every Wednesday in July and August of 1964 and 1965—a small devout group of women, black and white, would leave relatively comfortable lives in Baltimore, Boston, Chicago, New York, Minneapolis, and Washington, D.C., to fly to Jackson, Mississippi. This unlikely mission was called "Wednesdays in Mississippi."

The idea had actually been germinating for a while in the mind of Polly Cowan—a true doer, heir to the Spiegel catalog fortune, married to the future president of CBS, whose sons were Freedom Summer volunteers like the martyred Chaney, Goodman, and Schwerner (see June 21). Cowan and NCNW (National Council of Negro Women) president Dorothy Height had gone to Selma, Alabama, in October 1963 to investigate the treatment of women and children in Civil Rights movement protests. From that reconnaissance mission, Cowan came up with the idea of sending women into the South as observers and supporters of those in the trenches. Six months later, Height invited women activists from eight southern cities to Atlanta. There, she provided a forum in which they could voice their concerns and define the scope of the support they would find most helpful. At that meeting, an unnamed woman from Jackson, Mississippi, suggested that other women could provide a "ministry of presence." From that idea, "Wednesdays in Mississippi" was launched that summer—bringing together women of diverse backgrounds in a common concern for the welfare of children.

Each "Wednesday" was a compact effort that began with travel on Tuesday night, a Wednesday visit to a Freedom School or similarly relevant site, and a Thursday morning return. The effort supported demonstrators and Freedom Summer volunteers, and carried news back to cities across the country—not as "objective" news, but as real life should be, experienced and savored firsthand. After these Wednesdays, no one who participated ever saw life in quite the same way again.

JULY 22

IN THE REVOLT-RIDDEN SUMMER OF 1967, the Detroit riot began at 3:45 A.M. on July 22 when police raided a "blind pig" (after-hours club) and arrested eighty-two people at a private party for a group of black soldiers returning from Vietnam. The riot lasted three days and was extremely costly in lives and hope. Five days after the Detroit riot began, President Lyndon Johnson appointed a panel headed by Illinois Governor Otto Kerner to "investigate the origins of the recent disorders in our cities." Johnson addressed the nation via radio and TV that same night. "All of us know what [conditions breed despair and violence]: discrimination . . . not enough jobs," Johnson said. "We should attack these conditions—not because we are frightened by conflict, but because we are fired by conscience. We should attack them because there is simply no other way to achieve a decent and orderly society."

Johnson knew the right thing to say. But in his frankness was the deeper pain. Everyone *did* know the problem. Why study the obvious and further delay real action? Within weeks the Kerner Commission, as it became known, released its earliest findings: one way to control a riot was to control and properly train the police and the National Guard. A second way was to report riots accurately. Of the 164 disorders, only 41 were notable. The rest, they concluded, were not worth notice. But wasn't that the problem? Quiet protest was not worth notice; a major riot had to happen first.

"Let your search be free," wrote the president in his commission to the bipartisan panel of nine whites and two blacks—NAACP Executive Director Roy Wilkins and the North's first black senator, Edward W. Brooke of Massachusetts. "As best you can, find the truth and express it in your reports. . . . This matter is far, far too important for politics." Yet while police were never called "antiblack," black activists were called "antiwhite"; Newark's Spirit House, a cultural center, was called a "gathering place for . . . militants of every hue." Clearly, politics had played a part. For deeper understanding, so-called militants should have played a part as well.

JULY 23

BY THE SUMMER OF 1962, seven months after the Albany Movement began, an endless round of protests had failed to dislodge segregation. Yet, for overcoming fear, organizing, and mobilizing people to action, the movement was a success. So effective was its boycott of white businesses that local merchants begged Police Chief Pritchett for relief. As testimony, no movement boast could do better than this letter, dated July 23, 1962, by shop owner Leonard Gilberg:

> At least 90 to 95% of all the negro business I have enjoyed in the past years has been lacking for the last 7 months due to an obvious boycott on the part of the negroes. . . .
>
> Now . . . their constant harassment, sit-ins, demonstrations, marching, etc. are keeping all people . . . from Albany. Our business is at present suffering an approximate 50% decrease due to lack of customer traffic in Albany and it is an intolerable situation. This fear of mob violence and demonstration has made our situation a dire one.

With every jail in a fifteen-mile radius filled, a judge issued a restraining order on marches. In defiance, Reverend Samuel "Benny" Wells vowed to march anyway. "I see Dr. King's name," he said, waving the court order in the air. "But I don't see Samuel Wells and I don't see Miss Sue Samples. . . . Where are those names?" he roared, leading 160 people out of Shiloh Baptist Church that very night. But two days later, the unthinkable happened: Marian King, the pregnant wife of movement vice president Slater King, was taking food to jailed marchers. When she didn't move fast enough to satisfy a guard, he kicked and beat her so badly that she later miscarried. An appeals court lifted the order, but was too little too late for the two thousand people who claimed the streets. For the first time they violated the pledge of nonviolence, throwing stones and bottles at police, who backed off in surprise. In calling for a "Day of Penance," Dr. King diffused the situation with a move that clearly saved lives.

JULY 24

FIGURATIVELY SPEAKING, it had been just days since the death of Stepin Fetchit. Yet, as the *New York Times* opined on July 24, 1968, his resurrection could be dangerously imminent. Where American history and its on-screen imagery were concerned, blacks had certainly been given a heavy cross to bear. And one of the heaviest crosses was the character known as Stepin Fetchit (actor Lincoln Perry's alter ego). "Stepin Fetchit Calls His Film Image Progressive" was the article's headline. But if the grinning, shuffling, eye-bucking Fetchit was as "progressive" as Perry would have readers believe, what did he progress us to?

The 1930s reign of Fetchit and his colleague Sleep 'n' Eat was symptomatic of black stereotypes throughout the entertainment industry. No mere matter of economics, this was propaganda. In the 1920s, the buy-out of black "race record" companies and blues queen Bessie Smith's contract saved the record industry. Yet, Hollywood refused to equate honest black portrayals with profitability. This was the era when Hollywood owned the pictures and the screens on which they played. In sheer size and clout, black and white producers of quality alternative films for African American audiences could not compete with the Hollywood machine. Instead, Hollywood offered Stepin Fetchit—and he was funny. But he was a joke that wore very thin as blacks tried to shake the yoke of segregation.

To his credit, Lincoln Perry was clear on who he was as an actor. Stretching the truth and the length of his on-screen performance in the process, he told directors he couldn't read. They told him to improvise. With pragmatic genius, he improvised a character who thought, scratched, and moved so s-l-o-o-o-w-l-y that he quickly rallied box office profits. Perry knew how to take a joke, and he took it all the way to the bank. Sadly, he was often mistaken for his character. So were other blacks. In the context of his time and ours, Perry's creative visions on-screen and off are no laughing matter—especially when one considers the stereotypes that masquerade as African American life and humor to this very day.

Film   Self-portraiture

JULY 25

Twenty years after the Supreme Court ordered public schools desegregated in *Brown v. Board of Education*, it reversed itself on a plan that would have done just that. In a 5-to-4 split, the Court defeated the "Detroit case" on July 25, 1974.

The desegregation battlefront had pushed north. In 1971, Federal Judge Stephen Roth approved a Detroit Metropolitan school plan that linked the majority-black urban Detroit hub with its majority-white suburban rim. In all, fifty-four school districts and 780,000 students would be affected. With that scope, the Detroit case became a symbol in every area where white families had fled from city to suburb to avoid integrated schools. In 1972, the Nixon administration proposed outlawing busing for the purpose of racial integration. In a rare response, ninety-five Justice Department lawyers publicly opposed the White House. But the Supreme Court said no to the Detroit plan. Michigan Governor William Milliken called the move a "victory for reason." Supreme Court Justice Burger stated that "no single tradition in public education is more deeply rooted than local control over the operation of schools." Yet, clearly there was a flaw in this reasoning. Didn't most parents prefer to send their children to private school if they could afford it? And didn't most private school students leave their localities? Didn't most suburban and rural students ride school buses? The issue was race—not neighborhoods, not buses, not even education.

Into the fray stepped Nathaniel B. Jones, the NAACP's chief legal counsel, and Dr. Kenneth B. Clark, the sociologist whose 1940s "dolls study" demonstrating the negative effects of segregation on black children had been pivotal in deciding *Brown*. They argued that the Detroit decision did not license districts to "evade the constitutional requirement that schools be desegregated." But the damage had been done. Those who saw busing as a means to offer a greater range of programs proposed a new concept: "magnet" schools designed to attract children with unique offerings and thus overcome race as an issue.

JULY 26

On July 26, 1968, Americans met four new families: the Lords, Philadelphia Main Line and terribly rich; the Woleks, second-generation immigrants not doing too well; the Siegals, Jewish; and the Grays, the first African Americans ever on a daytime drama. In short, these were the families with *One Life to Live.*

Very early into the cliffhangers, it was disclosed that the Grays had a difficult past. Sadie Gray had lost her daughter. It was a terrible tragedy. *Stay tuned.* Then Carla Benari, an "exotic" and "glamorous" actress "in the throes of a nervous breakdown," turned up at Llanview Hospital, where poor dear Sadie worked. As related by Carla's alter ego and real-life actress/embodiment, Ellen Holly, in her autobiography, *One Life,* it was rumored that Carla's "mental fragility was caused by the burden of carried secrets." Her finances were shaky, she lived in a run-down apartment "customarily rented out to chorus gypsies from touring road companies," and exactly what was bothering her and why she came to Llanview remained a mystery. But Carla's glamour and "emotional neediness" soon made her irresistible to two doctors. *Stay tuned for weeks on end.* Marrying one doctor wasn't good enough for Carla Benari. (Nooooo) She had to fall in love with the other doctor, too, a black man—(Yesssss)—and kiss him on national television (the hussy). And as she confessed her love for him . . . switchboards at ABC affiliates across the country lit up. *Cut to commercial.* The main New York switchboard was jammed, as Holly would learn, "flooded with calls from irate white men defending Carla's . . . Caucasian virtue." And then, before sponsors had time to cancel, Sadie came on camera. "Clara!" she said. "Mama!" Carla gasped. No wonder the girl was a mess. Carla Benari was Sadie Gray's lost daughter, back from the "dead" of passing for white. This is what it took to get blacks on daytime TV.

Two more years would go by before Flip Wilson premiered his prime time variety show on September 17, 1970—a first since Nat King Cole's show in the 1950s.

JULY 27

O<small>N</small> J<small>ULY</small> 27, 1972, news of the now-infamous "Tuskegee Study of Untreated Syphilis in Negro Males" began to spread worldwide. For forty years, 1932 to 1972, the U.S. Public Health Service and local agencies denied over four hundred unsuspecting black men treatment readily available when the study began that would have cured the disease and stemmed its spread. Condemnation had raged over Nazi experiments on human subjects during World War II; the 1964 Helsinki Declaration noted that the U.S. was behind other nations in protections against human experimentation; provisions on informed consent were even endorsed by American agencies. Still nothing rescued the Tuskegee men.

The story of the Tuskegee experiment is the best argument for knowing one's history. In 1923, nine years before the study began, Dr. W. E. B. Du Bois had written an indictment of the facility, titled "The Tuskegee Hospital," which he published in *The Crisis*. The article criticized staffing the hospital with all-white doctors and nurses attended by "colored nurse-maids for each white nurse, in order to save them from contact with colored patients"! While early documents indicate that a black nurse was added and that the study was approved by Dr. R. R. Moton (Booker T. Washington's longtime aide), Du Bois's piece shows that Moton was more front than director. A white doctor was appointed superintendent and was sent to Tuskegee before Moton was even notified, and over his objections. Moton protested to the president and then needed armed guards around his home. "The only interest of white people in Alabama in this hospital is economic and racial," Du Bois wrote. "They want to draw the government salaries. . . . The contract for burying soldiers was given to a white undertaker from Greenville, South Carolina, before the bids of local colored undertakers had a chance even to be submitted. . . . Any Negro in such a hospital under southern white men and women of the type who are now fighting like beasts to control it, *would be a subject of torture and murder* rather than of restoration of health." [Italics added.]

Health   **Truth**

JULY 28

IN THE 1980s, when unregistered voters were asked what had finally inspired them to register, many pointed to Jesse Jackson's presidential campaigns—at last there was someone to vote *for* instead of two to vote against, they said. But when that same question was posed in the 1970s, memory would clock back to the pride felt as Representative Barbara Jordan of Texas held television audiences spellbound with her inspired analysis of the Constitution and the Watergate-related charges against President Richard Nixon during impeachment hearings. For two days, in order of seniority, each House Judiciary Committee member made an opening statement. Fate slated Barbara Jordan, whom many considered the committee's most accomplished lawyer, for the 9:00 P.M. prime-time slot on July 25, 1974:

> "We the people"—it is a very eloquent beginning. But when the Constitution of the United States was completed on the seventeenth of September in 1787, I was not included in that "We the people." I felt for many years that somehow George Washington and Alexander Hamilton just left me out by mistake. But through the process of amendment, interpretation, and court decision, I have finally been included in "We the people." Today I am an inquisitor. . . . My faith in the Constitution is whole. I am not going to sit here and be an idle spectator to the diminution, the subversion, the destruction of the Constitution. . . . The subjects of its jurisdiction are those offenses which proceed from the misconduct of public men, and that's what we're talking about. If the impeachment provision in the Constitution of the United States will not reach the offenses charged here, then perhaps the eighteenth-century Constitution should be abandoned to a twentieth-century paper shredder.

On Sunday, July 28, days after Jordan's historic speech, the first article of impeachment was front-page news and the Supreme Court blow to school integration (see July 25) was the top black issue. But the most talked about, prayed about, person was Congresswoman Jordan as people just beamed at "how she made us proud."

"OUR POLITICAL INDEPENDENCE is meaningless," warned Ghana's President Kwame Nkrumah, "unless we use it so as to obtain economic and financial self-government and independence." On July 29, 1957, four months after political independence, this new nation opened the Bank of Ghana.

In colonial times, Ghana had been known as "the Gold Coast" for its primary asset. For a view of precolonial Africa, an account by Arab geographer Al-Bakri of his visit to the palace of Ghana's eleventh-century king, Tenkamenin, proves the point: "When he gives audience to his people . . . he sits in a pavilion around which stand his horses caparisoned in cloth of gold; behind him stand ten pages holding shields and gold-mounted swords; and on his right hand are the sons of the princes of his empire . . . with gold plaited into their hair." Nine centuries later, plundered and poorer but free to chart her own course as a nation, Ghanians had championed freedom by putting aside as public savings and reserves, money which might otherwise have been spent privately. The Bank of England had helped set up the new bank, but let no one doubt its independence. Nkrumah was clear, "We intend our bank to be just what its name says, THE BANK OF GHANA," and Ghana would now attract foreign investors:

> In the early days of the development of any country . . . local savings were largely invested in government funds of the imperial power and in foreign enterprises. But I believe the time has come when it is as safe for the investor to invest in a harbor on the coast of Ghana as it was for him, twenty or thirty years ago, to invest in the docks of Liverpool or London. . . .

Within four months, Ghana's flag was raised on its seaworthy merchant ship, the *S. S. Volta River,* the first of its national shipping fleet—the Black Star Shipping Line. With that name, Ghana honored Marcus Garvey, the Caribbean-born "Back-to-Africa" nationalist whose plans for black economic empowerment had been anchored in the original Black Star Line of the 1920s (see August 13).

JULY 30

O<small>N</small> J<small>ULY</small> 30, 1976, Trinity AME Church—a modest brick building of undistinguished architecture— became an official National Historic Landmark. The church is located in Salt Lake City, Utah, where the Mormon religion is America's closest thing to a "state religion," so it is the very un- likelihood of the church's existence that made it so special. Trinity represents the spirit of a century of African Americans who nurtured it from the ground up and found in it a sanctu- ary and a sense of community.

Some of the whites who journeyed west in the mid-1800s to pioneer a Mormon community freed their slaves, but others kept blacks in bondage as a financial asset. One Mississippi group, for example, arrived in Utah territory as a party of fifty- seven whites and thirty-four enslaved blacks. Following Eman- cipation, the area remained home to many black families. But only one black man, Elijah Abel, was ever ordained a Mormon priest. With his death in 1884 came a total barring of blacks from the church hierarchy—a ban held into the late 1970s as Mormons declared the teachings of their faith to be based on a "revelation." Blacks, they said, "were not yet to receive the priest- hood [although] sometime in God's eternal plan, the Negro will be given the right to hold the priesthood."

With this history, it is significant that Trinity AME Church, the first black congregation in Utah, was founded just after Abel's death, meeting first in homes. The economic boom of the late 1880s brought the Gilded Age and construction on a building all their own in 1891—an event so notable that the territorial governor laid the ceremonial cornerstone. Sadly, the congregation ran out of money in the recession of the 1890s and was forced to abandon the unfinished church. Finally, in 1907, a generous donation by Mary Bright endowed the com- pletion of the existing structure. An ex-slave, Bright had made a fortune working as a cook and "restauranteur" in a Leadville, Colorado, mining camp. Hers was truly food for the soul.

W<small>HEN THE</small> Honorable Elijah Muhammad, spiritual leader of the Nation of Islam, ascended the podium at Harlem's 369th Armory before an overflow crowd on July 31, 1960, the energy in the hall was electric. Harlem Mosque #7 leader and national spokesman Malcolm X had publicized the event well. But the press had hyped it with such passion that it was difficult to tell who was a threat to whom. The top priority became safety for all those who braved the scene. William DeFossett, a policeman, recalled the Fruit of Islam's security procedures: "The armory must have had close to ten thousand people. And everyone that came in was searched. Male and female. Very efficiently and very quickly. If you had a nail file, they took it off you. When you came back out, you got your nail file. That armory, that afternoon, was one of the safest places in the world."

Of course, there was "danger" in those days of the late 1950s and early 1960s. As Alice Windom, who'd met Malcolm X in Africa, recalled "Suddenly those of us . . . who had grown up on Tarzan movies and all the degradation of African people were seeing these marvelous people coming into the United Nations . . . hearing speeches being made in perfect English that were striking home at what needed to be done for Africa to resume its rightful place in the world. And we realized that we had been lied to." And so, in this presidential election year, not only had Minister Muhammad come to address the lie, he had come to propose a plan. "When one group argues among themselves as to whether another group deserves basic Civil Rights, this is hypocrisy," said the Minister in his two-hour speech. "I am not asking you to choose me as your leader, but you need to choose a man who is unafraid to speak out the truth." His plan resurrected the promise made to blacks at the end of the Civil War by General Sherman's Field Order No. 15. That 1865 document set aside a tract of coastal land from South Carolina to Florida in order to provide "forty acres of tillable land" for each family formerly enslaved. All Elijah Muhammad wanted, he said, was a state of our own.

AUGUST ◈

Renaming the Park (1967). Courtesy of the
photographer. © Roy Lewis, 1967.

AUGUST 1

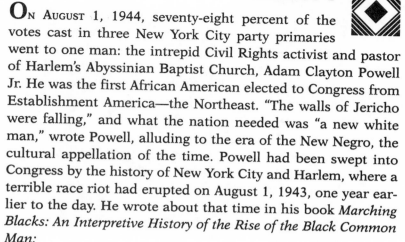

On August 1, 1944, seventy-eight percent of the votes cast in three New York City party primaries went to one man: the intrepid Civil Rights activist and pastor of Harlem's Abyssinian Baptist Church, Adam Clayton Powell Jr. He was the first African American elected to Congress from Establishment America—the Northeast. "The walls of Jericho were falling," and what the nation needed was "a new white man," wrote Powell, alluding to the era of the New Negro, the cultural appellation of the time. Powell had been swept into Congress by the history of New York City and Harlem, where a terrible race riot had erupted on August 1, 1943, one year earlier to the day. He wrote about that time in his book *Marching Blacks: An Interpretive History of the Rise of the Black Common Man:*

> America is in the midst of Civil War II. It began on December 7, 1941 [see December 7]. . . . When World War II broke out fifteen million black Americans found themselves politically disinherited . . . and confronted with the deepest hypocrisy in the field of religion. . . . Yet there at that most tragic hour when . . . Judas within the temple was selling him for thirty pieces, when the crutches upon which he had hobbled for seventy-five years of mythical freedom were taken away from him, there in that terrible hour of complete loneliness, abject poverty and black misery, the New Negro was born. For the first time since blacks were brought in chains to America they learned as a group to move under their own power. They found that it is better for a man to crawl than to walk on crutches provided for him by others. If he crawls, one day he will stand and walk.

Powell's mention of the chains left behind serves to remind us that on August 1, 1619, the first known black "indentures" had just left the African coast for the Middle Passage—a journey that would continue to consume African lives from that day through 1865 and survive in a legacy, mournful and magnificent, to this very day. May our consciousness of all that has gone before us swell into a national Day of Remembrance to honor those lives sacrificed to slavery.

AUGUST 2

W<small>HEN THE ROLL IS CALLED</small> of the most courageous people of the Civil Rights era, the name of Reverend George Wesley Lee will surely be on the list. Rev. Lee wasn't well-known—except, that is, in the tiny town of Belzoni, Mississippi. But to those who feared the potential of eleven million unregistered black voters, he was a symbol—a man of powerful influence—and they murdered him for it.

On May 6, 1955—a year after the Supreme Court had ruled that segregated schools were unconstitutional; two months before the lynching of a fourteen-year-old child, Emmett Till; and six months before Rosa Parks's courageous refusal to move to the back of a Montgomery bus ignited the year-long boycott that ended segregated buses—Rev. Lee voiced his intention to vote. As SCLC's Rev. Dr. Ralph Abernathy remembered him, Rev. Lee was a "stalwart hero who could barely read or write." But he knew that nothing would change unless those who had been wronged set things right. "If God gives me grace and I'm living on the second day of August, I'm going to march boldly to the courthouse and register," said Rev. Lee. The next day, a shotgun blast ripped off the left side of his face. No one was ever charged or convicted of his murder.

While we know the name of Rev. Lee, we know little more about him. In that, he is symbolic of the many African Americans claimed in the battle for human and Civil Rights. To remember him is to honor other black crusaders who were regularly kidnapped or who "disappeared." It is worth noting the 1964 FBI search for three well-publicized Civil Rights volunteers—Chaney, Goodman, and Schwerner, two of whom were white northerners. Dredging up rivers and old wounds, agents recovered the bodies of other black murder victims. But agents threw them back. Those unsung and unsought bodies remain buried along with centuries of guilt. On this memorial day for Rev. Lee—August 2, the day others registered in 1955 in his honor—we remember the nameless foot soldiers of the struggle who gave their lives to bring conscience and dignity to a careless world.

AUGUST 3

In the summer of 1936, Eslanda Goode Robeson fulfilled a lifelong dream to visit Africa—her "old country," as an African American. The granddaughter of a pioneering educator of former slaves, she had been "brought up in a household wide awake to every phase of the Negro problem in America." With a Columbia University degree in chemistry, she was richly educated for her breakthrough as a black woman in medical research. But, while visiting Europe with her husband, Paul Robeson, she was "startled" to find how censored her view of Africa had been in America. "In England, on the other hand, there is news of Africa everywhere." Living in Europe while her husband worked in film, she earned a degree in African anthropology from the London School of Economics, took the trip of a lifetime—three months touring South Africa, Swaziland, Basutoland, Uganda, and the Congo—and later published her travel diary as a photoessay. It is excerpted here:

Uganda, August 3, 1936: Spent the morning at the palace with Mukama (the King). . . . When he brought out the coronation robes for me to see I looked at them so longingly he laughed and said I could photograph [them]. Finally Mukama put on his robes and sat on the throne for me. He was terrific. He explained the tradition of coronation:

When a king dies the royal drum is turned upside down and remains so until the new king turns it right side up again. At three o'clock the morning of his coronation [he] went to the palace. There . . . a ceremonial fight took place. Defeating the guards, he took the royal drum and beat it, proclaiming himself Mukama. The people then gathered and saluted him the customary way: *"Zona Okale!"* ("Hail to the King!"). At nine o'clock the coronation procession went to Fort Portal, where all the people of Toro had gathered. Mukama then returned to the palace, where he put on his Crown-and-Beard and made the ceremonial walk to the Coronation House, a beautiful hut on an eminence in the palace grounds. He walked all the way on a handsomely woven grass matting through special gates to the hut, and was accompanied by young men of noble birth who shouted praise words *(okuswagura)* as they walked.

Adventure   Tradition

AUGUST 4

ON SUNDAYS IN SAVANNAH, you would find Reverend Dr. Ralph Mark Gilbert in the pulpit of First African Baptist Church. But on Mondays, you could tune out worldly worries and tune in to WTOC for Dr. Gilbert's radio ministry: "The Negro at Church." His weekly program was a regular feature of Georgia's Savannah Broadcasting Company. Dr. Gilbert took to the air on Monday, August 4, 1941. "Every once in a while, in this waste howling wilderness, we come to a spot that we call 'The Sweet Hour of Prayer,'" Dr. Gilbert would say. "Without God, this world indeed would be a desert place without an oasis."

For radio listeners, that station and precious few others nationwide brought the waters of cultural relevance to thirsting black souls. The first black radio show had logged on the air at 5:00 P.M. on November 3, 1929, when vaudeville's Jack L. Cooper pioneered and hosted "The All-Negro Hour" on Chicago's white-owned WSBC. But it was not until 1949 that the first black-owned station, Atlanta's WERD, went on the air. With a minimum $15 to $20 million required in start-up costs and limited access to FCC licenses, black-operated stations have long been white-owned and -programmed. But along the way, milestones have been set by those who broke through, giving on-air time and voice to the Civil Rights era. In 1961, Chicago's WGRT was acquired and operated by *Ebony* founder, John H. Johnson; 1973 saw the formation of the National Black Network, with sixty affiliate stations.

Black radio was not only ownership, it was also innovation. Perhaps the most lasting was that of "dialogue jockey" Leon Lewis, who brought talk to radio at New York's WLIB. On his evening show, "Community Opinion," people could voice opinions and grievances, and speak one-to-one with community leaders, activists, and politicians who were sometimes stunned by the depth and vehemence of the questions. In short, Lewis launched talk radio. With that pioneering effort, as the 1966 Peabody Award citation read, WLIB and Lewis "gave Harlem a safety valve."

"FREE HUEY!" For three years that alarm had sounded at rallies coast-to-coast. Then, on August 5, 1970, Huey P. Newton, cofounder of the Black Panther Party, was free. "Power to the People!" he shouted as he emerged from the Alameda County, California, jail to a hero's welcome. Newton's incarceration stemmed from an October 1967 police shootout that left one officer dead, one wounded, and Newton unconscious from four bullet wounds to the stomach and charged with murder.

In September 1968, as his eight-week trial wound toward the jury, Newton testified that the car he was in had been stopped in a predawn traffic check. When police recognized him, he was ordered out of the car and marched behind a patrol car, where an officer "hooked me in the face with his left arm." Dazed and down on one knee, "I saw him draw his service revolver and felt something like boiling hot soup spilled on my stomach." With that, Newton said, he fell unconscious, a claim supported by medical testimony on the nature of his wounds. Two years later that evidence proved critical on appeal. In his instructions, the judge had neglected to inform the jury that Newton's defense, if accepted, was sufficient to exonerate him. Had he done so, the Court of Appeals decreed, it was "reasonably probable" that Newton would have been acquitted.

The trial of Huey Newton had been the major media event of its time, and there was little doubt that politics had affected its outcome; FBI chief J. Edgar Hoover had publicly branded the Panthers "the greatest threat to the internal security of the country." From the conduct of the trial and the two years for appeal, the charge that Newton was a political prisoner gained credibility. And in 1976, it would be revealed that Hoover had targeted the Panthers for destruction under COINTELPRO (see April 6): of 295 acts against black groups, 233 had been made against the Panthers. Overturning Newton's manslaughter conviction was a major victory. Although he had needlessly served two years in prison, there were those who had been deprived of having him see the inside of a gas chamber.

AUGUST 6

It was 1964, Freedom Summer, and SNCC-sponsored programs were operating all across Mississippi. Freedom clinics offered free medical care from volunteer doctors; legal clinics provided free aid from volunteer students and lawyers from national organizations, including the NAACP Legal Defense Fund; and freedom schools advanced adult literacy in an ongoing voter education and registration drive. In all, one thousand volunteers had headed to Mississippi for what hostile Mississippians regarded as an "invasion." Tragically, three volunteers—Chaney, Goodman, and Schwerner (see June 21)—disappeared the very first day.

Rita Schwerner was training volunteers in Ohio when she received news that her husband, Michael, had disappeared. "It's tragic," she said, "that white northerners have to be caught up into the machinery of injustice and indifference in the South before the American people register concern. I personally suspect that if Mr. Chaney, who is a [black] native Mississippian, had been alone at the time of the disappearance, that this case, like so many others . . . would have gone completely unnoticed." She was right. Hundreds of sailors, FBI agents, and volunteers were called or came to search for the three. Newspapers kept daily vigil. Other bodies were found during the search and were reinterred in makeshift graves, nameless and unwanted; their relatives were still left to ponder their fate. Perhaps the nobodyness of everyday black life was best described by a twelve-year-old Biloxi girl:

> What is wrong with me everywhere I go
> No one seems to look at me.
> Sometimes I cry.
> I walk through woods and sit on a stone.
> I look at the stars and I sometimes wish.
> Probably if my wish ever comes true,
> Everyone will look at me.

But the good news that Freedom Summer was that the freedom teacher to whom she had presented the poem cherished her and it.

AUGUST 7

On August 7, 1970, a teenager too weary for his years entered the Marin County, California, courthouse at San Rafael in a desperate, disconsolate attempt to own a life that had spiraled out of control when he was seven. He never had a chance.

At about 11:00 A.M., he entered a courtroom in session. He removed pistols from his flight bag, unsheathed a carbine from his coat, and seized control. "This is it," he said, tossing a pistol to a defendant, who then forced deputies to remove his shackles at gunpoint. "Everybody line up," he ordered, arming two prisoner/witnesses. In minutes, the judge, the assistant district attorney, three female jurists, three prisoners, and the weary teen were on the elevator headed to a van. A stunning series of photos captured them exiting the building. "You take all the pictures you want," a prisoner called. "We are the revolutionaries." But the revolution was over before they could leave the parking lot when a caravan of nearly one hundred police officers, sheriffs, and prison guards opened fire. When it was over, four people were dead: the judge, two prisoners, and the teen. A San Quentin guard with the assault squad remembered seeing the weary teen visiting an imprisoned relative. From there an amazing saga etched history.

The teen was Jonathan Jackson. The incarcerated relative was his brother, George Jackson (see May 4). Jonathan's intent was not to murder, it was to trade hostages for the freedom of his idol, serving one year to life for a $70 gas station heist he always denied doing. George had been eighteen then; Jonathan was seven. Eleven years later, George had spent eight years in solitary with his growing political consciousness. When a Soledad prison guard fell to his death, George and two others were charged. The plight of these three Soledad Brothers drew UCLA professor Angela Davis to the prisoners' rights movement. As a political target and victim of death threats herself, she had purchased a gun for her own protection. When it was found among Jonathan's cache, the plight of political prisoners became a very personal cause (see February 28).

AUGUST 8

Twenty years after *Brown v. Board of Education* and continued resistance to school desegregation, how were black children faring emotionally?

Some educators and psychologists noted an improvement in the self-worth of the average child. The freedom movement had spawned a sense of empowerment, the feeling that one could change one's world. Continuing that growth meant educating children to become owners and decision makers rather than simply jobholders; giving children the tools with which to take charge of their destinies. But others warned that with limited integration had come a decline in the Black Is Beautiful movement. By attempting to blend into the larger society, blacks were becoming increasingly vulnerable to the emotional backsliding that had taken place during Reconstruction. White culture and white images became the standards by which blacks measured their societal progress. Clearly, nurturing healthy black children began with guiding parents. In August 1974, *Ebony* magazine published a special issue, "The Black Child," which included an article by Harvard Medical School's Associate Professor of Psychiatry, Dr. Alvin Poussaint, M.D.: "Building a Strong Self-Image in the Black Child."

"Racial pride is an important aspect of a child's self-concept," wrote Poussaint. "For children to develop a healthy self-concept, parents themselves must display self-respect for the child and racial pride." Otherwise, one could achieve outward success but inwardly hate blacks, and therefore oneself. Poussaint cited an *Ebony/Jet* survey that found blacks treated fairly in only one third of the nation's textbooks. "Black parents must expose their children to the positive side of their heritage." Such false images as the blaxploitation films of the period "too often emphasized self-defeating violence" and were cited for their negative effects. And finally: "Many black children have achieved despite the twin impact of racism and poverty on their psyches. . . . Black parents must teach [children] to constructively assert themselves when the odds seem stacked against them."

Parenting   Self-worth

AUGUST 9

L IKE MOST ARTISTS, Horace Pippin had a unique way of signing his paintings. Most often, his signature would look like this, "H. PiPPiN" or this, "H. PiPPiN: 1945." But when he completed a work on a date of particular historical significance, he documented it on the canvas: "H. PiPPiN, Aug 9." On August 9, 1945, as an atomic bomb fell on Nagasaki, Japan, bringing World War II to a close, Horace Pippin completed his work *The Holy Mountain III*. Lush and thick with the nighttime green of grass and trees, tiny flowers—red, white, and yellow—appear like stars dotting the night landscape as animals pause in pensive, tentative rest.

1945 proved to be the last year of Pippin's life. It was a tumultuous time for the artist. His personal life seemed to reflect the chaos of the world at large as his wife descended into madness and he escaped into his paintings. Responding to questions from his Quaker admirers about *The Holy Mountain III*, he wrote:

> To my dear friends:
> To tell you why I painted the picture. It is the Holy Mountain, my Holy Mountain.
>
> Now my dear friends, the world is in a bad way at this time. I mean war. And men have never loved one another. There is trouble every place you go today. Then one thinks of peace, yes, there will be peace, so I look at Isaiah XI—there I found that there will be peace. I went over it 4 or 5 times in my mind. Every time I read it I got a new thought on it. So I went to work. Isaiah XI, the 6th verse to the 10th gave me the picture, and to think that all the animals that kill the weak ones will dwell together, like the wolf will dwell with the lamb, and the leopard shall lie down with the kid and calf and the young lion and the fatling together. . . . Now my picture would not be complete of today if the little ghost-like memory did not appear in the left of the picture. As the men are dying, today the little crosses tell us of them in the First World War and what is doing in the South—all that we are going through now. But there will be peace.

In ALBANY, GEORGIA, the stage was set for a showdown on Friday, August 10, 1962. Both King and Abernathy had been jailed for two weeks of a forty-five-day sentence in lieu of a fine, and a charge of obstructing a sidewalk was still pending. Even the sheriff who had jailed them wanted them out. As political heat was applied from every direction, the issue became this: how to release them and save face.

Offstage, it was the motion filed by attorney William Kunstler forcing the city of Albany to dismiss the new charge or expedite King's trial that led to the August 10 date. With that, SCLC Executive Director Rev. Wyatt Tee Walker strategized a response to the pending verdict. If the two men were convicted, mass demonstrations were set to erupt. If they were freed, the movement would celebrate this victory. In either case, he developed plans for a dramatic Mother's March by the wives of Albany Movement leaders. In its own best interests, the Justice Department also sought to avoid being dragged into the fray by the city's ongoing attempts to seek an injunction banning demonstrations. The Justice Department came down on the side of the demonstrators, arguing that the city had been using police power to subvert federally mandated desegregation orders. They opposed the intent of the injunction: to ban demonstrators from accessing their constitutional rights. As the drama hurtled forward, guards delivered King and Abernathy into the courtroom. The spectacle did not last long. In a political settlement, the judge found them guilty as charged but suspended their sentences as long as they broke no other laws. Would they have to observe the laws of segregation? No, the judge declared; the Supreme Court had already invalidated Jim Crow law.

The movement had won—barely. City officials still fought the change that did not come until the Voting Rights Act of 1965. From the start, Albany was oddly recalcitrant—as though the city could always one-up demonstrators. Said Dr. King, "Every time I saw FBI men in Albany, they were with the local police force."

AUGUST 11

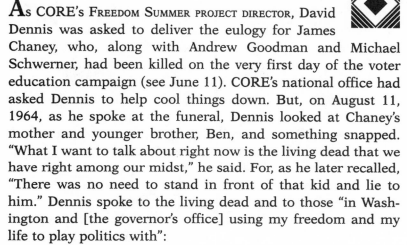

As CORE's FREEDOM SUMMER PROJECT DIRECTOR, David Dennis was asked to deliver the eulogy for James Chaney, who, along with Andrew Goodman and Michael Schwerner, had been killed on the very first day of the voter education campaign (see June 11). CORE's national office had asked Dennis to help cool things down. But, on August 11, 1964, as he spoke at the funeral, Dennis looked at Chaney's mother and younger brother, Ben, and something snapped. "What I want to talk about right now is the living dead that we have right among our midst," he said. For, as he later recalled, "There was no need to stand in front of that kid and lie to him." Dennis spoke to the living dead and to those "in Washington and [the governor's office] using my freedom and my life to play politics with":

> I am not here to pay tribute. . . . This has got to stop. . . . I have attended too many memorials, too many funerals. But the trouble is that YOU are not sick and tired and for that reason YOU, yes YOU, are to blame. I've got vengeance in my heart tonight, and I ask you to feel angry with me. . . . When they find the people who killed those guys [they will] have a jury of all their cousins and aunts and uncles. And I know what they are going to say: "Not guilty." I'm tired of that! Do YOU hear me, I am SICK and TIRED. . . . The best way we can remember James Chaney is to demand our rights. Don't just look at me and go back and tell folks you've been to a nice service. Your work is just beginning. If you go back home and sit down and take what these white men in Mississippi are doing to us . . . if you take it and don't do something about it . . . then God damn your souls! Stand up! Those neighbors who were too afraid to come to this service, pick them up and take them down there to register to vote! Go down there and do it! Stand up! Hold your heads up! Don't bow down anymore! We want our freedom NOW!

Although the murderers of the three martyrs had buried them together, Jim Crow law ironically forbid their legally sharing a grave—as their families had hoped. In lieu of that wish, a common memorial was held in Mississippi on August 16, 1964.

AUGUST 12

In 1965, eyes that equated despair and poverty with the tenements of Chicago or New York easily overlooked the pain of Watts, California, where neat rows of single-family bungalows stretched for blocks. There were no decaying tenement stoops on which the jobless languished. Instead, grassy lanes of lawn were spread with palm trees and exotic flowers native to the sunny scene. To the untrained eye, Watts seemed as pacific as its nearby sea. It was, however, a poor enclave in the midst of superwealth and supermyth, both courtesy of the resident film industry with its closed-door policy to positive black self-images. That Watts, angry Watts, went up in flames the week of August 11–16, 1965. In six days of rioting, thirty-five were killed, nearly nine hundred were injured, almost thirty-six hundred were arrested, and fire damage totalled $175 million. The worst of the American uprisings, it became the riot by which all others, before and since, are judged.

When Dr. King flew into riot-torn Watts in the midst of the siege, what struck him was "a class revolt of underprivileged against privileged." He met with the governor and city leaders, each of whom was more dismissive than the next of his efforts to address legitimate woes. Heading the list: police brutality. Six months after Malcolm's murder, five months after Selma (see March 7), two months after the president's "We Shall Overcome" speech, Watts hadn't. At a time when violent segregationist wars were still openly waged with police help, Los Angeles recruited too many southern policemen who brought their worst habits with them. Indeed, an incident of police brutality sparked the Watts melee.

Said the African American psychiatrist J. Alfred Cannon, "They have developed a feeling of potency. They feel the whole world is watching now. And out of the violence, no matter how wrong the acts were, they have developed a sense of pride." Said Dr. King, "The decade of 1955 to 1965 . . . misled us. . . . Everyone underestimated the amount of rage Negroes were suppressing, and the amount of bigotry the white majority was disguising."

Revolt!   Failure

AUGUST 13

IN THE 1920s, with a proud plan for African uplift, a fanciful plumed commodore hat, uniformed parades of the men and women of his African nation-in-the-making, and himself as its provisional president, Marcus Garvey had seized the imagination of the Pan-African world. Raised and educated in Jamaica, he had gone off to see the world. He returned home from his youthful travels in Europe and the Americas matured—disgusted with racism and determined to end it. In 1914, with superior skills as an orator and an organizer, he founded the Universal Negro Improvement Association. Within five years, his empowerment philosophy spread throughout the United States. In 1920, in New York's Madison Square Garden, his first convention attracted over 25,000 people. Challenging the crowd to rid itself of the shackles of colonialism and segregation, he issued the call: "Up you mighty race, you may be what you will."

Garvey was industrious. So successful was his weekly newspaper, *The Negro World*, that colonial governments meted out five-year jail terms to anyone caught reading it—and in Dahomey, the sentence was life! Still Garvey flourished, with an estimated six million active followers. He bought a Harlem auditorium to use as his headquarters and he launched the Negro Factories Corporation in industrial cities throughout the Americas. But it was the literal flagship of his Back-to-Africa campaign, the Black Star Lines, that ultimately sank him. When management floundered and the investment soured, rival black leaders in collusion with the white establishment destroyed him. In 1923, Garvey was imprisoned for mail fraud; he was later deported. In 1927, a Jamaican hero's welcome revived his spirit. In 1928, Howard University's symposium hailed Garveyism as "eternal." He tried to revive the UNIA (see November 29), but things were never the same. He died in 1940 in London—broke, and perhaps broken. But when a liberated Jamaica named its first national hero, it resurrected the memory of Marcus Garvey. His body, exhumed in London, was reinterred at home in Jamaica on August 13, 1964.

AUGUST 14

"I<small>F WE MUST DIE</small> . . ." Britain's Prime Minister Winston Churchill roared mightily, filling a joint session of the United States Congress with inspired awe in 1943, "If we must die, let it not be like hogs—Hunted and penned in an inglorious spot—Like men we'll face the murderous, cowardly pack—Pressed to the wall, dying, but fighting back!" Seeking aid from his World War II ally, Churchill was quoting one of the most famous poems of the Harlem Renaissance. Ironically, Claude McKay's call had urged blacks to fight against white mobs rioting through their communities in an effort to resubjugate them in that "Red Summer" of 1919 as the soldiers came home from World War I.

Churchill's call was not the first time allied British-American exhortations had left a hollow ring in black ears. In the summer of 1941, four months before the official entry of the United States into World War II after Japan bombed Pearl Harbor (see December 7), Britain's Churchill and America's President Franklin Delano Roosevelt held a secret meeting in Newfoundland to draft their war aims. On August 14, 1941, they signed that historic accord, the Atlantic Charter.

A brief document, the Charter represented much more than either of its signers intended. For its eight stated principles left little doubt that, to colonizers, the colonized do not merit consideration, and worse, they do not even exist in the consciousness of the colonizer. Why else would two colonialist, imperialist, and segregationist powers declare that they "wish to see sovereign rights and self-government restored to those who have been forcibly deprived of them"? Why else would they pledge to "endeavor . . . to further the enjoyment by all States, great or small, victor or vanquished, of access, on equal terms, to the trade and to the raw materials of the world which are needed for their economic prosperity"?

Whatever the intent of Britain and the United States, Africa, Asia, and the Caribbean took them at their word. In their push for independence, the Charter was always cited.

AUGUST 15

IRONICALLY, ONE OF THE most critical moments in the Civil Rights movement did not involve African Americans. It took place in India on August 15, 1947, as that five-thousand-year-old civilization retook its freedom from England.

The hero of India's freedom fight was undeniably Mohandas (or Mahatma) K. Gandhi, born to a prominent Hindu family. His grandfather and father were prime ministers of subjugated Indian states. Gandhi had studied law in London, returned to India to practice in 1891, emigrated to South Africa two years later, and become a successful lawyer within that country's Indian community—otherwise referred to as apartheid's "colored class." It was there that he honed his human rights activism. But as an Indian, he was, therefore, also a British subject. During the Boer War (between the British and Dutch for control of South Africa), he joined the British ambulance corps. He returned to India in 1914, during World War I, remaining loyal to the Crown. But it was the Amritsar Massacre of April 13, 1919, that changed his life. As South Africa's whites would do in Sharpeville (see March 21) and Soweto (see June 16), as America would do in Orangeburg (see February 7) and at the Pettus Bridge (see March 7), Britain did at Amritsar. The army gunned down twenty thousand Indian men, women, and children penned inside a walled garden to which they had come for a meeting on the suppression of their rights of speech and assembly. From that tragedy, the Indian revolution—a nonviolent crusade with Gandhi as its moral and strategic leader—was born.

Even if geographers had not yet found that the world was round and interconnected, consider this. Gandhi's activism began in Africa, where he read Henry David Thoreau, the American pacifist and Underground Railroad station master; Rev. James Lawson (see February 13) helped ground the "Civil Rights wars" in Gandhi's theory. And it is said that Jesus departed the Middle East (northeast Africa) to study in India. African America's crusade had found inspiration in a Hindu, a Hebrew, and a Christian disciple of both.

Independence   Legacies

AUGUST 16

Berry Gordy was a young boxer spending every day in the gym, working out, hoping against hope that one day he would get a shot at the featherweight title. Then he had the revelation that would make him a "heavyweight" with endless titles to his credit—some pure gold, others platinum. As he wrote in his autobiography, *To Be Loved:*

> One hot August day in 1950, a remarkable thing happened. The Woodward Avenue Gym was packed. I was training hard. Pitting myself against the big bag and feeling very much the victor, I decided my tired, profusely sweating body deserved a break. As I sat down on a bench, my eyes fell on two posters on one of the four square pillars that supported the gym's ceiling. I got up and walked closer. The top poster announced a Battle of the Bands between Stan Kenton and Duke Ellington for that same night. The one below was advertising a bout between two young fighters, scheduled for the following Friday night. There it was again: boxing versus music. This time it was visual.
>
> I stared at both posters for some time, realizing the fighters could fight once and maybe not fight again for three or four weeks, or months, or never. The bands were doing it every night, city after city, and not getting hurt. I then noticed the fighters were about twenty-three and looked fifty; the band leaders about fifty and looked twenty-three. The war that had been raging inside me—music versus boxing—was finally over. I had my answer. No more sweating in a hot gym every day, no more running those five miles around Belle Isle at 5:30 A.M. No more abstinence. No more abstinence!! That day I took off my gloves—for good.

For the next few months all Gordy could think about was songwriting. By the end of the decade, he would launch his own record company, and from then on all we would hear about was *Motown.*

AUGUST 17

Some months after the assassination of Malcolm X, Roy Wilkins, executive director of the NAACP, received a letter from an unidentified young man. "What he had to tell me was typical of the spirit of those times," said Wilkins. "Looking at that letter now, I still wince."

It was 1965—a time when conflict between movement factions was often so fierce that the true black-on-black crime was the politically charged round of accusations and counteraccusations that were destroying the movement. At one time, Malcolm X could have been blamed as the antagonist. But the situation had not abated with his death. At root, the problem was what it had always been—competition for funds, support, and media time. But it was also the decreased priority given to the movement in the wake of the escalating war in Vietnam.

"Dear Mr. Wilkins," ventured the student:

> You, Dr. M. L. King, and A. Philip Randolph and many others have done a marvelous and outstanding feat and I sincerely embrace you wholeheartedly for it, but there is a biblical connotation that I believe has pertinence to our revolution, that is, God replaced Moses when he couldn't communicate with his followers in the wilderness. He replaced him with Joshua, a young militant warrior, who led the children of Israel to the promised land. He was the same gentleman who made the sun stand still, destroyed the walls of Jericho. God Almighty knew he was a man, and indeed so was Malcolm X and most certainly is Stokely Carmichael.

The times were indeed changing. In the young man's words, the voices of the ancestors could be heard guiding him on:

> Joshua fit the battle of Jericho, Jericho, Jericho
> Joshua fit the battle of Jericho
> And the wall came a-tumbling down. . . .

Leadership   Alternatives

AUGUST 18

To SAY THAT THE CIVIL RIGHTS MOVEMENT is an era that begins in 1954, with school desegregation, and ends in 1968, with the assassination of Dr. King, is to distort history. For the African American freedom fight, a human rights movement, most certainly began in 1619 as the first boatload of Africans enchained were forced ashore at Jamestown. The Civil Rights movement began in the courts of colonial Virginia seven years later.

In the only documentation of the landing, John Rolfe wrote in 1619, "About the latter end of August, a Dutch man-of-warre [ship] . . . arrived at Point Comfort. He brought not any thing but 20 and odd negars which the Governor . . . bought for victualle [food]." The first known enslaved Africans were legally classed as indentures, like white indentures. But unlike the whites, whose seven years of indentured labor was either a criminal punishment or payment for passage to America, the blacks had committed no crime and made no such contract. Yet they, too, had to wait seven years to petition for their freedom. In 1626, these cases began coming into court, and in the first race-based court decisions, the court created a crime for which black indentures could be found guilty and sentenced to a second term: heathenism, not being a Christian. With these decisions, the courts forced blacks into added years of unpaid labor and gave colonial planters legal access to endless supplies of a renewable resource—human capital. A few Africans did receive justice in court; most did not. It is with these decisions that the Civil Rights movement begins. In 1626, therefore, the death knell for African sovereignty was also rung. Europeans and American colonists gave themselves license to violate their own Christian teachings by simply exempting blacks from them.

Freedom Days covers the years 1936 to 1976, but we honor all those who have paved the way. This day about the "latter end of August"—August 18, 1976—marked the 350th anniversary of the Civil Rights movement in the Americas.

AUGUST 19

Aˢᴷ ꜰᴏʟᴋˢ ᴡʜᴏ ᴡᴇʀᴇ ᴀʀᴏᴜɴᴅ in the early 1950s, and they all tell the same story. In the endless stiflingly hot summer known as Montgomery, Alabama, there was a Sunday when Vernon Johns, legendary pastor of Dexter Avenue Baptist Church, preached the sermon "It's Safe to Murder Negroes." How he came to deliver that word is a story in itself, a story retold by Taylor Branch in *Parting the Waters*.

Sometime in 1951 or 1952, an incident that began when a black motorist was stopped for speeding ended when police beat the man to near-death with a tire iron as other blacks looked on silently. Never one for silence when a whole lot of noise was called for, Johns posted the title of his sermon on a bulletin board outside the church. That night his phone never stopped ringing. In a counterpoint of white threats and black fears, each group urged Johns, in its own habitual way, to take down the sign. When a summons for his arrest was issued charging Johns with inciting a riot, he calmly escorted the policeman to court. There, the judge asked him why he had posted the sign. Johns replied, logically, that he had done so to attract congregants to the Sunday service. When the judge recommended removal of the sign, Johns gave a spontaneous lecture on signs—how officials had railed against the people's posted signs from ancient Greece through Martin Luther's Reformation. The judge asked why he would want to preach such a divisive, incendiary sermon. Johns replied, "Because everywhere I go in the South the Negro is forced to choose between his hide and his soul. Mostly he chooses his hide. I'm going to tell him that his hide is not worth it." With that, the judge issued a warning and dismissed Johns.

Frustrated by a peaceful outcome, the Klan took the opportunity to burn a cross on the church's lawn. But the sign had done its job. The next day churchgoers packed the pews, and Johns challenged the pastoral flock to action. Comparing the murder of blacks to the "lynching of Jesus," he predicted that the violence against them would continue for as long as they continued to "let it happen."

AUGUST 20

ON AUGUST 20, 1960, the end of French colonial rule and independence day for Senegal, the power and prestige of the presidency was vested in Léopold Sedar Senghor—poet, dramatist, and, arguably, one the greatest intellectuals of his day. He was also a leading exponent of "Negritude"—the literary expression of a Pan-Africanist political philosophy—so Senghor's Senegal was very much a reflection of this artistic integrity and intellectual curiosity. As he wrote in his essay, "Negritude and Modernity": "Objectively speaking, Negritude is the whole system of values not only of black African peoples but also of black Americans and even of black peoples of Asia and the Pacific. . . . Subjectively speaking, Negritude is a will to endorse the values of black civilization."

This carving of Senegalese identity was particularly apparent in its cinema. Several newly free nations had started television networks and begun to produce newsreels, but they often farmed out the operating task to foreigners—significantly, to African Americans. For example, Liberia and Ethiopia both named producer/filmmaker William Alexander (see June 9) their official state producer. In Ghana, Shirley Graham Du Bois (see December 22) helped develop the nation's television system. But Senegal created its own newsreel service, Actualités Senegalaises. Well supported by government funds, it made a difference in forging a postindependence industry where film was seen not only as a vehicle for self-expression but as an educational tool for the general public, many of whom were still illiterate.

A vital service to its nation and the world, Actualités Senegalaises was also a boon to young filmmakers. Within only three years, it had spawned an African cinematic identity and industry (see November 18). By 1963 the films were of such quality that film historians have called it a "watershed year" for Senegalese cinema. Among its important young auteurs: Blaise Senghor, Paulin Soumanou Vieyra, Momar Thiam, and Ousmane Sembène, still revered as "the Father of African Cinema" (see December 23).

AUGUST 21

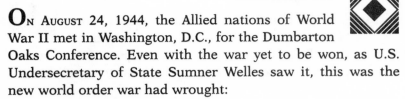

ON AUGUST 24, 1944, the Allied nations of World War II met in Washington, D.C., for the Dumbarton Oaks Conference. Even with the war yet to be won, as U.S. Undersecretary of State Sumner Welles saw it, this was the new world order war had wrought:

> The startling development of Japan as a world power, and the slower but . . . steady emergence of China as a full member of the family of nations, [and] notably India, all combined to erase very swiftly indeed the fetish of white supremacy cultivated by the big colonial powers during the nineteenth century. The thesis of white supremacy could only exist so long as the white race actually proved to be supreme. The nature of the defeats suffered by the Western nations in 1942 dealt the final blow to any concept of white supremacy which still remained.

Reviving the idea of the World War I–era League of Nations, Dumbarton paved the way for founding the United Nations in 1945. Most important, as Welles forecast, China demanded that the Allies declare unequivocal support for racial equality. Japan, the Allies' wartime enemy, also rallied Asian unity around white racism. And, as American Nobel laureate Pearl Buck, a forty-year resident of Shanghai, warned, Japan's call was successful because it was heard by people of color who'd had "unfortunate experiences" with Britain and the U.S.

> [The] white man . . . has too often behaved without wisdom or justice to his fellow man. . . . It is dangerous today not to recognize the truth, for in it lies the tinder for tomorrow. Who of us can doubt it who has seen a white policeman beat a Chinese coolie in Shanghai, a white sailor kick a Japanese in Kobe, an English captain lash out with his whip at an Indian vendor—who of us, having heard the contemptuous talk of the white man in any colored country, can forget the fearful bitter hatred in the colored face and the blaze in the dark eyes?

With global communication, people of color could see a common enemy—the theory of white supremacy. Racist superiority/inferiority propaganda was seen for what it was—a strategy based in brutality, not "scientific" reality.

AUGUST 22

I**T WAS** F**REEDOM** S**UMMER**, 1964. Three murdered voting rights volunteers—James Chaney, Andrew Goodman, and Michael Schwerner—had just been dredged from the Mississippi mud. Countless others had been tortured. Having sacrificed their all for freedom, there was no turning back for the Mississippi Freedom Democratic Party (MFDP). On August 22, 1964, Fannie Lou Hamer told her story in front of the Credentials Committee of the Democratic National Convention:

> Mr. Chairman. . . . It was the thirty-first of August in 1962 that eighteen of us traveled twenty-six miles to the county courthouse in Indianola to try to register to try to become first-class citizens. We was met in Indianola by Mississippi men, highway patrolmens, and they only allowed two of us in to take the literacy test at the time. [We] started back to Ruleville, we was held up by the city police and state highway patrolmens and carried back to Indianola, where the bus driver was charged that day with driving a bus the wrong color. After we paid the fine among us, we continued on to Ruleville. . . . The plantation owner . . . said, "Fannie Lou . . . if you don't go down and withdraw your registration, you will have to leave," he said. . . . I had to leave that same night.
>
> On the tenth of September, 1962, sixteen bullets was fired into the home of Mr. and Mrs. Robert Tucker for me. . . . And in June, the ninth, 1963, [I] attended a voter-registration workshop, was returning back to Mississippi [see June 10]. When we got to Winona . . . four of the people got off to use the washroom . . . I was carried to the county jail . . . and I could hear the sounds of licks and horrible screams . . . and it wasn't too long before three white men came to my cell . . . and he said, "We are going to make you wish you was dead." I was in jail when Medgar Evers was murdered.
>
> All of this on account we want to register, to become first-class citizens, and if the [MFDP] is not seated now, I question America, is this America, the land of the free and the home of the brave, where we have to sleep with our telephones off the hooks because our lives be threatened daily because we want to live as decent human beings in America? Thank you.

With tears in her eyes she left the witness table.

Politics   Human Spirit

AUGUST 23

In 1948, the mass arrest of Communist Party leaders for conspiring to overthrow the government went beyond politics: it threatened all who dared dissent. On August 23, 1948, "The First Line of Defense," a condemnation of the "hysteria-breeding arrests," was issued to black newspapers. Cosponsored by four hundred blacks, it was signed by *Crisis* editor Dr. W. E. B. Du Bois, Oklahoma publisher Roscoe C. Dunjee, Iowa lawyer Charles P. Howard, and actor Paul Robeson: "Our concern is to defend the right of [minorities] to fight for the kind of society they consider democratic and just. . . . We agree fully with [Communist leader] Henry A. Wallace: 'Defense of the Civil Rights of Communists is the first line in the defense of the liberties of a democratic people.'"

In fact, American communism had reached its heyday in the Depression-era 1930s. Onto a political landscape littered with such racist land mines like the case of the Scottsboro Boys (see October 25) had marched the Party with its policy crossing boundaries of race and class. Writers and artists often attended John Reed Club socials. Seeking an end to exploitation as cannon fodder in war and as underpaid labor in peace, other blacks—scorned and rejected by Democrats and Republicans alike—found support in the Party. Among them, New York councilman Benjamin Davis and Henry Winston (see July 5) had been arrested.

Long victimized by "way of life" campaigns, African Americans knew the attack on communists to be an attack on progress. In the 1930s, the target was unions. In the 1940s, as Civil Rights engines revved up on segregation, it was blacks. In 1942, ground was paved in an investigation of Mary McLeod Bethune, a highly visible member of President Franklin Roosevelt's "kitchen cabinet," Bethune-Cookman College founder, and head of the National Council of Negro Women with an outreach in the millions. In 1943, the House Un-American Activities Committee accused her of being a communist. Though she was cleared, this top-down approach to intimidation had made its point: all were vulnerable.

AUGUST 24

FROM THE REVOLUTIONARY WAR THROUGH VIETNAM, the treatment of returning black veterans and the effort to terrorize blacks into submissiveness after each conflict have provided a sad commentary on American life. In August 1944, as the recent D day landing on Normandy promised to draw the curtain on World War II's European theater, hope was high that every soldier would soon come home. In Colorado, the National Opinion Research Center of the University of Denver conducted a study of white attitudes and race.

Voices from the North: In Berkeley, California, a music teacher anticipated postwar trouble stemming from "propaganda and anti-Democratic forces who use the Negro question to 'divide and rule.'" In Chicago, Illinois, a woman pensioner feared that "Negroes will have had a taste of equality in the army and in war jobs, and will demand their rights as citizens. The white people will try to stop them, and there will be trouble." *Voices from the Southwest:* In Houston, Texas, a county official cursed "the damn-yankees [who] mingle with the Negroes too much and spoil 'em." In Tulsa, Oklahoma, a radio program director spoke of "a conflict between the supremacy of the whites and the newly found sense of freedom of the Negro due to the war." *Said others:* "Some people are now putting Negroes on a basis of equality with whites, and I think after the war there will be trouble with them." "Negroes will expect wartime privileges in time of peace." "The present administration has ruined the Negroes—making such an issue of equal rights." *And there was this voice of a southern grocer:* "After the war the Negroes are going to demand the equality we preach and don't practice."

The attitudes expressed above foreshadowed a season of lynchings as black soldiers returned home from 1945 into 1946. As was predicted, the attitudes of the soldiers forged the Civil Rights movement. But although the movement changed behavior, it did not erase deep-seated attitudes. Clearly, the reeducation of the entire nation on the subject of race—the human race—is a challenge long overdue.

Temper of the Times   Values

"BETWEEN FIVE AND SEVEN P.M. daily, the number-one question asked on subways is 'What was the figure today?'" a 1954 exposé in the *Amsterdam News* reported. The answer depended on where the train stopped and who got off. Wealthy whites were into the stock market; poor blacks were into the numbers racket.

In the early 1920s, the numbers came to Harlem with its West Indian founders and made wealthy men of number "barons" and "bankers." But with success came white mobs. After the stock market crash of 1929, two legendary mobsters, Dutch Schultz and Jimmy Hines, needed a new game. They saw a gold mine in Harlem's numbers racket and moved in. It was soon reported that the numbers game "employs more people than the nation's largest aircraft plants."

By the mid-1950s, in New York City alone more than twenty thousand people made a living from the numbers—or policy, as it was called. Bets ranged from a cent to a hundred dollars; odds ranged up to "600 to 1." The winning numbers were horse race results telegraphed or phoned from racetracks to bet-collecting drops. Numbers runners collected bets and paid off after each race. A half day's work earned up to $100 a day, but one risked raids. "It becomes a question of race, graft, and how and when to make the arrest," the *Amsterdam* wrote. "Precedence shows that this happens whenever there is 'a big downtown newspaper scare' making Harlem a crime-ridden area—a new top cop wants to make headlines." And while some whites also played the numbers, headlines were not made at their expense. "This fascinating industry runs into the billions of dollars, and [police and political] protection funds run higher than $50,000,000 a year. No system has yet been devised by [the police commissioner] which can stop this activity," the paper reported. Soon, they would not have to; numbers went legit. The state took it over and renamed it "Lotto," "Pick Four," and a host of other names. Now, when folks get the itch to play the numbers, they're not gambling, they're investing in the education of our children.

Social History   Enterprise

"THERE WAS A SHINING MOMENT IN THE STRUGGLE," said Dr. King of the mid-1960s, when the nation seemed driven by a moral agenda. Then came the Vietnam War, with its record highs in casualties and length of conflict as if "a society gone mad on war." Some had "gone mad" on war, but others had gotten mad about it.

Protestors took to the streets over the draft and the war itself, as hippies chanted "Make love not war," adopting the method and metaphor of the Civil Rights movement with its marches and "love" for one's oppressor. On the surface, it was about Vietnam; deep down, it was about class. Young draft-age whites unable to attend college and claim student deferments versus privileged young draft-age whites who were able to attend, resist the draft, flaunt society's taboos, damn drafted peers for being "part of the system," and taunt working-class police "pigs." Treatment usually reserved for blacks was meted out on such whites. A book about the National Guard assault on Ohio's Kent State campus was titled *Don't Shoot. We Are Your Children.* In Mayor Richard Daley's Chicago, they did. News of King's assassination erupted into a riot in April 1968, and Daley chided police restraint: Next time, he instructed them, "shoot to kill arsonists and shoot to maim looters."

That "next time" came on August 26, 1968, opening day of the Democratic National Convention. The demonstrators were white, the rioters were police, the results were violent as hippies, yippies, poets, and provocateurs camped in Lincoln Park for a Festival of Life, the counterculture counterconvention, and police, angered by an antiwar demonstration, swept through the park in riot gear. Wednesday, a mule train that had come cross-country from the Poor People's Campaign (see June 19) in Washington triumphantly inched up Michigan Avenue. As a crowd formed to greet it, police rioted anew. That was the official conclusion of the National Commission on the Causes and Prevention of Violence. If ever there was proof of the self-destructive power of hate, here it was. The Vietnam War was coming back to haunt the nation, tearing at it from within.

Social History   **Consciousness**

AUGUST 27

THE ANNUAL EAST-WEST GAME brought out families in droves for the high point of Negro Leagues baseball season—often more than forty thousand fans in all. These were the days when legends like Cool Papa Bell, Josh Gibson, and Satchel Paige (see July 9) had their turn at bat. For sport, for fun, for box office, there was nothing like it. And one of the greatest games ever was played on August 27, 1938.

There was nothing minor about the Negro Leagues, where, as it has been said, "only the ball was white." "They say that we were not organized," said Kansas City Monarch veteran Sammie Haynes. "We were organized. We had two leagues. We had a 140-game schedule. We played an all-star game every year in Chicago. We had sellouts. We had a World Series at the end of the season. If that's not organized, I don't know what is." And it was Rube Foster's idea. This visionary team owner invited other owners to join him at the Colored YMCA in Kansas City, where together they founded the National Negro League (NNL) on February 13, 1920. Thanks to Foster, the Negro Leagues were serious business—a business with a full spectrum of jobs on the playing field and off, in management and every other related field; a business that was lost when, as Foster always predicted they would, the white major leagues integrated the players, closing out black businessmen and leaving them behind.

We can learn a lot from the Negro Leagues. One lesson is this: too many blacks tricked themselves into seeing the white leagues as "major" and important, and the Negro Leagues as "minor" and unimportant. But if blacks had continued to support the NNL while cheering on our pioneers of integration, the NNL—a beacon of black entrepreneurism—would be alive today. By feeling minor to someone else's major, blacks have too often allowed the negativity of others to overtake our own positive self-interests. Just as savoring Italian food doesn't stop Greeks from cooking, we know this: integrated baseball is a good thing; segregated baseball is an unnatural thing; but a sense of self-worth is everything.

AUGUST 28

THE DRAMA AND SUSPENSE had been building for weeks. Far beyond conscience or commitment, fair weather or foul, whatever the day's outcome, history would remember August 28, 1963, for the March on Washington for Jobs and Freedom.

Scrolling back on that day, a sea of 250,000 people floods the Capitol Mall in front of the Lincoln Memorial. The largest political rally in U.S. history to that date, it is a highly orchestrated, sanitized affair. With the notable exception of Brooklyn, New York, CORE's thirteen-day, 230-mile trek, the demonstrators have marched "at" rather than "on" the capitol. Only John Lewis's speech damning pending legislation as "too little too late" will cause a stir. Martin Luther King's "I have a dream" incantation will be the emotional high. And, although the march may not erupt with the terror of the times, it does reflect it. For despite what some will later deride as a picnic, a quarter-million people will not risk thousands of miles at their own expense for a day's picnic in a hot, segregated capitol city. Within blocks of the White House are shacks dressed up as slums. Attacks on Freedom Riders are headline news. The likelihood of crazed antimarch minions storming buses en route is real. So is the fear that bus drivers and pilots will scuttle travel plans. Already desegregated bus depots in Maryland and Delaware will refuse service to black marchers. FBI chief J. Edgar Hoover's obsession with destroying the Civil Rights movement is known. And those who "march" will have braved land mines of fear to do so.

A pre–woman's liberation event, the march will feature only three women: the legendary dancer Josephine Baker (See September 28) speaks, wearing her French Legion of Honor medal; Marian Anderson, opera's noble contralto, and Mahalia Jackson, gospel's queen, sing. Yet, it is a magical day. As James Baldwin will write, "For a moment, it almost seemed that we stood on a height, and could see our inheritance; perhaps we could make the kingdom real, perhaps the beloved community would not forever remain the dream one dreamed in agony."

AUGUST 29

On August 29, 1957, Congress passed the Civil Rights Act of 1957. Despite some official efforts to limit Jim Crow, not since 1875 and the end of Reconstruction had the federal government made a definitive antisegregation strike. Yet the 1957 act was a step backward for the movement. In its language, if not its intent, it undermined the federal government's power to intercede in Civil Rights enforcement. Title III actually repealed an 1866 statute giving the president power to raise troops to enforce or to prevent violation of Civil Rights. While the president retained powers to the same end, the motive behind Congress's repeal of presidential powers at the same time that it was so reluctant to enforce desegregation was certainly suspect. For on this very day, a situation was bubbling over in Little Rock, Arkansas, that would reveal the city once considered one of the South's most progressive as one of its most racist. Three years after the Supreme Court rendered its school desegregation order (see May 17), a judge granted an injunction preventing the desegregation of Little Rock schools on August 29, 1957.

A week earlier, a rock had been thrown through NAACP chapter president Daisy Bates's living room window. Tied to the rock was a note: "STONE THIS TIME. DYNAMITE NEXT." It was the opening salvo of "The Battle of Little Rock." Georgia's governor had publicly praised segregationists for their stand on "states' rights" that night. The next morning, he and Arkansas Governor Orval Faubus would circle the wagons for a showdown. Faubus faced reelection that next year; Little Rock was great cannon fodder.

With the city's so-called progressiveness, no one predicted the violence, no one strategized a response, and no one prepared the chosen test children for what they would face. How did it happen, then, that those black students, the Little Rock Nine, could respond with such courage? As Melba Pattillo Beals remembered, "I simply raised my hand one day when they said, 'Who of you lives in the area of Central High School? Who has good grades?' It was an accident of fate."

AUGUST 30

As COLLEGE STUDENTS HEAD BACK to school on this day, we recognize the world's oldest university—at Sankore in Timbuktu, West Africa—as the original historically black college, and celebrate today's black colleges and universities (HBCUs) as protectors of the best that is ours. And nowhere else is that more beautifully in evidence than in our art. In 1868, Hampton University was the first to acquire works by black artists. Since then, the HBCUs have collectively become the greatest repository of black art, as this 1973 comment by Atlanta University's Professor Richard A. Long suggests: "[The] University is the happy possessor of the largest collection of paintings by black American artists. The collection, which presently totals approximately five hundred paintings, sculptures, and graphic works, is in large part the result of the . . . annual Atlanta University Exhibitions from 1942 to 1970." Extend this back to 1868 and multiply it by just a fraction of the number of schools and one begins to realize the artistic wealth that is our public trust.

It is difficult to overstate the importance of these archives to our history and our future. At a time when museums would not admit blacks to explore otherwise public halls, when gallery owners and museum curators refused to show works by black artists, and when—as Tom Feelings experienced (see September 30)—art schools disclaimed the validity of all black art, these college art archives quite simply meant everything to students, artists, and art lovers.

While the HBCUs began in 1854 and began collecting art in 1868, the first African American artist was not hired to teach art until Hale Woodruff joined the faculty of Spelman College (part of Atlanta University) in 1931. "Mr. Woodruff was very much like Frederick Douglass," said one student, assessing the impact of the venerated teacher. With library displays of student work, mounting an exhibit of nineteenth-century African American artists Edward Bannister and Henry Ossawa Tanner, and his special privilege forays to Atlanta's segregated High Museum, Woodruff led his young artists to freedom.

Art   Legacies

AUGUST 31

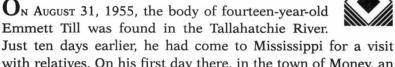

ON AUGUST 31, 1955, the body of fourteen-year-old Emmett Till was found in the Tallahatchie River. Just ten days earlier, he had come to Mississippi for a visit with relatives. On his first day there, in the town of Money, an incident took place that ended in his lynching—an event of international notoriety.

Having fun with some local boys, he showed them pictures of his interracial school friends in Chicago and identified one as his girlfriend. Kidding around, one of the local boys dared him to speak to a white woman in a nearby store. Emmett did just that. With this, the boys told him he'd better get away. Unaware of the rules of the South, Emmett didn't know to take their words seriously. Nor did he know to tell the relatives with whom he was staying what had happened. They would have known to get him out of town. The following Sunday morning at around four A.M., they were awakened by intruders who struck Emmett's grandaunt in the head with a shotgun and demanded that his granduncle, Mose "Preacher" Wright (see September 22), give them the boy "who did the talking." Kidnapping Emmett, they vowed to kill everyone in the house if Wright called the sheriff. When Emmett didn't return later that morning, his cousin called the sheriff, and his and Emmett's mothers in Chicago. Emmett was found dumped in the river that Wednesday; one eye had been gouged out, his forehead had been crushed, he'd been shot, and his badly mutilated body was swollen beyond recognition.

Without permission from the family, the sheriff ordered immediate burial. Emmett's mother, Mamie Till Bradley, called everyone up to the governor to stop the burial. Giving in, the sheriff shipped the body to Chicago with orders not to open the casket. Mamie Bradley did. And what she saw so sickened her that she wanted the world to see it too. *Jet* magazine published the brutal photo, thousands filed past the open casket, more gathered for the funeral. The burial was delayed four days to allow still more to see that a lynching was not a victimless, nameless act. It bore the face of a child.

Children   Innocence

SEPTEMBER

The Landsmark Girls (September 11, 1937).
Photographer unknown. Courtesy of the author.

For more information about the Landsmark Girls,
please see September 11.

SEPTEMBER 1

On September 1, 1976, one of the oldest and most sacred sites in the history of Africans in the Americas was officially recognized and preserved as a National Historic Landmark. Fortsberg, on St. John's Island in the Virgin Islands, was the site of the first successful slave rebellion.

In 1717, the Danish West India and Guinea Company established a plantation on the island at Coral Bay that was completely dependent on slave labor for its self-contained sugar industry. Sugar and bay rum were produced in an early-eighteenth-century state-of-the-art sugar factory. The ever-expanding scope of slavery produced a rebellion, which began on November 23, 1733, at the Estate Carolina plantation and soon consumed the entire island.

So superior in military strategy and strength were the enslaved Africans that their battle for independence lasted a full six months. In May 1734, they were finally overpowered when the French, the Dutch, and the Danes banded together to suppress the freedom fight. In the course of battle, much of the now-historic fort was destroyed. By 1760, however, it was rebuilt, as was the agribusiness of plantation life on the island.

Tragically, the Africans did not win their freedom. It would be another century before slavery ended throughout the West Indies. But the landmark status of the fort is a tangible reminder of the long road from slavery to freedom throughout the Caribbean, and the road from plantation slavery to human dignity in the Virgin Islands of St. Croix, St. John, and St. Thomas—now U.S. territories.

SEPTEMBER 2

A LETTER DATED SEPTEMBER 2, 1970, from Maybelle Wilcox, curator of the South Dakota Historical Society, to the Film Department of the Museum of Modern Art requests information on a pioneer of African American film: "Oscar Micheaux, who is a noted colored author, based his book *The Homesteader* on early day history in our county. We understand he filmed this story when he became a producer. Our county was opened to homesteaders in 1909 and we have now opened the Tripp County Historical Society."

From this intriguing little note, the story of Oscar Micheaux only gets better. Blessed with a confident, pioneering spirit, when most African Americans were leaving the South for the cities of the North, Micheaux moved west. In 1905, he settled in South Dakota. When drought dried up ranching opportunities, he turned his experiences into popular fiction—writing, publishing, and selling his own books. In 1918, *The Homesteader* attracted the attention of Lincoln Pictures, a major producer of "race movies" (films for, but not always by, blacks). Lincoln wanted the film rights to the book, but when Micheaux insisted on directing the film himself, the deal was off. Undaunted, he used his entrepreneurial skills to raise the money to produce and direct the film himself. Released in 1919, *The Homesteader* was the first African American feature film.

Micheaux was not the first black filmmaker, but he was the most prolific. In the forty-five films he wrote, produced, directed, and distributed, he used Hollywood genres to bring black characters to the screen. As other black companies died out with the advent of talkies, Micheaux took on white investors, toured with prints in hand, "four-walled" his films by renting theaters and self-promoting his latest sensation starring the "Negro Valentino" or the "Sepia Mae West." Well into the 1940s, Micheaux brought to black audiences "the colored heart from close range." Though his characters were stereotypical, his real achievement was in persistence, his body of work, and a 1925 feature, *Body and Soul*, with Paul Robeson in his screen acting debut.

Historiography/Film   Self-portraiture

SEPTEMBER 3

ON SEPTEMBER 3, 1957, Little Rock, Arkansas, was positioned for a showdown on school desegregation. The night before, Governor Orval Faubus had given a televised speech guaranteed to heat already seething racial passions to a full boil. He had called out the National Guard to surround Central High School "not as segregationists or integrationists, but as soldiers called to active duty to carry out their assigned tasks." In an obvious play to violence, he added: "But I must state here in all sincerity that it is my opinion, yes, even conviction, that it will not be possible to restore or maintain order and protect the lives and property of the citizens if forcible integration is carried out tomorrow in the schools."

With the Guard in place, the school superintendent asked black parents not to accompany their children to school the next day. "This is murder," a reporter told the NAACP's Daisy Bates late that night. He had seen a white mob swarming the school and feared that thousands more would join them by morning for the arrival of the Little Rock Nine. "I have been powerless to do anything," presidential aide E. Frederic Morrow wrote of the occasion in his diary, accurately expressing the mood. African Americans in powerful places had made powerful allies; yet, when the crucial moment came, the nine children were on their own.

Of the Nine, all but Elizabeth Eckford had gotten word that they would meet off-site and be escorted by a group of ministers. Taking the bus directly to school, she arrived alone and was soon circled by a screaming mob. The Guard allowed white students to enter and raised their bayonets to block her. Fleeing amid a flood of taunts, Elizabeth rested at a bus stop. There, *New York Times*'s reporter Benjamin Fine tried to interview her, but seeing her tears, he lifted her head and whispered, "Don't let them see you cry." Soon Grace Lorch, a white woman broke through. "Leave the child alone," she yelled to the crowd screaming "Nigger lover" and "Get the Jew!" When Fine and Lorch tried to get a cab, but couldn't, they stayed with Elizabeth until a bus took her to safety.

SEPTEMBER 4

"WE THOUGHT WE WERE about to be lynched." Huddled in a car with Paul Robeson, that's how fellow passengers—and, some alleged, "fellow travelers"—felt as they fled the infamous Peekskill Riot of September 4, 1949.

Robeson had previously headlined three successful concerts in Peekskill, New York. Then HUAC skewered him in its witch-hunt for "communists" (see July 20, August 23). When a fourth Robeson concert was announced for August 27—a benefit for the Harlem chapter of the Civil Rights Congress—the rabble-rousing and the violent sighted their chance for mischief. Peekskill's *Evening Star* led a front-page charge: "Robeson Concert Here Aids 'Subversive' Unit—Is Sponsored by 'People's Artists' Called Red Front in California." And the circus came to town. On the day of the concert, local Veterans of Foreign Wars (VFW), American Legion, and a Catholic high school troupe set out to break up the event. Thugs blocked entry to the outdoor concert site, some passengers were pulled from their cars into a rock-throwing crowd yelling "Dirty Commie" and "Dirty Kike." A cross burned on a hillside. And all this took place under the smiling gaze of police officers who arrested no one. As Robeson neared the site by car, his companions had their hands full preventing him from trying to perform, driving him to safety. And in the aftermath, even an FBI agent report that the riot had been "started by vets" was insufficient to get an investigation. The American Legion commander boldly stated, "Our objective was to prevent the Robeson concert and I think our objective was reached." Not quite. Robeson slated a rematch for September 4.

At 6:00 A.M., union guards arrived at the site to rim the stage, then came the state police, twenty thousand attendees, thousands of vet provocateurs, and two snipers (soon arrested). At 2:00 P.M. the concert began. Folk singer Pete Seeger, pianists Ray Lev and Leonid Hambro, and Paul Robeson, accompanied by Larry Brown, performed their historic, courageous best and were swept offstage, shoved onto the floors of cars, covered in blankets, and delivered 'cross the River Jordan.

SEPTEMBER 5

THE AUGUST 1971 KILLING of George "Soledad Brother" Jackson (see May 4) by guards as he walked across a San Quentin, California, prison yard sent shock waves through the prisoners' rights movement so deep that the ripples reached upstate New York and surged into the Attica prison rebellion of September 1971.

In July, Attica inmates had sent a "manifesto" to Governor Nelson Rockefeller and the state corrections commissioner, Russell Oswald, calling for such reforms as more than one shower per week, more than one bar of soap and one roll of toilet paper per month, library books, and increased visiting hours. Then came Jackson's death. The next morning, in spontaneous solidarity, prisoners wore black shoestrings as armbands and refused breakfast. Oswald recorded a taped message to be played over the intercom: Reform would take time. By September 5, 1971, anger at Oswald's "put-down" had percolated to a boil. On September 9, it erupted in rebellion as inmates seized hostages and took control of the prison. On September 13, rumors of castrated hostages got more credibility than they deserved. Over the objections of a team of observer/negotiators, the governor ordered state troopers to storm the prison. Tom Wicker of the *New York Times* was an observer. In response to his honest reporting about prisoner solidarity across racial lines, he was met by guards taunting him as a "nigger lover." That was the mind-set generating the rumors. He described the last minutes of the siege: "At 9:43:28 this morning the power went off in the small littered steward's room on the second floor of [Attica] . . . while officers put a bloody end to a massive uprising by about 1,500 inmates. . . . 'There's always time to die,' [Congressman] Badillo said. 'I don't know what the rush was.'"

When it was over, guards stripped the men and retaliated with such bestial acts that a civil suit was filed on the prisoners' behalf in 1974. In June of 1997, Frank Smith, an inmate released in 1973, working as a paralegal, was awarded $4 million in damages for injuries suffered.

Prisoners' Rights   Understanding

SEPTEMBER 6

O<small>N</small> S<small>EPTEMBER</small> 6, 1960, in Rome, Rafer Johnson made Olympic decathlon history, winning a gold medal. On merit alone, it was a stellar triumph, but what he did for African Americans in the throes of the Civil Rights era was what Jesse Owens had done at the height of Jim Crow. Of the sixteen records set in Berlin in 1936, Owens had set four. In the brutal Civil Rights era, Johnson won the ten-event decathlon, the most grueling of all the Olympic trials, and he, too, set a record. So definitive was each man's victory that it could not be misconstrued as a fluke. Yet, meaningful as this was, was as meaningless as it should have been. There seems something very wrong with viewing black achievement through the prism of white negativity, with burdening ourselves to prove things that we should have never admitted into doubt.

Muhammad Ali (né Cassius Clay) was also among the 1960 Olympians. Just as he would be called upon by life to show that the world's greatest fighter could be one of its greatest pacifists (see June 20), others have struck a blow for freedom from their Olympic platform by proving that there is more than one way to deliver a punch. In 1960, polio victim Wilma Rudolph made strides for the disabled with three golds as an Olympic runner. At the Mexico City games in 1968, gold and bronze medalists Tommie Smith and John Carlos raised a black power salute in memorial tribute to Dr. King. And in the spirit of *harambee!* (let's all pull together, Kenya's freedom chant) the fifteen-man Kenyan team galvanized world acclaim by taking home eight medals, three of them gold.

Although tennis was not an Olympic sport, we honor Arthur Ashe on this day for winning the men's U.S. Open championship at Forest Hills in 1968. That he was the first black man to do so is historic; that he was an army lieutenant at the time and unable to accept a $14,000 prize is ironic; but that he achieved *A Hard Road to Glory,* his three-volume history of the African American in sports, was, to him, his finest hour. And his human rights advocacy against racism and apartheid, and for AIDS research made him a man truly without peer.

From his days in the Marine Corps to his days as a Civil Rights organizer and president of the NAACP's Union County branch, Robert F. Williams had seen a lot and taken a lot. But Williams would take no more. He'd seen a court acquit a white man of kicking a black hotel maid down a flight of stairs—despite eyewitness testimony and the defendant's failure to appear at his own trial. The same court acquitted a white man of the attempted rape of a pregnant black woman—again, despite corroboration of the victim's testimony. When the Klan roared through town in 1957, each raid on blacks was led by police cars. He saw "cringing, begging" ministers go to the city fathers for aid, only to be told the Klan had a "constitutional right to meet and organize the same way as the NAACP." Only when news of "dangerous incidents between Klansmen and armed Negroes" appeared in the papers did the attacks stop.

In the face of such evil, Williams publicly challenged nonviolence and was suspended as chapter president by the national NAACP. In September 1959, *Liberation* magazine featured the story "Is Violence Necessary to Combat Injustice? For the Positive: Williams Says, 'We Must Fight Back'":

> Laws serve to deter crime and protect the weak from the strong in civilized society. Where there is a breakdown of law, where is the force of deterrent . . . ? Moral individuals respect the rights of others. The southern brute respects only force. Nonviolence is a very potent weapon when the opponent is civilized, but nonviolence is no repellent for a sadist.
>
> Negroes must be willing to defend themselves. . . . They must be willing to die and to kill in repelling their assailants. Negroes *must* protect themselves. . . . Some Negro leaders have cautioned me that if Negroes fight back, the racist will have cause to exterminate the race. . . . It is instilled at an early age that men who violently and swiftly rise to oppose tyranny are virtuous examples to emulate. I have been taught by my government to fight. Nowhere in the annals of history does the record show a people delivered from bondage by patience alone.

Ideals   Conscience

SEPTEMBER 8

In the fall of 1968, the murder trial of Black Panther Party cofounder Huey Newton was front-page news (see August 5). If Newton was convicted, he faced execution. If Newton was exonerated, high-level city, state, and federal officials faced their own demise in this presidential election year turned to riot over the assassination of Martin Luther King, the draft, and the war in Vietnam. The battle for public opinion was on. To raise both public consciousness and defense funds, Panthers and supporters crisscrossed the country in a frantic round of "Free Huey!" rallies. As the trial wound its way toward the jury and a verdict, FBI chief J. Edgar Hoover publicly declared war on the Black Panthers, topping the headlines for September 8, 1968.

The Black Panther Party is "the greatest threat to the internal security of the country," Hoover pronounced. "Schooled in the Marxist-Leninist ideology . . . leaders . . . travel extensively all over the United States preaching . . . not only to ghetto residents, but to students in colleges, universities and high schools as well." Clearly, the Panthers were a threat, but not for the reasons Hoover alleged. Their intelligence and discipline were yielding success, as Panther leader Elaine Brown related in this story about Chicago's Fred Hampton (see December 4):

> It was six, six-thirty in the morning, freezing Chicago weather. And Fred would have them out there doing push-ups and jumping jacks and getting themselves energized for the day's work, which included making the breakfast . . . selling papers . . . working in the medical clinic. . . . That was Fred Hampton . . . twenty-one years old. He was unbelievable. It was like Martin Luther King. You just had to see Fred Hampton mobilize people who wouldn't have moved for anything else that I could imagine on the planet, much less to get up and cook breakfast.

Poignantly enough, just as Brown admired King, King had admired the Panthers. As Harry Belafonte recalled: "Dr. King once said, 'Were I able to co-opt those minds into my cause, there is no question that victory would be swift and eternal.'"

Social History   Self-realization

SEPTEMBER 9

On Monday, September 9, 1968, a New York City Teacher's Strike began that paralyzed the city for six weeks and made the desegregation of northern schools front-page news. In all, one million children and fifty-seven thousand teachers were affected. But, contrary to published reports, the root problem was not really job security, it was years of disrespect and distrust.

In 1964, ten years after the Supreme Court desegregated schools (see May 17, May 31), the North remained aloof—regarding segregation as a southern issue (see February 18). But black children were equally victimized in the North. The methods differed, but the results could be just as bad, as in the case of Reverend C. Herbert Oliver's son. Oliver's duties as a Presbyterian minister had brought his family from Birmingham to Brooklyn in 1965. In the South, his son had scored far above the national average in math; in New York, he was failing despite his teacher's word that he was "doing fine." In the South, when Oliver went to school, he felt welcome as a parent; in the North, he was ignored and put off. The issue, as Oliver saw it, was not that the children, teachers, and principals were all black in the segregated South; it was that southern children, teachers, principals, and parents were all part of the same community, all shared the same values, and together supported their schools. Not so in the North.

As African Americans and Latinos began taking more responsibility for their children's academic growth, they were rebuffed at Board of Education meetings. When they spoke up, their microphones were shut off. They wanted integrated schools, but New York's "neighborhood school" policy kept their districts almost all black and Puerto Rican. With support from State Commissioner of Education James Allen, a compromise was struck in the spring of 1967 and was later funded by the Ford Foundation. Three pilot Community School Districts were created: two in Manhattan and one in Brooklyn—the Ocean Hill–Brownsville District that ignited the spark that touched off the strike (see November 24).

School Desegregation   Self-determination

SEPTEMBER 10

As NEW YORK'S TWO BIGGEST BLACK WEEKLIES went to press on September 10, 1937, there was no doubt about the lead story. Two rival religious leaders—one derided as a cultist, the other as too faithful a Christian—joined forces to rally thousands of disciples and dollars in defense of the "Scottsboro Boys." In 1931, nine young teenage boys had the misfortune of being on a train when the thought of rape crossed a stranger's mind. At a station near Scottsboro, Alabama, the nine were dragged from the train and into a snare of false arrest, imprisonment, lynch mobs, forced confessions, death-row convictions, Supreme Court reversals, and retrials that—despite the "victim's" recantation and medical evidence that no rape had occurred—consumed their lives for the next forty-five years (see October 25).

It was this international cause célèbre that forged the unlikely alliance of Father Divine and Rev. Thomas Harten, each a man of commitment to black freedom in his own right and on his own terms. Father Divine was the flamboyant leader of the Harlem-based Peace Mission, whose Depression-era formula for the "good life" for his flock of multiracial "angels" built cooperative businesses and outwitted segregation and poverty. Rev. Thomas Harten of Brooklyn's Holy Trinity Baptist Church was the fiery activist-preacher and founder of the Afro-Protective League, which fought lynchings and police brutality. For achievement and the size of their followings, few could stride among these two ecclesiasts in their day.

As Malcolm X would remind a later generation, "You don't catch hell because you're a Methodist or Baptist . . . you catch hell because you're a black man." It was a point Divine and Harten had crossed vast land mines of public pressure to reach. Said Harten, "There are a lot of people . . . who are going to talk about me for appearing here. They talk about you wherever you go. I want you to know that Father Divine will not convert to me tonight nor I to him. . . . I want you to know that we're not here to do battle. But we are here for a common cause. For the cause of justice, liberty, and righteousness."

SEPTEMBER 11

In 1891, TWIN SISTERS—Mabel and Lena Carlisle—were born on the Caribbean island of St. Kitts. As a young woman, Mabel came to the United States, vowing to send for her twin. She had come from a privileged family that had fallen on hard times after her father's death. Having grown up in a family with servants, she found herself working as a domestic in America. It did not stop her, she had a goal: to see her sister. It would take her five years to save the eighty dollars needed for her sister's first-class steamer passage. But she did it. Together in the States, each was married and gave birth to three children. And so the story of their first-generation progeny begins with a lesson passed on by their brother, Cyril, to their children pictured in family photos dated September 11, 1937 (see September's lead photo). "You children are born here," he would tell them. "Take a civil service exam."

When Lena's daughter, Muriel, graduated from high school, Mabel's daughter, Doris, gave her an exam application. One thing stood between Muriel and success: a watch. Her mother took her to buy one—a delicate, affordable wristwatch perfect for a seventeen-year-old honor high school graduate. The store was operated by Father Divine's Harlem Peace Mission (see September 10). Upon learning of the watch's special significance in the young girl's life, the saleswoman offered a blessing: "Don't worry, Father will see that you pass." And pass she did.

On July 6, 1943, Muriel began work as a New York City civil servant working for the Department of Welfare. These were the war years of good news and bad, and so the radio stayed tuned at work. There, on the radio, Muriel heard that *The Arthur Godfrey Show* needed a secretary. She got word to Doris—a fine typist and stenographer. Within days, listening to the radio again, Muriel's office mates heard Arthur Godfrey say, "And today we welcome our new secretary, Doris." When the story is told of "how we got ovah," family is high on the list. So, too, is the African maxim resurrected by Toni Morrison: *It takes a village to raise a child. . . .*

Family   Continuity

Hᴇ ᴡᴀꜱ ᴋɴᴏᴡɴ ᴀꜱ the best all-around boxer ever: Sugar Ray Robinson. "The greatest combination of brains, brawn, and boxing skill the modern prize ring has seen," said sportswriter Dan Parker. On the night of September 12, 1951, to that list of credits was added the record for gross receipts in a nonheavyweight fight: $767,626.17. For his rematch with England's black champ, Randy Turpin, 61,370 fans packed New York's Polo Grounds to see Sugar Ray retake his crown.

As a young athlete, Robinson learned critical lessons on the keys to success from his trainer, George Gainford—for example, how to circumvent the ban on prize money for amateur bouts: "They give you a watch and then buy it back for ten dollars." When sports officials in upstate New York asked the young athlete for his AAU card before a bout, not having one, Gainford convinced the unknown, who did not have one, to use a card registered to a Ray Robinson. He was young, poor, hungry to win, and didn't even have a name to call his own. But when sportswriter Jack Case commented to Gainford "That's a real sweet fighter you've got there. As sweet as sugar," Walker Smith was reborn as Sugar Ray Robinson.

Eleven career years later—with time out for service in World War II—the welterweight-turned-middleweight champ was a "homeboy" in communities throughout the United States. He was Everyman. Having literally fought his way from the very bottom to the top, he had stumbled and lost his crown just months before. Now he was back on top. As the *New York Times* reported:

> Thousands of persons who had waited patiently . . . for word of the outcome of the fight . . . transformed their favorite ringman's bailiwick into a screaming, cheering, back-slapping backdrop for their pent-up emotions last night. Shouts of . . . "Can't beat that man" rent the air as milling throngs pressed about. . . . Pedestrian and traffic lanes leading to the heart of Harlem, were jammed. . . . Vehicles, bumper to bumper, moved at a snail's pace . . . [Awaiting] their hero, the crowd in front of the hotel swayed, sang and danced to the rhythm of a band.

SEPTEMBER 13

Throughout 1961 and 1962, James Meredith's crusade to enter the University of Mississippi dominated the school desegregation news. A century after its founding, "Ole Miss" had never admitted a black student. In 1958, Clennon King (see November 17) tried to enroll. Declared "crazy," he soon found himself institutionalized, then forced out of state. A 1959 attempt left Clyde Kennard jailed and imprisoned in a penitentiary for the rest of his life. Then, in 1962, Governor Ross Barnett personally interceded to bar Meredith's registration. In the wake of *Brown v. Board of Education* (see May 17), Barnett's defiance of federal law on September 13, 1962, forged the most serious constitutional crisis since southern secession had caused the Civil War. As toughs from the statehouse to the streets begged for his blood, throughout this death-defying saga the calmest man was Meredith himself. How did this army veteran and acknowledged loner survive? As he wrote in his book *Three Years in Mississippi* he had a plan:

> How to engage in this war without becoming a casualty was of prime importance once the decision had been made to invade the enemy's most sacred and revered stronghold. . . . For a long time I had been impressed by [the] maxim, "The wise man learns by the mistakes of others, the average man learns by his own, and the fool never learns." The most obvious similarity in the fate of [those who had applied before me] was their willingness to collaborate with the enemy. There is always that element of trust in the "good faith" of one or of a few of the men who make up the backbone of the system. . . .
>
> Not once during the three years that I was in Mississippi did I have discourse with the enemy without the public as a witness. One fact that I prize highly, and it confirms my faith in the basic trustworthiness of all my people, is that no Negro ever approached me to make any deals for the "white folks." However, I must admit that I deliberately made myself unapproachable by anyone white or black. . . . The primary tactics that I chose to use were (1) to act secretly and quickly and (2) to capitalize on public concern and public opinion. The objective was to make myself more valuable alive than dead.

Turning Points   **Vision**

SEPTEMBER 14

W<small>E FIRST MET</small> A<small>LICE</small> W<small>ALKER</small>, *Revolutionary Petunia* and sage of the South, in 1968 and loved her work at *Once*, her first book of poetry. Since then, as she wrote in her poem *I Said to Poetry*, she's ridden the morning rails to the muse and the nighttime express to a Pulitzer Prize—a rough commute between the lands of fiction and non.

But it was *To Hell with Dying*, her first published story, that spread the news: Alice Walker had the gift, and, as folks would hope, we would have Alice Walker for a long, long time . . . *the good lord willin' and the creek don' rise.* . . .

A student at Sarah Lawrence, distraught at the death of a beloved elder and too poor to travel to his funeral, she wrote the fictionalized tribute to him on the day of his burial one sad Christmas season. Langston Hughes opened the world's eyes to her gift by publishing it in 1967, the year he died. In 1974, she returned the favor, opening children's eyes to the life of Hughes as his newest biographer. As in the story that Hughes so loved, the power of children's love would restore life to a dying man.

"To hell with dying," my father would say, *"these children want Mr. Sweet!"* Walker would begin her story. Twenty years later, as she finalized the details of its first illustrated children's edition, she would write, "When I met Langston Hughes I was amazed. He was another Mr. Sweet! Aging and battered, full of pain, but writing poetry, and laughing too, and always making other people feel better. It was as if my love for one great old man down in the poor and beautiful and simple South had magically, in the new world of college and literature and poets and publishing and New York, led me to another." It was as if the two elder artists, wracked by life's labors and pain, had breathed their last and best into the soulful artistry of Alice Walker. As if from the music of one and the lyric tome of the other, she had learned to sing.

SEPTEMBER 15

At 10:00 A.M. ON SEPTEMBER 15, 1963, four girls were in the basement ladies' room of Birmingham's Sixteenth Street Baptist Church excitedly preparing for their annual Youth Day service. Twenty minutes later, a truck driver known to the local Klan as "Dynamite Bob" bombed the church, killing the girls: Denise McNair, Addie Mae Collins, Carole Robertson, and Cynthia Wesley.

Historian Taylor Branch recounted the scene:

> "[Maxine] McNair stumbled through the church to the front door and then made [her] way around outside through the gathering noise of moans and sirens. McNair searched desperately for her only child until finally she came upon a sobbing old man and screamed, 'Daddy, I can't find Denise!' The man helplessly replied, 'She's dead, baby. I've got one of her shoes.' He held a girl's white dress shoe and the look on his daughter's face made him scream out, 'I'd like to blow the whole town up!'"

Since the start of the Birmingham demonstrations, the Sixteenth Street Baptist Church had served as the movement's headquarters. But there was more to the bombing than that. Not only had the high point of the era—the March on Washington—taken place just over two weeks earlier, but the desegregation of Alabama schools had been set for that week. In Birmingham that same day, police killed a black boy in the street with a shot to the back of his head. A white mob randomly attacked and killed a black man on a bicycle. Would there be no end to the violence? Why children? Why the innocents?

That Wednesday, eight thousand mourners attended the funeral of three of the four girls (Carole Robertson's family had decided on a private service). Among the mourners at the mass funeral was an interracial delegation of eight hundred clergy, the largest such assembly in the city's history. Months before, it had been the callousness of the clergy that had provoked Dr. King's "Letter from a Birmingham Jail" (see April 16). Perhaps they had at last understood "why we can't wait."

Children   Demons

SEPTEMBER 16

ALTHOUGH WE THINK OF SLAVERY as a southern institution, there was a time when the largest slaveholding
colony was Connecticut. How fitting that Connecticut should
be among the first to formally address Civil Rights. In mid-
September 1943, the Connecticut State Assembly passed House
Bill 1361, which established the Connecticut Inter-Racial Commission, called for the governor to appoint ten commissioners,
and allocated six thousand dollars for the first year's budget.

The Inter-Racial Commission was a response to Hartford's
black community and, in particular, to the leadership of Rev.
John C. Jackson of Union Baptist Church. From the start of his
activist ministry in 1922, Jackson pushed for fair employment
and achieved his first victory with the hiring of Union Baptist's
C. Edythe Taylor as Hartford's first black teacher. From his
congregation also came the city's first black policeman and
members of the city's school and welfare boards. After years of
relentless agitation, the statewide Inter-Racial Commission
(with Jackson as one of its board members) was created in
1943 and officially began its work on January 19, 1944, when a
black social worker, Dr. Frank T. Simpson, was hired as the
first paid staff person. Significantly, the commission was multiracial both in its membership and in its mission—to analyze
and recommend policy solutions on discrimination relating to
race, ethnicity, and religion. On September 8, 1944, a year into
its funding, the commission's first report focused on five key
areas: racial tensions in industrial employment, educational opportunity, housing, the use of public facilities, and the spread
of malicious rumors.

The commission's nursing school study sheds light on its
work. Six schools were asked "Do you accept Negro students?"
Two did not respond, two barred "colored students," one said
blacks "would be most unhappy," and only one, St. Francis, admitted students on merit. Clearly, the commission faced a
long-term challenge. In 1951, it became the Connecticut Commission on Civil Rights. In 1967, it was renamed the Connecticut Commission on Human Rights and Opportunities.

SEPTEMBER 17

Sɪɴᴄᴇ ᴛʜᴇ ᴅᴀʏꜱ of the Underground Railroad, images of "freedom" and "trains" had been inextricably linked. These two words conjured notions of space, distance, movement, and a long-awaited destination well worth the ride. And so it was that the inspiration for the Freedom Train chugged from dream to reality. An idea attributed to then–Attorney General Tom Clark, it would cross 23,000 miles of track through North and South. But true to the journey toward freedom in the United States, the Freedom Train, which rolled on September 17, 1947, would make more than a few stops along the way.

What made the specially equipped Freedom Train worth the ride for planners were its exhibits—authentic historical documents telling the story of freedom: the manuscript of the Declaration of Independence (1776); the Treaty of Paris, recognizing the independence of the United States from Britain (1783); a draft of the Constitution with George Washington's handwritten annotations (1787); the original manuscript of the Bill of Rights (1789); Abraham Lincoln's handwritten Emancipation Proclamation (1862), and the Declaration of the United Nations (1945).

But for African Americans, accustomed to empty words, freedom's meaning was best expressed by the planners' action: the Freedom Train would travel only to cities that accepted a no-segregation policy. To be an authorized depot, a city was asked to proclaim a "Community Rededication Week" of activities recommended by the American Heritage Foundation, a committee specifically organized to manage the project.

As with all trains, the tracks—in this case, theory and practice—did not converge. So although no colored or white signs affronted the eye, separate waiting lines often derailed the plan. Poet Langston Hughes's inspiring "Ballad of the Freedom Train," a sign of things on the right track, endures.

Social History   Values

"**I** WASN'T REALLY CHOOSING FRANCE," wrote James Baldwin, "I was getting out of America. I had no idea what might happen to me in France, but I was very clear as to what would happen if I remained in New York. I would go under." "I didn't expect any utopia," wrote Chester Himes. "After all, Americans were [Europe's] descendants. I just wanted out from the United States." In the postwar Paris of the 1940s and 1950s, what black artists who fled America would come to love about their adopted City of Light was that it offered them room to shine.

Among the first expatriates was Ollie Harrington. In 1944 he went to Paris as a war correspondent for the *Pittsburgh Courier*. He returned home after the war, only to find conditions worse than before as racists reasserted brutal dominance, unpunished. After nine lynchings of black veterans in one year, he joined the NAACP's antilynching campaign, only to be targeted for investigation on grounds of his alleged "communist ties." Warned, he self-exiled to Paris, where he flourished as the well-known cartoonist/creator of *Bootsie*.

Richard Wright exiled in 1947 (see June 28). As he wrote in his essay "I Chose Exile": "I live in voluntary exile in France and I like it. There is nothing in the life of America that I miss or yearn for. . . . I love my adopted city. Its sunsets, its teeming boulevards, its slow and humane tempo of life have entered deeply into my heart." In Paris, with his ties to the international community of black and white writers, he cosponsored *Présence Africaine*, the journal edited by Senegal's Alioune Diop. Under its auspices, with such West African and Afri-Caribbean Negritude writers as Léopold Senghor and Aimé Césaire, he co-organized the Congress of Negro Artists and Writers. It was a milestone. At the dawn of the American Civil Rights movement, six months before the Gold Coast took its independence as Ghana, the Congress allied intellectuals throughout the diaspora. On September 18, 1956, that world assembly would land in Paris and head for the Sorbonne, where the Congress opened the next day.

SEPTEMBER 19

For years, New York's black communities had been unofficially off-limits to diplomats—except, of course, for such segregated nightspots as the Cotton Club. But all that changed on September 19, 1960, when Dr. Fidel Castro, premier of Cuba, angered by the inappropriate treatment he'd received at a downtown hotel, moved uptown to a suite at Harlem's black-owned Hotel Theresa.

As reported in the *New York Times* the next day, the Cuban premier and his delegation had been booked at the Shelburne Hotel in central Manhattan near the United Nations. When hotel management breached diplomatic protocol by making "unreasonable cash demands" of the Cuban delegation, Premier Castro personally protested the affront to UN Secretary General Dag Hammarskjöld. After three hours of wrangling among the UN, the U.S. State Department, and Cuban officials, alternate arrangements were made at another midtown hotel at no cost to the Cubans. But by then it was too late. Dr. Castro and his full delegation had left the Shelburne for the Hotel Theresa. Asked why he did not take the other hotel, Castro answered simply: the Theresa had invited him first.

From his perch at the Hotel Theresa, Castro obviously enjoyed the moment for all it was worth—and the need for solidarity against the mistreatment of people of color worldwide was a point well worth making. Among those with whom he held audience at the hotel were Premier Nikita Khrushchev of the Soviet Union, Malcolm X, the press, and a grateful Harlem community, which maintained a steady vigil. As historian John Henrik Clarke recalled years later, "The symbols were absolutely magnificent. Fidel Castro in a black-owned hotel, Khrushchev meeting him in the lobby, the community surrounding the hotel day and night, Castro occasionally coming to the window to wave. It was an event in the development of consciousness in the community." Two weeks later, another appreciative, consciousness-raised crowd would rally in front of the Hotel Theresa to greet Ghana's president, Kwame Nkrumah.

International Relations   **Consciousness**

Mᴀʀᴛɪɴ Lᴜᴛʜᴇʀ Kɪɴɢ's ʙᴏᴏᴋ about the Montgomery Bus Boycott, *Stride Toward Freedom,* had just been published to excellent reviews, and its author was on the road promoting it. Detroit's crowds were eager to meet him. Chicago's were larger and even more eager. New York's liberals and literati were ready, too.

Dr. King had led a thirteen-month seige on segregated buses and, despite a lack of southern hospitality, survived. His home had been firebombed, and just two weeks before his book tour, he had been brutally arrested by police for attempting to enter the courtroom where his friend, Dr. Ralph Abernathy, was being tried on charges stemming from his Civil Rights activism. He had overcome that, too. But it all began spiraling down the Friday night he arrived in Harlem. Nonviolence was no eye for an eye for the sins of oppression; that is what a crowd of the distressed and vocal awaiting King wanted him to know. Then, on Saturday, September 20, 1958, disaster struck as he prepared to autograph his books in the shoe department of Blumstein's Store, located on 125th Street in the heart of Harlem. "Is this Martin Luther King?" asked Izola Curry as she pushed aside the adoring throng waiting to shake his hand and buy his book. Pulling a letter opener from the bodice of her dress, the deranged woman plunged it into King's chest. So close to his aorta had she struck that, as his doctors related, "He was just a sneeze away from death." Symbolically enough for the young pastor, the resulting surgical scar over his heart was shaped like a cross.

Happening so early in his freedom days, when he was only twenty-nine, this incident shaped King's view of his ever-imminent death. As his lieutenant and Atlanta's future mayor Andy Young would say, "The thing he talked about most was death. . . . 'Every morning when I look in the mirror,' he said, 'I realize that this day could be my last. It makes you realize, if you haven't found something you're willing to die for, you're not fit to live.' That was Martin's way of challenging us to live so we wouldn't mind dying for the things we were trying to do."

SEPTEMBER 21

IT IS SAID THAT you can't change the hearts and minds of men. There have always been leaders who knew that the first priority was often to change the *behavior* of men—hearts and minds could follow in their own due time. One such leader was Joseph E. Ritter, Catholic Archbishop of the Diocese of St. Louis.

On September 21, 1947, as he integrated parochial schools, Archbishop Ritter presented his diocese with an ultimatum. In short, he threatened to excommunicate those who actively protested the integration order of the diocese. Those who resisted school desegregation did so at peril to their eternal souls.

St. Louis did not have a good history where race riots were concerned. The "Red Summer of 1919," as the soldiers came home from World War I, had forever stained the city with blood as racist whites ran riot through the black community, unchecked and unapologetic, destroying everything and everybody in sight. In 1946, soldiers returning from World War II had been victimized by a flood of terror like the one that poured from the first war. Now, in 1947, Ritter was taking no chances.

With endless wrangling and harrumphs by religious leaders who managed to justify their racism in biblical chapter and verse, with all the words for why the thing couldn't be done, how refreshing it was to watch a man do so much and say so little.

Religion   Integrity

It was one of the most courageous acts ever. On September 22, 1955, Mose "Preacher" Wright stood up in the witness box of a Sumner, Mississippi, court. With fully extended arm and steady hand, he pointed to two white defendants. "Thar he," said Mr. Wright. There were the two men who had kidnapped and killed his grandnephew Emmett Till (see January 24, August 31). With that, the *New York Post* reported, Wright sat down "with a lurch which told better than anything else the cost in strength to him of the thing he had done." In the twentieth century, never had a black man accused a white in a Mississippi court of law. Never before had a black man held a white to account and lived. Whether this time would be different for the dirt-poor sharecropper, only time would tell. The kidnappers had threatened Wright with death as they took Till. He was fighting back. "I wan't exactly brave and I wan't scared. I just wanted to see justice done."

Added to the drama of Mose Wright's testimony was the scene upon the arrival of Detroit Congressman Charles Diggs, one of only three black representatives at the time. When Diggs couldn't enter the overcrowded courtroom, he gave his card to National Negro Press Association pool reporter James Hicks to hand to the judge. As Hicks later recounted for *Eyes on the Prize* researchers, while he was heading toward the bench, a deputy stopped him: "'Where you going, nigger?' And I said, 'I'm going to see the judge.' 'I was going to hand [this card] to the judge.' . . . He called another deputy over and said, 'This nigger said there's a nigger outside who says he's a congressman . . .' So this guy said, 'A nigger congressman?' 'That's what this nigger said, ha! ha! ha!' I said to myself, 'My God!' I had never seen anything like this in my life. The deputy went to the sheriff, who said, 'I'll bring him in here, but I'm going to sit him at you niggers' table.'" When the congressman entered, that's where he sat—at the black press table, where the victim's mother, Mrs. Mamie Bradley, had also been placed.

In the end, the two murderers were acquitted by an all-white male jury.

SEPTEMBER 23

I~N~ 1950, while on a tour of the West African colony of the Gold Coast, Britain's prime minister, Harold Macmillan, looked at the horizon and saw the future. "The wind of change," he predicted, was blowing through Africa; people there would not long tolerate colonial rule. To this, Osagyefo Dr. Kwame Nkrumah—revolutionary leader of the Gold Coast and future president of Ghana, the first colony to steer a course to freedom upon those winds—would add that what Macmillan saw ahead was "no ordinary wind, but a raging hurricane."

Ten years later, as that wind blew through the Congo, Nkrumah headed to New York to address the United Nations in defense of African sovereignty. The first African head of state to ascend the UN stage, Nkrumah was a riveting figure in his kinte robes, generously draped about him. It was the first time the traditional royal cloth had been so prominently displayed in front of the world. Along with the extraordinary tapestry, Nkrumah was the embodiment of Africa's future and the promoter of his nation's own distinctive means to that economic end—the ancient art of weaving the kinte with its unique "monograms" of pattern and color identifying the tribe and station of the wearer. For the Pan-African world, Nkrumah's appearance was an inspiring turning point.

As the Trinidadian scholar C. L. R. James would note, "Nkrumah is . . . one of the greatest of all the Africans. [He] was able to organize the revolution, and after Nkrumah some forty African states followed in ten years. . . . There were only five million people in Ghana, but it was one hundred million who followed in ten years. In other words, he was the catalyst that sent this thing rushing through." As catalyst, Nkrumah sent a message: Stay neutral in the cold war. "The Afro-Asian nations, if they act together, might prove strong enough to be the decisive force for peace. . . . But the whole of Africa must be free and united. Only then will we be able to exercise our full strength [for] peace and the welfare of mankind."

Pan-African World   Tomorrow

"Hollywood has taken millions of dollars of Negro money," wrote Earl J. Morris in the September 24, 1948, issue of the *Pittsburgh Courier*. It wasn't the first time blacks had criticized Hollywood racism. But why did blacks subsidize such racism?

From the turn-of-the-nineteenth-century dawn of American cinema well into the 1970s, the best that could be said for positive change was that white actors no longer worked in blackface, thereby creating jobs for black actors. From 1902 to 1920, the earliest films were celluloid minstrel shows. The few dramas were Jim Crow propaganda tracts. In the 1920s and 1930s, credible independent white producers like Norman Studios, the prolific Oscar Micheaux, and George Johnson's Lincoln Motion Picture Company made "race movies." But they were shut out of distribution by heavy-handed competition and by the high cost of the new talkies and, later, Technicolor. Why should blacks see positive images when Hollywood could serve up bucked-eyed frights and a kid with endless "bad hair days"? A few films featured such legends as Bessie Smith, the singer who saved Columbia Records with her *Downhearted Blues*. But others were still left to wail the same old demeaning tune. The 1940s brought *Gone With the Wind*, for which Hattie McDaniel's Mammy got an Oscar, and Butterfly McQueen's "I don' know nothin' 'bout birthin' no babies, Miss Scarlett!" Prissie got a slap. The 1950s brought Hollywood's answer to school desegregation: *Blackboard Jungle*. But, mercifully, the 1960s brought Sidney Poitier (see April 13).

In truth, Hollywood did not produce a better film; Hollywood had produced a better promotion and distribution network to which no independent filmmaker had access and with which none could compete. But, the either/or—either take the insults or have nothing—that was our *reel* world. Yet subsidizing nothing could prove as powerful a weapon as self-subsidy. In 1971 Melvin van Peebles's totally independent, highly profitable hit *Sweet Sweetback's Baadasssss Song* opened doors for black filmmakers and brought new options to black audiences.

SEPTEMBER 25

Weeks of political posturing and intimidation had delayed school for the Little Rock Nine (see September 3) at Arkansas's now-infamous Central High School. Then the dam broke. On September 23, 1957, President Dwight D. Eisenhower issued a proclamation to desegregate the school and to command "persons engaged in such obstruction of justice to cease and desist therefrom." On September 24, by Executive Order No. 10730, he authorized activation of the National Guard and Air National Guard.

Then, on September 25, 1957, the president and World War II general made known his intention to implement the law. Ten thousand Arkansas National Guardsmen and one thousand paratroopers stood guard as the 101st Airborne "Screaming Eagle" Division of the 327th Infantry Regiment escorted nine teenagers to their first day of school. The nine were: Minnijean Brown, Elizabeth Eckford, Ernest Green, Thelma Mothershed, Melba Pattillo, Gloria Ray, Terrance Roberts, Jefferson Thomas, and Carlotta Walls.

Melba Pattillo recounted the scene inside the school for the *Eyes on the Prize* team:

> I'd only been in the school a couple of hours [when] it was apparent that the mob was overrunning the school. . . . We were all called into the principal's office. . . . Someone made a suggestion that if they allowed the mob to hang one kid, then they could get the rest out while they were hanging the one kid. And a gentleman [Assistant Chief of Police Eugene Smith] said, "How are you going to choose? You're going to let them draw straws?" He said, "I'll get them out." And we were taken to the basement . . . and put into two cars. The drivers were told, "Once you start driving, do not stop." They told us to put our heads down. So the guy revved up the engine and came out of the bowels of this building and as he came up, I could just see hands reaching across this car. I could hear the yelling. I could see guns. The driver didn't hit anybody, but he certainly was forceful and aggressive. . . . He dropped me off at home, and I remember saying, "Thank you for the ride." I should have said, "Thank you for my life."

School Desegregation   Collective Responsibility

SEPTEMBER 26

Twelve days out of the United States, SNCC leaders Julian Bond, Ruby Doris, James Forman, Prathia Hall, Fannie Lou Hamer, Bill Hansen, Donald Harris, Matthew Jones, John Lewis, Robert Moses, and Dona Richards were tasting fresh air. They had given their all in the Freedom Summer project, lost three of their workers to murder (see June 21) and seen more brutalized. Their Mississippi Freedom Democratic Party had left its mark on the political process (see August 22). Now they were in Africa—Conakry, Guinea.

How was the trip possible? Singer Harry Belafonte, a devout supporter of both SCLC and SNCC, made it so. He raised $60,000 to fund the fall voter registration drive plus $10,000 for the trip. In Conakry, they were welcomed as guests of the Guinean people and their government.

Throughout the trip, James Forman kept a journal. On September 26, 1964, he recorded a surprise visit from President Sekou Touré the night before. Guinea's six years of freedom from French colonial rule offered unique insight. He saw in the freedom struggle a political problem "created by history, and history would decide its future." Solving it began with understanding then strategizing the step-by-step goals of their greater objective. Organization was key; everyone must pull in the same direction. Finally, freedom in the United States must evolve from tactics grounded in a study of the uniquely American sociopolitical landscape.

Later, Belafonte recalled that evening's most moving experience:

> After the meeting Fannie Lou started to cry and said that she didn't know quite what she would do with this experience. For so long she and a lot of poor black folk had tried unsuccessfully to meet with the president of her own country . . . and could never see him. And here in Africa, a head of state came to see her with great words of encouragement and hope and a declaration that this Africa was their home and its people their family. I don't think that anybody who was on that trip ever saw life in quite the same way again.

SEPTEMBER 27

In the revolving door that cycles African American culture in and out of vogue, the fall of 1968 produced a rebirth not unlike the flowering of arts and culture that generated the Harlem Renaissance of the 1920s. As the demand for Black Studies swept campuses, the publishing and music industries responded by opening dusty vaults to reveal long-lost treasure troves. Spoken-word albums and early sound jazz were restored; out-of-print books were republished, and with them the DuBoises, Robesons, Wrights, and others were resuscitated from the obscurity imposed by the Red Scare politics of the 1950s. Open-heart surgery to the soul, these missing voices pumped a life-sustaining continuity through our veins. It was a vibrant time, full of intellect, energy, and a quest for possibility.

In September 1968 alone, Arno Press, in cooperation with the *New York Times*, published forty-five "forgotten" books. And *for the record*, the Folkways label released a twenty-seven-volume set of spoken-word albums from its series "Afro-American History and Culture."

In the cycle of things, ready access to these resources was proof and reward in one of a major symbiotic phenomenon. Just as Black Studies had generated the demand for these works, the resurrection of our printed and recorded history and culture empowered entire academic disciplines. For without books, college courses could not be accredited. Without accredited courses, advanced study could not be legitimatized. Without advanced degrees, the academic matrix could not generate new scholars to produce new books, and so forth. Without advanced degrees in a discipline, that area of study was rendered invalid, considered inappropriate for serious study. In this self-fulfilling prophecy, there could be no professors to teach undergraduates, no new teachers to impart the knowledge to those in elementary through high school.

Is it any wonder that thirty years later the process has only just begun?

SEPTEMBER 28

On September 26, 1976, a Black Leadership Conference of 130 men and women, convened by the Congressional Black Caucus, was held in Washington, D.C. Two days later the idea that would take shape as TransAfrica, Inc. was gnawing at the mind of its future executive director, Randall Robinson, then on the staff of Michigan Congressman Charles Diggs, chairman of the Africa subcommittee of the House Foreign Affairs Committee.

Leaders at the two-day conference had been mulling over issues relating to the African diaspora. They concluded that the need existed for a private advocacy group on matters crucial to Africa, the Caribbean, and U.S. foreign policy in those regions. An ad hoc committee led by Randall Robinson, Herschelle Challenor, and Willard Johnson went into a huddle, strategizing a working plan and developing funding sources. With underwriting from the National Council of Churches and the United Methodist Church, TransAfrica was incorporated and began formal operations on July 1, 1977. Since that time, it has grown to a membership organization of forty thousand devoted to its mission of "monitoring legislative activities and lobbying for more progressive U.S. foreign policy towards Africa and the Caribbean." To date, its greatest achievement has been its effort to overturn the white apartheid regime in South Africa through economic sanctions and the release of Nelson Mandela. Typically and significantly, Robinson was unable to be in South Africa for Mandela's historic walk to freedom. He was on a hunger strike, his own personal commitment to the people of Haiti.

As one magazine has said of the Harvard-educated lawyer, Robinson is "polished brass." As Randall Robinson has said of himself and his mission, "If we love ourselves, we love Africa and the Caribbean. We are indissolubly joined."

SEPTEMBER 29

WHEN ALEX HALEY WAS A BOY in Henning, Tennessee, the stories his grandmother told were not always welcome. "Oh, Maw," Alex's mother would say. And his grandmother would snap back, "If you don't care who and where you came from, well, I does!" But then would come the days of summer when other, older aunts came to visit the Henning homestead and young Alex would "sort of scrunch myself down behind the white-painted rocker holding Grandma." That was a first call to adventure for the boy who would retrace her stories back to Africa and write *Roots*, the book that launched the great American genealogical quest.

On September 29, 1967, he stood on the dock overlooking the Annapolis, Maryland harbor, where his great-great-great-great-great-grandfather was dragged ashore on September 29, 1767, two centuries ago. How he came to know that was a story in itself—a story that began on the porch with Grandma:

> The time would be just about as the dusk was deepening into the night, with the lightning bugs flickering on and off around the honeysuckle vines, and . . . always they would talk about the same things. . . . The farthest-back person they ever talked about was a man they called "The African," whom they always said had been brought to this country on a ship to some place that they pronounced "Naplis." They said he was bought off this ship by a "Massa John Walker." . . . This particular African's name was "Toby." But they said anytime any of the other slaves called him that, he would strenuously rebuff them, declaring that his name was "Kin-tay." . . . He would point at the river that ran near the plantation—actually the Mattaponi River—and say what sounded like "Kamby Bolongo."

Those wondrously woven threads would knot themselves into the tapestry of who Alex was and the adventurer–folk historian–writer he would become. The strange words would beckon a trail to "Naplis," Annapolis. Massa John's plantation records dated the arrival of his *cargo*, "Toby," who knew himself as "Kintay," Kunte Kinte, and who was born four days upriver from "Kamby," Gambia.

Adventure/Family   Memory

Tom Feelings grew up in love with art. For inspiration, he looked to the thrill of life outside his own front door, scenes from Fulton Street and Nostrand Avenue in Brooklyn, New York. Returning home from the air force in the late 1950s, he went to art school for formal training in painting and illustration. But the noses of the people he drew were never straight enough, the lips always too thick.

> We were told that we should paint the things we felt most deeply about, but that encouragement was not meant for me. . . . When I brought in black subject matter, I either got the cold shoulder or was told that I was "overly sensitive." One day in art history class, I asked the lecturer, "Weren't there any black artists of significance?" "No," he said. "Well, what about African Art?" I asked. . . . "That's primitive art," the lecturer replied. I walked out of the class. I *had* to reject a history that did not include me.

Fortunately, Feelings was an adult when this incident occurred. What would such an attitude have done to a child? Ironically, it was from children that Feelings found his own artful solutions when he, his wife, Muriel, and their son lived in Ghana from 1964 to 1966. To this day, his sketches of children are among his most enduring images as an artist:

> I knew that [warmth and] spirit was in the young black children at home, but it was buried deep under layers of frustration and alienation. I saw none of this in the faces of children I drew in Ghana, and I do not feel I "read something into" the faces. As soon as I saw them I knew what I had come there for . . . to re-affirm a feeling I had deep within me that this is where the warmth and strength must have originated: the knowledge of knowing *who* you are and *where* you have come from—that you have the security of an extended family. It's a way of looking at life. As someone once said, "Africa turns all knowledge into a living experience." Once you have seen that, it cannot be taken away from you.

OCTOBER

Little Boy with a Big Message (1967). Courtesy of the
photographer. © Roy Lewis, 1967.

OCTOBER 1

IN 1961, friends leaked word to Dr. W. E. B. Du Bois that his passport would soon be revoked by the U.S. State Department, making travel impossible. At age ninety-three, Du Bois was highly visible, articulate, and determined to agitate in the cause of Pan-African liberation to his dying day. For that he was considered a threat—and worse. Despised for being vocal and black, he was branded a communist as well (see November 19). He never was. Yet his persecutors kept on. Six weeks after the warning, William and Shirley Du Bois left the United States for Ghana. As Dr. Du Bois departed, never to return, with irony and total contempt for those who had hounded him under the cloak of government authority, he joined the Party on October 1, 1961, with this letter:

> I have been long and slow in coming to this conclusion. . . .
>
> I joined the Socialist Party in 1911. . . . I attacked the Democrats and Republicans for monopoly and disfranchisement of Negroes; I attacked the Socialists for trying to segregate the southern Negro members; I praised racial attitudes of the Communists, but opposed their tactics in the case of the Scottsboro boys and their advocacy of a Negro state. I was early convinced that Socialism was an excellent way of life, but thought it might be reached by various methods. . . . Today I have reached a firm conclusion: Capitalism cannot reform itself; it is doomed to self-destruction. No universal selfishness can bring social good to all.
>
> Communism—the effort to give all men what they need and to ask of each the best they can contribute—this is the only way of human life. The path of the American Communist Party is clear: it will provide the United States with a real third party and thus restore democracy to this land. It will call for public ownership of natural resources; public ownership of transportation and communications; abolition of poverty; no exploitation of labor; social medicine, with hospitalization and care of the old; free education; training for jobs; discipline for growth and reform; freedom under law; and no dogmatic religion. These are not crimes. They are practiced increasingly all over the world. No nation can call itself free which does not allow its citizens to work for these ends.
>
> —William Edward Burghardt Du Bois

In the fall of 1968, as the school year began, a fiery tempest engulfed the University of California at Berkeley. What might otherwise have been a passing storm loomed over the state well into the 1990s. The storm had flared over an invitation to the Black Panther Party's Eldridge Cleaver to conduct a series of ten lectures at Berkeley. The clouds had been seeded by then-governor Ronald Reagan. The site of the erosion was "academic freedom."

In September, news of Cleaver's lecture series intensifed an ongoing conflict between the governor and a coalition of students intellectually and politically armed to combat racism and the Vietnam War. In a deft move, white conservatives denounced Cleaver as an "advocate of racism and violence." It was a presidential election year, and backlash politics peppered every conversation. Eager to keep the governor out of such academic daily fare, the state Board of Regents took to high academic ground and offered a compromise: Cleaver could do a one-time guest lecture. But this was a time when students were taking over campus buildings, determined to make universities more consumer-friendly, "relevant," to their predominately young, adult student bodies. In such a mood, students stood firm on a bed of quicksand, demanding that Cleaver appear without restriction.

On October 2, 1968, Eldridge Cleaver accepted an invitation to speak to an overflow crowd of twenty-five hundred at Stanford University, a private institution forty miles outside Berkeley. In a seventy-six-minute address, Cleaver predictably blasted his lead detractor: "Ronald Reagan is a punk, a sissy, and a coward, and I challenge him to a duel to the death or until he says Uncle Eldrige. I give him a choice of weapons—a gun, a knife, a baseball bat, or marshmallows." In the end, Cleaver's single Berkeley lecture, "The Roots of Racism," was well received, adjudged "scholarly and moderate." But the political agenda aimed at quashing voices like Cleaver's continued. In the 1990s, it soared anew in the debate over affirmative action in admissions and faculty hiring.

OCTOBER 3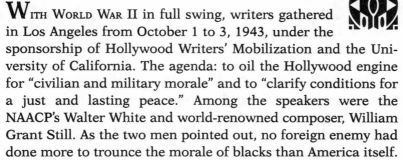

With World War II in full swing, writers gathered in Los Angeles from October 1 to 3, 1943, under the sponsorship of Hollywood Writers' Mobilization and the University of California. The agenda: to oil the Hollywood engine for "civilian and military morale" and to "clarify conditions for a just and lasting peace." Among the speakers were the NAACP's Walter White and world-renowned composer, William Grant Still. As the two men pointed out, no foreign enemy had done more to trounce the morale of blacks than America itself.

"In a sense," said Walter White, "the importance of these media by which ideas are formed and propagated is more crucial than the making of guns and planes." Mindful of the hostilities engendered by Hollywood's demeaning stereotypes, he continued, "Men shoot guns and fly planes because of ideas, good or evil, which the spoken and written word and the image on the screen have planted in the minds of the gun-shooters and plane-flyers. Because of this fact, an enormous opportunity—and an appalling responsibility—faces the coiners of words and the makers of media which will help to shape the world to come."

"I don't know exactly where the line of demarcation comes: what is racial prejudice and what is inherent in the business of filmmaking," said William Grant Still. As composer of the *Afro-American Symphony*, theme music for the 1939 World's Fair, he was one of the most respected blacks in Hollywood. Yet, "Every suggestion I made was disregarded . . . thrown out with the statement that it was 'too good.' One orchestration . . . was not used because 'Negro bands didn't play that well' according to the musical director. I protested that I was playing in Negro bands [at the time] and that the men played better then than they do today. My comment was simply ignored, and the orchestration never [used]. I, who for more than thirty years have been intimately associated with [African American] music have had to give way to the hasty verdicts of [whites who] doubt my 'authenticity.'" Clearly, the armistice would have to begin very close to home.

Film   Authenticity

OCTOBER 4

IN 1955, baseball's "fall classic" was another subway series, as the World Series was called when two New York teams—the Dodgers or Giants and the Yankees—won their respective league's pennant. In the sixth Yankee/Dodger series in baseball history, it looked like the Yanks would beat the eight-time pennant-winning Dodgers, who had never won a World Series, again . . . until October 4, 1955.

"Please don't interrupt, because you haven't heard this one before—honest," wrote the *Washington Post*'s Shirley Povich. "At precisely 4:45 P.M. today, in Yankee Stadium, off came the fifty-two-year slur on the ability of the Dodgers to win a World Series, for at that moment the last straining Yankee was out at first base, and the day, the game, and the 1955 Series belonged to Brooklyn." For Povich, one of the few sportswriters who had argued for the integration of baseball, it was a special victory. In the Dodger line-up were five blacks: Sandy Amoros, Junior Gilliam, Don Newcombe, and Hall of Famers Roy Campanella (a three-time MVP) and Jackie Robinson, who had opened the door for all other black players. But Povich wasn't the only emotional reporter that day. "I was the one who was able to say on television, 'Ladies and gentlemen, the Brooklyn Dodgers are the champions of the world,' " recalled veteran broadcaster Vin Scully. "That's all I said, not another word. And all winter people said to me, 'How could you have been so calm at such a tremendous moment?' Well, I wasn't. I could not have said another word without breaking down in tears."

But while blacks had taken their rightful place on the playing field, it would be years before owners would give them similar opportunities off the field. In 1962, Negro Leaguer Buck O'Neil became the first black coach in major league history. In 1974, the Cleveland Indians hired Frank Robinson as the first black manager. After retirement, O'Neil added another historic first to his personal best—preserving the story of African Americans in baseball as founder of the Negro Leagues Baseball Museum in Kansas City, Missouri.

OCTOBER 5

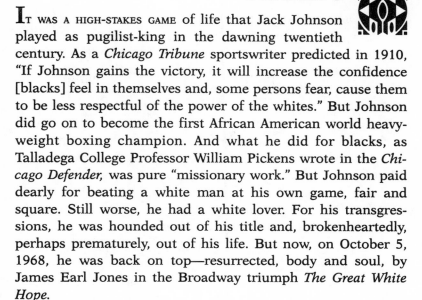

It was a high-stakes game of life that Jack Johnson played as pugilist-king in the dawning twentieth century. As a *Chicago Tribune* sportswriter predicted in 1910, "If Johnson gains the victory, it will increase the confidence [blacks] feel in themselves and, some persons fear, cause them to be less respectful of the power of the whites." But Johnson did go on to become the first African American world heavyweight boxing champion. And what he did for blacks, as Talladega College Professor William Pickens wrote in the *Chicago Defender*, was pure "missionary work." But Johnson paid dearly for beating a white man at his own game, fair and square. Still worse, he had a white lover. For his transgressions, he was hounded out of his title and, brokenheartedly, perhaps prematurely, out of his life. But now, on October 5, 1968, he was back on top—resurrected, body and soul, by James Earl Jones in the Broadway triumph *The Great White Hope*.

For his performance, Jones would regain the title for Johnson and himself. On April 20, 1969, he took home Broadway's highest honor, the Tony Award, for Best Actor in a Drama. Two weeks later, playwright Howard Sackler was honored with a Pulitzer Prize for his dramatic script. Once vanquished, now vindicated, the spirit of Jack Johnson had returned victorious!

Theater/Sports   Resurrection

OCTOBER 6

A ONE-WOMAN ARMY, Ernestine McClendon was relentless in her crusade to gain more work for black actors and better black images for black audiences. Her battlefront: television ads. After years of opposition, in October 1974, one dramatic last-ditch push finally opened the door.

An actress herself, McClendon knew the business well when she formed her talent agency. She actively recruited clients and was vigilant in her attempts to place them. But every Hollywood door seemed bolted by the same rusty old lock. She had to do something, and in one audacious move, she did. She wrote an open letter to Hollywood media producers and casting agents, and made it the text of two ads she took out in entertainment industry trade journals:

> I'm not a rip-off artist. I cannot afford to pay money under the table so that my clients will be cast. I've worked hard and honestly and that has to be enough. If it's not, then there is something dreadfully wrong with our industry.

Her bravado worked—so did her clients. McClendon Enterprises was up and running, and Ernestine McClendon an acknowledged trailblazer without whom many of our most recognizable actors—whether on her client list or not—might never have succeeded in the business, for breakthroughs like McClendon's are the hard-fought precedents that empower countless others.

How important it is, then, that we look at contemporary shows and contemporary images, that we put them to the test. Do they honor the path so many sacrificed so much to blaze?

OCTOBER 7

Authority versus personal identity and integrity. That was the issue fourteen black college football players faced at the University of Wyoming on October 7, 1969. In a test of the coach's authority, they violated his ban on protest for any reason and were dropped from the team.

The mitigating incident was a scheduled game between Wyoming and Brigham Young University—a school operated by the Mormon Church, which barred blacks from its ministry on "theological" grounds best summarized as racism. In an approach not unlike that of athletes who protested apartheid by refusing to play South African teams, Wyoming's Black Students Alliance decided to protest Mormon racism and the insensitivity of those who either supported it or ignored it to the detriment of blacks. But the coach's ban put team members in a difficult position. What to do: to support their peers in the Black Students Alliance on moral grounds; to support their team on the basis of loyalty; to uphold the disciplinary dictates of the coach; to satisfy their own integrity. Straddling a precarious middle ground, the black players arrived at the stadium ready to play, but wore black armbands in solidarity with their cause. The coach dropped them from the team—a move that cost most of the young players their athletic scholarships and, in effect, forced them to drop out as full-time college students. All this in the middle of the Vietnam War, when attending college part-time meant losing one's student deferment, being reclassified 1A, and facing the draft. It is doubtful that the students had thought through their protest this far, nor should they have had to. But this was the price they paid. This was the solidarity shared by thousands of college-age crusaders of the Civil Rights era.

An interesting sidebar: those who argued against the black athletes' moral stand would later follow their lead in 1980 when President Jimmy Carter protested the Soviet Union's invasion of Afghanistan by withdrawing all U.S. athletes from the 1980 Summer Olympics in Moscow.

OCTOBER 8

"THIS ONE'S FOR THE DUKE!" musicians asserted as they gathered at Yale University from October 6 to 8, 1972, in honor of Duke Ellington and the tradition of African American music to which they had all contributed so much.

Who else but Ellington could command the appearance of so many of the greats all at one event: Eubie Blake, Ray Brown, Benny Carter, Kenny Clarke (in from Europe for the event), Richard Davis, George Duvivier, Harry Edison, Dizzy Gillespie, Sonny Greer, Milt Hinton, Elvin Jones, Jo Jones, the Mitchell-Ruff Duo, Thelonious Monk, Odetta, Max Roach, Willie "The Lion" Smith, Slam Stewart, Sonny Stitt, Billy Taylor, Lucky Thompson, Joe Williams, Mary Lou Williams, Tony Williams, and the Duke Ellington Orchestra.

With this unprecedented gathering, Yale inaugurated the Duke Ellington Fellowship program to preserve and perpetuate the legacy of African American music—the early chants, ceremonial songs, slave codes, blues, jazz, and gospel music—in an academic setting. For years, black musicians who had not studied at a formal conservatory had been devalued as "untrained." Now Yale paid its respects to the oral tradition that had honed the finest musicians of African descent:

> Traditionally, the performers who have studied in this unstructured institution have developed their talents beyond the confines of a classroom—in cotton fields, in the ghetto, in nightclubs and in churches. . . . Membership in this school involves paying heavy dues. No degrees are conferred, and there are no Phi Beta Kappa keys awarded for excellence. There is, however, a . . . society of performers who are recognized by their peers as truly great musicians [who] exert informal leadership and become the "professors" in the "conservatory without walls," providing inspiration and giving guidance to the next generation of students.

With this initiative, Yale's distinguished guests comprised a true "master class."

OCTOBER 9

"THE URBAN LEAGUE'S LINE: Bias Is Bad Business." That was the story in the October 9, 1954, edition of *Business Week.*

Five months after the *Brown v. Board of Education* (see May 17) decision that was already beginning to give schools a much-needed shaking up, leaders of the National Urban League (NUL) arrived at its annual conference in September armed. Now, word was spreading through its network in the media to affirm its "determination to remove the blight and stain of segregation from our national life." Behind the Supreme Court decision lay no new revelations, said the NUL. "Segregation has not suddenly become wrong. It has always been wrong."

Second only to the NAACP in longevity, the National Urban League had begun as a civil rights–social work organization in 1910. As blacks fled the Jim Crow South, the NUL's earliest incarnations offered assistance in the transition from rural to city life, helping people find jobs and housing. It was particularly helpful to those with no street-smart relatives to protect them from the unscrupulous, to whom they were easy prey. In structure, the NUL began and continued a pattern it continues to this day. It is traditionally led by a white man as president and a black man as executive director. What began as a women's "protective" league is now an "interracial, nonprofit community service organization that uses the tools and methods of social work, economics, law, and other disciplines, to secure equal opportunity in all sectors of our society for black Americans and other minorities." In short, the NUL was designed to work within, and deeply vest itself in, the system. It is for this reason that the NUL could have the ear of *Business Week* in 1954. Whites with clout in all phases of business used their leverage for social change in order to provide fair employment and fair housing opportunities. Without question, "conflicts of interest" arose; without question, from a pragmatic standpoint, the NUL was uniquely qualified—not as an agitant but as a participant—to get the job done.

OCTOBER 10

In one of the most unusual initiatives of the period, the W. E. B. Du Bois Department of Afro-American Studies of the University of Massachusetts at Amherst invited seven professional artists to join the faculty in order to infuse the campus with a burst of creative inspiration. In an October 1972 brochure, this Institute for Pan-African Culture staked its ground:

> To create institutions among black people which will permit us to understand and preserve the culture that strengthened and preserved our ancestors, to analyze its elements, identify its roots and sources, and to outline its forms and interpret their meaning in terms, language, and a critical vocabulary of our own. If [we can] do these things in a systematic way, then other things will follow: the development of black talent in all the arts which will perpetuate the culture by creating new forms from its rich resources, the development of mechanisms to end the exploitation of black culture by the general society.

Seven artists, seven visions. Charting the route were: Paul Carter Harrison, playwright; Ed Love, sculptor; Eleo Pomare, dancer and choreographer; Diana Ramos, dancer and choreographer; Max Roach, percussionist and composer; Archie Shepp, saxophonist and playwright; Nelson Stevens, graphic artist.

Empowering the institute was Dr. Randolph Bromery, the school's African American chancellor. A geologist, Bromery knew how to mine precious black gold. Also on the faculty were Nigerian novelist Chinua Achebe (see July 16), anthropologist and future Spelman College president Dr. Johnnetta B. Cole, author Julius Lester, and scholars Acklyn Lynch and Michael Thelwell (see April 30). In 1973, Bromery's ultimate coup was to welcome author Shirley Graham Du Bois (see December 22) to the faculty of the department named for her late husband, and to commit university resources to catalog, archive, and publish the eight four-drawer file cabinets of Du Bois's papers that accompanied Mrs. Du Bois from Egypt back home to the area where her husband had been born.

OCTOBER 11

Who said the thrilling days of rough riding were gone? Who said we'd never again see the likes of such legendary cowboys as Deadwood Dick and Bill Pickett? Certainly not the folks who frequented state and county fairs in 1973. Certainly no one who experienced the joy of watching Tracy Latting do her riding routine. Tracy, ten years old, was one for the history books.

A trick riding superstar, Tracy could get out there with the best. In fact, she was the best at barrel racing and goat tail-tying rodeos held for children aged seven to seventeen. Known throughout the county fair and state fair circuits in Illinois, Iowa, Michigan, and Wisconsin, she had won three trophy buckles. And by the time she entered fifth grade at the Blue Island, Illinois, St. Benedict School, Tracy was a near legend— and it showed in the fancy rodeo stunts that attracted major crowds. Performing on a prancing horse, her repertoire included such picturesquely named tricks as the "Hippodrome," the "Butterfly," and the "Apache."

How did she learn all this so well and so young? The daughter of Thyrl Latting, owner of the Latting-Burkholder Rodeo Company, based in Robbins, Illinois, Tracy, one of three children, had begun to ride at a very young age. The family that rodeos together . . .

OCTOBER 12

By 1938, Germany had written its preamble to the Holocaust with the erosion of rights for its "undesirables": Jews, Gypsies, gays, the disabled, and people of color. But while Germany had crossed the line on human rights, it had not yet carried its campaign across its borders. The United States and the rest of Europe, with abuses of their own, struck a "gentleman's agreement" guaranteeing each nation sovereignty within its borders and territories—a decision that, at times, denied Hitler's victims haven from persecution. Yet, even as these nations turned an official deaf ear to the rumored atrocities, a growing number of their citizens did not.

In the United States, Arthur W. Mitchell bore a unique burden as the only black congressman. As a solo agitant, Mitchell could neither sway a vote nor influence one. But he could be the voice of controversial issues from which the other ninety-nine percent of Congress that was white, Christian, and male felt insulated. Congressman Mitchell was just that voice when he sent a letter to President Franklin Delano Roosevelt on October 12, 1938:

> As a representative of a minority group in America, an underprivileged group . . . subjected to prejudice and mistreatment . . . we are interested in the attitude of majority groups throughout the world toward minority groups. We are greatly disturbed [by] the intolerance of certain majority groups toward the Jewish people residing in European countries and wish to have our voice heard in the interest of justice and fair play for all. . . . We believe that the same spirit . . . working so tremendously against the safety and sacred rights of the Jewish people, if permitted to go unchallenged, will manifest itself sooner or later against all minority groups, perhaps in all parts of the world. [We] request you . . . to use every . . . means at your command in securing protection for the Jewish people in this hour of sad calamity.

Mitchell was unique among elected officials. For while his congressional district was Chicago, as Congress's sole minority he crossed racial, religious, state, and party lines to represent the disfranchised American millions.

Human Rights   Responsibility

FOR THE ARTIST WHO HAD SPENT his teens in a haven called the library, the controversy brewing in the October 1970 issue of *School Library Journal* seemed absurd. Jacob Lawrence's illustrated children's book, *Harriet and the Promised Land,* had just been published, and his view of slavery and escape was raising concern. How far should art go to depict truth when children are the audience? people asked. No matter how accurate the depiction or how gruesome their own gleeful fantasies, how should an artist reveal the nightmare of historic truth to children?

Harriet and the Promised Land was based on Lawrence's Harriet Tubman series on the Underground Railroad heroine's daring rescue missions, which helped three hundred people escape from slavery to freedom. *Time* praised it as a "tour de force." And it was a stellar example of the work for which he had been awarded the Spingarn Medal that June. Yet the book took deep hits of criticism from children's librarians for its "disturbing" images. By the time the book saw print, Lawrence had already sanitized the violence of slavery. At the request of his publisher, no blood was shown, and contradicting history, Tubman did not carry a gun. Still, the art was considered "too grim." For children, detractors argued, the book should have taken a more traditional graphic approach with Tubman cast in what artists deride as "Cinderella-like" images. A New England librarian wrote that Tubman's image was "grotesque and ugly." Lawrence responded:

> If you had walked in the fields, stopping for short periods to be replenished by underground stations; if you couldn't feel secure until you reached the Canadian border, you, too, madam, would look grotesque and ugly. Isn't it sad that the oppressed often find themselves grotesque and ugly and find the oppressor refined and beautiful?

Beyond the ability of children to digest history, perhaps the first step begins with retraining adults to cope with, communicate, and transcend painful realities.

OCTOBER 14

Oₙ October 14, 1964, an emotionally and physically drained Martin Luther King was resting in Atlanta's St. Joseph Infirmary when this announcement was made to the world: "The Nobel Committee of the Norwegian National Assembly has decided to award the Peace Prize for 1964 to Martin Luther King Jr. The sum of the prize is 283,000 Swedish Kroners [$54,600]." Word had first reached Coretta King when an Associated Press reporter telephoned the King home. She, in turn, phoned the hospital. "How is the Nobel Peace Prize winner for 1964 feeling this morning?" she asked history's youngest laureate, giving him the news.

One of the world's highest honors, the Nobel Prize was created by Alfred Nobel, the Swedish chemist who discovered dynamite in 1863. In his lifetime, Nobel's more than one hundred patents earned him a fortune, the bulk of which he willed to the benefit of humanity. Every December 10 since 1901, the fifth anniversary of his death, prizes have been awarded in Chemistry, Literature, Physics, Medicine or Physiology, and Peace. Each laureate is awarded a gold medallion engraved with a likeness of Nobel on the front and the symbol of the field on the reverse side. The amount of the award is determined by the interest earned on the principal that year divided by the number of fields awarded. Not every field is awarded each year, but each field is honored no less than once every five years.

These sons of Africa have received the Nobel Peace Prize: Dr. Ralph Bunche, the United Nations undersecretary and highest ranking American UN officer, who negotiated an Arab-Israeli truce (1950); South Africa's Albert Luthuli, President-General of the African National Congress (1960); Rev. Dr. Martin Luther King Jr. (1964); Bishop Desmond Tutu, South Africa's conscience (1984); and Nelson Mandela, South Africa's future president (1993). The Nobel Prize for Literature was awarded to Wole Soyinka of Nigeria (1986); Naguib Mahfouz of Egypt (1988); Derek Walcott of the Caribbean (1992); and the first black woman so honored in the history of the Nobel Prize, African American author Toni Morrison (1993).

OCTOBER 15

A COLLEGE MEANS MORE than students, faculty, mortar, and books. As a gateway to learning, a college is a resource for all who come through its doors and a gift for generations to come. With its closing comes a tragedy for an extended community. When that community was founded by former slaves whose sacrifices raised the school and the race, the tragedy can rock the foundations of hope itself. For witness, visit Harpers Ferry, West Virginia. On a hill overlooking the town known for its pre–Civil War arsenal and made famous by John Brown's antislavery raid, stands a ghostly spectacle: Storer College.

From its humble start in a vacated Civil War barracks, Storer had grown to a full campus. For nearly a century, it honored its postwar lineage and legacy. Then, in 1955, Storer became an early casualty of the Civil Rights era. With victory had come defeat. Reacting to the Supreme Court's *Brown v. Board of Education* school desegregation order of 1954, state authorities closed Storer College in apparent retaliation. Who would have thought it? At a time when authorities could not find the means to desegregate schools that educated whites, it could find a way to close a college that educated blacks.

And what a loss Storer was. Frederick Douglass had lectured there, donating his fees to establish a professorship in freedom's honor and in tribute to John Brown, whose antislavery blow was struck by the only integrated brigade in two centuries of American military history. Dr. Du Bois had led his NAACP cofounders on a Barefoot March from Storer to the old fire engine house site of the John Brown Raid on the fiftieth anniversary of emancipation. Generations had made pilgrimage to the college. It was gone, but not forgotten. With a groundswell of support, not only did the loyal remember, they ensured that others would never forget Storer's legacy as a historically black college. On October 15, 1966, Storer College was designated a national treasure, a landmark sustained by the National Park Service, providing inspiration for generations to come.

OCTOBER 16

For a vast majority of southerners playing at politics, it has been not necessarily the democratic process in action, so much as a thoroughly delightful sport.
—Thomas D. Clark

THE CITY OF ATLANTA had long prided itself the most progressive city in the South, but attempts to dislodge segregation's worst habits usually proved it otherwise. By the late 1960s, the federal Civil Rights Act had finally been signed. Still, the political shenanigans of 1966 literally made a federal case out of denying SNCC's Julian Bond his duly elected seat in the Georgia House. The Voting Rights Act mandated that Bond could not be barred for race, so he was attacked for his opposition to the Vietnam War. Only after a Supreme Court decision in Bond's favor did the state give in. So, imagine the "fun" when Maynard Jackson ran for mayor of Atlanta. And imagine the victory celebration on October 16, 1973, when he was elected the first African American mayor of a southern city since Reconstruction.

During his tenure as mayor, Jackson's greatest test came in a three-month strike by city employees. Firing one thousand, 98 percent of whom were black, was something "I had to pray over," said Jackson. Settling the strike and rehiring the workers, he handily won a second term. Before Jackson, no women headed city departments, and despite a fifty-fifty racial mix only 0.5 percent of city contracts were awarded to blacks. He rectified those issues with affirmative action and secured jobs for the most undereducated of Atlantans. Among his triumphs: Atlanta's airport, with the world's biggest terminal building complex.

What a powerful date October 16 has been in African American history. In 1859, John Brown's biracial army struck a blow to slavery with the historic raid on the arsenal at Harpers Ferry, West Virginia. In 1995, African American men headed to Washington, D.C., and the unprecedented success of the Million Man March, at the call of Minister Louis Farrakhan of the Nation of Islam.

Politics   Continuity

OCTOBER 17

Before Greensboro (see January 31), the sit-in had been used as a protest tactic in sixteen cities over a three-year period. But the North Carolina A & T sit-in was different—and no one has been able to say why for sure. Whatever the unique chemistry that made it so inspiring to so many students, in its purity of spirit, its spontaneity, and its lack of rules, it found authenticity. In an age when going to college was taken for granted by a very few, it dramatized a simple truth: well-mannered students who had played by the rules all their lives, willing to pay for their wants and needs with no favors asked, were being refused the most basic of human rights—to eat when they were hungry.

Within two weeks the message and the method had spread to Nashville. A. Keith Guy, a Fisk University student, wrote of his movement experiences in a letter to Lawrence Landry, his friend and an editor of *New University Thought*. The letter was published in the magazine's spring 1960 issue. "When one is faced with the threat of bodily harm, imprisonment, or intimidation, the decision is not an easy one to make," wrote Guy. "It gives me confidence though to see the number of those who are willing to undergo the hardships for what they believe to be right. And the beauty of the movement is that it is nonviolent and for an ideal. Just think, fighting a reality with an ideal." By fall, the strategy and the sacrifices of the students were yielding results.

On October 17, 1960, four national department store chains desegregated 150 lunch counters in 112 cities in Florida, Kentucky, Maryland, Missouri, North Carolina, Oklahoma, Tennessee, Texas, and the Virginias. An army of seventy thousand sit-in demonstrators had served notice—a message well summed up by Carl Blair, president of the Chamber of Commerce in Montgomery, Alabama, a city still recovering from its historic year-long bus boycott. "The South is in a time of change, the terms of which cannot be dictated by white Southerners," he said. "There's a revolution of the Negro youths in this nation."

OCTOBER 18

O<small>N</small> O<small>CTOBER</small> 18, 1976, eighteen months after the death of the Honorable Elijah Muhammad, Wallace D. Muhammad, his son and heir as leader, announced the end of an era. Henceforth the Nation of Islam (NOI) would be known as the World Community of al-Islam in the West, a transformation that was to be both symbolic and substantive. The religious teachings of the reformed organization would be more in keeping with those of contemporary international Islam. Operating as a multiracial religious community, it would cease to function in exclusive service to the African American community as it had in the past. The businesses groomed and grown under the Nation would be liquidated.

The Nation of Islam had been founded by W. D. Fard in the 1920s, rooted in the Islamic faith, based on cooperative economic principles much like those of Marcus Garvey (see November 29), and operated as a religious institution. When Fard mysteriously disappeared in the 1930s, Elijah Poole—later known as the Honorable Elijah Muhammad—succeeded him and was responsible for the Nation's expansion in membership and economic interests. In his lifetime, the NOI built an empire throughout the United States, the Caribbean, and Central America, with interests in publishing, real estate, dairy, poultry, fish, produce farms, restaurants, retailing, trucking, apparel, schools, and mosques—worked by and for the common good of its members. By the time of Elijah Muhammad's death in 1975, the Nation had grown to 160,000 members, amassed $46 million in assets, and, at a weekly circulation of 600,000 copies, its official organ, *Muhammad Speaks*, had the largest circulation of any African American weekly or daily newspaper.

Wallace D.'s reformation was difficult for many of the elder Muhammad's loyal followers. Friends said of Louis Farrakhan, then leader of the Chicago mosque, that he seemed dazed. He said he seemed "already dead." But, as he came back to life in 1977, he brought the Nation of Islam back with him—reviving its membership, reassembling its assets, and resurrecting it to reach new heights.

Turning Points   **Resurrections**

OCTOBER 19

In 1964, SNCC's John Lewis and Donald Harris were in the New Stanley Hotel in Nairobi, Kenya, when into the lobby walked Malcolm X accompanied by Kenya's president, Jomo Kenyatta. That evening into the next day, October 19, 1964, three people were free to do in Africa what they had never before done on their native American soil: relax in a supportive environment, dream better days, and—strengthened and united by their diverse insights—strategize a future.

In Africa, Malcolm had visited eleven countries, met eleven heads of state, and addressed most of their parliaments. Lewis and Harris had visited Guinea with their SNCC delegation (see September 26), then Ghana, Zambia, and now Kenya, and would travel to several other nations. All three found Africa supportive of the Civil Rights movement as part of a larger "human rights struggle." But, as Malcolm confirmed, none of the nations would "tolerate factionalism"—support for one group above the others. This idea had helped Malcolm structure his newly formed Organization of Afro-American Unity. In the hotel, in a little coffee shop nearby, the three talked on. As John Lewis observed, "I had a feeling . . . that Malcolm was in the process of becoming a changed man. He kept saying . . . that he really wanted to be helpful and supportive of the Civil Rights movement." Within months, he accepted the invitation of SNCC Chairman Stokely Carmichael to speak at a Selma, Alabama, rally (see February 4).

That chance meeting in Nairobi would alter the texture of the movement. On December 20, the Committee in Support of the Mississippi Freedom Democratic Party Challenge held a Harlem rally at which Malcolm X spoke. That day, Fannie Lou Hamer and SNCC's Freedom Singers were honored guests at Malcolm's Organization of Afro-American Unity meeting. SNCC-sponsored high school students came to Harlem from Mississippi that month and were welcomed by Malcolm on New Year's Eve (see December 31). Along with the coming new year, the freedom movement was facing a brand-new day.

OCTOBER 20

It was DIFFICULT TO SUPPORT Jelly Roll Morton's claim that he alone invented jazz in 1901. But his talent as a pianist, composer, and arranger was unimpeachable. So were the stories he told the Library of Congress in a series of recordings back in 1938:

> In New Orleans we would often wonder where a dead person was located. At any time we heard somebody was dead we knew we had plenty good food that night. Those days I belonged to a quartet and we specialized in spirituals for the purpose of finding somebody that was dead, because the minute we'd walk in, we'd be right in the kitchen where the food was—plenty ham sandwiches slabbered all over with mustard. . . . Of course, the dead man would always be laid out in the front and he'd be by himself most of the time and couldn't hear nothing we would be saying at all. He was dead and there was no reason for him to be with us living people. And very often the lady of the house would be back there with us having a good time, too. . . . Then we would stand up and begin—*Nearer my God to thee*—very slow and with beautiful harmony, thinking about that ham—*Nearer to thee*—plenty of whiskey in the flask and all kinds of crazy ideas in the harmony, which made it impossible for anybody to jump in and sing. We'd be sad, too, terribly sad. *Steal away, steal away to Jesus.* I tell you we had beautiful numbers to sing at those wakes. . . . Everybody in the city of New Orleans was always organization minded . . . and a dead man always belonged to several organizations. So when anybody died, there was a big band turned out on the day he was supposed to be buried. You could hear the band come up the street taking the gentleman for his last ride, playing different dead marches like "Flee as the Bird to the Mountain." They would always bury them in a vault. . . . Then the band would get started and you could hear the drums, rolling a deep, slow rhythm. A few bars of that and then the snare drummer would make a hot roll on his drums and the boys in the band would tear loose, while second line swung down the street, singing *Didn't he ramble? He rambled 'til the butchers cut him down.*

Music   Tradition

THE WORLD WAR II fight for freedom ended in 1945, but the battle for liberty had just begun. Italy's aggression against Ethiopia had been repulsed, but the rest of Africa was still, in the main, divided, conquered, and colonized. The colonial powers, England, France, Holland, and Belgium, had won the war, but it would be years before they could resurrect their decimated economies and imperial seats. With her fleet in ruin, Britain no longer "ruled the waves," as she had long boasted. And as the sun set on the British Empire for the first time in five centuries, Prime Minister Harold Macmillan felt the chill. "Winds of change," he predicted, were altering the course of history; peoples of color would never again be subjugated to Europe. He was right.

On October 21, 1945, seven weeks after the war's end, delegates throughout the African diaspora headed to Manchester, England, for the Fifth Pan-African Congress. Gathering at the call of black trade unionists, the congress was organized by Trinidadian scholar-activist George Padmore. When the gavel sounded, among those in attendance were Ghana's Kwame Nkrumah and Kenya's Jomo Kenyatta and Tom Mboya. Within two decades, each would lead his country to freedom. There, too, was the venerated elder and warrior Dr. W. E. B. Du Bois. Then seventy-seven, he had steered the congress movement since its inception in 1900. For his vision, the meeting hailed him the Father of Pan-Africanism.

The agenda: independence. The strategy: implementation of the Atlantic Charter. In the 1941 charter, Britain and the United States had agreed to "Respect the right of all peoples to choose the form of government under which they will live, and they wish to see sovereign rights and self-government restored to those who had been forcibly deprived of them." When the charter was cited by Asians and Africans, Britain's Winston Churchill recanted. Colonial peoples had never been included, he said, only the "States and Nations of Europe under Nazi yoke." In his duplicity, the winds of change turned blustery. Colonialism was on its last wobbly leg.

Freedom   Foundations

Bᴏʙʙʏ Sᴇᴀʟᴇ ʜᴀꜱ ꜱᴀɪᴅ that were it not for the assassination of Malcolm X, there might never have been a Black Panther Party. With Malcolm's murder came the disenchantment of millions. "I think that I was following not Elijah Muhammad or the Muslims, but Malcolm X himself," said Huey Newton. Newton and Seale rooted the Black Panther Party for Self-Defense in Black Muslim teachings. Inspired by Malcolm, they were descendants of Marcus Garvey's 1920s Black Nationalism (see November 29), with its adherence to self-discipline, economic empowerment, and the call "Up you mighty race, you may do what you will!"

Building on the powerful impact of young people in the southern-based Civil Rights movement, they knew their western-based Oakland, California, movement must organize the young. On the night of October 22, 1966, Newton and Seale outlined a ten-point Black Panther Party platform:

"What We Want; What We Believe:"

1. We want freedom. We want power to determine the destiny of our Black Community . . .
2. We want full employment for our people . . .
3. We want an end to the robbery by the CAPITALIST of our Black Community . . .
4. We want decent housing, fit for shelter of human beings . . .
5. We want education for our people that exposes the true nature of this decadent American society. We want education that teaches us our true history and our role in the . . . society . . .
6. We want all Black men to be exempt from military service . . .
7. We want an immediate end to POLICE BRUTALITY and MURDER of Black people . . .
8. We want freedom for all Black men held in prison . . .
9. We want all Black people when brought to trial to be tried in court by a jury of their peer group or people from their Black Communities, as defined by the Constitution . . .
10. We want land, bread, education, justice and peace. . . .

It is little wonder they were so admired and so dangerous.

OCTOBER 23

THE YEAR 1946 defined the depths of brutality to which white America would stoop to uphold segregation and the heights of self-assertion to which blacks would have to rise to end their victimization. In a move uncharacteristic of its history, and over the objections of former First Lady Eleanor Roosevelt, an important board member, the NAACP sponsored a petition to garner world support for the fight against racism in America. That petition, "An Appeal to the World," was presented to the UN at Lake Success, New York, on October 23, 1947.

In six essays by five authors, edited with an introduction by Dr. W. E. B. Du Bois, the Appeal targeted American oppression and the nation's hypocritical view of itself as "leader of the free world." The Appeal called for UN intervention on the side of justice for an oppressed minority. A hearing was supported by the Soviet Union and blocked by the United States. But, the Appeal's existence represented a major evolutionary step in the black human rights struggle. As historian Lerone Bennett wrote, "What this all meant—the NAACP petition, the Randolph crusade (see March 3), the Robeson challenges (see December 17)—was that the pain was becoming unbearable and that somebody had to do something."

Three pivotal events then occurred in rapid succession. First was a series of suits brought by the NAACP's Legal Defense Fund that culminated in the historic *Brown v. Board of Education* Supreme Court decision of 1954. Outlawing segregated public schools, this case brought the overthrow of segregation within reach. Second was the lynching of Emmett Till and the dredging up of his body from the Tallahatchie River in August 1955, which put the violence in perspective. The world suddenly saw the violence for what it was: the face of a child, battered beyond recognition. And third was the refusal by Rosa Parks to yield her seat and self-respect to racism in December 1955, which launched the 385-day Montgomery Bus Boycott and brought a recent divinity school graduate in his first pastoral assignment to world prominence—Dr. Martin Luther King Jr.

OCTOBER 24

THE VISION OF a "chicken in every pot" may have chased away Great Depression woes, but often as not, by the time the chicken came home to dinner, it had spoiled. With the inventions of one man all that would change.

U.S. patent number 2,526,874, registered on October 24, 1950, tells the story. This "apparatus for heating or cooling the atmosphere within an enclosure" was invented by Frederick McKinley Jones—the man who also invented the refrigerated truck and refrigerated railroad boxcar, which revolutionized the nation's food-delivery systems and made possible the frozen food industry. For years, in the proverbial manner of such stories, everyone said "it couldn't be done." While trucks and railroads were long-established successes, and air-conditioning was being perfected for wider applications, refrigerated transport was thought to be impossible because of the delicate nature of the cooling systems that would bounce around in transit. Jones solved the problem and patented his plan.

Orphaned at age ten, a sixth grade school dropout forced to support himself at an early age, Jones was known to have one good idea after another. A movie theater wanted to make the transition from silent films to talkies; Jones's device to adapt the projector was so successful that he was hired by a movie sound systems manufacturer to enhance their products. Jones also designed the first portable X-ray machine and shock-proofed racing cars with junkyard treasures. The list goes on for a total of sixty-one patents registered in his lifetime.

But while Jones liberated the food industry, he was only slightly more free to profit from his ingenuity than early black inventors racially barred from registering patents, and nineteenth-century inventors like the engineer Elijah McCoy, who died penniless, despite patents for the lawn sprinkler and other lucrative inventions. Joint ventures, licensing agreements, and investment capital were a long way off for the black inventor. Sadly, that too, like Elijah, was the real McCoy.

OCTOBER 25

THE CASE OF THE "SCOTTSBORO BOYS" was one of the most flagrant abuses of the legal system in history. Begun in 1931, it dragged on until October 25, 1976, when Alabama Governor George Wallace pardoned the last "Boy."

In 1931, nine black boys aged thirteen to nineteen hopped a freight train with Depression-era drifters in search of work, like themselves. When the white drifters insisted the blacks get off the car, a fight broke out. The blacks won and put their adversaries off the train. The losers demanded vengeance. At the next station, just outside Scottsboro, sheriffs dragged the boys from the train. Two white female drifter/riders then cried rape and trapped the boys in a web of political and legal injustice that ensnared them for life. With only fifty dollars for their defense, the boys' families hired a white lawyer who arrived drunk half an hour before trial. Despite a lack of evidence, the white male jury found them guilty of rape in twenty-five minutes. All but the thirteen-year-old were then scheduled for execution. Famed attorney Clarence Darrow offered to appeal, but resigned over "communist exploitation of the case." The NAACP Legal Defense Fund came. So did the International Labor Defense, a Communist Party team that filed and won three Supreme Court appeals. In a ruckus between the two groups, the case became a cause célèbre (see September 10). "Victims" recanted and medical evidence proved that no rape had occurred, yet the Scottsboro Boys remained in prison, paroled or freed, one by one through 1950. Clarence Norris, the last to be cleared, had fled parole in 1948; he was pardoned by Wallace on this day in 1976.

Wallace's pardon had a note of irony. In the early 1960s, there had been no greater grandstander or instigator of racist violence than Wallace. The governor had pardoned Norris, but who could pardon the governor for all the lives lost? And how would blacks pardon themselves for being unable to protect nine children? Little wonder that throughout the Civil Rights era, the word repeated like a mantra again and again, lest we forget, was *Scottsboro . . . Scottsboro . . . Scottsboro . . .*

OCTOBER 26

O<small>N</small> O<small>CTOBER</small> 26, 1975, Dr. Ruth Wright Hayre was celebrating her sixty-fifth birthday and contemplating her retirement after thirty-three years in the Philadelphia public schools. But this wasn't the close of a lifetime of service, it was a turning point—a new beginning powered by an incident in her grandfather's life more than a century earlier. Shortly after Emancipation, "boxcar" schools—classes for ex-slaves held in converted railroad boxcars—began to dot the South. Dr. Hayre's grandfather, Richard Robert Wright, was attending an Atlanta boxcar school in 1865 when Union General O. O. Howard—the future director of the Freedmen's Bureau and founding president of Howard University, for whom it is named—came on inspection. The general asked the students, "Now, what message shall I take back north?" After tortured silence from teachers and students alike, young Wright took a "leap of faith" to answer: "Sir, tell them we are rising." Extremely moved, the general carried the message so far and wide that John Greenleaf Whittier immortalized it in his poem "Howard at Atlanta":

> The man of many battles,
> With tears his eyelids pressing,
> Stretched over those dusky foreheads
> His one-armed blessing.
> And he said: "Who hears can never
> Fear for or doubt you;
> What shall I tell the children
> Up North about you?"
> Then ran round a whisper, a murmur,
> Some answer devising;
> And a little boy stood up: "General,
> Tell 'em we're rising!"

In 1988, Wright's inspiration was further immortalized by his granddaughter's "Tell Them We Are Rising" pledge to pay college tuition for the students in two Philadelphia schools who would be accepted to an accredited four-year institution.

Education   Empowerment

IN THE EARLY 1950s, two Montgomery, Alabama, men stood out for their activism. The first was Rev. Vernon Johns, pastor of Dexter Avenue Baptist Church. His defiant anti-segregationist agitation (see August 19) put him in constant conflict with his congregants, shook up the status quo, and created the vacancy that brought a new reverend, Martin Luther King Jr., to town. The second man was E. D. Nixon.

Long before the historic Bus Boycott, Nixon was Montgomery's race relations mentor—founder of its NAACP chapter and its voters' league. He had championed the Brotherhood of Sleeping Car Porters, the first union of black men to achieve a national charter, from its threadbare start in the late 1920s. A skillful organizer, he modeled himself on his hero, union founder A. Philip Randolph. He worked as a Pullman porter, enduring humiliation from the white clientele. But, like most porters, he was highly esteemed among blacks. Well traveled, sophisticated, porters had seen a world others could only imagine. In Montgomery, Nixon built a reputation for knowing every member of the city's white power structure: judges to policemen. So respected was he by blacks, that every issue worth note was first brought to him for resolution. He might not be able to get justice, but he got noticed. With small, consistent, cumulative acts, he and others had begun to get things moving. He was the first black man since Reconstruction to put himself on a ballot, a sign of his daring. Another sign, for which he became legendary, was barging into the governor's office—all six feet, two inches of him—to make a point.

When Rosa Parks was arrested for her refusal to give up her bus seat to racism, she notified her mother, and her mother called E. D. Nixon. It was he who asked his fellow NAACP member Mrs. Parks to be a test case to break bus segregation, who suggested a boycott, and who dubbed King leader. Why King? In the polished young man who had just completed his doctorate, Nixon saw someone unknown to the city, unbeholden to local whites (an asset in closing off avenues of intimidation), and thus beyond the reins of their direct control.

THE 1946 NAACP annual report condemned that year as "one of the grimmest years in the history of the NAACP." Founded in 1909, the nation's oldest Civil Rights organization had weathered the infamous "Red Summer of 1919," when marauding whites destroyed black communities with impunity. While terror had been the homecoming meted out to every generation of black soldiers since the Revolutionary War, the blowtorching and eye-gouging of black World War II veterans in 1946 had been unequalled in sheer savagery. The race riots of Columbia, Tennessee, and Athens, Alabama, had left scores dead and wounded. But although African Americans were admittedly "disillusioned over . . . official recession from all of the flamboyant promises of postwar democracy and decency," the NAACP report also noted that nothing would deter the ongoing freedom fight on the homefront. With mounting world pressure, President Harry Truman issued Executive Order No. 9808, commissioning the Committee on Civil Rights. On October 28, 1947, its report, "To Secure These Rights," was finalized; it was submitted to the president the following day.

The presidential commission acknowledged: "We were not asked to evaluate the extent to which civil rights have been achieved in our country." Because its purpose was not to "praise our country's progress" but to assess the nation's "most immediate needs," the commission "did not, therefore, devote ourselves to the construction of a balance sheet. . . . Instead, we have almost exclusively focused our attention on the bad side of our record—on what might be called the civil rights frontier."

Arguing in favor of the Bill of Rights and the Constitution, "To Secure These Rights" was based on a fundamental principle: "The protection of civil rights is a NATIONAL problem which affects everyone. We need to guarantee the SAME rights to every person regardless of who he is, where he lives, or what his racial, religious, or national origins are."

OCTOBER 29

IT WAS THE HEIGHT of Black Panther phobia, the aftermath of the Chicago police riot that embarrassed leaders of the 1968 Democratic National Convention (DNC), time for retribution, and the wrong people were on trial—the "Chicago Eight"—leaders of the antiwar and anti–race war movements, all known to be more victim than villain, yet charged with conspiracy to incite a riot at the DNC.

Then, on October 29, 1969, came the shot seen 'round the world—a news artist's sketch of Bobby G. Seale, codefendant and chairman of the Black Panther Party, bound to a chair and gagged as ordered by Judge Julius J. Hoffman. For days the judge and Seale had been engaged in verbal combat. Seale argued that if the judge refused to stay the trial until his lawyer recovered from emergency surgery, he wanted to invoke his constitutional right to defend himself and cross-examine a key witness. The judge ordered that he be represented by the attorney for his codefendants, the noted activist William Kunstler. Seale refused, insisting that he was being denied his right to his own attorney. The judge overruled him. Seale jumped to his feet in protest, cursing the judge as a racist. As this went on, the judge ordered guards to "deal with him as he should be dealt with in these circumstances." Marshals removed Seale to an anteroom and returned him gagged and shackled. It was clear that the response had been prearranged; clearer still that sentencing Seale to four years for contempt imprisoned him without having to find him guilty of conspiring to do anything. Legal pundits could think of no precedent for shackling a nonviolent defendant in a nonmurder case. But the precedent spoke for itself as Seale sat in Hoffman's slave pen—a black man shackled to a chair hand and foot, silenced, and sentenced to be three-fifths a man.

Yet there was television, and there was witness. The next day, as Seale again "disrupted" the court for the right to have rights, a parade of multiracial protesters spirited Seale's message to the outside world. Mouths gagged, hands tied, they brandished signs: FREE BOBBY! POWER TO THE PEOPLE!

Quiet as it's kept, there were no marigolds in the fall of 1941. We thought, at the time, that it was because Pecola was having her father's baby that the marigolds did not grow. A little examination and much less melancholy would have proved to us that our seeds were not the only ones that did not sprout; nobody's did. Not even the gardens fronting the lake showed marigolds that year. But so deeply concerned were we with the health and safe delivery of Pecola's baby we could think of nothing but our own magic: if we planted the seeds, and said the right words over them, they would blossom, and everything would be all right.

WITH THESE OPENING LINES, Toni Morrison began her first novel, *The Bluest Eye*, published in October 1970. Profoundly rooted in the American psyche, it was, as Morrison would say, "like Pecola's life: dismissed, trivialized, misread." An accident? Probably not. Morrison's marksmanship, as precise as her imagery, was evident at the start. Twenty years later, she wrote an afterword to a new edition:

> We had just started elementary school. She said she wanted blue eyes. I looked around to picture her with them and was violently repelled by what I imagined she would look like if she had her wish. The sorrow in her voice seemed to call for sympathy . . . I "got mad" at her instead. . . . It must have been more than the face I was examining. . . . In any case it was the first time I knew beautiful. . . . Beauty was not simply something to behold; it was something one could do. . . . Implicit in her desire was racial self-loathing. And twenty years later I was still wondering about how one learns that. . . . The reclamation of racial beauty in the sixties stirred these thoughts. . . . I focused on how something as grotesque as the demonization of an entire race could take root inside the most delicate member of a society: a child. . . . I believed some aspects of her woundability were lodged in all young girls . . .

For, as she writes in the novel's second paragraph, "Once we knew, our guilt was relieved only by fights and mutual accusations about who was to blame. . . ."

OCTOBER 31

Paul R. Williams was one of the century's finest architects. Based in Los Angeles from 1927 to 1973, he was known as the "Architect to the Stars," having designed homes for actors Lon Chaney and Cary Grant; the Polo Lounge of the Beverly Hills Hotel; actress Hattie McDaniel's church, First AME Church; and Danny Thomas's children's hospital in Memphis, St. Jude, for which Williams donated the design.

Williams was licensed as an architect in California in 1921 and opened his design firm the following year. As his roster of commissions clearly attests, he was gifted. Well schooled not only in his primary field, he had studied such ancillary skills as interior design, color harmony, and landscaping, as well as business. He was born in 1894, at the dawn of Jim Crow, and he walked in the footsteps of that long march of African Americans considered quite capable as craftsmen while enslaved only to find themselves "incompetent" when payment was required for their services. How did he break the incredible racial barriers? He cultivated unusual skills.

People would happen into his office, perhaps knowing his reputation but not his race, and back out mumbling phrases like "Just shopping around" or "Thinking of spending about eight thousand dollars." For these potential clients Williams had a trick. He'd welcome them with a disclaimer. "I am sorry, but I have been forced to make it a rule never to do houses costing less than $10,000—but won't you sit down for a moment? Perhaps I may be able to give you a few ideas." While the illusion of being too busy for the job intrigued the potential client, the time spent *listening* to him gave them a chance to relax, and sometimes they gave him the commission. Like other African Americans creative enough to succeed at whatever their chosen endeavor, he learned to do the impossible. In another relaxation (and job realization) technique, he had learned to draw upside down. Sketching opposite the client also let the story of their homes unfold before their eyes. His work spoke for itself. And what it said people wanted desperately to hear—and own.

Architecture   Survival

NOVEMBER

Bring the GI's Home, Chicago (1966). Courtesy of
the photographer. © Roy Lewis, 1966.

NOVEMBER 1

"In 1942," John H. Johnson recalled, "my mother and I were recent graduates of the relief [welfare] rolls. And I decided I was never going down that road again." He had a dream of an idea—he wanted to publish a magazine. For his dream, his mother risked hers—the furniture she'd saved for and paid for with a lifetime of work. In 1942, she pledged her furniture as collateral to empower her son with a $500 secured bank loan. That year, on November 1, he published his first issue of *Negro Digest*. With its success, he dubbed the date his "good luck" day. On November 1, 1945, he launched *Ebony*. And on November 1, 1951, came *Jet*.

To begin to view the magnitude of all he had surveyed, one had only to look at *Ebony*'s November 1975 thirtieth anniversary cover—a summary spread of thirty years of covers. There it was, our story—our history. And while Johnson Publications was not the first black magazine publisher—that distinction belongs to the abolitionist David Ruggles, who launched his *Mirror of Liberty* in 1838—Johnson was the breakthrough publisher who achieved the first competitive success in attracting white advertisers. In business terms, *Ebony* and *Jet* were in a class by themselves in number of full-color pages, advertising ratio, newsstand distribution, supermillion circulation, and international name recognition. Notably, Johnson's achievement also empowered others—witness the success of the next largest general market magazines, *Essence* and *Black Enterprise*. Each made its own distinctive mark in the industry; each extended the reach of black publishing into communications media and other business ventures.

Underwriting these successes was the confidence of investors and advertisers, which began in 1942 with Mrs. Johnson's leap of faith. From that root branched not only publishing interests but, lest we forget, the highly visible crossover story in television. In 1956, the *Nat King Cole Show* became the first network show with a black host. NBC's sales department could sell the show to advertisers by pointing to Johnson's success. And in a sixty-four-week run, Cole never lost a sponsor.

NOVEMBER 2

A$_{\text{GE-OLD}}$ A$_{\text{FRICANS}}$ $_{\text{TELL THE TALE}}$ of a mother lion and her cubs. Sad and dejected, the youngsters cuddle against her back. They ply her with what they have heard other animals say about lions—terrible things heard in the jungle, at play. Are they rumors? Could what they have heard be true, the cubs ask, in two yelps just above a purr. It is not the lion life they have seen with their mother and father. It is not like the stories of majestic beauty, strength, and wisdom they so love to hear. In the time of your great-father's father, she has told them. In the land of your mother's mother, their father has said of the place of high grass and cool waters. This is the world they know. In this history and in this present is all that they are meant to someday be. But these strange voices seem to own a different calling. What is to become of them, they wonder. How will they each find their way to being the lions their elders have told them they are meant to be, they worry, burrowing under her. The mother lion listens to her young ones, lapping their ears, soothing their hurt. Then she stands. It is time to move on. Shaking the dust from her belly, she nudges her cubs to their height. Do not listen to what others who do not know you say of you. Wait, she roars, one day your time will come to tell the tale. With that, mother and cubs press on toward their pride.

On this day, November 2, 1971, twin girls were born: Ayodele Nailah and Dara Rashida Roach, this author's children. It is from their need and the depth of their questions that this and many other books have been born. It was from the wisdom of their great-grandparents and grandparents that the answers have come. Pressing on toward their pride, together we have rediscovered the roots and routes that would bring them across the pass undeterred by misdirection and the voices of the misinformed—no matter how great the creature chatter.

On this symbolic birthday for all our sons and all our daughters, let us remember that what we tell our children as they approach life's crossroads begins with what we tell ourselves. Happy birthday to us all!

Family   Truth

NOVEMBER 3

IN THE LATE 1950s and early 1960s, as racists railed against school desegregation in Mississippi, the state constitution was amended to authorize officials to close schools to avoid desegregation. Common-law marriage was outlawed, rendering many black children "illegitimate" and, by statute, ineligible for public school. Whites obsessed with the idea that a black boy might date a white girl joined Citizens' Councils and appropriated $5,000 each month in state funds to campaign for segregation. In this environment, black voter registration was a must. It was also dangerous. Among the volunteers leading the drive was a New York City math teacher, Robert Moses, who was jailed for "disturbing the peace." On November 3, 1961, a secret letter he had written reached fellow volunteer Tom Hayden:

> We are smuggling this note from the drunk tank of the county jail in Magnolia. Twelve of us are here, sprawled out along the concrete bunker. . . . Later on Hollis will lead out with a clear tenor into a freedom song; Talbert and Lewis will supply jokes; and McDew will discourse on the history of the black man and the Jew. McDew—a black by birth, a Jew by choice, and a revolutionary by necessity—has taken on the deep hates and deep loves which America, and the world, reserves for those who dare to stand in a strong sun and cast a sharp shadow. In the words of Judge Brumfield, who sentenced us, we are "cold calculators" who design to disrupt the racial harmony (harmonious since 1619) of McComb into racial strife and rioting; we, he said, are the leaders who are causing young children to be led like sheep to the pen to be slaughtered (in a legal manner). "Robert," he was addressing me, "haven't some of the people from your school been able to go down and register without violence here in Pike County?" I thought to myself that Southerners are most exposed when they boast.
>
> It's mealtime now; we have rice and gravy in a flat pan. . . . Water comes from a faucet and goes into a hole. This is Mississippi, the middle of the iceberg. Hollis is leading with his tenor. . . . This is a tremor in the middle of the iceberg—from a stone that the builders rejected.

NOVEMBER 4

AHH! THE BEAUTY OF GRENADA, the Caribbean island nation "just south of paradise, just north of frustration," as the saying goes. There, on November 4, 1973, thousands gathered for a People's Congress at Seamoon in St. Andrew's Parish. Two months before the island's long-awaited independence, there was trouble in paradise. It was an unusual circumstance. Instead of rallying around the new prime minister, who had brought the country to freedom and victory against their evil oppressors—as the story was told everywhere in the world where people had fought for and won their freedom—in Grenada people were rallying against him. The Afri-Caribbean one-time island hero, Sir Eric Gairy, was now the enemy of the people. What had happened?

In the late 1960s, sailor-author Carleton Mitchell was greeted in Grenada's harbor by Premier Gairy. "Changes since your last visit?" asked Gairy. In 1967, Grenada had been one of six semiautonomous British colonies to become Associated States of the British Commonwealth. Change had indeed occurred, as Gairy would note. While foreign affairs remained under British control, "We fly our own flag, and are responsible to no one else for the conduct of our internal affairs. Outside investors are aiding our development, diversifying the economy, and opening new fields of employment. Improved communication brings us closer to the world, and the world to us. You can say there have been more changes here in the last four years than in the last century."

It was only partly true. In his twenty-year journey, Gairy had gone from labor leader to people's hero to premier to despot. When one more, last straw, victim was shot and killed by police, the People's Congress—led by the dissident New Jewel Movement (NJM) leader Maurice Bishop—convened to "indict" Gairy for twenty-seven crimes. Found guilty in a mock trial, Gairy was sentenced to resign. His violent response was the "Bloody Sunday" beating of NJM leaders. It was also the sign that the country was on its way from independence to revolution.

NOVEMBER 5

O**N** N**OVEMBER** 5, 1968, in one record-breaking day's testament to the power of the black vote unleashed by the 1965 Voting Rights Act, seven black men and women were elected mayor, nine went to Congress (eight to the House and one to the Senate), ninety-seven were elected to state legislatures, and four hundred were elected to local governments in the former Confederate States.

Although no one had dared predict such sweeping success, the 1968 results had been foreshadowed by the 1967 election of the first two black mayors—Richard Hatch of Gary, Indiana, and Carl Stokes of Cleveland, Ohio. And few could deny the repercussions—pro and con—from the slaughter of the Orangeburg students by the National Guard (see February 7), the assassinations of Martin Luther King Jr. and Robert F. Kennedy, and the appearance of Fannie Lou Hamer at the Democratic National Convention (see August 26). The energy ushering Richard Nixon into the presidency on a "law and order" campaign also brought a generation of blacks into party politics. A network of community organizers had succeeded in forging the national Civil Rights agenda into an election platform.

Among the highlights, New York's Shirley Chisholm (see July 13) became the first black woman elected to Congress. Louis Stokes of Ohio (brother of Carl Stokes, Cleveland's mayor) and William Clay of Missouri were also new. And, in defiance of those who would hold back the tide of black electoral power, Harlem returned its beleaguered congressman of twenty-three years, Rev. Adam Clayton Powell Jr. (see March 1), minus his seniority, as a virtual freshman. Determined to dethrone the powerful black congressman, ranking majority leader, and third in line of succession to the presidency, the House leadership had forced Powell's expulsion in a move that was suspicious on its face—a fact the Supreme Court would later confirm. In rallying behind Powell, Harlem voters—like their southern cousins—were fighting for the fundamental right of a people to elect the qualified candidate of their own choosing.

NOVEMBER 6

THIS WAS GORDON PARKS's moment to celebrate. His son had safely returned home from the Vietnam War. A daughter had just been born. But how were others faring? The photojournalist decided to chronicle a much less fortunate family. After others had turned him down in embarrassment, he met a family almost too desperate to care. Convinced that their story might help others, the Fontenelles agreed. He stayed with them for eight days—even providing rent money. He began keeping a diary on November 6, 1967:

> Bessie Fontenelle appears to be a strong woman, especially in the early part of the day, when she looks younger than her age. As the day wears on she seems to age with it. By nightfall she has crumpled into herself. "All this needing and wanting is about to drive me crazy," she complained today. "Norman's a good man but when he's broke he takes it out on me and the kids . . . especially little Norman. . . . The boy keeps saying he'll kill him if he keeps beating on me. And I wouldn't be surprised if he didn't up and do it some day." Bessie tries to give warmth to the place, but it remains a prison of filth. . . . It's a losing battle for her. I have yet to see the whole family sitting down and eating together. One of the kids will cry out his hunger and Bessie will scrounge up a sandwich of some kind. Little Richard was eating a raw potato today. Sometimes the kids will hungrily share one apple.

By December 1, Norman had beaten Bessie so many times that the ominous sign of her stirring of "a large cauldron of boiling water" is hardly surprising. The next day, everyone is left wondering. Bessie wonders if Norman broke her ribs kicking her around the night before. Norman wonders why she fought back this time and scalded him. Parks wonders about the effect of his intrusion into their lives. When the story is published in the March 1968 issue of *Life*, readers send in contributions sufficient to secure furniture and a home with grass and fresh air for the children. Norman Sr. gets a good job. As Parks tells us, "An entirely new world had suddenly raced in upon them."

NOVEMBER 7

On November 7, 1972, Andrew Young was elected to the House of Representatives from Atlanta's Fifth Congressional District. He was the first black congressman from the South since the late nineteenth century. Then, in a flurry of political chicanery that ended Reconstruction, every black elected official was expelled from office in a systematic campaign of fear, deception, rumor, and outright fraud. But as a member of Dr. King's SCLC inner circle, as a tireless fighter for black voting rights and voter registration, and as a man who was on the balcony of the Lorraine Motel with King when he was assassinated, Young did not need an election to tell him how very much alive was the push to keep blacks from the polls and, definitely, off the ballot.

Young had first attempted the seat in 1970. His opponent, Fletcher Thompson, campaigned on a platform that equated a vote for Young with a vote for the demise of Western Civilization. With this strategy, Thompson, a Republican, beat Young by 20,000 votes on what was once southern Democrat turf. In 1972, incumbent Thompson admitted that in two years in office he had never met with one black group. Even racism couldn't save him, and he bowed out of a reelection bid. Just as the Voting Rights Act had activated the black vote in 1965, Supreme Court–backed redistricting unlocked the power of that vote. Now there were districts that demanded that attention be paid to black voters. Atlanta's redrawn Fifth Congressional was one such district, making it ripe for Young's second try. With a substantial, though still minority-black, vote, the Fifth District elected Young when 23 percent of the white vote allied with his solid black plurality.

In the aftermath of the National Black Political Convention (see March 11), a solid black political agenda and strategy was having positive effect. Other election gains brought two black women to Congress—Barbara Jordan of Texas (see July 28) and Yvonne Brathwaite Burke of California—and reelected the only black senator, Edward Brooke of Massachusetts.

NOVEMBER 8

An obscure Alabama law still on the books in 1965 permitted a political party to form in a specific county. In 1966, that handy bit of research by SNCC led to the founding of the Lowndes County Freedom Organization (LCFO). It also marked a turning point in the story of African Americans, voting, and party politics that, whether Democrat or Republican, had too long best served to exclude them. LCFO set its sights on the court and tax assessment offices. By May, it had a slate of black primary candidates, and political education classes were organized. On election day, November 8, 1966, the showdown vote came. Each white candidate won by the same margin over each black candidate—600 votes—with poll results of roughly 2,200 to 1,600 for each office.

Even though LCFO lost, it had won. Twenty months earlier, not one black was registered to vote; now there were 3,900, of whom 40 percent had risked their lives and livelihoods to actually vote. To intimidate the daring, twenty families had been thrown off their sharecropper plots and spent the winter months in tents in subfreezing cold. Yet fear was matched by determination. With LCFO came a new form of "third-party politics" that, if played to win, could lead majority-black districts to election victory. As Stokely Carmichael and Charles V. Hamilton wrote in their book, *Black Power: The Politics of Liberation in America*, that victory required a "patronage system"—a network of support to release blacks from the stranglehold of white economic supremacy: "Only so many black people will rush to the banner of 'freedom' and 'blackness' without seeing some way to make ends meet, to care for their children." That was the task of the new era now begun—political self-determination required economic development.

With passage of the Voting Rights Act, the southern Democratic Party was still in denial over black Civil Rights, arguing that blacks "owed" them votes for being "allowed" to vote. But, Carmichael and Hamilton argued, they did not *give* black people the right to vote; they *stopped denying* black people the right to vote.

Voting   Empowerment

NOVEMBER 9

THE DETROIT COUNCIL FOR HUMAN RIGHTS was planning a Northern Negro Leadership Conference for November 9 and 10, 1963, with New York's Congressman Adam Clayton Powell as its main speaker. But when the council refused to encourage a cross section of black views and excluded nationalists, Rev. Albert Cleage balked and planned a Northern Negro Grass Roots Leadership Conference for the same two days. From leader to laity the question was this: Where do you stand, brothers and sisters? Those who stood with Cleage heard Malcolm X's last great speech before exiting the Nation of Islam, "Message to the Grass Roots." It was the speech historian John Henrik Clarke has called "the finest revolutionary message delivered by a black man in the twentieth century."

Ever the preacher and the teacher, Malcolm spoke on unity: "What you and I need to do is learn to forget our differences. . . . You don't catch hell because you're a Methodist or Baptist . . . a Democrat or Republican . . . a Mason or an Elk . . . you catch hell because you're a black man. . . . We have a common oppressor, a common exploiter, and a common discriminator." On history: "Of all our studies, history is best qualified to reward our research. . . . All you have to do is examine the historical method used all over the world by others who have problems similar to yours. Once you see how they got theirs straight, then you know how you can get yours straight." On strategy: "There is nothing in . . . the Koran that teaches us to suffer peacefully." On nationalism: "It's based on land. A revolutionary wants land so he can set up his own nation."

In 1965, Rev. Cleage cofounded the Organization for Black Power. One year after that, seeing James Meredith shot down on his courageous March Against Fear (see June 6), Stokely Carmichael would call for "Black Power!" popularizing the phrase that would become the battle cry of a new age. It was an era of change that Cleage would help guide by cofounding the Shrine of the Black Madonna, a community-building institution with a strong spiritual and educational agenda.

NOVEMBER 10

In 1961, divide-and-conquer tactics had separated workers by caste who should have been aligned by class. Unions once positively influenced by the communist stand on workers' rights and racial equity were now strictly Jim Crow and hostile to blacks. White supremacy had infiltrated every union issue from seniority and wage differentials to apprenticeship opportunities. The AFL-CIO even segregated its conventions in southern cities.

Once the dependence of black groups on the contributions of wealthy white industrialists had kept African Americans out of the union movement. No longer. That bond had been strained as the Civil Rights movement attacked racist institutions nationwide. Twenty-five years after founding the Negro National Congress and the Brotherhood of Sleeping Car Porters, A. Philip Randolph was president of the Negro American Labor Council. As delegates gathered in Chicago for the Council's convention on November 10, 1961, Randolph set the tone in this keynote address:

> No greater tragedy has befallen the working class anywhere in the modern world than that which plagues the working class in the South. Both white and black workers turned against their own class and gave aid to their enemy, the feudalistic-capitalist class, to subject them to sharper and sharper exploitation and oppression. . . . By poisonous preachments by the press, pulpit, and politician, the wages of both black and white workers were kept low and working conditions bad, since trade union organization was practically nonexistent. . . . When unions improved northern labor conditions, corporate capital fled south into the land of [the] nonunion, low wage, low tax, race bias, mob law, and poor schools, namely Dixie. Southern [politicians] make special appeals in the northern press to industries to come south for nonunion, cheap labor. But this antitrade union condition in the South is labor's fault. It is the direct result of the fact that neither the old AFL, nor the CIO, nor the AFL-CIO ever came to grips with the racial-labor problem in the South.

The last of the old warriors, Randolph alone could tell the truth—and survive.

Labor   Survival

NOVEMBER 11

A PLAQUE READS:

PRESENTED TO ED DAVIS, INC.
DETROIT, MICHIGAN
To My Husband Upon Appointment By Chrysler Corporation as a
Franchised Dealer
November 11, 1963
"Who made the impossible possible" and helped give a new sense
of direction to the automobile business in these United States. A
new sense of hope and inspiration to scores of Negro youths who
have yet to enter the mainstream of the American economy
With Admiration
Mary Agnes

Ed Davis was a trailblazer. In 1939, he opened a Studebaker
dealership, the first African American franchisee of any U.S.
car manufacturer. Born into a comfortable family in Louisiana,
where his father owned a 500-acre farm and a Model-T Ford,
Ed grew up in love with the magic and newborn potential of
cars. Those were the days when seeing a car was as rare as
owning one. Following his love, at sixteen he left Louisiana to
attend Detroit's Cass Technical High School and study auto
mechanics. But graduating during the Depression era made it
impossible to find a job. After he was refused a job washing
cars on the ground that the gas station owner was losing too
much money in equipment and supplies, the business skills he
had learned from his father kicked in. He struck a deal to
"rent" space for $1 per day and keep what he made on washes,
for which he charged fifty-nine cents. He washed three cars
that first day, six cars the second. By the end of the first week,
he was earning $6 per day. The owner soon complained, "You
are making more money than I am." The owner didn't see his
own potential to increase sales to people who came in for a
wash. Instead, his racism got in his way. His concern was who
made more money. Davis was offered $15 a week plus ten
cents for every car washed, and he took it. With initiative, he
had created a job for himself when there was none to be had.
It was that start that launched him on his way.

NOVEMBER 12

IN THE 1880s, there were eight African American delegates to the General Assembly of Virginia. In 1882, one such member, the Honorable Alfred W. Harris of Dinwiddie County—a Howard University Law School alumni—proposed and passed through the legislature a "radical" bill that chartered Virginia Normal and Collegiate Institution. Unique among historically black colleges, it was the first four-year college funded by the state. The others had been founded under the federal Freedman's Bureau or by missionaries. In 1957, its seventy-fifth year, the school—renamed Virginia State University (VSU)—was as "radical" as ever in pursuing its founder's stated mission: "We will demonstrate to that class of gentlemen in Virginia who do not believe that we can comprehend the higher training, that we are their intellectual equals; and will ease the fears of those who yet think that it will not comport with the dignity of old aristocratic families to give the Negro a fair show." Yet, as the Civil Rights movement began its rise, at VSU and elsewhere, one could discern frustration and discouragement among black alumnae. Why? That was the subject of an address at VSU on November 12, 1957, by one of the century's premier spiritual leaders and theologians, the Rev. Dr. Howard Thurman, dean of the Marsh Chapel at Boston University.

In a speech titled "The New Heaven and the New Earth," Thurman argued the frustration grew out of the "cult of inequality." It even impacted course offerings that deliberately discouraged students from dissecting the ethical dilemmas posed by a segregated society. As an alternative and antidote to the frustration, Thurman welcomed the new age of activism:

> The forces that are at work in the environment . . . are at last beginning to work in [the frustrated and discouraged], causing him to be able to make an unconditional response to the fruits of learning . . . to the impact of truth and to follow that truth wherever it leads, transcending all barriers and all contexts—it is into this new earth that the . . . Negro is catapulted in his encounter with higher education.

NOVEMBER 13

THE MONTGOMERY BUS BOYCOTT was over eleven months old. People were weary, worn down by having to walk up to twelve miles a day and by the threats, the lost jobs, the lost car insurance on the few cars available. But they were bolstered, too, by those foreign underwriters who issued insurance when American companies would not, by those whites who risked their lives to cross the color bar, and by gradual support in the nation's courts of law and public opinion. Early in 1956, the campaign to break the boycott led a state court to hand down eighty-nine indictments under an archaic law on conspiracies to boycott "without just cause." To segregationists, blacks had no rights, much less a cause. The only one indicted was the boycott's leader, Martin Luther King Jr.

On November 13, 1956, the international press, along with boycott leaders and supporters, crowded into a Montgomery courtroom for King's sentencing. Under the Fourteenth Amendment to the Constitution, Congress had the right to intercede when rights of citizenship were denied (see March 15). But Congress wasn't willing. Following hard on the heels of its school desegregation order of 1954, the Supreme Court was better positioned for change—to again harness the power of federal law over state law. As King sat pessimistically awaiting his fate, a reporter broke into court in a scene straight out of the movies, Associated Press wire copy in hand. He handed King the news. The Supreme Court had just declared Alabama's segregated bus laws unconstitutional, nullifying the charges against him. Spreading the word, a spectator cried out, "God Almighty has spoken from Washington, D.C.!" Undoubtably, that must have been true. For without divine intervention, the state of Alabama would have most certainly imposed the stiffest possible prison term on King. Celebrating that night, boycotters were as jubilant as they were cautious. No mere news wire copy would steer them off course. The issue was bus desegregation, not one vacated prison sentence. That night's unanimous vote continued the boycott until a signed desegregation order was in hand.

NOVEMBER 14

ON NOVEMBER 14, 1961, as vicious attacks on Freedom Riders continued to make headlines, Betty Rice
Hughes committed an unbelievable act of faith despite centuries of proof that her faith was unwarranted:

> It was mostly curiosity that caused me to set out from Los Ange-
> les on a tour of the South by bus just twelve days after the Inter-
> state Commerce Commission's order went into effect forbidding
> separation by races in interstate buses and terminals. . . . I wanted
> to see . . . if a female Negro tourist traveling alone—unheralded
> and unprepared for—would receive a different reception [from]
> the Freedom Riders. I traveled straight across the middle of Ar-
> kansas and saw no "White" or "Colored" signs on the rest rooms
> or waiting rooms. I could sense the hostility brought on by my
> presence in some towns, but I was served without incident. In
> Memphis I encountered the first separate waiting rooms. There
> were stares from other passengers when I went into the main
> waiting rooms, but nothing more. In Monteagle, I saw the first
> evidence that the signs had recently been removed.
>
> I realize now that my naïveté about southern customs was a
> protective cloak. I was subjected to my first real attempt at dis-
> crimination in South Carolina. As I walked into the restaurant
> the cashier looked up, turned red, and started pointing and yell-
> ing. "There's another one just across the waiting room!" Stalling
> for time, I feigned innocence and asked her, "What's the differ-
> ence? This one's fine, thank you." A tall white counterman fol-
> lowed. "Just go on over to the other restaurant and you'll find out
> the difference." A customer got up from the counter and I sat
> down. Just before the end of my lunch break, a waitress came
> over and took my order. My bravado had paid off [but] I was no
> longer optimistic and I dreaded the next bus stop. And yet at
> Charleston and Savannah, I received service. The other Negro
> passengers had started watching to see what I was going to do at
> the lunch stops. Several asked me, "Are you riding for us?" I said
> in a sense I was. I believe that what must happen next is for
> southern white people to get used to seeing Negroes. And it is just
> as necessary for southern Negroes to get used to seeing other Ne-
> groes bypassing the segregated areas so that they may take
> courage and insist on the best facilities for their money.

NOVEMBER 15

In 1969, young Bay Area Californians seething over society's inequities adopted a two-pronged strategy to combat injustice. As Black Panthers took to the streets of Oakland, Black Studies seized imaginations on nearby campuses. With the first student generation to come from a land beyond the "Talented Tenth" of W. E. B. Du Bois's 1920s and the "Black Bourgeoisie" of E. Franklin Frazier's 1950s, a new era had begun. A Purdue student assessed the plight of his generation. These black students, he said, were "sharecroppers of the American dream." The assassination of Dr. Martin Luther King forged a turning point. Nonviolence was out; self-defense was in. "Integration into what?" they asked, questioning society's basic premises. No longer grateful for college acceptances, "Relevance!" was their demand; "Black Studies!" was their cry.

For perspective, KRON-TV's *Like It Is* asked three scholars—Drs. St. Clair Drake, Nathan Hare, and Andrew Billingsley—to answer the question "What is Black Studies?" The program aired on November 15, 1969. Defining Black Studies as a systematic study of the black experience in the world through the eyes of blacks and the perspectives of blacks, each added further insight. "Black Studies is a social movement—action-oriented versus purely academic," said Drake, adding that it went beyond history. Black people must be viewed as having a present and a past. To Hare, it was knowledge "useful to black students." He outlined three department models: "'Negro studies' for whites; 'polka-dot,' intermediate; and 'Afro-American,' the study of the black race for black students." "Autonomy is essential," noted Billingsley. Far beyond textbook teaching, blacks had to not only define the experience, but develop it. "Each campus must ask the question, 'Black Studies for whom!'"

In 1970, in the midst of the push to add Black Studies and achieve academic reform, Mills College, a private Bay Area women's school in Oakland, awarded the nation's first graduate degree in Black Studies to Janus Adams.

NOVEMBER 16

ON NOVEMBER 16, 1941, Edward Margetson, a prolific composer and organist, was honored by the Schubert Music Society in New York at the American Academy of Arts and Letters. A child prodigy, he was composing at age five. In 1919, he left St. Kitts to study at Columbia University. In 1920, he was named organist and choirmaster of Harlem's Church of the Crucifixion, where he remained for thirty-five years. As a composer of hundreds of anthems and string quartets in the European classical tradition, he was celebrated for his use of West Indian folk music and for his eloquent simplicity. His talents echoed in these remarks:

> In my early boyhood I loved to wander deep within the dark bosom of the mountain on which my home looked out one way, and by the shores of the sea on which my home looked out another way. I was born and lived in an Eden situated between these two symbols of the Everlasting. . . . The mountain appalled me by its majestic immobility and its incredible silence; while the sea struck terror in my heart by reason of its incessant striving and the note of menace in its voice. And so my wanderings were always done in company with other children. That was the secret of my pleasure in them. . . . I have never cared to walk alone.
>
> Music is a sanctuary; a haven of contentment for the spirit; a realm into which the clash and clang of life's uneven warfare, the heart cries of its wounded, may, and do surely enter; but, entering, they are muted first, then hushed. And this is the reason why I have always longed that those whose lives touch mine—all my friends and acquaintances . . . should come "home" to it and find in it the platform for a perfect sympathy; so that truly . . . "we might all be together."
>
> No large masterpieces have dripped from my pen. . . . I have simply tried to work uncommonly well in the smaller forms. But whether my thoughts survive or perish, believe this: that it has been joy unspeakable to have lived with them, and loved them, and sometimes set them down. I know the loving thoughtfulness which has been the origin [of this tribute]. To the little band of fellow pilgrims who comprise the Schubert Society, I thank you very, very kindly.

Music   Beauty

NOVEMBER 17

As SEGREGATED AS ALBANY, GEORGIA, WAS, life for its 40 percent black population was different in important ways—blacks had steady work on local farms and in nightclubs and resorts, they owned their own small mom-and-pop businesses, and they could even attend historically black Albany State College. But in the early 1960s, as the Civil Rights movement became an ongoing nationally televised drama, progress—school desegregation, lunch counter sit-ins—had passed Albany by. On November 17, 1961, the Albany Movement woke up the town and kept its *minds stayed on freedom.*

Things had begun heating up in the spring of 1961. Black students protesting the harassment of women students by off-campus whites were further politicized by officials who retaliated by suspending student leaders. That summer, students asked SNCC's young leaders for help organizing an Albany voter registration drive. But the relatively "better" life in Albany found few willing to risk their livelihoods—much less their lives—for the vote. Local NAACP leaders railed against "outsiders," like SNCC, who were condemned for getting folks stirred up and arrested, then leaving the costs of bail and legal defense to the NAACP. What distinguished Albany was the source of conflict itself. "We're working for the same things, aren't we?" young Bernice Johnson asked, honing the voice and vision that would yield her international acclaim as a founding member of the singing group Sweet Honey in the Rock. It was a good question. In answer, an "organization of organizations" was founded to unite the factions. It was called the Albany Movement. Its mission was to desegregate city facilities and ensure equal educational and economic opportunities.

Dr. William Anderson was named president. A doctor and drugstore owner, he was sufficiently grounded in a black economic structure to have a degree of financial autonomy. Slater King—a builder and real estate broker—became vice president.

NOVEMBER 18

To WANDER THROUGH CENTRAL PARK and happen upon Cleopatra's Needle, a two-thousand-year-old obelisk, to visit the Metropolitan Museum of Art's Egyptian Wing, with its ancient temple rebuilt and encased in its own pyramid scaffold of glass and steel, is to marvel at the wonder of African civilization and to wonder at all the marvels now lost to the continent. In all, more than nine hundred objects created during the Amarna and post–Amarna Periods—circa 1353 to 1295 B.C.—open a window on an unmatched period of artistic creativity. But the story of how these treasures came to light is as old as time—need and greed. One such real-life story was retold in the Egyptian film *The Night of Counting the Years*, directed by filmmaker Shadi Abdelsalaam. The film was made in 1969, but it would be another six years before it premiered in the United States. To watch it at the Regency Theater on November 18, 1975, was to hear the ancestors weep.

As the story of the actual event is retold, a series of ceremonial revelations unfolds with the opening of door after door into the secret burial chamber of an ancient Egyptian tomb. From a conversation in the Antiquities Department in Cairo, Egypt, we retrace the tale back to the Mountain of the Dead, near Thebes, where an ancient royal cache was discovered in 1881.

At the time, Egyptian and British archaeologists were disturbed and enthralled by rare art pieces that began to mysteriously present themselves, illegally, to art dealers. With no record of the existence of these obviously ancient treasures, it was conjectured that they must be from a newly opened tomb. The mystery unfolds. The source is the people of a once-prosperous ancient village. Pressed by starvation, for years village elders had robbed the graves of their ancestors to sell first one piece, then another. With the death of their leader, the secret is passed to his son. Repulsed, he reports it to the Antiquities Department, saving the past by betraying the present. His truth causes the destruction of his people, who are left without their means of survival . . . as we ponder the dilemma and its treasures.

Film   Values

NOVEMBER 19

On November 19, 1951, the world-renowned eighty-three-year-old Dr. W. E. B. Du Bois sat in a Washington, D.C., courtroom, indicted by the U.S. government as a secret foreign agent facing a $10,000 fine and five years in prison. He noted, with irony, that as one of the world's most prolific writers and social critics, he'd never been secretive. But this was the McCarthy era. Just because the situation was ludicrous did not mean the government was not out to get him.

How had things spiraled so far out of control? Just the year before, the eighty-two-year-old Du Bois had run for the Senate on a platform of world peace. Amazed, he found that 205,729 New Yorkers had voted for him. Those courageous people, he wrote, "without the prejudice against color which I always expect and usually experience faced poverty and jail to stand and be counted for Peace and Civil Rights." The summer before the campaign, in fact, the government had demanded he register as a foreign agent. He wasn't one, so he didn't. Then, on February 9, 1951, probably in response to his added popularity, he was charged with failing to register and was indicted. "A shameful proclamation to the world that our government considers peace alien and its advocacy criminal," wrote Du Bois. "I have faced . . . many unpleasant experiences: the growl of a mob . . . threat of murder. . . . But nothing has so cowed me as that day, November 8, 1951, when I took my seat in a Washington courtroom as an indicted criminal."

The major hurdle came in jury selection. While courts regularly excluded blacks from jury pools, Du Bois's had been stacked with black civil servants. A federal employee who acquitted him was in danger of being accused of "disloyalty" and of being similarly indicted and jobless. If Du Bois declined black jurors, he would face an all-white jury and violate the principles of equity for which he had long fought. Du Bois decided to put his faith and fate with the majority-black jury. On November 19, after five trial days, the government rested its flimsy case. The next day, the judge directed the jury to acquit Du Bois and his four codefendants.

NOVEMBER 20

IN THE FRONT PORCH AND KOOL-AID DAYS of girlhood and Mississippi, Carrie Ann, Marva Ann, Nola Ann, and Hattie Mae knew they would always be together. When they were grown, only the one without the Ann in her name went away. Even then she was as different as her name, Hattie Mae. Twenty-plus years united and reunited the four whenever Hattie Mae felt her accent coming on and headed home for a breeze. The four girls had become girlfriends, the front porch Marva Ann's den, the giggles deep dangerous woman-laughs, and the Kool-Aid margaritas. Together again after all these years, little and a lot had changed. Nola Ann remembered a story about Hattie Mae and *Carmen Jones*.

Nola Ann and Hattie Mae were in Catholic elementary school, Sacred Heart, when the archdiocese sent down word that any child who went to see the movie *Carmen Jones* would be committing a venal sin worthy of possible excommunication. Now, as Nola Ann remembered it, this presented serious problems for the black children in the diocese—especially because so few movies ever featured blacks in starring roles; especially because *this* movie had Pearl Bailey, Harry Belafonte, and the siren herself, Dorothy Dandridge. Nola Ann decided to avoid eternal wrath. Not so Hattie Mae, who reared back on preadolescent hips to declare, "I ain' stud'n 'bout no excommunica'n. I'm gon' see *Carmen Jones*." Now the problem was Nola Ann's, so she stayed away from Hattie Mae for days because the nuns knew how close they were as friends and Nola Ann did not want Hattie Mae's troubles to rub off and get her excommunicated, too. Nola Ann told her friend, "I knew you had gone, Hattie Mae, because very soon thereafter you took a liking to red dresses." But, as she later determined, maybe it wasn't so bad after all: "Given your life, Hattie Mae, I'm certain the Lord has forgiven you by now."

How could the Lord do otherwise, having destined Hattie Mae to become Miss Hattie Winston, cabaret singer, Broadway leading lady, and star of film and TV?

Women and Womanhood   **Friendship**

NOVEMBER 21

"THIS ARMY IS SOMETHING ELSE. I've been in it for three days now and it feels like three years." Writing these words on Sunday, November 21, 1965, David Parks began his military service and a diary of his two-year sojourn. From basic training at Fort Dix, New Jersey; his tour of duty; seeing people killed; returning home safe but scarred, here was an African American soldier's Vietnam in his own words:

November 21, 1965: It was a bad scene at the draft board, all these cold, shivering jokers looking lost and scared. A lot of mothers and fathers standing around crying like we were on our way to Vietnam already. I stayed in the car until the very last minute. It would be at least two years before I was a free man again.

January 16, 1966: Three more funerals this week for soldiers killed in Vietnam.

March 4, 1966: "Parks, you look like you just came off a block in Harlem." "Why, Sergeant?" I asked. "What gives you that impression?" "You're all the same."

September 29, 1966: Hot damn! Made the football team today.

March 2, 1967: Last night we got our first mortar attack. . . . I had no control over my body. I shook like jelly as the shrapnel burst all around our bunker. There would be that awful *shruuuump* of the hit, then the sound of steel spraying the air . . .

September 9, 1967: I take off for home day after tomorrow. Yowie! The chopper ride back to Zulu is probably the last one I take in Nam. Looking down over the rice paddies I knew so well made me wonder if I had a right to be there. When I came into the army I had no questions, but I am leaving with some.

September 13, 1967: Homeward bound. . . . The white guy who sold me my ticket at the airport . . . pitched it at me like I was dirt. . . . He reminded me of how some of my white officers treated me. . . . Thought I'd left all my problems behind. Hell, the new ones will just have to wait. I'm going to enjoy myself for a few days.

The idea for Parks's diary had been suggested by his father, the photojournalist Gordon Parks (see March 22, November 6). Upon David's safe return home, the two men smoothed the diary and sifted photos for his book, *GI Diary.*

NOVEMBER 22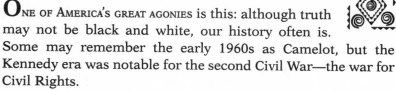

ONE OF AMERICA'S GREAT AGONIES is this: although truth may not be black and white, our history often is. Some may remember the early 1960s as Camelot, but the Kennedy era was notable for the second Civil War—the war for Civil Rights.

On November 22, 1963, as a traumatized nation absorbed the assassination of its bright young president, reporters sought to put the legacy of John F. Kennedy in context by interviewing key figures. Responding, Malcolm X characterized JFK's murder as "a case of chickens coming home to roost." Tactless as it seemed to grieving ears, it was hardly inaccurate. Kennedy had launched the siege on Vietnam, which Buddhist monks protested with public self-immolations. His CIA had helped capture South Africa's Nelson Mandela (see June 12). On the homefront, his infamous FBI director, J. Edgar Hoover, had approved the wiretapping (see April 15) and sabotage (see April 6) of Civil Rights leaders.

Yet, even with this racism-as-usual, blacks knew that Kennedy's intervention during the 1960 election had freed Dr. King from jail. Northern blacks who could vote, cast ballots of faith for Kennedy in the name of their southern cousins who couldn't, and that block vote gave Kennedy a narrow winning margin over Richard Nixon. As president, Kennedy lifted his sights from the nation's blood-soaked racial landscape to denounce segregation and decry the Birmingham church bombing that killed four girls. When southern senators filibustered for racism and "states rights," JFK cast his political lot with segregation's victims. In so doing, he might have also cast his personal lot with its many casualties.

In the end, Kennedy did not deliver on the promise for which blacks had helped elect him. For all he offered in glamor and hope, Kennedy too often sacrificed black justice for southern votes. It took his successor, a Southerner, Lyndon B. Johnson, to break the mold and enact the Civil Rights Act (1964), Executive Order No. 11246 on affirmative action (1965), and the Voting Rights Act (1965).

In 1973, Howard University hosted a conference and celebration of composer W. C. Handy on the centennial of his birth. As Dr. Sterling Brown made a presentation challenging the historical basis for calling Handy the "Father of the Blues" yet honoring the composer's work undeterred, in that moment, Bernice Johnson Reagon has said, she understood the venerated educator's greatness. In Brown's work, she realized teaching as the art of "taking great risks to open the way to a usable truth. . . . I knew I wanted my work to be cleansing like that." For two years, she had been conducting a vocal workshop at Robert Hooks's DC Repertory Company and evolved a working group of women singing traditional music a cappella. When Reagon was asked to sing at the closing session of the Handy conference on November 23, 1973, the lesson she garnered from Brown crystallized a mission for the group she had begun to call Sweet Honey in the Rock. She decided to premiere Sweet Honey at that closing session.

To hear the group is to cease to ask why it, or "she," as Reagon calls the ensemble, has "her" name. As in the tradition of naming a child by capturing some unique experience that took place at the moment of its birth, "Sweet Honey in the Rock" was the first song Reagon had taught her group. As the song and the voices took to one another, she knew she had found a name for a group in the process of being born. After the first rehearsal, she called her father, Rev. Jessie Johnson, a Baptist minister, to ask the derivation of the song. It was a religious parable, but one not taken directly from the Bible. The parable described a land so rich that when a rock was cracked, honey poured from its veins.

"As African Americans and as women we have had to have the standing power of the rocks and the mountains," Reagon has written. "This quality often obscures the fact that we are sweet like honey. Inside the strength partnering the sturdiness, we are—as honey is sweet—sweet. If our world is warm, honey flows, and so do we; if it is cold, honey gets stiff and stays put, and so do we."

NOVEMBER 24

In 1967, as New York City began desegregating schools via its Community School District (CSD) plan (see September 9), the nation's largest school system had no black superintendent-level personnel and only a few black principals. As John Powis, a Catholic priest and the only white member on the pilot Ocean Hill–Brownsville CSD Board, noted, "New York wasn't ready for that." Indeed, when veteran teacher Rhody McCoy became the district's superintendent, each of the principals in his district, subordinates all, refused him office space in their schools. McCoy had to set up shop in an unsuitable, unheated storefront. If that was the way a boss was treated, what was being done to the children? McCoy and his CSD board decided to remove those who provided the greatest impediment to cooperative progress. Nineteen in all, thirteen teachers and six administrators, they were as racially mixed a group, proportionately, as the school personnel city-wide: seventeen whites, one Puerto Rican, and one black.

This "reassignment," as the CSD called it—or firing, as the union saw it—ignited the New York City Teacher's strike. Ironically, the only district to operate undeterred was Ocean Hill–Brownsville. It had recruited 350 new teachers that summer, a mix of white Christians, Jews, blacks, and Puerto Ricans. Despite negative publicity, neither the issue nor the solution was all black or white, as an article, "A JHS 271 Teacher Tells It Like He Sees It," in the *New York Times* of November 24, 1968, confirmed. Charles Isaacs, one of Ocean Hill's new white hires, saw as the problems the police and press in school, helicopters overhead, and this: "Our experiment will be evaluated in terms of the established conventional criteria: reading scores, standardized achievement tests . . . some of which measure what they are intended to measure, for middle-class children. . . . If the conventional criteria measure the wrong things, their effect is harmful to our students, yet they will determine to a great extent whether or not we will ever be free to develop our own yardsticks. In effect, we must miseducate the children before we will be allowed to educate them."

Education   Standards

NOVEMBER 25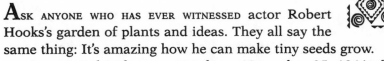

ASK ANYONE WHO HAS EVER WITNESSED actor Robert Hooks's garden of plants and ideas. They all say the same thing: It's amazing how he can make tiny seeds grow.

As papers hit the newsstands on November 25, 1964, the verdict was in: LeRoi (Amiri Baraka) Jones's play, *Dutchman*, with Robert Hooks in the lead, was a hit! With his actor's hours—home in the day, out at night—Hooks became friends with the high school kids who frequented the playground across the street from his apartment. He offered to show them what he did, planting a seed. As these informal workshops grew, Hooks took out a wall in his apartment to build a rehearsal space for the kids. These lessons in acting were *building character*—presentation skills, diction, self-confidence—and it was time to showcase his teens for their parents. He asked the producers of *Dutchman* for use of the Cherry Lane Theater on a "dark" night—a Monday, when the production was traditionally off. For his group (now called the Group Theater Workshop), he developed *We Real Cool*. And to give his young actors a chance to work with professionals, he asked to stage a reading of *Happy Ending*, one of a pair of unproduced one-act plays by his friend Douglas Turner Ward. At the parents' showcase was *New York Post* critic Jerry Talmer, unknown to Hooks, who wrote a resounding review. A sprout. Hooks coproduced Ward's plays with Gerald Krone, again to such success that Ward was asked to write an article for the *New York Times*. "American Theatre: For Whites Only?" was published on August 14, 1966, and caught the eye of Ford Foundation executives, who saw an opportunity for problem solving. A bud. A Hooks-Krone-Ward proposal, funded by the Ford Foundation, gave birth to the Negro Ensemble Company—a resident repertory troupe and training center for theater professionals, which premiered on January 2, 1967. From its perennial bloom have come actors Laurence Fishburne, Barbara Montgomery, Phylicia Rashad, Denzel Washington, Hattie Winston; directors; playwrights; and Charles Fuller's Pulitzer Prize–winning play-turned-film, *A Soldier's Story*.

NOVEMBER 26

Nᴏᴠᴇᴍʙᴇʀ 26, 1965, marks the death of Wendall "Winks" Hamlet, a man who for forty years gave blacks the time of their lives. Pack up the family, head off to the hills above Pinecliffe, and find peace in Winks Panorama, a Colorado mountain lodge as unique in architecture as it was in clientele.

Local census records published in the *Denver Republican* on April 4, 1866, listed sixty "colored" people in a census of seven thousand in this gold mining countryside. But while black families could work, they were not accepted in the region's general life. Sixty years into the area's boom, black real estate developers advertised a planned community for blacks: Lincoln Hills. For five dollars down and five dollars per month, for a total of fifty dollars, blacks could buy land and build. Endorsed by such respected groups as Denver's Shorter AME Church and the YMCA, the plan was a success. In 1925, it attracted Wendall Hamlet and inspired his vision of a lodge for blacks, free from the racial indignities of the day.

Architectural historians have cited the lodge, prized for its "careful siting" on the land, for "its sensitive use of indigenous and imported materials, its creative combination of rustic and contemporary structural techniques . . . its restrained yet thoughtful use of color, harmony, contrast, and accent [which] allow it to sit naturally in its environment." In short, it was breathtaking. Despite hard times brought on by the Depression and World War II, the lodge survived with national publicity and ads in *Ebony*. To its expansive vistas came tourists from the East—for the fun, the fraternal atmosphere, and some of the best peach cobbler west of the Mississippi. Seated around the fireplace, guests enjoyed jazz on the jukebox and live readings by such giants as Countee Cullen and Langston Hughes.

In 1980, for its significance to black history and culture and its architectural integrity, Winks Panorama, though no longer in business, was designated a landmark and was listed on the National Register of Historic Places.

NOVEMBER 27

THE FIRST BLACK presidential aide in U.S. history, E. Frederic Morrow (see April 26), had navigated uncharted miles of historic ground during the Eisenhower years. Throughout his tenure as Administrative Officer for Special Projects, from 1955 to 1960, he kept a diary. In the first entry he wrote, "This is not to be a Jim Crow office solely made up of Negroes." But it had been a Jim Crow time—a transitional era in which violent resistance to the Supreme Court–mandated end of segregation was captured by a brand-new medium called TV, with pictures that glared for all the world to see. Now, following his party's defeat in the presidential election of 1960, Morrow prepared to exit center stage with his Republican colleagues. His diary entry from November 1960 closed the book on the Eisenhower years:

> I begged [Richard] Nixon's managers, by memo and in person, to have the Vice-President [and presidential candidate] make a statement deploring the situation under which [Dr. Martin Luther] King was jailed. They demurred. They thought it bad strategy. . . . I even drafted a telegram for the Vice-President to send to the mayor of Atlanta. The press secretary put the draft in his pocket to "think about it." Twenty-four hours later, King was freed from jail. His freedom came after the intercession of the Democratic presidential candidate, John F. Kennedy [see November 22]. *This act won the election.* Kennedy's action electrified the entire Negro community and resulted in tens of thousands of Negro voters going over to the Democrats' banner. . . . He had keen, intelligent Negro advisers, and he obviously listened to them. In the Republican headquarters everybody was an expert on the Negro.
>
> The results of this campaign should hold many valuable lessons for Republican . . . politicians. The strategy of wooing the solid South and ignoring the available Negro vote was a costly blunder. The South is still too emotional over slavery and Reconstruction to come over to the Republicans in a wholesale manner. And white people must stop believing they "know the Negro." For a long while to come in this country, it would be well to ask knowledgeable Negroes for an objective assessment of the Negro attitude and mood on a given subject.

NOVEMBER 28

As Malcolm X wrote in his autobiography, "If ever a state social agency destroyed a family, it destroyed ours." But at long last, over the weekend of November 28, 1964, they were together again for the first time in twenty-five years.

Young Malcolm Little had enjoyed a close, loving family. His father was a Baptist preacher from Georgia. His mother, born to a West Indian mother and a Scottish father who never acknowledged her, grew up in Canada. In Omaha, Nebraska, where Malcolm was born, the Littles were active in Marcus Garvey's Pan-Africanist UNIA (Universal Negro Improvement Association) (see August 13, November 29). As soon as their views became known, the Klan warned them to leave Omaha. They relocated to Lansing, Michigan, still active in the local UNIA. Their house was burned down by whites who refused to have black neighbors. By 1931 the family had a new home in East Lansing. But Earl Little was killed by a streetcar on September 28, 1931. The police termed it an accident, but his death was quite likely the work of a white supremacist group. Louise Little worked as a seamstress until the threads of her own sanity finally unraveled under the pressure. When social workers began parceling out her seven children, she snapped and was committed to Kalamazoo State Hospital. That spring of 1939, Malcolm told his teacher he wanted to be a lawyer, only to hear, "That's no realistic goal for a nigger." His father dead, mother hospitalized, older siblings in one place, younger in another, Malcolm's behavior deteriorated. He was placed in juvenile detention and a series of foster homes.

Malcolm visited his mother when he could until he realized "she didn't know who I was." That was in 1952. Years later, Malcolm's sister, Yvonne Woodward, recalled, "I'd tell Malcolm . . . none of us is ever going to amount to anything until we get our mother out of Kalamazoo. It had preyed on my mind for years. The next thing I knew I got a call, my mother was in Lansing at my brother Philbert's. And we went to see her. It was a joyous time."

Family   Healing

NOVEMBER 29

As one scholar wrote in 1927, "After all the tinsel is brushed away, the fact remains that the grandiose schemes of Marcus Garvey gave to the race a consciousness such as it had never possessed before." By the late 1930s, however, the Universal Negro Improvement Association (UNIA) was in disarray (see August 13). Gone were the proud parades up Harlem's Lenox Avenue. Gone were the power and majesty of his command: "Up you mighty race." Even Garvey himself seemed exhausted of funds and spirit—but not ideas.

From his London base, he kept his magazine, *The Black Man*, going. In its November 1938 issue, an ad promoted his School of African Philosophy, which offered live sessions in his Beaumont Crescent UNIA headquarters and correspondence courses for a limited number of students worldwide. Garvey had been quieted, but he was hardly quiet. Nor had he ceased to be a "threat" to white world rule, as a colonial Kenyan intelligence report would confirm. Dated June 1939, the report from a local commissioner to British colonial authorities raised concern that the people of North Kavirondo, Kenya, had taken up a collection to pay for Garvey's course. To his Kenyan disciples would be added other graduates in London, Nigeria, Uganda, South Africa, and the United States. Impoverished and forgotten by all but a stalwart few, Garvey could not make a financial success of the course. But, he'd certainly documented a powerful legacy.

All the time-honored Garvey principles were there. Preserved was a wealth of experience and lessons garnered and honed over a thirty-year career as visionary organizer, activist, and entrepreneur. In twenty-one lessons he mapped out not only the philosophy of the UNIA, but a model plan for the liberation of Africans the world over—including the directive to turn (reinvest) a dollar three times before it left black hands. At the root of everything was this: "Number One—Intelligence, Education, Universal Knowledge and How to Get It: You must never stop learning."

Ideas   Enterprise

NOVEMBER 30

In 1957, a hospital building at the corner of Eighth and Webster Streets in Yazoo City, Mississippi, had the patina of failure. But to those who knew its history, it was a monument to thirty years of successful innovation.

In the South of the 1920s, medical care for the black rural poor was inadequate at best and malevolent at base—as the infamous "Tuskegee Experiment" (see July 27) would later confirm. The traditional African medicine based on a knowledge of roots and herbs passed on during slavery had since been tossed aside by waves of "progress" unfulfilled. All the while, such treatable conditions as rust infection and low birth weight proved fatal to blacks from whom care was either withheld on account of race or was denied on account of poverty. In 1924, T. J. Huddleston—Delta farmer, teacher, and founder of the Humphreys County Training School—came up with an alternative cure: Mississippi's first hospital for blacks. During World War I, Huddleston had become a top war bonds salesman. In this door-to-door nickel-and-dime fund-raising formula, he saw the means to his end. "Us gon' have our own hospital?" people would marvel as he detailed his plan for a fraternal order that would pool resources to ensure care by trained physicians and nurses. Affordable monthly dues entitled members to office visits and hospitalization. In 1924 the Afro-American Sons and Daughters Fraternal Organization was chartered, and within four years the hospital was a reality.

A forerunner of today's managed care facilities, this cooperative medical plan was revolutionary in its day. Thirty years later, when Huddleston died in 1957, the hospital had fallen on hard times born of deepened segregation and worsened poverty. In 1972, it closed. But by then, as Huddleston's granddaughter Dr. Patricia C. Murrain would later write, people had changed. "They would never again be satisfied with hopelessness." The "little I's" had come together to become "strong WE's." As the Civil Rights era broke new medical ground, it did so on the firm foundation of Huddleston's Afro-American Hospital.

DECEMBER

DECEMBER 1

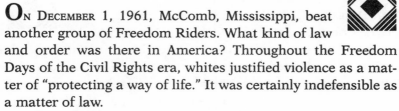

On December 1, 1961, McComb, Mississippi, beat another group of Freedom Riders. What kind of law and order was there in America? Throughout the Freedom Days of the Civil Rights era, whites justified violence as a matter of "protecting a way of life." It was certainly indefensible as a matter of law.

Looking back on history, the violence of slavery is condoned as having been "legal then." Legal to whom? one might ask. As important as is majority rule, no majority-black vote ever "legalized" slavery. Thus, if one accepts slavery as legal, when the Freedom Rides are discussed one should note that the Freedom Riders were the "law-abiding" parties. Racists argue the Constitution's "states' rights" provisions, but the Constitution also established the supremacy of federal law in interstate commerce. The Interstate Commerce Commission, as upheld by the Supreme Court, had desegregated interstate travel. It was the law. When Freedom Riders were attacked, the mobs were violating that law. Each infraction compromised not only the courts but the signed order of a president— the commander in chief. By act and intent, these "partial coups" in effect acted to overthrow the government.

This is the story as it should be told. Yet instigators were pandered to, the violent were coddled, subversion was tolerated. Lawful Freedom Riders were tormented while the disloyal went free. No wonder the heroic Freedom Riders became folklore, as Juan Williams confirmed in *Eyes on the Prize:*

> For several years after the Freedom Rides, Civil Rights workers in the deepest South, from Louisiana bayous to the Florida Keys, would be asked by local blacks, "Are you one of them Freedom Riders?" The answer might be, "No, ma'am, we're working for voter registration," or "No, sir, we're doing legal research for the NAACP," or "No, son, we're here to teach folks how to read." But if the workers were seen as part of the Civil Rights movement, the people called them Freedom Riders. The courage and tenacity of those pioneers had captured the imagination and awe of blacks throughout the Southland.

DECEMBER 2

On December 2, 1952, in testimony before the Supreme Court, Secretary of State Dean Acheson made the following statement: "The continuation of racial discrimination in the United States remains a source of constant embarrassment to this government in the day-to-day conduct of its foreign relations, and it jeopardizes the effective maintenance of our moral leadership of the free and democratic nations of the world." At last, a government official had said the right thing, albeit for the wrong reasons.

Just two years earlier, Acheson had supported the revocation of Paul Robeson's passport (see July 20). He had presided over the heating up of the Cold War into the boil of Korea. Left simmering in the domestic pot was the stew of Civil Rights. Testifying just weeks after the presidential election had unseated his Democratic party and its hard-core segregationist block, Acheson's weighing-in on the side of image signaled increased federal support for Civil Rights. But it did not mean the end of Cold War propaganda as Race War politics. It was the 1950s—the age of McCarthyism and euphemism, when a "red menace" was said to "threaten" the American way of life, a way of life sustained by Jim Crow, lynching, and taxation without representation for people of color. "Outside agitators" were said to be "fomenting unrest" through the Civil Rights movement (as though black "insiders" were unaware of their own plight or incapable of addressing it without "alien" Soviet "influence"). It would be two more years before Gandhi's philosophy of nonviolence (see August 15) inspired the confrontational pacifism of Martin Luther King, which inspired the Freedom Rides, sit-ins, marches, and cries of "Revolution!" that pushed an embarrassed America to s-l-o-w-l-y parse out bits of human dignity in individually wrapped bitter pills labeled "travel," "education," "housing," and "voting."

Acheson's awakening did not lead the way; it recognized what was under way—a turning of the tide.

DECEMBER 3

Using strategic legal attacks on segregation to undermine its foundations in "separate but equal" law (see December 11), Charles H. Houston had become one of the major architects restructuring a nonracist America. His 1944 appointment to the Fair Employment Practice Committee (FEPC) was hailed as a major step forward. Then things began to crumble. "Aside from the emasculation of the Full Employment Bill," wrote Herbert Aptheker, a noted historian and Du Bois protégé, "the most dramatic occurrence in the fight for fair employment" came with Houston's intense public criticism of President Truman's wobbly stance and a letter of resignation dated December 3, 1945. From that letter:

> On November 23, 1945, in the Capital Transit Company case . . . the committee voted to [direct] Capital Transit to cease and desist from practices and policies which have resulted in the denial of employment policy declared for industries essential to the prosecution of the war by Executive Order. Without . . . a chance for the [FEPC] to present its views, on November 24 you ordered the committee not to issue the decision. . . . Since the effect of your intervention is not to eliminate [discrimination] but to condone it, to that extent you not only repudiate the committee but more important, you nullify the Executive Orders themselves. . . . The issue of the Capital Transit case far transcends the question whether a few Negro workers shall be placed on the platforms of street cars and buses and as traffic checkers. . . . It raises the fundamental question of the basic government attitude toward minorities. The failure of the government to enforce democratic practices and to protect minorities in its own capital makes its expressed concern for national minorities abroad somewhat specious, and the interference in the domestic affairs of other countries very premature.

"[Legal challenges] mean little unless supported by public opinion," Houston once said. "The really baffling problem is how to create the proper kind of public opinion." With his letter's release, Houston sacrificed personal gain to seriously influence the public's opinions and enhance its depth of thought.

DECEMBER 4

Those of us who want to love our country are not anxious to ask whether our police are capable of murder. So we do not ask. . . . We are aware . . . that hundreds of us are killed every year by police. We assume the victims are mad killers and that the officers fired in self-defense or to save lives. . . . Does the truth matter . . . ? This report pursues the truth of an episode that occurred early on December 4, 1969, at 2337 West Monroe Street in Chicago, Illinois. It was a time of darkness, cold, rage, fear, and violence. Facts are not easily found in such company. . . .

So BEGAN "Search and Destroy: A Report by the Commission of Inquiry into the Black Panthers and the Police," a 1973 study by Roy Wilkins, Executive Director of the NAACP, and Ramsey Clark, former Attorney General of the United States. At 4:45 A.M. on December 4, 1969, fourteen plainclothes Chicago police officers, with floor plans provided by a police informant, led a predawn raid on an apartment in which the occupants were asleep. Two young men—Fred Hampton and Mark Clark—were killed. Nearly one hundred shots had been fired into the apartment; only one was fired out. In conflicting testimony, a police photo released to show bullet holes from Panther weapons was found to show nail holes in the wall. A massacre had taken place. After endless complaints of police brutality, after too many blacks shot in the back by police had been declared "justifiable homicides," a groggy nation slowly awakened to ask why.

Eight black members of Congress held special hearings that led to the formation of the Congressional Black Caucus. In 1971, fourteen police officers were indicted for conspiracy to obstruct investigations. But not until 1976 would news of the FBI's COINTELPRO operation (see April 6) reveal the depth of the plot: had the victims been police, not Panthers, what was minimized as self-defense would have been prosecuted as murder. In 1982, the government settled the case for $1.85 million. It was "an admission," said an attorney for the victims' families, of the conspiracy by "the FBI and [Chicago police] to murder" Hampton and Clark.

DECEMBER 5

J UST FOUR MOMENTOUS DAYS EARLIER, a seamstress boarded a Montgomery, Alabama, bus bound for history. Taking the last available seat in the "colored" section, she relaxed for the trip home and thought of Christmas. When the white seats were filled, the driver told the blacks in her row to get up so that a white passenger could be seated in a row with no blacks. Three of the black passengers moved; one did not. "You'd better make it light on yourselves and let me have those seats," the driver warned. "If you don't stand up, I'm going to have you arrested." The woman who held on to her seat and her self-respect even as she was removed from the bus, arrested, jailed, and fingerprinted was Rosa Parks. Would she allow hers to be the test case that could bring the degrading system of segregated bus seating to an end? Yes.

Parks had not planned her protest. But Montgomery's blacks spent the weekend planning a response. Flyers were mimeographed for students to distribute, a local newspaper headlined the story, ministers took to pulpits in support: a one-day bus boycott would begin Monday morning as Mrs. Parks went to court.

Just after 6:00 A.M. on December 5, 1955, as the first bus prowled the dim morning street in search of former victims, Coretta Scott King called her husband, Martin, to the window. "Darling, it's empty!" she exclaimed. By afternoon, Martin Luther King Jr., the new minister in Montgomery, would be elected to lead the newly formed Montgomery Improvement Association. By evening a one-day protest became a movement: the Montgomery Bus Boycott. A historic mass meeting was held at Holt Street Baptist Church that night. Martin Luther King Jr. gave his first Civil Rights movement speech:

> When the history books are written . . . somebody will have to say, "There lived a race of people, black people, fleecy locks and black complexion . . . who had the moral courage to stand up for their rights." And thereby they injected a new meaning into the veins of history and of civilization. And we're gonna do that. God grant that we will do it before it's too late.

DECENBER 6

IN 1899, Henry Sylvester Williams, a Trinidadian-born barrister and founder of African Associates, an organization of West Indian expatriates like himself living in London, coined the term "Pan-Africanism" to define "a feeling of unity" and "to facilitate friendly intercourse among Africans in general; to promote and protect the interests of all [British] subjects claiming African descent, wholly or in part, in British colonies and other places." The term and concept were popularized the following year at a three-day meeting—the first Pan-African Congress (see December 22). In the closing address the African American whose clarity of scholarship and vision would help chart the course of the era, Dr. W. E. B. Du Bois, later revered as "the Father of Pan-Africanism," made a memorable prophesy: "The problem of the twentieth century is the problem of the color line."

As the century progressed, the continent began its slow, arduous emergence from European domination. Ethiopia narrowly escaped being colonized, maintaining her sovereignty over Italian aggression in 1941. Sudan became independent in 1956. A year later, in 1957, Ghana became the second nation to achieve modern-day independence. By 1958, five Pan-African Congresses had taken place, largely at the prodding of African Americans with Du Bois in the lead. But not one congress event had taken place on the African continent. The following year, Ghana changed that by hosting the first gathering of the diaspora on sovereign African soil in centuries, the All-African People's Conference.

With all this, is it any wonder that Tom Mboya, a liberation leader of the still-colonized Kenyan people, would not only remember December 6, 1958, as the proudest moment of his life but also as "a date of the greatest historical importance for every one of the two hundred million people of Africa"? Arriving at Ghana's Accra Airport for the All-African People's Conference on this day, he learned that he had just been named its chairman.

DECEMBER 7

Wᴏʀʟᴅ Wᴀʀ II was raging throughout Europe, Northern Africa, and Asia. Still an undeclared combatant, the United States placed an embargo on Japan that was tantamount to an act of war. On Sunday, December 7, 1941, Japan retaliated, bombing the United States military installation at Pearl Harbor. It was "a date which will live in infamy," said President Franklin D. Roosevelt. And it was surely that for African Americans, albeit for a different reason. That difference was deeply underscored by the story of Dorie Miller of Waco, Texas, an African American assigned to the USS *Arizona* as messman.

Miller was going about the business of his routine laundry tasks when the Japanese air raid began. Hauling his wounded captain to safety, he returned to the deck, voluntarily manned a machine gun for which he had not been trained, and downed four planes. Miller was the first American hero of World War II. Like Crispus Attucks, his heroic predecessor and the first martyr of America's Revolutionary War, Miller, too, was not given the credit due him historically. Miller was awarded the Silver Star and the Navy Cross for his heroism, but he was neither promoted nor transferred to a rank that better befit his aptitudes and achievements. He was promoted to Mess Attendant Third Class and remained a messman throughout the war. He was killed in action in 1943 when the aircraft carrier *Liscome Bay*, to which he'd been reassigned, went down in the South Pacific with no survivors.

The pride and the shame of the navy, Miller had been confined, like most blacks, to a subservient role in a segregated military. Others who "jumped ship," so to speak, on their racially relegated military roles as "noncombatants" included Navy Cross recipients Leonard Roy Harmon of the USS *San Francisco* and William Pinckney of the USS *Enterprise*, and Silver Star medalist Elbert H. Oliver of the USS *Intrepid*.

Military   Initiative

DECEMBER 8

Dᴇᴄᴇᴍʙᴇʀ 8, 1964, found Dr. and Mrs. King, their family, and their friends landing in Oslo, Norway, for the Nobel Prize ceremonies. As they gathered for a private dinner party two days before the event, Rev. Martin Luther King Sr. rose in tribute to his son and the moment. "I want to say something to all of you now, and I want you to listen," said Daddy King in a manner befitting the patrimony for which he had become so respected and loved. As he spoke, invoking the spirit of the ancestors watching over them, tears welled in the eyes of the faithful:

> I came from nowhere. My father was a sharecropper, and I didn't get the opportunity to get much formal training when I was growing up. . . . It wasn't until I left the farm and went to Atlanta that I was able to get any real education. I was a man . . . with my wife and three children [when I finished college]. . . . I wanted my children to have all the things I had not had. I prayed for the Lord to let them do the things I could not do. This young man here became a minister, and I wanted him to have the best training available, so he would be able to get his Ph.D.
>
> I always wanted to make a contribution, and all you got to do if you want to contribute, you got to ask the Lord . . . and the Lord heard me and in some kind of way I don't even know, He came down through Georgia, and He laid His hand on me and my wife, and He gave us Martin Luther King, and our prayers were answered. . . . You don't know how it feels where some stranger calls you on the phone and he tells you he wants to kill you, or kill your son. . . . Even though I feel so proud tonight about what is happening here in Oslo, I also must be humble. I don't want to get puffed up with pride. I am not that kind of person. . . . The devil is busy out there, and we have to pray that God will keep my son safe.

Radiant in the glow of his family's pride, he concluded, "When my head is cold and my bones are bleached, the King family will go down not only in American history but in world history as well, because Martin King is a Nobel Prize winner." Two days later (see December 10), he would see those words fulfilled. . . .

Parenting   Building Dreams

DECEMBER 9

"WHOM THE GODS WOULD DESTROY, they first call promising," it is said. Sadly, this saying applies to the story of the sculpture (and the sculptor) called up and destroyed by the 1939 World's Fair. The story begins on December 9, 1937, when Augusta Savage, one of only four women commissioned, and the only African American, was commissioned to sculpt a large work reflecting "the American Negro's contribution to music, especially in song" for the fair. *Lift Every Voice and Sing* was the result. Art historian Debra Spencer's description of the monumental nineteen-foot sculpture explains why:

> The metaphorical content of the sculpture is remarkable. A chorus of people form the strings of a harp; the soundboard of the harp is the right forearm of a figure that we infer to be the Celestial Harpist, creating human reality out of sound. The soaring vertical figures are modeled in an austere volumetric style whose antecedents are the statues that adorn the walls and porticoes of Romanesque churches. Yet the portrait heads speak with the sculptural force of African carvings. This is especially true of the kneeling male who holds in his hands a bar on which are inscribed musical notes. The posture, gesture, and modeling of this figure, its symmetry and contained energy, clearly mark it as a legatee of the African sculptural tradition.

Lift Every Voice and Sing was one of the most popular attractions at the fair. Yet, as it closed, a now famous but still very poor Savage could not afford to have her sculpture moved. It was bulldozed, forever lost. Artist-scholars of no less stature than Romare Bearden have even alleged that Savage's commission may have been awarded as a political ruse to remove her from her government-sponsored WPA position as director of the Harlem Community Center, where she was far too diligent an advocate for other black artists. To the Hampton University Museum, therefore, a debt is owed for purchasing, thus rescuing, and continuing to exhibit a ten-inch cast-iron maquette of *Lift Every Voice and Sing*, Savage's only surviving representation of the work. What power and genius are ours.

Art   Collective Responsibility

DECEMBER 10

ON THURSDAY, OCTOBER 10, 1964, eight hundred guests joined King Olaf of Norway and Queen Louise of Sweden in the University of Oslo's Festival Hall for the Nobel Peace Prize ceremony honoring Rev. Dr. Martin Luther King Jr. The day before, in a lighter moment, he had introduced the world press to his friend and fellow soldier Rev. Ralph Abernathy, his "perennial jailmate." Now, stoically attired in waistcoat, pinstriped trousers, cravat, and patent leather shoes, he sat alone at the apex of the glare as a parade of luminaries extolled the "undaunted champion of peace." As ceremonial trumpets blared, Dr. Gunner Jahn of the Norwegian Parliament read the citation: "The first person in the western world to have shown us that a struggle can be waged without violence. . . . Without Dr. King's confirmed effectiveness of this principle, demonstrations and marches could easily have been violent and ended with the spilling of blood." King would deliver his Nobel Prize acceptance speech the next day. In brief thanks, he said:

> I accept the Nobel Prize for Peace at a moment when twenty-two million Negroes of the United States are engaged in a creative battle to end the long night of racial injustice. . . . I am mindful that only yesterday in Birmingham, Alabama, our children, crying out for brotherhood, were answered with fire hoses, snarling dogs, and even death. . . . Therefore, I must ask why this prize is awarded to a movement which is beleaguered and committed to unrelenting struggle; to a movement which has not won the very peace and brotherhood which is the essence of the Nobel Prize. After contemplation I conclude that this award, which I receive on behalf of the movement, is a profound recognition [of] the need for man to overcome oppression without resorting to violence. I accept this award today with an abiding faith in America and an audacious faith in mankind. . . .

Some had derided his award. He wasn't even Pan-American, they charged. But, as he left the hall that night, hundreds of torch-bearing students chanting "Freedom now!" and "We shall overcome!" made the point: his King-dom was global.

DECEMBER 11

In 1935, the NAACP Legal Defense Fund's Charles Houston declared, "A lawyer's either a social engineer or he's a parasite on society." Attacking Jim Crow law in court was an idea whose time had come, he argued. Convinced that white harassment of black children would not soon change, W. E. B. Du Bois argued an alternative: separate schools had to become better schools. In the end, the either/or conflict forced a changing of the guard at the NAACP. Du Bois— NAACP cofounder and editor of its official magazine, *The Crisis*—resigned.

On Sunday, December 11, 1938, the nation, poised on a precipice, awaited the next day's Supreme Court ruling in *Missouri ex rel. Gaines v. Canada, Registrar of the University of Missouri*. Lloyd Gaines, a graduate of Pennsylvania's historically black Lincoln University, had been denied admission to the state-run law school in his home state of Missouri on grounds of race. State law technically required the school to provide an all-black equivalent for the all-white one. It did not. Hence, the Legal Defense Fund (LDF) argued, the state must either admit Gaines or be in violation of the "separate but equal" law. How would the Supreme Court decide Lloyd Gaines's fate the next day? The Court ruled in favor of Gaines. Points had been scored all around: NAACP lawyers were proved to be engineers; their foes were shown to be parasites. And Du Bois's concern about white harassment of black students was, tragically, reinforced. Immediately after the decision, Gaines disappeared, never to be heard from again. He was presumed dead. The LDF strategy, however, was very much alive. It reappeared again and again until 1954 (see May 17) when Thurgood Marshall, carrying the baton for his deceased mentor, Houston, won the landmark *Brown v. Board of Education* Supreme Court decision ending school segregation at all levels.

As social engineers, this was the NAACP's first test of the Houston Plan, a step-by-step strategy to dismantle segregation by chipping away at its foundation. After three years of litigation, *Gaines* loosened the "separate but equal" cornerstone.

Strategy   Alternatives

DECEMBER 12

In December 1947, Bredu Pabi was a customs officer in the Gold Coast at the port of Takoradi. There, Pabi regularly welcomed his countrymen home and came into contact with visitors from the world over. That contact and a newspaper story about Brooklyn College in the *African Morning Post* inspired his dream to attend college in America. But that was before his two children were born, and sadly, too, before his wife died. And so when a scholarship from New York's Academy of Arts and Research was offered to him in 1949, Brooklyn College was the place he wanted to be. With his mother taking care of his children, he sailed for America and started college in the fall semester of 1949—a thirty-five-year-old freshman. His goal: to major in economics and political science, with which he proudly hoped to help his country after independence. As the *New York Times* reporter who interviewed him during December 1949 wrote, "The stocky freshman claimed the distinction of being the sole Gold Coast scholarship student in this country where he feels education 'gives students a sense of leadership and direction.'"

Bredu Pabi might have been the only Gold Coast student, but he was not the first. Unknown to him, he was following in the noble footsteps of one who had recently graduated from Lincoln University.

In December 1947, that man had passed through customs at Takoradi as he returned home for the first time in twelve years. He had spent more than half those years earning his way through college, gone on to work with the London-based West African National Secretariat, and become increasingly active in "The Circle," a movement of pro-independence revolutionaries. As he passed through the port at Takoradi to help liberate his country, the man destined to be the new nation's first president—Kwame Nkrumah—fully expected to be detained. But the customs officer was African! A native of the Gold Coast like himself! Delighted to see him and eager for news from abroad. Could it be . . . *"Let the circle be unbroken, by and by . . ."*

DECEMBER 13

FOR THE ELDER STATESMEN OF ALBANY, Georgia's black community, the students and SNCC were new kids on the block—and resented for it. Before them, vets from World War II and Korea had come home eager to forge change, and organized into such local groups as the Criterion Club, Ministerial Alliance, Negro Voters League, and the regional NAACP. All played important roles—as would be appreciated once they pooled resources. For what the younger group offered in brash courage, the elder groups had in strategy. Slowly trust began to build. Wherever people gathered—in churches, bars, nightclubs, or pool halls—SNCC's Charles Sherrod and Cordell Reagon told the story of their movement experience. "There were worse chains than jail," said Sherrod. "We mocked the system that teaches men to be good Negroes instead of good men." When they were arrested with local students in a test of federally desegregated travel facilities, wave upon wave of demonstrators marched and were arrested. When arriving Freedom Riders were arrested and roughed up for attempting to integrate railway waiting rooms, 267 high school students marched and went to jail in support.

On December 13, 1961, the Albany Movement's vice-president, Slater King, led two hundred protesters to City Hall. Stopping at the courthouse to pray for the release of jailed students and Freedom Riders, they, too, were arrested. The charge: parading without a permit. As the numbers in jail grew, the Albany Movement's president, Dr. William Anderson, phoned an old college chum, who agreed to attend a rally that Friday night. That chum was Martin Luther King.

With the Freedom Riders and Dr. King, the Albany Movement took on national significance that marked the emergence of a coordinated city-by-city strategy. It was rough going for the nationally chartered groups, each of which competed for daily press notice to raise needed troops and bail and defense funds. From the Albany experience SNCC founded the Freedom Singers in 1962. The singers traveled the nation raising morale and funds for the freedom fight.

DECEMBER 14

Sncc's John Lewis and Donald Harris had toured the African continent—first Guinea with their benefactor, singer/actor Harry Belafonte, and nine other SNCC members (see September 26), then on their own. Now it was time to assess all they'd done and become on this pilgrimage to Africa and themselves.

On December 14, 1964, they filed their report: "We in SNCC have been teaching what is called 'Negro and African history,' completely disregarding the potential of the many African embassies and thousands of African students already in the country." In Africa, they made contacts. Perhaps more important, they made *connections*—the closing of a gap called history. Now they saw themselves at one with a larger whole. At a time when "colored" was still scrawled on the closed doors of a segregated America, they left the United States as Negroes—alienated people, isolated and with no real homeland. They returned as African Americans—people integral to the total liberation of Africa and her diaspora from the yokes of colonialism and slavery.

They had arrived in Ghana just as Malcolm exited. His stellar example remained, but when they spoke to their own successes, they too were met with great support. In Zambia, they discovered a special niche. That was the country to which South Africans escaped to train for the freedom fight. It was, as they reported, the "last refuge before entering a hell beyond description for any man who had the audacity to be born with a skin that was black. . . ." Zambian nationalists hungered "to know that the efforts and lives that they are expending are also being heard and supported." Connected, they now envisioned an expanded role for SNCC with these proposals: (1) establish an international wing, specifically, an African Bureau that would (2) maintain and increase SNCC's contacts with other groups or countries "helpful to us or the Cause" and (3) upgrade SNCC communications to tell the world what SNCC and others were doing. With their trip and new perspective on the struggle at home, they would help refocus the movement.

Pan-African World   Self-portraiture

DECEMBER 15

As PRODUCED BY Ellis Haizlip, PBS's *Soul!* was a milestone in African American and television history. Never before (and rarely since) had Pan-African culture been displayed with such honesty, enthusiasm, respect, and range. Here was a people enjoying their artful best and sharing it with the world, both in performance and in reflection. In many ways *Soul!* was the people's voice—the Civil Rights movement without the headlines, as it was felt deep inside.

On December 15, 1971, *Soul!* aired the first half of a two-part conversation between author James Baldwin and poet Nikki Giovanni. Taped on November 4 in London, this talk between two writers—older and younger, male and female, expatriate and U.S.-based, world-renowned and about-to-be—was later published in book form as *A Dialogue*. From the book:

> BALDWIN: It takes a long time before you accept what has been given to you from the past. What we call black literature is really summed up for me [in music] because that's how it's been handed down. We had to smuggle information, and we did it through our music and we did it in the church . . .
>
> GIOVANNI: I'm stuck with Chester [Himes] because he's one of my favorite writers. He went into the Coffin Ed, Gravedigger Jones books, which everybody assumed was safe . . . just a detective story. Then he did the master detective story, *Blind Man with a Pistol,* and they said, Who's the murderer? He said, The State's the murderer.
>
> BALDWIN: It's not a detective story at all; it's an allegory.
>
> GIOVANNI: Exactly. Chester could say, Okay, I will pursue truth in this way . . . so that you can make a movie out of it if you want to and it'll still be true.
>
> BALDWIN: But, sweetheart, it's the same thing we were doing on the plantation when they thought we were singing "Steal Away to Jesus" and I was telling you it's time to split.
>
> GIOVANNI: Why do we, as black writers, seem to be so hung up on the truth?
>
> BALDWIN: Because the responsibility of a writer is to excavate the experience of the people who produced him. The act of writing is the intention of it; the root of it is liberation.

Television   Self-concept

DECEMBER 16

Even when we seemed most powerless, African Americans used boycotts, or "selective buying campaigns," as empowerment tools. In the Depression-era 1930s, "Buy Where You Can Work" forced Harlem's Jim Crow employers to hire blacks. Marcus Garvey's UNIA (see August 13, November 29) used "buy black" campaigns to power its industries. Even in slavery days, free blacks used their power of the purse. And so, when the article "Unsheathing the Consumer Sword" was published in the December 1946 issue of the *Crisis*, more notable than the strategy proposed was the man proposing it—James Farmer, who had, in 1941, founded the Congress of Racial Equality (CORE).

Black dollar power was its own mighty sword, wrote Farmer. "The oppressors can remain masters only so long as dark folk can be duped into thinking . . . 'We thank you for our daily bread, by your sufferance must we be fed.' The greatest compulsive force in Negro life is *fear*. But the deepest fear is not one of bodily harm . . . but seeing one's family starve is a living torture worse than death." For remedy, Farmer notes the strengths and weaknesses of the agricultural South and proposes replicating the alliances of black family-owned farms in the consumer "co-op," examples of which were just beginning to dot the scene from Texas to Georgia. "Sixty-one . . . colored farm families were organized into a co-operative," wrote Farmer. "They purchased a grist mill, rented a two-compartment store, equipped one half with a soda fountain and luncheon tables and the other half with facilities for processing and selling their farm products. It is *their* store. They supply it with goods, and they, among others, are its patrons. They are doing thousands of dollars worth of trade. The profit is theirs. At the end of the year it goes to them, or into expansion of the store and the expansion of their lives."

Predictably, such co-ops were often undermined as "communist" as soon as they experienced success. But once the march to a different drum had begun, the co-op movement kept its "eye on the prize," and held on.

Business   Respect for Use of Power

DECEMBER 17

IN THE AFTERMATH of World War II—with its extermination of eleven million civilians—the UN redefined the term "genocide." In its definition, the UN term exceeded state-sponsored mass murder to include the "serious bodily and mental harm" done to groups of people targeted by race, ethnicity, religion, or nationality. Mindful of centuries of genocide practiced against blacks in the United States, simultaneous delegations led by William L. Patterson in Paris and Paul Robeson in New York delivered a historic 225-page petition to the UN on December 17, 1951.

Entitled "We Charge Genocide," this petition was the third attempt to bring the plight of Africans throughout the Americas before the world body. An appeal on behalf of Caribbean peoples was drafted and blocked in 1945 (see May 25). The NAACP-sponsored "An Appeal to the World" received public notice but little more in 1947 (see October 23). Each time, the United States used its seat on the Security Council to block recognition. And despite its hundred prominent cosigners, "We Charge Genocide" met the same fate. Among them, Mary Church Terrell's career as an activist and journalist had been provoked by the lynching of a friend in 1892. Other cosigners could recite similar incidents—and did. Utilizing Robeson's training as a lawyer, Article II (a) of the petition, "Killing Members of a Group" documented 150 incidents over six years in painful detail. Still the petition received no hearing. Despite its stand on genocide, the UN had cast itself as the arbiter of grievances *between* nations, not *within* nations. The problems of colonized peoples and oppressed minority groups were ignored as internal, domestic affairs. The violence of the powerful fell beyond censure.

Although unsuccessful at the UN, Patterson and Robeson made their charges known to French radio audiences and to the African American and European presses. In doing so, they raised awareness about the cause for which people would soon sacrifice their lives in the Civil Rights movement wars of the 1950s and 1960s.

DECEMBER 18

FOLLOWING DR. KING'S DEATH, a contest of leadership between Ralph Abernathy and Jesse Jackson began simmering at SCLC. On December 18, 1971, it boiled over into Jackson's resignation and his founding of PUSH (People United to Save Humanity).

Since the first days of the Black Power movement, Jackson had been convinced that the key to realizing that power lay in economics. "We are the margin of profit of every major item produced in America from General Motors cars down to Kellogg's Corn Flakes," said Jackson. And, in 1966, his plan of attack, Operation Breadbasket, became the economic arm of SCLC. Retooling the "Buy Where You Can Work" campaign of the Depression-era 1930s, he led a selective buying campaign to press for jobs. Now, with PUSH, his "civil economics" organization, the objectives were jobs, organizing the working poor earning less than a living wage, encouraging the growth of existing black businesses, and launching new ones. Again, he used boycotts to leverage specific goals. "Covenants" were signed with such major white-owned conglomerates as Coca-Cola and Coors to increase the number of black employees, open the door for black-owned subcontractors, and donate moneys to black colleges and organizations. The Chicago-based PUSH was also designed to open the door to political power.

"You can call me a gadfly if you wish," said Jackson. "The job of a doctor is to show up where sick people are." For all that Operation PUSH had done in a scant three years, a reality checkup on January 15, 1975, revealed a serious disease. Jackson was leading young people in a protest march on the White House for jobs that day, when he realized that too many marchers were drunk or on drugs. Stopping mid-step, he sent everyone home while he searched for a cure. Months later, he found it: PUSH for Excellence, PUSH/Excel, a national campaign to save black youth by attacking the growing drug culture, encouraging pride in self, and celebrating education. There was far too much work to be done to heal society to be able to afford the loss of even one young soul.

Organizing   Values

DECEMBER 19

I<small>T WAS WARTIME</small>, C<small>HRISTMASTIME</small>, and a church in Portland, Maine, that dated its ancestry back to the incorporation of the first Abyssinian Society meetinghouse in 1828 was celebrating its one hundred and fifteenth birthday with the gift of a new name. In 1943, the congregation formerly known as the Abyssinian Congregational Church was reborn for Christmas as Green Memorial AME Zion. The name change was particularly significant. For with it, the black community was preserving its own history—a history that includes the home in which John B. Russwurm lived while attending Bowdoin College in nearby Brunswick. Graduating in 1826, he was the second African American to earn a college degree. In 1827, the year after graduation, he cofounded *Freedom's Journal*, launching the history of African American journalism.

In choosing the name Green Memorial, the church honored the continuity of its story and community from slavery to freedom as personified in the life of Moses Green. Born into slavery in Maryland, Green lived a simple, honorable life, working at Union Station in Portland for fifty-two years and devoting himself to the welfare of the church until his death in 1943 at age eighty-nine. In honoring Green, the congregation also paid homage to its own tradition, best stated by Ruth McIlwain, a woman who joined the church the year Green died: "We are a church where everybody is somebody."

Thirty years later, on January 17, 1973, Green Memorial African Methodist Episcopal Zion Church was formally designated a National Historic Landmark. As Maine's only black church, and a member of a historically black denomination, its landmark status symbolized the pivotal role of the church in establishing a sense of community for Maine's African American citizens.

AT LAST! With the Supreme Court–backed desegregation order in hand, the "foot soldiers" of the 385-day Montgomery Bus Boycott of 1955–1956 gathered at St. John A. M. E. Church. A one-day protest 385 days earlier in support of Rosa Parks's courageous refusal to forfeit her seat to racism had exploded into a year-long movement of civil disobedience. That Alabama boycott took a front seat to history as the official start of America's Civil Rights era, catapulting a newly ordained twenty-seven-year-old strategist, Reverend Dr. Martin Luther King Jr., to world acclaim.

On December 20, 1956, King stood at the precipice of a long climb. After more than a year of protest, he spoke for his noble troops: "We came to see that, in the long run, it is more honorable to walk in dignity than ride in humiliation." For weeks they had known of the coming Supreme Court bus desegregation order. Still they held out, walking thirty more days, until the decision was final. "These twelve months have not been easy. . . . We can remember days when unfavorable court decisions came upon us like tidal waves, leaving us treading waters of despair. . . . Now our faith seems to be vindicated. . . . The Negro citizens of Montgomery are urged to return to the buses tomorrow morning on a nonsegregated basis!" In his book, *Stride Toward Freedom: The Montgomery Story*, King wrote:

> This is . . . the chronicle of 50,000 Negroes who took to heart the principles of nonviolence, who learned to fight for their rights with the weapon of love, and who, in the process, acquired a new estimate of their own human worth. . . . And of the Negro followers, many of them beyond middle age, who walked to work and home again as much as twelve miles a day for over a year rather than submit to the discourtesies and humiliation of segregated buses. The majority . . . were poor and untutored, but they understood the essence of the Montgomery movement. One elderly woman summed it up for the rest. When asked after several weeks of walking whether she was tired, she answered, "My feets is tired, but my soul is at rest."

DECEMBER 21

Throughout the 1970s, the Alvin Ailey Dance Theater was performing somewhere in the world on December 21—usually New York. Ailey's masterpiece, *Revelations*, was often on the bill, closing the performance, bringing down the house. And when that experience was afforded the audience, there would come the moment that left them totally stunned, the moment for which they would return year after year—that moment when Judith Jamison would dance "Cry," choreographed by Ailey for both Jamison and Consuelo Atlas in 1971. Jamison premiered this solo and made it her own; it made her the most well-known dancer in a company prized for its ensemble work and lack of "stars."

An elegant figure, tall for a dancer (five feet ten inches), with closely cropped hair, ebony skin, and stunning features, Judith Jamison was regal—in her bearing and in the gifts she brought to bear upon her work. As Ailey said of her in 1972, "Judy is a lady who came to my company in 1965. A tall, gangly girl with no hair. I always thought her beautiful." In 1966 and 1967, the company toured Africa. Said James Truitte, one of the original Ailey dancers, "In Africa, she was clearly a great beauty as well as an outstanding dancer. And it has to do something for your image when [Kenyan president] Jomo Kenyatta debates whether you look more like a Kikuyu or a Masai." And through Judy Jamison's awareness of herself came the glory of black womanhood in "Cry." As the dancer, choreographer, and dance critic Deborah Jowitt wrote in the *New York Times:*

> When, with a few lashes, not just of her arms and hands, but of her whole torso, she wraps a long piece of cloth around her head in a turban and strides about the stage, by God, she *is* the African Ancestress. When she arches her back, stretches up her long arms, and slowly circles her head, she projects with singular purity the anguish of women who have lost their men to death. . . . This ability to maintain a human dimension and to project superhuman power and radiance is perhaps one of her most impressive skills.

Dance   Stature

DECEMBER 22

In 1900, Dr. W. E. B. Du Bois closed the first Pan-African Congress with this prophesy: "The problem of the twentieth century is the problem of the color line." In 1958, six Congresses and conferences later, the Pan-African world was loosing the stranglehold of white domination. The Civil Rights movement was sweeping the U.S. South. Africa and the Caribbean were moving toward independence. For the first time in centuries, the diaspora gathered on free African soil as a year-old independent Ghana hosted the All-African People's Conference (see December 6). Du Bois was ill and unable to attend. His wife, the author Shirley Graham Du Bois, delivered his message on December 22, 1958—words of wisdom from the ninety-one-year-old "Father of Pan-Africanism":

> Here then, [the] decision: Will you [opt] for temporary advantage—for automobiles . . . and Paris gowns—spend your income in paying interest on borrowed funds; or will you sacrifice your present comfort . . . in order to educate your children, develop such industry as best serves the great mass of people, and make your country strong in ability, self-support, and self-defense? Such . . . strength calls for sacrifice and self-denial, while the capital offered you at high price by the colonial powers like France, Britain, Holland, Belgium, and the United States will prolong fatal colonial imperialism, from which you have suffered slavery, serfdom, and colonialism. You are not helpless. You are the buyers, and to continue existence as sellers of capital, these great nations, former owners of the world, must sell or face bankruptcy. You are not compelled to buy all they offer now. You can wait. . . .
>
> Forget nothing. . . . Your nearest friends . . . are the colored people of China and India, the rest of Asia, the Middle East and the sea isles, once close bound to the heart of Africa and now long severed by the greed of Europe. Your bond is not mere color of skin but the deeper experience of wage slavery and contempt. So, too, your bond with the white world is closest to those who support and defend China and India and not those who exploit the Middle East and South America. You have nothing to lose but your chains! You have a continent to regain! You have freedom and human dignity to attain!

Independence   Building Dreams

DECEMBER 23

Suspended somewhere among snatches of tribes-men in outdated issues of *National Geographic* are images of Africa headlined and framed in disaster—famine (Ethiopia), war and refugees (Rwanda), superhuman courage (South Africa's Mandela). Rarely are Africans seen as everyday people. Changing that view for postcolonial Africans themselves and the outside world was the mission of Senegal's premier filmmaker, Ousmane Sembène, director and screenwriter of several dramas documenting the transition from colonial life to independence. The film that had its U.S. premiere in December 1974 was a breakthrough even for Sembène: *Xala, (The Hex)*. This comedy of manners satirized a corrupt business-man in modern Dakar, the capital city. It was spoken in Wolof (an indigenous Senegalese language) with French and English subtitles.

In a film arsenal built on eight films in ten years, Sembène has been ever the keen observer—and for that, ever the out-cast. "In the schools they have yet begun to teach our history," he once said. And with each work, he had begun to tell the story of modern Africa, particularly Senegal, rich, varied, and complex. Twenty years, two novels, and three feature films later, Sembène, who had begun his film career at age forty, was honored at the San Francisco International Film Festival with a lifetime achievement award. From the official citation:

> There are some expressions that are overused, but no other term so aptly fits Senegalese filmmaker Ousmane Sembène as "the Father of African Cinema." As a militant filmmaker, as a godfa-ther to younger African directors, and as a writer of international renown, he has never wavered from his basic goal: the desire for his art to serve his suffering compatriots by . . . helping to trans-form their lives and exposing the pretenders who claim to bring salvation but feast on power. In . . . lost financial support, censor-ship, problems with international distribution, and police surveil-lance, he has paid the price for his boldness. . . . Through it all his creative will has not been broken, and his vision remains intact.

DECEMBER 24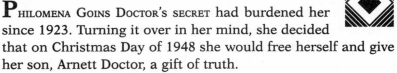

Philomena Goins Doctor's secret had burdened her since 1923. Turning it over in her mind, she decided that on Christmas Day of 1948 she would free herself and give her son, Arnett Doctor, a gift of truth.

There was a place called Rosewood, Florida, mother told son. It was a tiny black town right across the road from Sumner, which was white. They said a black man raped a white woman, but that's what they always said so they could do what they did that New Year's Day 1923, torching every black home, starting the Rosewood Massacre. We children hid in the swamps until they got us away. A few whites helped but they were afraid too. They knew what would happen to them too once a mob starts. It's a terrible thing to hate so much you don't know what you're doing and when to stop. And what's all the hating about? It was about black Rosewood being better off than white Sumner. That's why they lynched us.

Philomena Doctor's was not the only secret about Rosewood. Actually, there were three. Who you are said which you kept. Robie Mortin was also a child of Rosewood. As she confided seventy-three years later, "My grandma told me not to say a word. My grandma said never to look back. We weren't supposed to talk about Rosewood." For survivors, your secret was about being black and terrified, knowing justice would never call your name. For others, yours was about being white and terrified that your neighbors would call you a "nigger lover" and run you out of town or worse for helping blacks. And for the guilty third group, your secret was fear that someday someone would not know how to let things be.

With her gift to her son, all would know. Blacks regained the truth of why all they had built up was lost. Her son began a crusade for Rosewood survivors that led to a *St. Petersburg Times* exposé, pressure on Florida's legislature, and the first reparations ever paid African Americans for injustices done. And John Singleton's 1997 film told the world: Once there was a place called *Rosewood*. . . .

DECEMBER 25

IT WAS A CHRISTMAS MIRACLE. On December 25, 1956, the home of Rev. Fred Shuttlesworth was bombed. So violent was the blast that the reverend and his deacon, who had stayed the night to plan a march, fell into the basement and were unhurt. Amazing grace, indeed. This was "Bombingham," as Birmingham was known. Police advised Shuttlesworth to leave town. "God erased my name off that dynamite," said he. He'd been spared at the eye of a bomb; he had work to do.

He had been one of the major supporters of the Montgomery Bus Boycott. When it ended, just five days before the bombing (see December 20), he knew the task had just begun. Four days later, a teenager stood alone at a bus stop on Christmas Eve. Five white men jumped out of a car, beat her, and fled. In response, Shuttlesworth had called for the march that nearly cost his life. He had long been on the front lines. He and his wife had attempted to register two of their children in school after the desegregation order. Mobbed, the children were attacked, his wife was stabbed, he was beaten to near death with metal chains, and his youngest child saw it all on the evening news. Despite incriminating news footage, no one was prosecuted. The Shuttlesworths persevered. When Alabama outlawed the NAACP in 1956, he knew that "they could not outlaw the movement of a people determined to be free," and cofounded the Alabama Christian Movement for Human Rights (ACMHR). As its leader, he supported the Montgomery Boycott and ACMHR launched its own campaign to desegregate Birmingham. And in 1957, he cofounded SCLC with King.

After the bombing, Shuttlesworth returned home from the hospital by bus and sat in a front seat. Said Rosa Walker, an early ACMHR member, "When I went to the meeting the next morning Rev. Shuttlesworth was the first thing I saw. I knowed as how their house was blowed up, and I couldn't figure out how he was there. And I said then that I'm going into it. And I went into it on that day." The gift of his life that Christmas invigorated the newborn Civil Rights movement.

DECEMBER 26

Dᴇᴄᴇᴍʙᴇʀ 26: ᴛʜᴇ ꜰɪʀꜱᴛ ᴅᴀʏ ᴏꜰ Kᴡᴀɴᴢᴀᴀ, the annual celebration of heritage created in 1966 by Maulana Ron Karenga, a University of California Ph.D. candidate in political science. As the freedom movement evolved from its religious-based thrust of the 1950s and early 1960s into the politics and culture of the Black Power movement, there was a need to make the ideology relevant in everyday, life-affirming terms. Karenga conceived of a seven-day cultural celebration, each day of which would be dedicated to one of seven principles, the *Nguzo Saba*. Using Swahili words, he called the celebration *Kwanzaa*, meaning "first fruits," a time to harvest the gifts of heritage and life itself. On this, the first day of Kwanzaa, we honor the principle of *Umoja*. In its spirit of unity, our task is "to strive for and maintain unity in the family, community, nation, and race."

In the cause of human rights, one leader spans the better part of the century from her work with the YWCA in the late 1930s through the late nineties—Dorothy Height, president of the National Council of Negro Women (NCNW) since 1957. Founded in 1935 by Mary McLeod Bethune (see January 3), the NCNW benefitted from Bethune's vast abilities and outreach through 1949. Mary Church Terrell (see June 8) also took her turn presiding. But Height's stewardship of the largest African American women's network united black women across class and turf. It is she who took off the gloves—the white gloves, that is—ending the era of the "ladies' club." As she said in 1958, "The problem we have is that the level of thinking women have about the Council is beneath the level that women should be operating on. They think of it more like a club and if many women saw things that women's organizations were doing . . . they would have more respect and understanding." Such was her level of understanding that when an in-the-trenches activist like Unita Blackwell was turned off by "what I call these 'highly elites,'" it was the openness to change fostered by Height that brought Blackwell back to stay, in the true spirit of *Umoja* and Height's maxim: "Leave no one out."

DECEMBER 27

DECEMBER 27: KWANZAA DAY TWO. The day of *Kujicha-gulia*, self-determination. This is the day "to define ourselves, create for ourselves, and speak for ourselves."

In 1839, Africans bound for slavery mutinied and took control of the *Amistad*. For weeks the schooner zigzagged off U.S. shores—steering a route back to Africa by day. By night the crew member whose life they had spared headed back toward the American shore. Finally intercepted, the *Amistad* was brought to shore at Long Island; its cargo was charged with murder and was imprisoned in New Haven, Connecticut. At trial, the judge surprisingly found in their favor. The fact that the importation of slaves had been outlawed in 1808 made their kidnap illegal and they were, therefore, free. Violating all U.S. canon against double jeopardy, the president intervened to retry them. Again they were exonerated, and again the government appealed the case, this time to the Supreme Court, where their freedom was again affirmed. In 246 years of American slavery, the *Amistad* mutineers were the only Africans to win the legal rights of free human beings.

Why do we tell this story in a book on the Civil Rights era, 1936 to 1976? Because abolitionists inspired by the courage of the *Amistad* captives would found the American Missionary Association (AMA) in 1846. After the goal of emancipation was achieved in 1865, their AMA then raised funds to start over five hundred freedom schools in the post–Civil War era South. To this day, those who have attended Atlanta, Dillard, Fisk, Hampton, and Howard Universities, and Berea, LeMoyne-Owens, Talladega, Huston-Tillotson, and Tougaloo Colleges, have the courageous *Amistad* mutineers to thank for their legacy. And the story goes on. In 1966, Dr. Clifton H. Johnson and Warren Marr II, former editor of the *Crisis,* secured AMA papers related to the *Amistad* to found the Amistad Research Center and Archives in New Orleans. To honor our *Amistad* heroes is to know that the spirit of Kujichagulia, self-determination, lives on . . . and on . . . and on . . .

DECEMBER 28

DECEMBER 28: KWANZAA DAY THREE. The day of *Ujima*, collective work and responsibility. As envisioned by Dr. Maulana Ron Karenga, this is the day "to build and maintain our community together, to make our sisters' and brothers' problems our problems, and to solve them together."

Since the founding in 1909 of the NAACP, the oldest Civil Rights organization in the United States—followed in 1912 by South Africa's African National Congress, the oldest in the diaspora—the NAACP has symbolically represented the consistent spirit of *Ujima* and the determined fight for liberation by Africans the world over. Ironically, while the NAACP is thought of as moderate today, it was considered "radical" by its detractors throughout the Civil Rights era. So radical—read "effective"—was this collective force that it was outlawed by the state of Alabama in 1956 as a subversive organization. Its activities were condemned as injurious to peace in the state—this, in response to an NAACP antilynching campaign after the murder of fourteen-year-old Emmett Till in nearby Mississippi. To encourage participation, dues were always minimal, with most people paying less than five dollars annually well into the 1950s. But membership itself was a major commitment for which black men and women lost their jobs and often their lives.

Although the NAACP was often cited for its reliance on donations from major white sponsors, its high-ticket fund-raising was empowered by the tremendous number of modest donations that justified the effort. In that, the survival of the NAACP and the numerous descendant organizations that have followed in its footsteps is the embodiment of African American collective work and responsibility—an inspiration to people of conscience and goodwill crossing lines of race, class, and gender in pursuit of a common goal. And, lest we forget, with such editors as Dr. W. E. B. Du Bois, Roy Wilkins, and Warren Marr II, its magazine, the *Crisis*, has chronicled our sojourn since 1910.

DECEMBER 29

DECEMBER 29: KWANZAA DAY FOUR. The day of *Ujamaa*, cooperative economics. This is the day "to build and maintain our own stores, shops, and other businesses and to profit from them together."

Thomas Farrington had a dream. Born into an entrepreneurial family, he had grown up watching his father run his lumber and sawmill logging operations. His grandfather had been an independent farmer, his great-grandfather had been a veterinarian and a farmer, and young Farrington also wanted to build his own business. In 1966, with an engineering degree from historic North Carolina A & T (see January 31), this son of the segregated South was recruited by RCA and relocated to Massachusetts. There, in March 1969, he founded Input Output Computer Services, Inc., a software production company. In June 1969, he was operational, and within less than ten years, Input Output was on *Black Enterprise* magazine's "BE 100" list—one of the nation's top black businesses.

Asked what components are essential to business success, Farrington cited three: a strong strategic plan; the need to be analytical and stay on top of details; and how an entrepreneur manages and motivates others for success.

Most people who failed, he said, failed to learn to make the entrepreneur's ambition his or her employee's ambition; to recognize the employee's problems as the entrepreneur's woes. As a child, he watched his father motivate people to reach their highest potential. In short, his father often had to do "everything" for his workers—picking them up, worrying about their children. With his engineering and computer concern, Tom Farrington's employees were more skilled and had greater resources, but their life problems were no different from those of his father's employees. Working with people was the most serious challenge—and, ultimately, the key to the most rewarding success for all concerned. With this philosophy, he not only made the "BE 100" list, he stayed on it for twelve years.

DECEMBER 30

D ECEMBER 30: KWANZAA DAY FIVE. The annual day of *Nia*, purpose. This is a time "to make as our collective vocation the building . . . of our community . . . to restore our people to their traditional greatness."

Of Nomzamo Winnie Mandela, a woman of extraordinary courage, dignity, and beauty, these stories are told. The first was related by Dr. Nthatho Motlana, a member of South Africa's Black Parents Association, formed in the wake of the Soweto uprising:

> Winnie is powerful; she is faithful and honest. She would stand before police captains with machine guns and tell them to go and get stuffed. In fact . . . when they threatened to lock her up she just said, "Do it, man!" When this Major Visser in Protea police station said to her that she had started the [Soweto] riots [see June 16], she threw a book at him, her shoe, anything and everything she could lay her hands on—"You bloody murderer, killer of our children, and you tell us *we* started the riots. You go and stop those bastards killing our children in the street!"

In August 1976, after the Soweto uprising, Sally Motlana was detained with Mandela, who united others in protest:

> Winnie was a pillar of strength to most of us political detainees. . . . [When] the other prisoners came to clean the yard . . . they were not allowed to wear panties, they were not given any shoes and stockings, and she stood up for those poor women. She was really at loggerheads with the lieutenant herself, who was the top woman in that prison, saying that the people are not animals, they are human beings, and even if they are in jail they still want their dignity and you cannot strip them like that. After a week they were given shoes and stockings and panties. She was just out and out to fight for the underdog.

For these and other extraordinary acts, Winnie Mandela became known as the Mother of South Africa's freedom movement.

DECEMBER 31

Dᴇᴄᴇᴍʙᴇʀ 31: Kᴡᴀɴᴢᴀᴀ, ᴅᴀʏ sɪx. The day of Kuumba, Creativity: "to do always as much as we can in whatever way we can in order to leave our community more beautiful and beneficial than when we inherited it."

At the century's dawn Dr. W. E. B. Du Bois had closed the first Pan-African Congress with the line that has come to define our time: "The problem of the twentieth century is the problem of the color line." The years 1936 to 1976, the era of Civil Rights in America, the age of a global move for the liberation of people of African descent worldwide, fulfilled Du Bois's view of the global Pan-African mission. In the United States, on December 31, 1964, Malcolm X welcomed teenagers from McComb, Mississippi, to Harlem. In his words, one cannot help but hear the echo of the hope of Du Bois:

> In my opinion, the greatest accomplishment that was made in the struggle of the black man in America . . . toward some kind of real progress was the successful linking together of our problem with the African problem, or making our problem a world problem. . . . The same repercussions that you see all over the world when an imperialist or foreign power interferes in some section of Africa . . . nowadays, when something happens to black people in Mississippi, you'll see [those] same repercussions all over the world. I wanted to point this out to you because it is important for you to know that when you're in Mississippi, you're not alone. As long as you think you're alone, then you take a stand as if you're a minority or as if you're outnumbered, and that kind of stand will never enable you to win a battle. . . .

The Christian-based Dr. King was inspired by the Hindu-based nonviolence of India's Gandhi, who evolved his strategies as a "colored" lawyer in South Africa. The Islam-based Elijah Muhammad helped reinstill Caribbean-based Garveyism into a reclaimed Malcolm X. From voting rights to exposing terrible wrongs, nonviolence to self-defense, new musical forms to new personal images of black women loving their unstraightened hair. Wherever and whenever you looked, *freedom* was the word. Freedom for a new day, a whole new way of life.

BIBLIOGRAPHY

Archives, Libraries, and Private Collections
Beinecke Manuscript Library: Yale University, New Haven, Connecticut
Connecticut Historical Preservation Commission
Katonah Museum: *Revisiting American Art: Works from the Collections of the HBCUs,* 1997
Library of Congress, Manuscript Division, Washington, D.C.
Maine Historical Preservation Commission
Metropolitan Opera Archives, New York, New York
Museum of Modern Art Film Library and Archives, New York, New York
Museum of TV and Radio, New York, New York
National Park Service, Jamestown, Virginia
U.S. Dept. of Interior—National Park Service: National Register of Historic Places
Utah Historical Preservation Commission

Books
Abernathy, Ralph David, *And The Walls Came Tumbling Down.* New York: Harper & Row, 1989.
Adams, Janus, *Glory Days.* New York: HarperCollins, 1995.
Anderson, Marian, *My Lord What a Morning.* New York: Viking Press, 1956.
Angelou, Maya, *I Know Why the Caged Bird Sings.* New York: Random House, 1970.
Aptheker, Herbert, ed., *A Documentary History of the Negro People in the United States,* 7 vols. New York: Citadel Press, 1951–1994.
Ashe, Arthur R., Jr., *A Hard Road to Glory: A History of the African-American Athlete.* 3 vols. New York: Amistad Press, 1988–1993.
Baldwin, James, and Nikki Giovanni, *A Dialogue.* New York: J. B. Lippincott Co., 1973.
Baldwin, Lewis, and Aprille Woodson, *Freedom Is Never Free: A Biographical Portrait of E. D. Nixon Sr.* Nashville: UPS/Office of Minority Affairs, Tennessee General Assembly, 1993.
Bates, Daisy, *Long Shadow of Little Rock.* New York: David McKay Company, Inc., 1962.
Beals, Melba Patillo, *Warriors Don't Cry.* New York: Pocket Books, 1994.
Bearden, Romare, and Harry Henderson, *A History of African-American Artists.* New York: Pantheon, 1993.
Bennett, Joan Frances, and Tobi G. Sanders, *Members of the Class Will Keep Daily Journals: The Barnard College Journals of Tobi Gillian Sanders and Joan Frances Bennett, Spring 1968.* New York: Winter House, 1970.
Bennett, Lerone, *Before The Mayflower: A History of Black America.* Chicago: Johnson Publications, 1962, 1988.
———, *What Manner of Man: A Biography of Martin Luther King, Jr.* Chicago: Johnson Publications, 1964.
Bernotas, Robert, *Amiri Baraka.* New York: Chelsea House, 1991.
Bishop, Jim, *The Days of Martin Luther King, Jr.* New York: G. Putnam's Sons, 1971.
Branch, Taylor, *Parting The Waters.* New York: Simon & Schuster/Touchstone, 1989.
Burt, McKinley, Jr., *Black Inventors of America.* Portland: National Book Co, 1989.

Carmichael, Stokely, and Charles V. Hamilton, *Black Power: The Politics of Liberation in America.* New York: Vintage/Random House, 1967.

Carruth, Gorton, *Encyclopedia of American Facts and Dates.* New York: Harper & Row, 1987.

Carson, Clayborne, et al, eds. *Eyes on the Prize Civil Rights Reader.* New York: Viking Penguin, 1991.

————, *Malcolm X: The FBI File.* New York: Carroll & Graf Publishers, 1991.

Christian, Charles M., *Black Saga: The African American Experience, a Chronology.* New York: Houghton Mifflin, 1995.

Clark, Septima, *Ready From Within.* Navarro, Ca.: Wild Trees Press, 1986.

Coram, Robert, *Caribbean Time Bomb: The United States' Complicity in the Corruption of Antigua.* New York: William Morrow, 1993.

Davis, Angela Y., *An Autobiography.* New York: Random House, 1974.

Davis, Edward, *One Man's Way.* Michigan: Edward Davis Associates, 1979.

Dent, Tom, *Southern Journey: A Return to the Civil Rights Movement.* New York: William Morrow, 1997.

Duberman, Martin Bauml, *Paul Robeson.* New York: Alfred E. Knopf, 1988.

Edwards, Adolph, *Marcus Garvey 1887–1940.* London: New Beacon, 1967.

Ellington, Edward K., *Music is My Mistress.* New York: Doubleday, 1973.

Evers, Charles, and Andrew Szanton, *Have No Fear: A Black Man's Fight for Respect in America.* New York: John Wiley & Sons, 1997.

Fanon, Frantz, *Wretched of the Earth.* New York: Grove Press, 1963.

Farred, Grant, ed. *Rethinking C. L. R. James.* Boston: Blackwell Publishers, 1996.

Feelings, Tom, *Black Pilgrimage.* New York: Lothrop, Lee & Shepard, 1972.

Folson, Franklin, *Black Cowboy: The Life and Legend of George McJunkin.* Niwot, Co.: R. Rinehart.

France-Nuriddin, and Traylor-Herndon, series directors, *African Americans: Voices of Triumph.* Alexandria, Va.: Time-Life Books, 1993.

Gaines, Ernest J., *Autobiography of Miss Jane Pittman.* New York: Dial Press/Bantam, 1971.

Giddings, Paula, *When and Where I Enter: the Impact of Black Women on Race and Sex in America.* New York: William Morrow, 1984.

Gordy, Berry, *To Be Loved.* New York: Warner Books, 1994.

Gregory, Dick, *No More Lies.* New York: Random House, 1971.

Hampton, Henry, and Fayer, Steven with Sarah Flynn, *Voices of Freedom: An Oral History of the Civil Rights Movement from the 1950s through the 1980s.* New York: Bantam, 1990.

Haskins, Jim, *Diary of a Harlem Schoolteacher.* New York: Grove Press, 1969.

Hayre, Ruth Wright, and Alexis Moore, *Tell Them We Are Rising.* New York: John Wiley & Sons, 1997.

Hill, Robert, ed. *Marcus Garvey: Life and Lessons.* Berkeley, Ca.: Univ. of California Press, 1987.

Holiday, Billie, and William Duffy, *Lady Sings the Blues.* New York: Popular Library, 1958.

Holly, Ellen, *One Life.* New York and Tokyo, Kodansha America, 1996.

House, Ernest R., *Jesse Jackson and the Politics of Charisma.* Boulder, Co.: Westview Press, 1988.

Hudson, Karen, *Paul R. Williams, Architect.* New York: Rizzoli, 1996.

Huggins, Nathan I., ed., *Du Bois Writings*. New York: Literary Classics of the U.S., 1986.

Hunter-Gault, Charlayne, *In My Place*. New York: Farrar Straus Giroux, 1992.

Hurston, Zora Neale, *Dust Tracks on the Road*. Philadelphia: J. B. Lippincott, 1942.

————, *Mules and Men*. Philadelphia: J. B. Lippincott, 1935.

————, *Their Eyes Were Watching God*. Philadelphia: J. B. Lippincott, 1937.

Jackson, George, *Soledad Brother: The Prison Letters of George Jackson*. New York: Bantam, 1970.

Jones, James, *Bad Blood: The Scandalous Story of the Tuskegee Experiment*. New York: Free Press/Macmillan, 1981.

Jordan, Barbara (w/Shelby Hearon), *Barbara Jordan: A Self Portrait*. New York: Doubleday, 1979.

Kasher, Steven, *Civil Rights Movement: A Photographic History 1954–68*. New York: Abbeville Press, 1996.

Kent, George E., *A Life of Gwendolyn Brooks*. Lexington, Ky.: University Press of Kentucky, 1990.

Kenyatta, Jomo, *Facing Mount Kenya: Tribal Life of the Kikuyu*. London: Heinemann, 1971.

King, Martin Luther, Jr., *Stride Toward Freedom*. New York: Harper & Row, 1958.

————, *Why We Can't Wait*. New York: New American Library, 1968.

Klinkowitz, Jerome ed., *The Diaries of Willard Motley*. Ames, Ia.: Iowa State University Press, 1979.

Lanker, Brian, *I Dream A World*. New York: Stewart, Tabori & Chang, 1989.

Lecky, Sheryle, and John Lecky, *Moments: The Pulitzer Prize Photographs*. New York: Crown Publishers, 1978.

Lester, Julius, ed., *The Seventh Son: Thought and Writings of W. E. B. Du Bois*. New York: Random House, 1971—p. 666–671.

Lewis, David Levering, ed., *W. E. B. Du Bois Reader*. New York: Henry Holt, 1995.

Luthuli, Albert, and Charles Hooper, *Let My People Go*. Glasgow: Fontana, 1987.

Magida, Arthur J., *Prophet of Rage: A Life of Louis Farrakhan and His Nation*. New York: Basic Books/HarperCollins, 1996.

Makeba, Miriam, and James Hall, *Makeba: My Story*. New York: New American Library, 1987.

Malcolm X, and Alex Haley, *Autobiography of Malcolm X*. New York: Grove Press, 1965.

Mandela, Nelson, and Richard Stengel, *Long Walk To Freedom*. Boston: Little, Brown & Co, 1994.

Mandela, Winnie, *Part of My Soul Went With Him*. New York: W. W. Norton & Co, 1984.

Mark Bego, *Aretha Franklin: Queen of Soul*. New York: St. Martin's Press, 1989.

Mayfield, Julian, *The Hit: A Novel*. New York: Vanguard Press, 1957.

Mays, Benjamin E., *Born to Rebel*. New York: Charles Scribner's, 1971.

Mazrui, Ali, *The Africans*. Boston: Little, Brown & Co., 1986.

Mboya, Tom, *Freedom and After*. Boston: Little, Brown & Co., 1963.

McKissack, Patricia, and Fredrick McKissack, *Red Tail Angels: Story of the Tuskegee Airmen of WWII*. New York: Walker & Co., 1995.

Mills, Kay, *This Little Light of Mind: The Life of Fannie Lou Hamer*. New York: Dutton, 1993.

Mitchell, Carleton, *Isles of the Caribbees*. Washington, D.C.: National Geographic Society, 1971.

Morrison, Toni, *The Bluest Eye*. New York: Alfred E. Knopf, 1993.

Morrow, Everett Frederic, *Black Man in the White House*. New York: Coward, McCann, 1963.

National Park Service, *African American Historic Places*. New York: Preservation Press/John Wiley & Sons, 1994.

Nkrumah, Kwame, *I Speak of Freedom: A Statement of African Ideology*. New York: Praeger, 1961.

O'Shaughnessy, Hugh, *Grenada: Eyewitness Account of the U.S. Invasion and the Caribbean History that Provoked It*. New York: Dodd, Mead, 1984.

Oates, Stephen B., *Let the Trumpet Sound: The Life of Martin Luther King, Jr.* New York: Harper & Row, 1982.

Parks, David, *GI Diary*. New York: Harper & Row, 1968.

Parks, Gordon, *Voices in the Mirror*. New York: Doubleday, 1990.

Patterson, William L., *We Charge Genocide*. New York: International Publishers, 1970.

Perry, Bruce, *Malcolm: Life of A Man Who Changed Black America*. Barrytown, N.Y.: Station Hill, 1991.

Ploski, Harry A., Warren Marr II, et al, eds., *Negro Almanac*. Detroit: Gale Research, 1976.

Poitier, Sidney, *This Life*. New York: Alfred A. Knopf, 1980.

Powell, Adam Clayton, *Marching Blacks: An Interpretive History—Rise of the Black Common Man*. New York: Dial Press, 1945.

Rampersad, Arnold, *The Life of Langston Hughes, vol. 2: 1941–1967, I Dream A World*. New York: Oxford University Press, 1988.

Reagon, Bernice Johnson, and Sweet Honey in the Rock, *We Who Believe in Freedom*. New York: Anchor/Doubleday, 1993.

Rights in Conflict: The Walker Report to the National Commission on the Causes and Prevention of Violence. New York: Bantam, 1968.

Riley, James A., *The Biographical Encyclopedia of the Negro Baseball Leagues*. New York: Carroll & Graf, 1994.

Robeson, Eslanda Goode, *African Journey*. New York: John Day, 1945.

Robeson, Paul, *Here I Stand*. New York: Othello Press, 1958—reprint, Boston: Beacon Press, 1971.

Schoener, Allen, *Harlem on My Mind: Cultural Capital of Black America 1900–1978*. New York: Dell Publishing, 1968, 1979.

Shange, Ntozake, *for colored girls who have considered suicide/when the rainbow is enuf*. New York: Macmillan, 1977.

Stein, Judith E., *I Tell My Heart: The Art of Horace Pippin*. Pa.: Penna. Academy of the Fine Arts, 1993.

Stovall, Tyler, *Paris Noir: African Americans in the City of Light*. Boston: Houghton Mifflin, 1996.

Strickland, William, with the Malcolm X Documentary production team, *Malcolm X: Make It Plain*. New York: Viking, 1994.

Taylor, Clarence, *The Black Churches of Brooklyn*. New York: Columbia University Press, 1994.

Taylor, Stephen, *Shaka's Children: A History of the Zulu People*. London: HarperCollins, 1995.

Thomas, Coffey, *Lion By The Tail*. New York: Viking, 1974.

Turnbull, Walter, with Howard Manly, *Lift Every Voice*. New York: Hyperion, 1995.

Tutu, Desmond, and John Allen, ed., *Rainbow People of God: The Making of a Peaceful Revolution*. New York: Doubleday, 1994.

U.S. Riot Commission Report, Report of the National Advisory Commission on Civil Disorders. New York: Bantam, 1968.

Ward, Geoffrey C., and Ken Burns, *Baseball*. New York: Knopf, 1994.

Washington, James Melvin, *Conversations with God: Two Centuries of Prayers by African Americans*. New York: HarperCollins, 1994.

Weston, M. Moran, *Who Is This Jesus?* New York: Columbia University Press, 1973.

Wheat, Ellen, *Jacob Lawrence, American Painter*. Seattle: University of Washington Press and Seattle Art Museum, 1986.

Williams, Juan, *Eyes on the Prize*. New York: Viking Press, 1987.

Witherspoon, William Roger, *Martin Luther King, Jr—to The Mountaintop*. New York: Doubleday, 1985.

Wright, Richard, *American Hunger*. New York: Harper & Row, 1977.

Film, Audio, Video

All Power to the People: A Documentary Film by Lee Lew-Lee.

Malcolm X: Make It Plain, PBS/"American Experience" rebroadcast 2/1/1995.

Moms Mabley at Geneva Conference (phonograph album), Chess Recording Corporation, Chicago, Illinois.

The Music of Trinidad, Washington, D.C.: National Geography Society, 1971 (liner notes by Percival Borde, "Trade Winds, Steel Drums and 'Mme Ophélia,'").

"Rosewood," *Oprah Winfrey Show*, King Features Syndicate 2/27/97.

Periodicals and Other Sources

"1923 Horror Haunts Books and Films," *New York Times*, 28 December 1996.

Adams, Janus, *Cassia Tree*, 1977.

"African Foods," *Ebony*, August 1976.

Annual Report, 1990–1991, Virginia State University.

Bailey, Peter, "Malcolm Bailey Finds a Father," *Ebony*, August 1974.

Chicago Defender, 1936–1976.

"The CIA Report the President Doesn't Want You To Read," *The Village Voice*, February 1976.

Clark, Benjamin F., "The Editorial Reaction of Selected Black Newspapers to the Civil Rights Movement," Diss., Howard University, 1969.

Congressional Record, 1938–1964.

Crisis Magazine, 1932–1954.

Daily Gleaner, 1964.

Davis, Ossie, "Our Shining Prince: A Eulogy for Malcolm X," 1965.

Ebony Magazine, 1957–1976.

Huie, William Bradford, "The Shocking Story of Approved Killing in Mississippi," *Look*, 24 January 1956.

Isaacs, Charles S., "A JHS 271 Teacher Tells It Like He Sees It," *New York Times Magazine*, 24 November 1968.

Jowitt, Deborah, "Call Me a Dancer: Judith Jamison," *New York Times Magazine,* 5 December 1976.

Liberation Magazine, 1959.

Life Magazine, 1944–1970.

Lomax, Louis, "The Negro Revolt Against the Negro Leaders," *Harper's Magazine,* June 1960.

Lyon, Danny, "Ain't Gonna Let Nobody Turn Me Round: Use and Misuse of Southern Civil Rights Movement," *Aperture 115,* Summer 1989.

Murrain, Patricia C., Ph.D., "Us Gon' Have Our Own—Hospital?!? The Story of T. J. Huddleston" (unpublished).

New York Age, 1937–1938.

New York Amsterdam News, 1936–1976.

New York Times, New York Times Magazine.

Pittsburgh Courier, 1936–1976.

Poussaint, Alvin, M.D., "Building A Strong Self-Image in the Black Child," *Ebony,* August 1974.

Sanchez, Sonia, "For Malcolm," 1965.

School Library Journal, October 1970.

"Setting the Record Straight on the History of the Negro," *New York Times,* 15 September 1968.

Walker, Alice, "I Said to Poetry," *Her Blue Body Everything We Know: Earthling Poems, 1965–1990.* Orlando: Harcourt Brace & Co., 1993.

Weltner, Rep. Charles Longstreet, "Report from Washington: 24 July 1964," *Congressional Record.*

Williams, Paul R., "I Am a Negro," *American Magazine,* July 1937.

Williams, Robert, "Is Violence Necessary to Combat Injustice? For the Positive: Williams Says 'We Must Fight Back'" *Liberation Magazine,* September 1959.

GENERAL INDEX

INDEX OF SUBJECTS

INDEX OF INSPIRATIONAL THEMES